£ 55.00

AF835881

UNIVERSITY OF SUNDERLAND
WITHDRAWN

UNIVERSITY OF
SUNDERLAND

UNIVERSITY LIBRARY

HANNAH ARENDT AND THE LAW

This book fills a major gap in the ever-increasing secondary literature on Hannah Arendt's political thought by providing a dedicated and coherent treatment of the many, various and interesting things which Arendt had to say about law. Often obscured by more pressing or more controversial aspects of her work, Arendt nonetheless had interesting insights into Greek and Roman concepts of law, human rights, constitutional design, legislation, sovereignty, international tribunals, judicial review and much more. This book retrieves these aspects of her legal philosophy for the attention of both Arendt scholars and lawyers alike. The book brings together lawyers as well as Arendt scholars drawn from a range of disciplines (philosophy, political science, international relations), who have engaged in an internal debate the dynamism of which is captured in print. Following the editors' introduction, the book is split into four Parts: Part I explores the concept of law in Arendt's thought; Part II explores legal aspects of Arendt's constitutional thought: first locating Arendt in the wider tradition of republican constitutionalism, before turning attention to the role of courts and the role of parliament in her constitutional design. In Part III Arendt's thought on international law is explored from a variety of perspectives, covering international institutions and international criminal law, as well as the theoretical foundations of international law. Part IV debates the foundations, content and meaning of Arendt's famous and influential claim that the 'right to have rights' is the one true human right.

Volume 4 in the series Law and Practical Reason

Law and Practical Reason

The intention of this series is that it should encompass monographs and collections of essays that address the fundamental issues in legal philosophy. The foci are conceptual and normative in character, not empirical. Studies addressing the idea of law as a species of practical reason are especially welcome. Recognising that there is no occasion sharply to distinguish analytic and systematic work in the field from historico-critical research, the editors also welcome studies in the history of legal philosophy. Contributions to the series, inevitably crossing disciplinary lines, will be of interest to students and professionals in moral, political, and legal philosophy.

General Editor

Prof George Pavlakos (Antwerp and Glasgow)

Advisory Board

Prof Robert Alexy (Kiel)
Prof Samantha Besson (Fribourg, CH)
Prof Emilios Christodoulidis (Glasgow)
Prof Sean Coyle (Birmingham)
Prof Mattias Kumm (New York and Berlin)
Prof Stanley Paulson (St Louis and Kiel)
Prof Joseph Raz (Columbia Law School)
Prof Arthur Ripstein (Toronto)
Prof Scott Shapiro (Yale Law School)
Prof Victor Tadros (Warwick)

Editorial Assistant

Triantafyllos Gouvas (Antwerp)

Volume 1: The Normative Claim of Law
Stefano Bertea

Volume 2: Community and Collective Rights: A Theoretical Framework for Rights held by Groups
Dwight Newman

Volume 3: New Essays on the Normativity of Law
Edited by Stefano Bertea and George Pavlakos

Hannah Arendt and the Law

Edited by
Marco Goldoni
and
Christopher McCorkindale

•HART•
PUBLISHING
OXFORD AND PORTLAND, OREGON
2012

Published in the United Kingdom by Hart Publishing Ltd
16C Worcester Place, Oxford, OX1 2JW
Telephone: +44 (0)1865 517530
Fax: +44 (0)1865 510710
E-mail: mail@hartpub.co.uk
Website: http://www.hartpub.co.uk

Published in North America (US and Canada) by
Hart Publishing
c/o International Specialized Book Services
920 NE 58th Avenue, Suite 300
Portland, OR 97213-3786
USA
Tel: +1 503 287 3093 or toll-free: (1) 800 944 6190
Fax: +1 503 280 8832
E-mail: orders@isbs.com
Website: http://www.isbs.com

© The editors and contributors severally 2012

The editors and contributors have asserted their right under the Copyright, Designs and Patents Act 1988, to be identified as the authors of this work.

All rights reserved. No part of this publication may be reproduced, stored in a retrieval system, or transmitted, in any form or by any means, without the prior permission of Hart Publishing, or as expressly permitted by law or under the terms agreed with the appropriate reprographic rights organisation. Enquiries concerning reproduction which may not be covered by the above should be addressed to Hart Publishing Ltd at the address above.

British Library Cataloguing in Publication Data
Data Available

ISBN: 978-1-84946-143-6

Typeset by Compuscript Ltd, Shannon
Printed and bound in Great Britain by
TJ International Ltd, Padstow, Cornwall

MIX
Paper from responsible sources
FSC® C013056
FSC www.fsc.org

UNIVERSITY OF SUNDERLAND
SP LIBRARY
Class No.
340.1092 A72
Access No.
11112511752
Order No.
ND11003039

Foreword

Richard J Bernstein

When Hannah Arendt died in December 1975, she had a small group of admirers and a much larger group of vociferous critics. The stormy controversy provoked by the publication of *Eichmann in Jerusalem* in 1963 continued to overshadow virtually everything else she had written or done. Outside of the United States and Germany she was barely known and rarely discussed in intellectual circles. Today, almost 40 years later, the situation has radically changed. There is scarcely a place in the world where there aren't enthusiasts and critics of Arendt—from Helsinki to Beijing, from Belgrade to Lima, from Dublin to Seoul. She is now considered to be one of the major and most provocative political thinkers of the twentieth century. Both her advocates and her critics write passionately about her. What is it about Arendt that elicits such striking reactions? How is one to account for her ever-growing popularity? I don't think there are any simple explanations, but let me suggest one key reason. Arendt, by her own account, was an independent thinker (*Selbstdenker*). She did not belong to any school or associate with any dominant ideology. She wasn't a Marxist, liberal or communitarian. She resisted any simple classification as a left or right thinker, a radical or a conservative. Neither was she simply a philosopher, political theorist, literary critic or a journalist. She defied any and all classifications. But she grappled with some of the most serious issues of her (and our) time, including totalitarianism, evil, war, revolution, violence, power, and the meaning of action and politics. Arendt is an exemplar of a contemporary intellectual who was not afraid to take on the most pressing issues, to think about them in fresh ways and to bring all her intellectual resources—philosophy, political theory, literature, and history—to illuminate them. She was never afraid to express her strong views on controversial questions. One of her favorite phrases was 'thinking without banisters' (*denken ohne Geländer*)—and this is what she so eminently practised.

The word that I associate with Arendt's writings is 'fecundity'. She perfected the literary form of the essay—many of her books read like a series of loosely connected essays. But her essays are always packed with meaning—and one can always make new discoveries in careful reading and rereading. This fecundity has been reflected in the reception of her thinking and the growing body of international scholarship. There have been critical discussions of her reflections on imperialism and totalitarianism; politics and society, labour, work and action; thinking, willing and judging. There have been scholars who have focused on the ways in which she has appropriated and has been influenced by Socrates, Plato,

Aristotle, Augustine, Kant, Nietzsche and Heidegger. But with a few notable exceptions there is one topic in Arendt that has not been examined in a sustained and systematic manner—her thinking about law, jurisprudence and the creating of constitutions. This neglect is striking, because there is scarcely a major book or essay of Arendt that doesn't deal with some aspect of the law. From her earliest to her latest work, this was clearly one of her most central concerns. And typically she discusses law in novel and imaginative ways. Let me mention just a few of the many ways in which she probed legal and juridical issues. Her discussion of law pervades *The Origins of Totalitarianism.* She has a deep concern with how the major political catastrophes since the First World War have created masses of people who are no longer protected by law and are excluded from political communities. This is what led to her critique of abstract appeals to human rights and her insistence that the fundamental right of human beings is 'the right to have rights'. When she explores the role of the concentration and extermination camps in Nazi totalitarianism she emphasises how the 'manufacture' of living corpses begins with the killing of the 'juridical person'. There are no rights in the camps. Arendt explores the way in which totalitarianism corrupts the idea of law when it appeals to the laws of history and nature. Law is equally important in her discussion of *polis* in *The Human Condition*—for law in prepolitical condition forms the space of appearance in which political action takes place. In her *Introduction into Politics* she examines the limitations of the Greek *polis* and the differences between the Greek *nomos* and Roman *lex*, which is based on treaties and alliances. She argues that the Romans introduced a new concept of law that became the basis of Western European law. And, of course, in *Eichmann in Jerusalem* there is a constant reflection on law and its limits. Arendt argued for the need for international tribunals and yet defended the right of Israel to try Eichmann. Throughout her 'report' she questions whether any legal system is adequate to try the crimes of the Nazis. And in her postscript she reflects her understanding of 'crimes against humanity'. In *On Revolution*, she understands the American Revolution as culminating in the writing and ratification of the Constitution. It is the 'constituting act—the act by which a people … constitutes itself into a body politic' that she emphasises. She argues that part of the reason for the 'success' of the American Revolution is the long pre-revolutionary tradition of 'covenants and agreements' dating back to the Mayflower Compact. Throughout her writings Arendt returns over and over again to Montesquieu and his understanding of the 'spirit of the laws'. In her famous essay 'Civil Disobedience' she argues that the establishment of civil disobedience in the United States 'might be the best possible remedy for the ultimate failure of judicial review'.[1] These are just a few of her many rich discussions of law and jurisprudence. I emphasise what I said earlier, virtually *all* of her writings deal with some aspect of the law.

[1] H Arendt, 'Civil Disobedience' in *Crises of the Republic* (New York, Harcourt Brace, 1972) 101.

This is the first collection of essays to be dedicated *exclusively* to Hannah Arendt and the law. The editors have gathered papers from an outstanding group of international scholars who come from a variety of disciplines. These essays are at once appreciative, incisive and critical. Collectively they explore many of 'thought trains' that constitute Arendt's complex, subtle, unconventional and controversial thinking about law, jurisprudence and the creation of constitutions. They demonstrate the fecundity and relevance of her thinking about the law for our own time.

Richard J Bernstein
New School for Social Research

Summary Contents

Table of Contents

Acknowledgements

The origins of this book were to be found in a casual conversation about the dearth of legal engagement with Arendt's work which we had over one drink at the inaugural Glasgow–Antwerp Doctoral Colloquium in 2008. It was some time later that we set an aspiration to address that lacuna, and with this volume we hope to have achieved just that: the first systematic engagement with the many, varied and interesting things which Hannah Arendt had to say *about*, but also *to*, the law.

It goes without saying that we could not have reached this point without the help and support of a great many people. First, then, we must thank those who have so inspired us throughout our doctoral studies: Emilios Christodoulidis and George Pavlakos, whose energy and enthusiasm in creating a vibrant doctoral exchange between Glasgow and Antwerp made that initial conversation possible, and to Adam Tomkins whose support and advice both as a supervisor and as a friend have been invaluable. We hope that, in some small way, they can see in this book a reward for their own efforts.

The publication of the book was preceded by two events: an introductory reading group at Glasgow Caledonian University, and a workshop for contributors to the volume, held at the University of Antwerp. The former provided some beneficial insights for us in the initial stages of the project, and we would therefore like to thank those who attended—Tony Lang, Rhonda Wheate, Chris Nottingham, Richard Collins, Alessandra Asteriti, Hayley Hooper, Paul Scott, Haris Psarras and Francisco Saffie—as well as those whose financial, administrative and moral support made the day such a success: in particular, Jackie Tombs, Director of the Institute for Society and Social Justice Research at Glasgow Caledonian, Kirsty Cameron and Anne Gilfillan, who sadly passed away before the book could be completed. She remains in our thoughts and our prayers. The latter saw many of the contributors gather for two days in Antwerp for what was an extremely engaging, rich and—dare we say it—enjoyable exchange of papers and views in a remarkable setting. The event was generously supported by the Odysseus Program of the FWO (Research Foundation Flanders).

Chris McCorkindale
Marco Goldoni
Glasgow and Antwerp
January 2012

List of Contributors

Charles Barbour Lecturer in the School of Humanities and Languages at the University of Western Sydney.

Seyla Benhabib Eugene Meyer Professor of Political Science and Philosophy at Yale University.

Richard J Bernstein Vera List Professor of Philosophy at the New School for Social Research, New York.

Samantha Besson Professor of Public International and European Law and Co-director of the European Law Institute at the University of Fribourg, Switzerland.

Leora Bilsky Professor of Law in the Law School at Tel Aviv University and editor-in-chief of *Theory and Criticism.*

James Bohman Danforth Professor of Philosophy and International Studies at the University of Saint Louis.

Keith Breen Lecturer in Political Theory in the School of Politics, International Relations & Philosophy at Queen's University, Belfast.

Hauke Brunkhorst Professor for Sociology at the University of Flensburg.

Emilios Christodoulidis Professor of Legal Theory in the School of Law at the University of Glasgow.

Lawrence R Douglas James Grosfeld Professor of Law, Jurisprudence and Social Thought at Amherst College.

Marco Goldoni Research Fellow at the Centre for Law and Cosmopolitan Values of the University of Antwerp.

Florian Hoffman Franz Haniel Professor of Public Policy at Erfurt University.

Jan Klabbers Professor of International Law and Director of the Academy of Finland Centre of Excellence in Global Governance Research, University of Helsinki.

Vivian Liska Professor of German Literature in the Department of Literature and Philosophy at the University of Antwerp.

Christopher McCorkindale Lecturer in Law at Glasgow Caledonian University.

Patricia Owens Reader in the Department of International Relations, University of Sussex, and Senior Research Associate at the Oxford-Leverhulme Programme on the Changing Character of War.

Kari Palonen Professor at the Academy of Finland (2008–12), and Professor of Political Science in the Department of Social Sciences and Philosophy at the University of Jyväskylä, Finland.

Andrew Schaap Senior Lecturer in Politics at the University of Exeter.

William Smith Assistant Professor at the Department of Government and Public Administration of the Chinese University of Hong Kong.

Johan van der Walt Professor of Philosophy of Law at the University of Luxembourg.

Michael Wilkinson Lecturer in Law at the London School of Economics and Political Science.

Introduction

MARCO GOLDONI AND CHRIS MCCORKINDALE

THE SHEER VOLUME of secondary literature dedicated to the life and work of Hannah Arendt—which has been growing exponentially since her death, and which was reinforced by various events held in 2006 to mark the centenary of her birth—is truly impressive. However, and as Christian Volk has so sharply observed, whilst this literature has explored the question 'What is Politics?' from multitudinous vantage points, the question 'What is Law?' seems almost entirely to have been neglected, both by the legal academy and by Arendt scholars alike.[1] For sure, there are some plausible explanations for this. It is true, for example, that Arendt never took the time to develop in her *corpus* any detailed theory of law, and indeed lacked the legal background to do so; and yet—as we shall see—a close reading of her work shows Arendt to have had a keen interest in the law, and in particular its relationship with politics.

It must be said that in recent years this trend seems slowly to be changing. Some pieces on Arendt's views of international law and constitutionalism have been published by influential scholars such as Jan Klabbers and Jeremy Waldron,[2] whilst others have used Arendt's insights in order to treat specific legal problems.[3] Building on these developments, what we hope to provide in this volume is the first dedicated and systematic (if not comprehensive) treatment of the many, varied and interesting things which Arendt had to say on law and legal processes, and in so doing somehow to find law's place within the broader scope of her political thought. The contributors invited to participate in the project reflect our intention to spark a dual dialogue *between* 'Arendtians' and lawyers, simultaneously asking the former 'what does Hannah Arendt say *about* law', and to the latter 'what might Arendt's work say *to* the law'. As we shall see, arriving at answers to these questions is not straightforward—for here Arendt was no less elusive, no less inconsistent,

[1] C Volk, 'From *Nomos* to *Lex*: Hannah Arendt on Law, Order and Politics' (2010) 23 *Leiden Journal of International Law* 759, 759.

[2] J Klabbers, 'Possible Islands of Predictability: The Legal Thought of Hannah Arendt' (2007) 20 *Leiden Journal of International Law* 1; J Waldron, 'Arendt's Constitutional Politics' in D Villa (ed), *The Cambridge Companion to Hannah Arendt* (Cambridge, Cambridge University Press, 2000) 201–20.

[3] See, eg, L Bilsky, *Transformative Justice: Israeli Identity on Trial* (Ann Arbor, University of Michigan Press, 2004).

no more developed and yet for it no less fascinating than she was throughout her political and philosophical reflections. We can think of nowhere better to begin, then, than with an attempt to trace the roots of that ambivalence.

I. ARENDT'S POLITICAL TURN

Given her reputation as a theorist of action, it seems appropriate to introduce the work with a reflection not on her political thought *per se*, but rather on the experiences, and—in response to those experiences—the actions which led to her political awakening. It is, after all, in these experiences that we find the roots of Arendt's ambivalence towards law, her belief in action and—putting the two together—what she saw as being the constitutive (or at least, the creative) force of action, even *against* constituted law(s).

Considering the breadth and depth of her political thought, it is perhaps a little surprising to learn that a passion for, even an interest in, politics came to Hannah Arendt relatively late in her formative years. Attending university from 1924–29, 'exactly the years of greatest stability for the troubled Weimar Republic,'[4] Arendt was at this time, and by her own admission, as little concerned by the theoretical underpinnings of the public realm taught to her by Karl Jaspers as she was inattentive to the general political climate which surrounded her.[5] It was not until the early 1930s that Arendt took her first steps in the direction of politics. At this time, her biographical work on Rahel Varnhagen coincided with a developing interest in Marx and Trotsky, and a curiosity about the major political questions of the day, in particular those which impacted most upon her identity: the Jewish question and the (as she saw them, dubious) achievements of the women's rights movement.[6] What exasperated Arendt more than any other issue, however, was the 'darkening political situation' which surrounded her in Nazi Germany and, more than this, the failure of even leading intellectuals to understand the gravity of the situation which faced them.[7] In a revealing interview with the journalist Günter Gaus, Arendt was able to pinpoint the precise moment of her political awakening:

> GAUS: Your interest in political theory, in political action and behavior, is at the center of your work today. In this light, what I found in your correspondence with Professor Scholem seems particularly interesting. There you wrote, if I may quote you, that you 'were interested in [your] youth neither in politics nor in history.' Miss Arendt, as a Jew you emigrated from Germany in 1933. You were then twenty-six years old. Is your interest in politics—the cessation of your indifference to politics and history—connected to these events?

[4] E Young-Bruehl, *Hannah Arendt, For Love of the World* (London, Yale University Press, 1982) 42 (hereafter 'EYB').

[5] EYB 44.

[6] *Ibid* 92–97.

[7] *Ibid* 98.

ARENDT: Yes, of course. Indifference was no longer possible in 1933. It was no longer possible even before that …

GAUS: For you as well?

ARENDT: Yes, of course. I read the newspapers intently. I had opinions. I did not belong to a party, nor did I have need to. By 1931 I was firmly convinced that the Nazis would take the helm …

…

GAUS: Is there a definite event in your memory that dates your turn to the political?

ARENDT: I would say February 27, 1933, the burning of the Reichstag, and the illegal arrests that followed during the same night. The so-called protective custody. As you know, people were taken to Gestapo cellars or to concentration camps. What happened then was monstrous, but it has now been overshadowed by things that happened later. This was an immediate shock for me, and from that moment on I felt responsible.[8]

For Arendt, taking up the mantle of responsibility would manifest itself in two ways. For one, she published what remains, to many, the *magnum opus* of her vast body of work: *The Origins of Totalitarianism.* As she said in response to one (particularly stinging) review of the book, 'my first problem was how to write historically about something—totalitarianism—which I did not want to conserve but, on the contrary, *felt engaged to destroy*'.[9] Her solution, she continued, 'was to discover the chief elements of totalitarianism and to analyze them in historical terms.' Not a history of totalitarianism as such, '[t]he book … does not really deal with the "origins" of totalitarianism—as its title unfortunately claims—but gives a historical account of the elements which crystallized into totalitarianism',[10] with the express hope of eradicating them from the human condition.

A second manifestation of Arendt's taking of responsibility, however, one for which she is far less renowned, came in the shape of her own resistance to the Nazi regime, in the spring of 1933. Whilst thinking gravely of her own emigration, 'acting', for Arendt, would mean covertly offering her Berlin apartment as a welcome stop to Jews and Communists fleeing Germany, as tensions heightened in the immediate aftermath of the conflagration. Risky though her participation in this underground railroad undoubtedly was, her action took an altogether more flirtatious relationship with danger when the German Zionist Organization approached her to undertake illegal work on their behalf. As Young-Bruehl tells it:

They wanted her to collect materials at the Prussian State Library which would show the extent of anti-Semitic action in nongovernment organizations, private circles, business associations, and professional societies. She was to make a collection of the sort

[8] '"What Remains? The Language Remains": A Conversation with Günter Gaus' (hereafter '*with Gaus*') in P Baehr (ed), *The Portable Hannah Arendt* (London, Penguin, 2000) 3, 5.

[9] H Arendt, 'A Reply to Eric Voegelin' (hereafter '*Reply to Voegelin*') in Baehr (ed), above n 8, 158.

[10] *Ibid.*

> of anti-Semitic remarks which would be unlikely to make their way into the German or foreign press.[11]

At the point of undertaking this work Arendt had already come to full consciousness of the predicament in which she and her compatriots had found themselves. Along the path of the underground railroad she had witnessed many arbitrary arrests, particularly of Communists who would be sent to the cellars of the Gestapo or to the concentration camps, recalling them as 'monstrous' events overshadowed only by what was still to come. All at the same time, Nazi legislation continued to alienate Germany's Jewish population, depriving them, amongst other things, of key university posts and civil service appointments.[12] Where ordinary existence was increasingly suffocated *by* the law, and where even a life lived in apathetic legality could no longer guarantee the minimum liberal protection *of* the law, the opportunity to take on such an illicit task was one which Arendt embraced with positive relish. Recalling this climate of indeterminate il/legality as that which 'marked her [personal] turn to the political', when invited to explain the nature of her work for the Zionists she confided in Gaus about the arrest which had preceded her own flight from Germany:

> I was found out. I was very lucky. I got out after eight days because I made friends with the official who arrested me. He was a charming fellow! He'd been promoted from the criminal police to a political division. He had no idea what to do. What was he supposed to do? He kept saying to me, 'Ordinarily I have someone there in front of me, and I know what's going on. But what shall I do with you?'
>
> … Unfortunately, I had to lie to him. I couldn't let the organization be exposed. I told him tall tales, and he kept saying, 'I got you in here. I shall get you out again. Don't get a lawyer! Jews don't have any money now. Save your money!' Meanwhile the organization had gotten me a lawyer. Through members, of course. And I sent this lawyer away. Because this man who arrested me had such an open, decent face. I relied on him and thought there was a much better chance than with some lawyer who himself was afraid.[13]

Whilst Arendt was thankful for that piece of good fortune which had led to her release from custody, she was also astute enough to recognise the limits of that luck. Within days she had joined those exiles who had already made their way to Prague, on a journey that would not end until she received American citizenship some 18 years later.

There are three initial (and related) observations that we should like to make about Arendt's tale of 'good' fortune here. First, that the climate in Germany, in particular for Jews and Communists, was, in 1933, one of complete uncertainty.

[11] EYB 104.

[12] *Ibid* 104. Take, for example, *Gesetz zur Wiederherstellung des Berufsbeamtentums* (Law for the Restoration of the Professional Civil Service), passed on 7 April 1933, by which 'non-Aryan' members of the civil service were removed, or forced to retire, 'even where there would be no grounds for such action under the prevailing Law' (s 1).

[13] Arendt, *with Gaus*, 7.

'Conscientious, thoughtful people,' reflected Young-Bruehl, 'were shocked into the realization that legality no longer mattered'.[14] For the unfortunates this meant not just arrest but indefinite detention—and often torture. For those who might, for want of a better term, be thought 'fortunate', there still remained the immediate and burning appreciation that their fortune might desert them at any time.

Secondly, when we stop to reflect on Arendt's own arrest, we can appreciate her predicament not only in terms of the State's actual interference with her, but also as one in which Arendt's awareness of her relationship with the State, her knowledge that she was dominated, told her that she had to act accordingly in order to 'play safe'; to avoid, if at all possible, the terrifying consequences brought to bear upon so many of her compatriots. 'I *had* to lie to him,' she said, knowing full well that if she did not, not only would the 'organization be exposed' but her personal well-being would have been gravely endangered. In other words, Arendt could not act freely, could not speak openly about her business with the Zionists, nor of her opinions on the regime for whom her arresting officer worked. She had to censor herself in order to facilitate her own release and protect those closest to her from the regime's interference. Arendt was unfree, of that there can be little doubt. In 1933, however, that domination was not yet total.

Thirdly, then, despite the fact that she understood clearly the nature of her condition, despite the fact that the range of actions available to Arendt was restricted when she came face to face with the State via her arresting officer, it is difficult not to detect, as Arendt recounts the tale, a sense, almost, of perverse excitement. So—whilst we might be tempted to rebuke Arendt's abasement here—rather than cringe at a tale of servility, as she is forced to lie and beg her way out of capture, one is left with a sense that, at a micro-level—in *this* encounter—Arendt was the victor. Indeed, it is not impossible to lose sight of the context and feel some pity for the young officer, as the fullness of his naivety in dealing with her, revealed by his eagerness to 'get her out again', becomes apparent. The point, however, is this: Arendt was undoubtedly fortunate—she could just as easily have been arrested by a cold, charmless jobsworth, unresponsive to her lies and unimpressed by her character (little wonder, then, her later fascination with Adolf Eichmann and what she famously described as the banality of (his) evil). Nevertheless, the very fact of there being a face to face encounter, a human encounter, at least permitted the *possibility* of action, exercised extraordinarily, and capable of breaking the cycle of arbitrary arrest and the monstrous consequences which followed.

On this last matter, let us make three further points. First, this was an *extraordinary* encounter. *Normally*, said the police officer, he would know how to dispose of the person in front of him; but Arendt was different. If this was her fortune, her virtue was to grasp the chance, securing her release without betraying her Zionist colleagues. Secondly, Arendt could hold sway over this officer only *because* of the

[14] EYB 103.

extraordinary nature of the encounter. *Normally*, someone in Arendt's position would accept the legal representation paid for by the Zionists and offered to her. Yet Arendt seemed to sense (in the lawyer's 'fear') that normal channels would not serve her well. What is more, it would seem that Arendt saw the lawyer as an obstruction between the officer and herself: as a barrier, in other words, to action. Through a lawyer her encounter would have to have been refracted, she would have been unable to *act* (with all of its performative connotations) with fullest effect on the officer, and thereby would have been less confident of breaking a cycle which might, ultimately, have led her to the concentration camps. Far from debasing her, one might say that here the opportunity for self-censorship vis-à-vis Arendt's arresting officer itself constituted a moment of action. Thirdly, it was nevertheless at this precise moment—when she discovered law's *futility*—that Arendt was awakened to its importance, and even to its meliorative *potential*. It was, after all, the *juridical* person in man which stood as the first and most resistant obstacle to total domination and, worse still, extermination. Let us return then to *The Origins of Totalitarianism* to explore this thought a little further.

II. THE JURIDICAL PERSON

It is in the third book of *The Origins* that we find Arendt's first explicit statement of the *function* of law in a system of government:

> Positive laws in constitutional government are designed to erect boundaries and establish channels of communication between men whose community is continually endangered by the new men born into it. With each new birth, a new beginning is born into the world; a new world has potentially come into being. The stability of the laws corresponds to the constant motion of all human affairs, a motion which can never end as long as men are born and die. The laws hedge in each new beginning and at the same time assure its freedom of movement, the potentiality of something entirely new and unpredictable; the boundaries of positive laws are for the political existence of man what memory is for his historical existence: they guarantee the pre-existence of a common world, the reality of some continuity which transcends the individual life span of each generation, absorbs all new origins and is nourished by them.[15]

In this account, law is needed in order to secure stability: a sort of counterbalance to the constant movement of political action. Given the importance of the concept

[15] H Arendt, *The Origins of Totalitarianism* (New York, Schocken, 2004) 599–600 (hereafter 'OT'). It is not clear here whether Arendt embraced a positivist or natural law-based approach to law. She states, somewhat ambiguously, that '[b]y lawful government we understand a body politic in which positive laws are needed to translate and realize the immutable *ius naturale* or the eternal commandments of God into standards of right and wrong. Only in these standards, in the body of positive laws of each country, do the *ius naturale* or the Commandments of God achieve their political reality' (*ibid*, at 598).

of totalitarianism in Arendt's political theory,[16] her remarks on the special legality established by totalitarian government cannot pass unnoticed. It is not that totalitarian government was in itself lawless. Rather, for Arendt, its legality was based on the law of movement and not of stability. For this reason, totalitarian government could not respect the rule of law:

> At this point the fundamental difference between the totalitarian and all other concepts of law comes to light. Totalitarian policy does not replace one set of laws with another, does not establish its own *consensus juris*, does not create, by one revolution, a new form of legality. Its defiance of all, even its own positive laws implies that it believes it can do without any *consensus juris* whatever, and still not resign itself to the tyrannical state of lawlessness.[17]

This legality was instrumental in *dissolving* the community of men, and in opening the way to their domination. Thus, she said, the 'first essential step on the road to total domination is to kill the juridical person in man'.[18]

To be sure, Arendt did not believe and barely feared that totalitarianism could achieve its aims outright. Totalitarianism, in its fullest, most terrifying form of total, global domination, could not tolerate even the simple plurality of two concurrent totalitarian regimes:

> [T]he chances are that total domination of man will never come about, for it presupposes the existence of one authority, one way of life, one ideology in all countries and among all peoples of the world. Only when no competitor, no country of physical refuge, and no human being whose understanding may offer a spiritual refuge, are left can the process of total domination and the change of the nature of man begin in earnest.[19]

In the isolated context of the concentration camps, however, albeit for a fleeting moment, and restricted to limited spatial bounds, the totalitarian regime *had* succeeded in rendering men superfluous, in creating what she called 'living corpses', whose individuality, whose very humanness, had somehow been stripped from them; so much so that their march to the gas chamber seemed no different—from the perspective of neither the murderer nor the murdered—than the procession of a herd to the slaughterhouse: 'There are no parallels to the life of the concentration camps. Its horror can never be fully embraced by the imagination for the very reason that it stands outside of life and death…'[20]

Arendt traced the creation of living corpses to three key moments. The first, the killing of man's 'juridical person', was carried out by selecting for the camps inmates who had, in no real demonstrable way, violated what one might understand as a law or penal code. 'Criminals,' she explained, 'do not properly belong

[16] On this, see M Canovan, *Hannah Arendt: A Reinterpretation of Her Political Thought* (Cambridge, Cambridge University Press, 1992).
[17] OT 596.
[18] *Ibid* 577.
[19] *Ibid* 617–18.
[20] *Ibid* 572.

in the concentration camps, if only because it is harder to kill the juridical person in a man who is guilty of some crime than in a totally innocent person'.[21] The criminal, this was to say, was *already* a 'legal' person: his crime was defined by law; his criminal status was determined by the legal process; his punishment (should he be found to fall within that category) was both contestable (for example, by appeal) and predictable (as prescribed by law). The criminal, therefore, was by definition a rights-bearing individual judged for his unlawful *actions*. What made the status of the 'innocent' in the concentration camp so drastic was that his detention was brought about not because of his *actions*, something which he could control—to which he could consent—but because of his *identity*, something outwith one's control and also, in Arendt's words, something 'outside the normal judicial procedure in which a definite crime entails a predictable penalty'.[22] Jews could not consent to, and therefore could not contest, their identity *qua* Jews; the carriers of disease could not consent to their illness and therefore could not contest the reason for their detention. Consent, then, was rendered meaningless, and with it the very right of those individuals *to have* the (legal) rights and protections afforded to the criminal. Thus, the aim of arbitrary detention was, she said, to pave the way for the total domination of the whole population by destroying the founding myth of social contract: free consent: 'The arbitrary arrest which chooses among innocent people destroys the validity of free consent, just as torture—as distinguished from death—destroys the possibility of opposition.'[23]

With the legal personality of man destroyed, with the basis of his legal protection in free consent rendered meaningless, the next step in the preparation of living corpses is to destroy man's 'moral person'. 'This,' Arendt said, 'is done in the main by making martyrdom, for the first time in history, impossible'.[24] By making it impossible to find out whether an inmate was dead or alive, Arendt suggested that death itself was robbed of its significance. After a man has shed his mortal coil, after all, it is only by remembrance that his death takes on his significance, that his (individual) life story can be told. By making death 'anonymous', the SS 'took away the individual's own death, proving that henceforth nothing belonged to him and he belonged to no one. His death merely set a seal on the fact that he had never really existed'.[25]

With the destruction of man's legal and moral person, the final step, the overcoming of man's individuality, that which makes him human, '[was] almost always successful'.[26] This could be, and was, achieved by a variety of means, all of which served to transform the victim from human to 'beast': pointless torture designed neither to kill nor to extract information; the herding of hundreds of

[21] *Ibid* 577.
[22] *Ibid*.
[23] *Ibid* 581.
[24] *Ibid* 582.
[25] *Ibid* 583.
[26] *Ibid* 586.

human beings into cramped trains, like cattle, for transportation to the camps; the shaving of the head and the issue of intentionally ill-fitting camp clothing, all served to destroy human dignity and individuality.[27] Indeed, the common experience reported by tour guides at Auschwitz today—that visitors to the camp often find the mugshots of the inmates less harrowing than, say, the collections of their glasses, their shoes, or the briefcases which contained their home address and with them traces of identity—perhaps points precisely to the effectiveness of the SS in destroying even the physical individuality of the camps' inmates.

III. CRISES OF THE REPUBLIC

If Arendt despaired not that totalitarianism would succeed, ultimately, in achieving total domination, she remained concerned that by asserting itself, and by finding an awful reality in the confines of the concentration camps, totalitarianism had

> brought forth an entirely new form of government which is a potentially and an ever-present danger [and which] is only too likely to stay with us from now on, just as other forms of government which came about at different historical moments and rested on different fundamental experiences have stayed with mankind regardless of temporary defeats…[28]

It is unsurprising, then, that she came to warn against the emergence of many such pro-tototalitarian elements in that republic which she so cherished above all, the United States of America. The Vietnam War era, she said, had seen the secret service act almost as a shadow government, whose over-classification of sensitive information had deprived 'the people and their representatives [of access to] what they must know to form an opinion and make decisions'.[29] Detached from the people and their representatives,[30] detached even from the intelligence community,[31] the National Security Council operated in a culture of secrecy. Unlike the imperial bureaucracies, however, for whom effectiveness (however perversely defined) superseded democratic legitimacy, the National Security Council was concerned *not even* with this question. Not democracy, not effectiveness,

[27] *Ibid* 584.

[28] *Ibid* 616.

[29] H Arendt, 'Lying in Politics: Reflections on the Pentagon Papers' (hereafter 'LIP') in H Arendt, *The Crises of the Republic* (San Diego, New York, London, Harcourt Brace & Company, 1972) 30.

[30] LIP 21. 'Even when, under Johnson, foreign governments were thoroughly briefed on our plans for bombing North Vietnam, similar briefing of and consultation with congressional leaders seem never to have taken place.'

[31] *Ibid* 22: 'The fact-finding branches of the intelligence services were separated from whatever covert operations were still going on in the field, which meant that they at least were responsible only for gathering information, rather than for creating the news themselves. They had no need to show positive results and were under no pressure from Washington to produce good news to feed into the public relations machine … They were relatively independent, and the result was that they told the truth, year in and year out.'

but maintaining the *image* of the US as the leading world superpower became the overwhelming aim of their involvement in the region.[32]

Turning her mind to the question of *how* this could come about, Arendt focused her ire on 'the evils of bureaucracy'—what she called 'rule by nobody'—making explicit its cross-fertilisation with the concept of representative democracy:[33]

> The internal world of government, with its bureaucracy on one hand, its social life on the other, made self-deception relatively easy. No ivory tower of the scholars has ever better prepared the mind for ignoring the facts of life than did the various think tanks for the problem-solvers and the reputation of the White House for the President's advisers … [T]he truth of such decisive matters could be successfully covered up in these internal circles—but nowhere else—by worries about how to avoid becoming 'the first American President to lose a war' and by the always present preoccupation with the next election.[34]

What Arendt found to be novel about totalitarianism was not (only) its domination of the public realm but with it, its ravishing of the private realm. This malevolent seed, she warned, was precisely what was to be found in the McCarthy era, when many US citizens, from government officials to high-profile entertainers, to educators, trade unionists and private industry employees, found themselves to be the victims of rigorous investigation, on the basis of often false or exaggerated claims that they were either active Communists or passive sympathisers:

> Informing is a duty in a police state where people have been organized and split into two ever-changing categories: those who have the privilege to be the informers and those who are dominated by the fear of being informed upon.[35]

As she saw it, the adoption of *this* element of totalitarianism was a quite deliberate, but wholly ill-conceived, attempt to defeat the totalitarian spectre of Communism:

> It is the old story: one cannot fight a dragon, we are told, without becoming a dragon; we can fight a society of informers only by becoming informers ourselves …

[32] One memo to the US Secretary of Defense, Robert S McNamara, from his closest adviser, the then United States Assistant Secretary of Defense for International Security Affairs, John McNaughton, leaked to the *New York Times*, famously listed the US aims in Vietnam in order: 'US aims: 70%—To avoid a humiliating US defeat (to our reputation as a guarantor). 20%—To keep SVN (and then adjacent) territory from Chinese hands. 10%—To permit the people of SVN to enjoy a better, freer way of life. ALSO—To emerge from crisis without unacceptable taint from methods used. NOT—To "help a friend," although it would be hard to stay in if asked out.' (*The Pentagon Papers*, Gravel Edition, vol 3, 694–702. Available online, in full, at <http://www.mtholyoke.edu/acad/intrel/pentagon/pent1.html>.)

[33] LIP 20.

[34] *Ibid* 36.

[35] H Arendt, 'The Ex-Communists' in H Arendt, *Essays in Understanding 1930–1954* (Jerome Kohn ed) (New York, San Diego, London, Harcourt Brace & Company, 1994) 394.

> [However, if] we became dragons ourselves, it would be of small interest which of the two dragons should eventually survive. The meaning of the fight would be lost.[36]

For Arendt, the answer to these creeping 'crises of the republic' was—*contra* her contemporary, Ayn Rand's, virtues of selfishness[37]—not to be found by retreating to our private pleasures and peaceful enjoyment, but rather in a call to arms: a (re) invocation of the very soul of republican government; to find a *virtue* of (for want of a better word) 'publicness'. After all, to each of the crises which attracted her attention Arendt had attributed the *absence* of the public:

> [S]even years of an *undeclared* war in Vietnam; the growing influence of *secret* agencies on public affairs; open or *thinly veiled* threats to liberties guaranteed under the First Amendment; attempts to deprive the Senate of its constitutional powers, followed by the President's invasion of Cambodia in open disregard for the constitution, which explicitly requires congressional approval for the beginning of a war …[38]

to say nothing of the 'quicksand of lying statements of all sorts, deceptions as well as self-deceptions … apt to engulf any reader who wishes to probe' the top secret *Pentagon Papers*.

Where the injustices of government lurked in the shadows, remaining illicit, Arendt demanded *of* citizens that the shining light of publicity be cast upon those acts—the citizens themselves the final limitation on the tyrannical corruption of office. Where that injustice was open, defiant even, Arendt demanded *from* citizens the assumption of responsibility: she demanded that they *act*. Perhaps it is an oversimplification, but we can conclude this introduction with a simple proposition which (whether explicit or implicit, whether reaffirmed or denied) will act as a point of reference throughout this volume: that for Arendt the very point of law is to constitute and to preserve a common world—a public realm—where the spirit of action, that defining character of the human condition, can endure.

[36] *Ibid.*

[37] A Rand, *The Virtues of Selfishness: A New Concept of Egoism* (New York, New American Library, 1964).

[38] H Arendt, 'Civil Disobedience' in Arendt, *The Crises of the Republic*, above n 29, 74.

Part I

Between *Nomos* and *Lex*: The Concept of Law in Hannah Arendt's Political Thought

1

Law beyond Command? An Evaluation of Arendt's Understanding of Law

KEITH BREEN

I. INTRODUCTION

HANNAH ARENDT'S ENTIRE body of thought is motivated by one central impetus—the recovery of experiences and modes of perceiving and being in the world that were either lost to time, displaced by theoretical prejudices or tragically erased by events. Her goal, as she saw it, was not to return us to the past but instead to recover forgotten treasures, to retrieve the 'pearls and the corals in the depths' so that we might better understand where we are and where, more importantly, we went wrong.[1] This is why time and again she reaches back into the pre-philosophical experience of the ancient *polis* to lay bare what she sees as the true meaning of action and politics. For Arendt the true meaning of political action consists in 'the joy and the gratification that arise out of being in company with our peers, out of acting together and appearing in public'.[2] This meaning was lost on account of venerable misunderstandings that distorted the basis of political life and were to prove fateful for the course of Western history. The most important of these was the substitution of action understood in terms of 'making', of instrumentally crafting nature and human beings in accordance with a preconceived image, for intersubjective 'doing' and 'speaking', action-in-concert. This substitution proved fateful insofar as it replaced plurality and freedom, the essence of the *polis*, with the fundamentally anti-political categories of violence and domination, and thereby cast rule and command as legitimate political phenomena, a legitimation twentieth-century totalitarianism was to drive to its horrific, logical extreme.

As I understand her work, Arendt's chief objective is to counter the traditional assumption that politics equates with violence by effecting a radical revaluation of political life as a whole. At the heart of this endeavour lies the idea of law.

[1] H Arendt, 'Introduction—Walter Benjamin: 1892–1940' in W Benjamin, *Illuminations* (London, Pimlico, 1999 [1968]) 54.

[2] H Arendt, *Between Past and Future: Eight Exercises in Political Thought* (Harmondsworth, Penguin, 1977) 263 (hereafter 'BPF').

Just as philosophers have misconceived the basis of political life, so too have they misunderstood law. Indeed, the 'traditional concept of law', Arendt argues, reflects and reinforces the assumption that collective action is a matter of ruling and being ruled because it understands law in terms of commandment and of obedience.[3] Under this conceptualisation, law becomes assimilated to coercion, and coercion in turn becomes the basis of all politics. More problematic still, law is seen as requiring for its authority an absolute, a sovereign, whose will is deemed unquestionable and omnipotent. This is troubling not only because such absolutes threaten to efface the plurality and relativity definitive of the mundane, human world, but also because the appeal to absolutes has historically occasioned extreme cycles of violence. Hence Arendt's turn to alternative and earlier conceptualisations of law, to the Greek notion of *nomos* and the Roman idea of *lex*. As she sees them, the Greek idea of law as setting boundaries and the Roman view of law as establishing relationships differ significantly from law as command and obedience. In returning to them, Arendt therefore hopes, as she does with her account of the *bios politikos*, the 'political life', generally, to sidestep the appeal to absolutes and embrace of violence that have been axiomatic for so much of Western thought and practice.

Here I offer an assessment of Arendt's retrieval of *nomos* and *lex*. It is not my claim that she sought to arrive at a systematic theory of law, nor that her reflections on *nomos* and *lex* are fully integrated. Rather, I wish to suggest that when thinking of law in relation to the political, she understood it simultaneously in terms of boundaries and relationships, and that it was this understanding she believed we should endorse if we are to shake off traditional prejudices. I begin by setting out the broader context of Arendt's reflections on law, focusing on her distinctions between *praxis* and *poiēsis* and, relatedly, power and violence, and also on her account of the 'traditional concept of law', a concept whose origin is to her mind less political than theological. This leads to a discussion of *nomos*, the originary act of delineating the internal and external contours of the polity, and of *lex*, the mutual determination and establishment by citizens and strangers of appropriate modes of being-together. Of particular significance here are Arendt's account of the American Revolution and her claim that the 'Founding Fathers' avoided the aporias that doomed the French Revolution by implicitly rejecting the assumptions underpinning the traditional understanding of law, above all the idea of sovereignty. In her view the foundation of the American republic is of immense significance insofar as it reveals the possibility of constitutional beginnings that do not rely upon violence and command. However, this claim should be treated with scepticism. While much can be said for Arendt's account of constitutional beginnings and law, there is very good reason to question whether she has in fact freed law from the problems of sovereignty. Viewing her reflections on *nomos* and *lex* with a critical eye, it becomes clear that law cannot be purged of

[3] H Arendt, *On Revolution* (London, Penguin, 1963) 195 (hereafter 'OR').

the appeal to absolutes, and that the potential for exclusion and therefore violence necessarily remains ever-present.

II. THE PREJUDICES OF THE 'GREAT TRADITION'

> If philosophers … were ever to arrive at a true political philosophy they would have to make the plurality of man, out of which arises the whole realm of human affairs ... the object of their *thaumadzein*.[4]

The 'Great Tradition' of Western political thought, beginning with the Socratic School and in particular Plato, is for Arendt marked by an ironic wish not to understand the political as such but instead to 'escape from politics altogether'.[5] The mistake underlying this wish is the stress on rulership and, consequently, domination, a stress that continues to inform our understanding of the nature of politics. To Arendt's mind this entails a fundamental category error since politics has nothing to do, strictly speaking, with domination. As understood by the Greeks, it was the private realm of the *oikos* or household where domination held sway, the master compelling his slaves to provide the necessities of bare life (*zōē*). The public realm (*ecclesia*, *agora*), by contrast, was the space for freedom, for a genuinely human life (*bios*) lived through engagement with one's peers in endeavours of common concern. Action here consisted in *praxis*, that is, acting and speaking in public, whereby citizens revealed to the world their unique identities, 'who' they were. Such speaking presumed an audience, and in doing so presumed plurality, that the citizens comprising the *polis* were simultaneously equal and yet different, holding irreducibly diverse opinions on public matters. It also presumed the frail 'web of relationships' defining the intersubjective aspect of a world held in common, the fact that actors are necessarily interdependent and the freedom of one secured only through the freedom of all.[6]

Suspicious of the contingency, unreliability and frailty of political life, Plato sought an alternative grounding for politics so as to make it amenable to philosophy and its dictates, and thereby fundamentally altered the meaning of the *bios politikos*. His major innovation consisted in modelling political action in terms not of *praxis* but of *poiesis*.[7] *Poiesis* or 'work' comprises for Arendt both 'fabrication' and 'art' in the sense of *technē* or technical skill. In distinction to *praxis*, which has no determinate object, *poiēsis* is typified by an instrumental logic or rationality inhering in the calculation of means to determinate ends. The model applicable

[4] H Arendt, 'Philosophy and Politics' (1990) 57 *Social Research* 73, 103.

[5] H Arendt, *The Human Condition* (Chicago, University of Chicago Press, 1958) 222 (hereafter 'HC'). See also H Arendt, 'The End of Tradition' in H Arendt, *The Promise of Politics* (J Kohn, ed) (New York, Schocken Books, 2005) 81; and H Arendt, 'The Great Tradition II. Ruling and Being Ruled' (2007) 74 *Social Research* 941, 945 (hereafter 'GTII').

[6] HC 181–90; and H Arendt, 'Introduction *into* Politics' (hereafter 'IP') in Arendt, *The Promise of Politics*, above n 5, 117–18.

[7] HC 195, 222–23.

here is of the lone craftsman or architect—the philosopher king—moulding and disciplining natural and human material in accordance with pre-given ideas or plans.

From this innovation three regrettable consequences followed. First, because *poiēsis* entails seizing material and forcing it to accord with a pre-given image or plan, 'an element of violence is inevitably inherent' in its operation.[8] Violence, which in ordinary Greek experience was pre-political, therefore moved to the heart of political life. This is deeply problematic, Arendt contends, because violence has nothing to do with the real basis of politics, which is power. Power requires 'the living together of people' dependent on plurality and vocal interchange; it 'comes into being only if and when men join themselves together for the purpose of action'.[9] Violence, by contrast, is the use of implements by individuals or groups to coerce others into conforming with their ends and desires. Having no connection to speech or plurality as such, it is in fact power's 'opposite', a mode of interacting with the world destructive of genuine solidarity.[10] The second, and related, consequence was that the division between masters and subjects in the private household was transported into the public realm as a division between rulers and ruled. With this a despotic authority relation, appropriate only in a sphere of life concerned with necessity, with servicing bodily existence, became legitimate across all realms of human life.[11] Thus, in place of a relation of peers defined by equality, there now appeared a hierarchy between those who lead, because they possess the knowledge to 'mould' the polity, and those who follow, who obey. The third consequence was an elementary revaluation of the meaning of freedom. Where once freedom was understood to inhere in the ability spontaneously to begin, to initiate, dependent upon speech and thus the presence of others, the Western philosophical tradition gradually came to identify freedom with 'sovereignty, the ideal of a free will, independent from others and eventually prevailing against them'.[12] With this the original experience of the *polis* was finally lost, so much so that it has become received wisdom to understand politics in terms of ruling over others and its means as necessarily coercive.

Here law, or rather one vision of law, also played a key role. This is because Plato's transformation of the political was later 'strangely confirmed and fortified by the addition of the Hebrew-Christian tradition and its "imperative conception of law"'. Gaining ascendancy over all other conceptions, this theologically inspired concept of law stemmed from an 'almost automatic generalization of God's "Commandments", according to which "the simple relation of command

[8] BPF 111; HC 139–40.
[9] HC 201; OR 175.
[10] H Arendt, *Crises of the Republic* (New York, Harcourt Brace Jovanovich, 1970) 155 (hereafter 'CR').
[11] BPF 105–09; GTII 945.
[12] BPF 163; HC 234.

and obedience" … sufficed to identify the essence of law'.[13] As Arendt sees it, the Hebrew-Christian tradition is important for two basic reasons. First, and most obviously, it enshrines within the heart of law the ruler-ruled relation, taking as self-evident all that that relation entails. Second, it supposes that law requires 'a transcendent source of authority for its validity … an origin … beyond human power'. Here the idea of *poiēsis* and its correlates come to the fore, the origin of mundane law being a figure, a Creator God or Immortal Legislator, who in the mode of an architect both fashions the law and yet stands outside, above, that creation. And as with an architect's creation, the law's basis is seen to lie in imperatives, 'sanctions', that must be obeyed 'regardless' of 'consent or mutual agreements', since the originator of law is necessarily superior to ordinary human beings and therefore sovereign.[14] The ultimate authority of law lies, consequently, in the first mover's unparalleled strength and irresistible ability to punish transgressions. Thus, law under this conception is intimately connected with, if not identical to, coercion, its wellspring being a creative force and a fabricating violence.

So long as the authority of the Church remained intact, the traditional imperative concept of law remained largely unproblematic. However, once the authority of the Church was supplanted by early modern processes of secularisation, there appeared a pressing need to find alternative sources of authority for the newly-emancipated secular realm and its commanding law. Hence Bodin's and later Hobbes's novel claim that the source and legitimation of all earthly power was the sovereign, absolute monarch. To Arendt's mind this transference of absolute authority from the divine to the mundane realm set in train events that could only conclude in misfortune. For when the authority of the monarch was in turn itself challenged, as in French Revolution, there arose two seemingly irresolvable problems: how to ensure the legality of the new laws heralded by the revolution, which still required an absolute for their validity; and how to secure the legitimacy of the new revolutionary bodies themselves, which, being prior to any constitution, were clearly unconstitutional.[15] Sieyès's famed solution to these perplexities was to separate the new order or 'constituted power' (*pouvoir constitué*) from the sovereign 'constituent power' (*pouvoir constituant*), and to locate this sovereign power in the 'will of the nation', which, remaining 'outside and above all governments and all laws', therefore became simultaneously the source of all power and law.[16]

[13] CR 138. For present purposes I take Arendt's characterisation of the 'Hebrew-Christian' notion of law as commandant and obedience at face value. It is worth mentioning, however, that Arendt in a relatively early text attributes this notion of law not only to the Hebrew-Christian tradition but also to pre-Socratic thought, to Heraclitus' claim that '"All human laws are nourished by the one divine law"' (H Arendt, 'The Great Tradition I. Law and Power' (2007 [1953]) 74 *Social Research* 713, 718–19 (hereafter 'GTI').

[14] OR 189.

[15] *Ibid* 161, 183–84.

[16] *Ibid* 163. See EJ Sieyès, 'What is the Third Estate?' (1789), in M Sonenscher (ed) *Sieyès: Political Writings* (Indianapolis, IN, Hackett Publishing Company, 2003).

As Arendt sees it, this turn was ruinous because it rested the validity of an imperative law on an entity whose will is fickle, 'ever-changing by definition', with the result that the new French order was doomed to instability and continual usurpation.[17] Moreover, insofar as the will of the nation was the source of all power and law, the ultimate sanction, it became permissible, indeed a duty, to coerce or even eliminate those who offended against this sanctioning will.[18] Thus, oppression and terror became legitimate, normal, political tools. When under totalitarianism 'Nature' or 'History', governed by ineluctable 'laws of movement' discerned by nineteenth-century ideologies, subsequently replaced the nation as the absolute source of law, such terror would cease to be just a tool and transform instead into the very essence of government.[19]

III. LIMITING WALLS AND LASTING TIES—*NOMOS* AND *LEX*

> The common dilemma—either the law is absolutely valid and therefore needs for its legitimacy an immortal, divine legislator, or the law is simply a command with nothing behind it but the state's monopoly of violence—is a delusion.[20]

To escape this 'common dilemma' generated by the absolutism and violence inherent in the traditional Occidental understanding of lawmaking, Arendt advocates a return to the Greek and Roman conceptions of law. Although 'very different' in implication, 'even contrary' to one another, these ideas reveal a path out of the quandaries that beset the French Revolution and most political beginnings before and since then.[21] They do so, Arendt contends, because neither presumes the need 'to introduce an absolute, a divine or despotic power, into the political realm'.[22] Indeed, for the ancient Greeks and Romans the problem of transcendent sources of authority could not even arise, since they both viewed law as the result of this-worldly action. For both civilisations law was conventional, an 'artificial' and 'man-made' component of the human condition that, being essentially mundane, required no appeal to divinity or some universal norm beyond the human realm.[23] Thus, in the Greek and Roman concepts of law Arendt sees ideas that avoid equating law with sovereign command, and this because they reflect and feed into two primary features of the 'common world', for her the basis for all political life.

Nomos lies at the heart of Arendt's political thought insofar as it corresponds to the first aspect of what she means by 'world'. This is the world as 'human artifice',

[17] OR 163, 183.
[18] *Ibid* 164.
[19] H Arendt, *The Origins of Totalitarianism* (New York, Harcourt Brace & Company, 1966) 461–67 (hereafter 'OT'). See also CR 79–80; GTI 719–20.
[20] CR 193.
[21] IP 178.
[22] OR 188.
[23] *Ibid* 186.

the things and objects that physically connect and yet separate human beings, thereby providing an objective home or 'in-between' for their common life.[24] Law as *nomos* contributes to this artifice in delineating the boundaries and limitations of the polity, the very place where it can be said to be. 'All laws first create a space in which they are valid', a tangible range or enclosure where human beings can interact freely, and what lies beyond this 'is without law and, even more precisely, without [a] world'.[25] To the Greek mind, law consisted of 'hedges', 'walls' or 'boundaries [that] men establish between themselves or between city and city'.[26] The law, in other words, determines the internal and external topography of the polity, on the one hand internally demarcating the private from the public realm, the boundaries between citizens themselves, and on the other hand externally delineating the contours of the polity, separating it off from foreign spaces and cities. *Nomos* in this sense has two interwoven 'dimensions': a 'physical' aspect, the compartmentalisation of inner and outer territory, and a 'normative' aspect, the determination of a specific community with a unique identity defined by particular interests.[27] Indeed, Arendt writes that law actually creates the political community as a 'unity' as such by first determining 'the character of its inhabitants, setting them apart and making them distinguishable from the inhabitants of all other cities'.[28] *Nomos* is therefore 'constitutive' for all political action insofar as it is *nomos* that brings the space for such action into being and thereby 'sires' the citizen.[29] This is why the Greeks understood lawmaking as 'pre-political', a task engaged in prior to the existence of the *polis* and in like manner to the erection of a city's physical walls.[30] Viewing lawmaking as lying at the beginning of all polities, but having nothing to do with political activity or life per se, the Greeks therefore deemed it acceptable to task non-citizens and strangers with the foundation of the *polis*. But whilst this task may not have been the concern of the citizen, it nonetheless had enormous significance. For it was *nomos*, with its stabilising walls and boundaries, that gave the political realm durability and permanence, ensuring that men's words and deeds would not be forgotten, and also that the community itself would survive the 'onslaught' of new generations and unforeseeable events. Hence the Greek belief that violating the law represented the greatest vice, an act

[24] HC 95–96, 182.

[25] IP 190.

[26] GTI 716. See also HC 63–64.

[27] H Lindahl, 'Give and Take: Arendt and the *Nomos* of Political Community' (2006) 32 *Philosophy & Social Criticism* 881, 886.

[28] GTI 717; IP 180–81.

[29] IP 180, 182. This sits uncomfortably with Arendt's assertion elsewhere that the 'space of appearance … predates and precedes all formal constitution of the public realm and the various forms of government, that is, the various forms in which the public realm can be organized'. Under this alternative account, law does not bring community into being; instead, law only cements an 'already existing' political community (HC 198–99).

[30] HC 194; IP 179; OR 186, 313.

of supreme hubris, since in breaching the law transgressors imperilled the identity and survival of the community as a whole.[31]

In discussing *nomos* Arendt is not simply reporting the Greek view of law, but also affirming it as a concept. To appreciate law properly is to register its primordial spatial and limiting quality, a quality wholly expunged by totalitarianism's perverse identification of law with ineluctable and limitless movement.[32] Only within a stable polity and determinate place, hemmed in and guaranteed by laws that protect the citizenry from themselves and outsiders, can freedom be realised. Yet the idea of law as *nomos* is not without difficulty. Along with their fractious agonal spirit, it was the Greeks' exclusive understanding of law as a boundary or wall which separates, rather than bridges, distinct spaces and peoples that prevented them from joining city with city and establishing a cohesive Hellas. As Arendt sees it, politics for the Greeks could consequently exist only within the *polis*; outside the polity's walls, in interactions with different cities and communities, the logic of rivalry, subterfuge and violence necessarily reigned unchecked.[33]

The Greek inability to envision the possibility of an external politics prompts Arendt's turn to the Roman notion of *lex*. For her the undoubted 'political genius of Rome' stemmed precisely from its understanding of law as a bridge or bond.[34] *Lex* occupies a similarly significant position within Arendt's thought as *nomos* because *lex* coincides with the second elemental aspect of 'world'. This is the 'world' understood as an intersubjective 'in-between' that 'overlays' and complements the objective human artifice. It consists of the 'web of human relationships' engendered by the intersection of 'innumerable' perspectives through speech and action.[35] Because innately relational, *lex* contributes to and sustains this web, thus permitting a politics not only between citizens but also between strangers. In essence, law as *lex* denotes an '"intimate connection" or relationship' that 'connects two things or two partners whom external circumstances have brought together'. This intimate connection takes the form of '"lasting ties" or "contracts"' that come 'into being not by diktat or by an act of force but rather through mutual agreements'.[36] In sharp distinction to *nomos*, which is 'conceived by a lawgiver' prior to the birth of the polity, *lex* presumes and emerges from a 'back-and-forth exchange of words and action'.[37] Thus, for the Romans lawmaking represented the most political of activities, since it was by way of an agreement or treaty concluded between the warring patricians and plebeians that Rome had originally come into being, an alliance itself preceded in Roman self-consciousness by the

[31] HC 191; IP 181, 187.
[32] OT 464.
[33] GTII 950; IP 165, 182, 187; OR 12.
[34] HC 195. See also J Taminiaux, 'Athens and Rome' in D Villa (ed), *The Cambridge Companion to Hannah Arendt* (Cambridge, Cambridge University Press, 2000) 172; and R Tsao, 'Arendt against Athens: Rereading *The Human Condition*' (2002) 30 *Political Theory* 97, 109.
[35] HC 183–84; IP 161.
[36] OR 187; IP 179.
[37] IP 180.

legendary compact between Aeneas' Trojans and the native Latins.[38] In fact, it was law as *lex* that enabled them to see in conflict and war not the end of politics but its very beginning. Through agreements and joint undertakings erstwhile enemies could break the chains of hostility and come together as 'allies' (*socii*), thus giving birth to 'a cooperative community that fostered relationships between partners', the *societas Romana*.[39]

The importance of this view of law lies, for Arendt, in its total opposition to the idea of law as command. As Montesquieu correctly perceived, underpinning law as *lex* are mutual rapports enacted by parties who are equal yet nonetheless different from each other.[40] Its basis therefore is not rule and obedience but rather reciprocal persuasion and speech, *praxis* in the true sense of the term. It was this notion of law that the American revolutionaries alighted upon in founding the American republic and which helped them to avoid the aporias that later bedevilled the French. Although theoretically still under the spell of the traditional idea of law, on the level of practice the Americans escaped the need for a sovereign absolute because they discovered the legitimation of their new laws and of the constitutionality of their revolution 'in the act of foundation itself'.[41] Harkening back to the earlier experiences of the Pilgrims and the Mayflower Compact, in constituting the republic the 'Founding Fathers' uncovered the 'principle' that was to save their efforts from 'arbitrariness' and give them enduring 'validity'. Born of 'the combined power of the many', that principle was simply 'the interconnected principle of mutual promise and common deliberation'.[42] Enjoying the 'great good fortune' of never having their constituent power seriously questioned, the 'Founding Fathers' provided in the form of the Constitution an enduring, tangible source for law that quickly became an object of common reverence and 'worship', *pietas* in the 'original Roman sense'.[43] In doing so they avoided the French conflation of law and power, and subordination of both to the capricious will of the 'nation'. Just as importantly, they allowed for the natality of future generations, their 'capacity for building, preserving, and caring' for the world, in conceiving of the Constitution as a living document and thus as an object of subsequent amendment and augmentation.[44] Understood in its totality, what the 'unforgettable story' of the foundation of the American republic reveals is that 'all laws', in particular constitutional law, are essentially '"directives" rather than "imperatives"' whose 'ultimate guarantee' rests in 'the old Roman maxim *Pacta sunt servanda*'.[45] Law therefore requires no immortal legislator, no sovereign ruler,

38 OR 188; IP 183.
39 IP 185–86.
40 OR 170, 188, 302.
41 *Ibid* 204.
42 *Ibid* 212, 214.
43 *Ibid* 165, 198.
44 BPF 95; OR 202.
45 OR 213; CR 193–94.

and its authority does not rest on coercion; instead, its true wellspring is mutual consent and a promise between citizens.[46]

IV. LAW WITHOUT AN ABSOLUTE, FOUNDATION WITHOUT COMMANDMENT?

> 'A law', Pindar says …, 'is the king over all, the mortal and the immortal alike, and in creating justice it wields the most powerful force with overpowering strength'.[47]

In recounting the foundation of the American republic and returning to the ideas of *nomos* and *lex*, Arendt hopes to contest the assumption that all polities have their 'origin in crime', in violent confrontation, an assumption which, if not logically implied by the imperative concept of law, is nonetheless germane to it.[48] Moreover, while *nomos* and *lex* have very different meanings, it is clear she attributes to them equal importance.[49] The Greeks were unable to link city with city through treaties on account of their understanding of law as *nomos*, yet the Romans 'were also victims of their law', which, because lacking the Greek emphasis on limits, impelled them to found an empire that 'once achieved could only collapse'.[50] For Arendt, then, law is at one and the same time limiting and relational, creating a space bounded by rules and establishing relationships between distinct actors. This is the implication of the claim that actors need to constitute, through 'binding and promising [*lex*]', 'a stable worldly structure to house [*nomos*] … their combined power of action'.[51] To that extent it is better to understand her discussion of Greek and Roman law less as an accurate historical account and more as an extended reflection on the nature of law.[52] And although she nowhere attempts systematically to interrelate the concepts of *nomos* and *lex*, the general portrait of law that emerges is undoubtedly suggestive and illuminating. It disputes the celebration of violence as a creative, originary force that Arendt rightly sees as informing much of Western thought, from philosophy, through political theory, to psychology and

[46] CR 92–93. Indeed, Arendt believes that 'perhaps the greatest American innovation in politics as such was the consistent abolition of sovereignty within the body politic of the republic, the insight that in the realm of human affairs sovereignty and tyranny are the same' (OR 153).

[47] IP 181–82.

[48] OR 20.

[49] In stressing the coequality of *nomos* and *lex*, I take issue with Lindahl's (above n 27, 884) claim that *nomos* is Arendt's primary conception of law, *lex* being merely 'derivative', and also Taminiaux's belief (above n 34, 173–77) that she prized the Roman concept of law over the Greek.

[50] IP 187.

[51] OR 175.

[52] There is actually very good reason to doubt Arendt's historical assertions regarding Greek and Roman law. The Greeks clearly had an understanding of the law as 'lasting tie', as Thucydides' (Thucydides, *History of the Peloponnesian War* (London, Penguin, 1972) 356–63) description of the 'Peace of Nicias' and other treaties concluded during the Peloponnesian War shows; and the Romans, too, were conscious of the importance of limits, of, to quote Arendt herself, the 'old sanctity of the hearth', the 'boundaries surrounding each property … [and] house' (HC 29. See also *ibid* 63, fn 62).

biology.[53] Doing so this understanding of law also contests the idolatry of strength underpinning the commonplace yet hubristic belief that human beings can create their world in common simply through imposing their will. It shows that the ideal of sovereignty, *at least* as traditionally conceived in the sense of having just one source and being the attribute of one agent, is a dangerous chimera, more a despairing retreat from genuine freedom than its realisation. All law is brought into being by action-in-concert, by individuals who cooperatively establish elements of their common world, even if these individuals comprise merely a few and not the polity as a whole. And no law can endure, Arendt correctly observes, that relies solely upon coercion, since the authority and endurance of law ultimately depend upon citizens' acquiescence and support. Such acquiescence is not deference to a transcendental power or norm, whether in the form of an omnipotent deity or Kant's categorical imperative, but instead commitment and consent to a mundane reality that simultaneously relates one to all and yet places limits on what can be done and to whom.

Arendt, therefore, certainly de-dramatises the 'common dilemma' she thinks at the heart of Western legal thought. However, it is questionable whether this dilemma is merely a 'delusion' and whether she herself can fully escape the appeal to command or absolutes. The first reason for thinking this relates more to her understanding of politics than of law per se. As explained above, she draws a very strong contrast between political action and power, characterised by speech and equality, on the one hand, and violence, the use of implements to coerce others into compliance with one's will, on the other. This contrast is based upon an equally strong division between a political realm defined by freedom and non-political realms—the household in ancient times, the 'social' sphere in modernity—defined by necessity, where technical mastery rather than speech and deliberation fittingly holds sway. If these rudimentary divisions or binaries are rejected, then Arendt's political theory as a whole stands in need of fundamental revision. Predictably, there are very good grounds for rejecting them. As many have argued, Arendt's division between supposedly political and non-political realms rests on an untenable, essentialist partitioning of natural necessity, the needs of the body, from worldly culture and citizenship.[54] The effect of this dualism, perversely, is to rid politics of its substantive content and to legitimate hierarchy and

[53] CR 156–75.

[54] See, eg, S Benhabib, *The Reluctant Modernism of Hannah Arendt* (Thousand Oaks, Cal, SAGE, 1996); R Bernstein, 'Rethinking the Social and the Political' in R Bernstein, *Philosophical Profiles: Essays in a Pragmatic Mode* (Cambridge, Polity, 1986); J-P Deranty and E Renault, 'Democratic Agon: Striving for Distinction or Struggle against Domination and Injustice?' in A Schaap (ed), *Law and Agonistic Politics* (Farnham, Ashgate, 2009); J Habermas, 'Hannah Arendt's Communications Concept of Power' (1977) 44 *Social Research* 3; HF Pitkin, 'Justice: On Relating Private and Public' in LP Hinchman and SK Hinchman (eds), *Hannah Arendt: Critical Essays* (Albany, NY, SUNY Press, 1994); and S Wolin, 'Hannah Arendt: Democracy and the Political' in LP Hinchman and SK Hinchman (eds), *Hannah Arendt: Critical Essays* (Albany, NY, SUNY Press, 1994).

technocratic rule in large areas of human life.[55] A similar charge can be levelled against Arendt's all too easy separation of power from violence, a separation she herself frequently calls into question. Although seeing them as absolute contrasts, she concedes they 'usually appear together'.[56] More than this, violence is understood as a 'rational' and apposite collective response in many circumstances, including defence against aggression, liberation from tyranny and resistance against injustice. Speaking of 1968, for example, Arendt acknowledges that France 'would not have received the most radical bill since Napoleon to change its antiquated education system if the French students had not rioted'.[57] Here and elsewhere in her work the rigid contrast between instrumental *poiēsis* and collective *praxis* breaks down, an undeniable instance of genuine acting-in-concert occurring within and being impelled by a campaign of hostile confrontation. Hence the eventual concession that neither power nor violence 'is a natural phenomenon', that both 'belong to the *political realm* of human affairs whose essentially human quality is guaranteed by man's *faculty of action*'.[58]

It is therefore no exaggeration to claim that 'Arendtian politics remains haunted by the violence it supposedly excludes'.[59] This being so, it would be surprising if violence were not also to haunt her understanding of law, and in truth it does. We can see this most noticeably in her account of *nomos*. Law as both *nomos* and *lex* is said to have 'an altogether different meaning' from the imperative concept of law and its presumption of command, sovereign rulership and an absolute source.[60] Yet Pindar, Arendt observes, was not wrong to see in *nomos* a '"king"' having '"the most powerful force"'. For the Greeks, but also for Arendt insofar as she affirms the idea of *nomos*, the 'law ... has something violent about it in terms of both its *origins* and its *nature*'.[61] This is so because law in the form of *nomos* issues not from *praxis* but from a process of fabrication, *poiēsis*, the lawmaker acting in the guise of an architect or craftsman in determining the contour and identity of the polity. Creating boundaries and inscribing a distinct communal identity, the lawgiver's laws consequently function as 'masters and commanders

55 K Breen, 'Violence and Power: A Critique of Hannah Arendt on "the Political"' (2007) 33 *Philosophy & Social Criticism* 343, 351–55.

56 CR 151.

57 *Ibid* 176.

58 *Ibid* 179, emphasis added. This finds further reinforcement in the observation that 'even the most despotic domination we know of, the rule of master over slaves, who always outnumbered him, did not rest on superior means of coercion as such, but on a superior organization of power ... the organized solidarity of the masters' (*ibid* 149). Here power and violence are not opposed; they are mutually implicated.

59 E Fraser and K Hutchings, 'On Politics and Violence: Arendt contra Fanon' (2008) 7 *Contemporary Political Theory* 90, 94.

60 OR 189; HC 63.

61 IP 181, emphasis added. It could be retorted that Arendt is merely reporting the Greek view and not endorsing it. However, given that she affirms the notion of *nomos* generally, and given, too, that *nomos* corresponds to the world as fabricated artifice, the objective in-between, this retort lacks plausibility. Moreover, note her use of the present tense here: the violence intrinsic to law is not ascribable to Greek understanding alone but to law in general.

in the *polis*' whose authority all must obey and 'fear'. Indeed, the law is 'both father and despot in one', bringing the polity into being and ensuring its continuance through prohibitive barriers—'walls' or 'fences'—that none may transgress without incurring retribution.[62]

These remarks are striking for two reasons. First, despite lamenting Plato's substitution of *poiēsis* for *praxis*, Arendt concurs with him in thinking law, or at least one crucial aspect of it, a product of making, fabrication. Second, the terms and images employed in describing *nomos* here are heavily redolent of the terms and images employed in her account of the traditional concept of law. The origin of *nomos*, like that of the Decalogue and its precepts, lies in an act of creation that is definitive for all that follows, the lawgiver of the *polis*, similar to the Hebrew-Christian God, standing outside or beyond his creation. The nature of *nomos*, as with the imperative idea of law, is essentially despotic, presuming rule and necessary subordination to rule—its '"force"' consisting in an '"overpowering strength"'—and therefore some notion of sovereignty, of a predominant, albeit impersonal, commander. And just like the traditional concept, *nomos* consists of absolutes, of limits that are unconditionally valid for all within its reach and province.

There appears, then, to be a deep-seated tension in Arendt's understanding of law insofar as she simultaneously spurns the imperative concept of law and yet sees command and obedience as inherent features of *nomos*. This tension stems, I believe, from her overriding wish to purge politics of violence, which motivates her rejection of law as command, and yet a partial recognition of the ramifications of viewing law, quite appropriately, as the setting of limits and boundaries. For viewing law in this way necessarily means seeing elements of command, even violence, lying at its heart. Of course, to emphasise these features of law as *nomos* is not nihilistically to celebrate violence or to embrace a Schmittian ideal of sovereignty, which Arendt properly rejects.[63] It is, instead, to recognise the ever-present possibility of violence and the fact, lamentable or not, that for the law to endure there must be some effective sanction, some temporally located absolute, that counters violations and transgressions.

Arendt was unaware of the tension in her account of law because she failed fully to think through the implications of law as *nomos*. One plausible explanation for this failure lies in her suggestion that law as *nomos* is 'pre-political', that its imperative dimensions do not intrude upon politics itself, and also her view that in subordinating ourselves to law's mastery we do not submit to rulership but instead give voluntary 'consent', 'support', to an impartial body of rules.[64] So conceived, command and coercion lie outside the political properly understood, at the

[62] *Ibid* 182.

[63] We should note that rejecting Schmitt's view of sovereignty does not necessitate a rejection of sovereignty per se. Arendt could not see this because she understood sovereignty entirely in Schmittian terms.

[64] CR 139–40.

moment when the 'rules of the game' were set, these rules being less imperatives and more the condition for our entering 'human community' and 'the great game of the world'.[65] The problem here, first, is that Arendt's characterisation of *nomos* as pre-political misrepresents what is in truth the *arch-political* moment and event.[66] In laying down the law, the lawgiver, whether a single individual or a group of actors, establishes, to use Arendt's own words, the 'character' of the community itself, stabilises it as a 'unity', thereby giving expression to a unique 'identity', what the community is and is not, and, just as importantly, demarcating what belongs in public from what lies in the household and private realm.[67] To do all this is to constitute, in short, what 'politics' essentially is, an act which in no wise can be said to stand above or somehow before that which it constitutes. Moreover, the spatial and normative constitution of a polity does not occur simply at its beginning but is an ongoing process, the polity's wall of law, like a physical wall, requiring maintenance, revision and addition over time.

However, the more serious problem here is Arendt's neglect of a vital aspect of fixing identities and setting boundaries. The creators of law, because finite and embedded in the world, give shape to an identity that reflects and reinforces a specific constellation of interests that is attributable to a distinct collectivity or group inhabiting a particular time. Such is an unavoidable aspect of all lawmaking and should not therefore be decried. But what needs to be acknowledged is the inescapability of *exclusion*, that the identity embedded in law as *nomos* shuts out and silences alternative communal self-conceptions and interests. There will consequently always be those who, whilst perhaps of the polity, are not recognised in its laws, whether justly or unjustly. This was the case, as Arendt notes, in the ancient polity, just as it is in modern states ('displaced persons' being merely one of many instances).[68] But to see in law as *nomos* the arch-political event and to admit, as well, that this ongoing event entails exclusions, is to accept the ineradicability of command and coercion and such at the core of political life. This is because a polity, in order to endure as a unity, must where necessary be willing forcefully to assert its physical and normative identity against challenges from within and without. It is also because those excluded from that identity, or who find themselves distorted within it, may dissent and eventually rebel, resorting to coercion to resist coercion by the existing polity and its supporters. Arendt is right to say that laws, the 'rules of the game', depend upon consent, but this consent is rarely ever to an impartial body of rules that encompasses all in an equal manner, and it is consent to laws that we think should be *valid*, absolute in an important sense, not only for ourselves but also for others, regardless of whether they themselves consent.

[65] *Ibid* 193.
[66] Lindahl, above n 27, 885.
[67] IP 180–81; GTI 717.
[68] GTII 949; OT 279–302.

In her discussion of civil disobedience in *Crises of the Republic*, for example, Arendt does acknowledge the exclusionary aspects of law. Nonetheless, she omits to register exclusion, and therefore the potential resort to command, as inevitable aspects of all law.[69] This omission is apparent in her account of *nomos*, but even more conspicuous in her account of *lex* and her prime example of political foundation, the American Revolution. Arendt's narrative of that event is in terms of an entire people, through 'mutual promise and common deliberation', consensually settling upon 'an agreed purpose' and deciding the terms of their shared existence.[70] Doing so, she declares, they not only avoided Sieyès's invocation of sovereign power and secured the legitimacy of their common endeavours, but also ensured the stability of the republic by separating law from power, the source of law being the Constitution and the source of power, very differently, 'the people'. The foundation was thereby laid for '"a Commonwealth for increase"'.[71] However, as Frank points out, this happy narrative is at best a partial and distorting history, one that hides 'the sharply agonistic politics' of revolutionary and post-revolutionary America.[72] Little mention is made of the conflict between the Federalists and the Anti-Federalists and the historical truth that the term 'the people' was subject to opposed invocations, which, *contra* Arendt, both questioned the constituent power of the 'Founding Fathers' and *in extremis* gave rise to outright rebellion (Shays's Rebellion, the Whiskey Rebellion and so forth). There is little recognition, either, that this '"Commonwealth for increase"' and its precursor, the pre-revolutionary colonies, rested and subsequently grew upon the brutal subjugation of rival peoples—native American nations, Hispanic cultures, African slaves—who were deliberately left to languish outside the scope and terms of the Mayflower Compact and later the Constitution.[73] Nor, just as strangely, is there any reflection upon the American Civil War, a conflagration which saw the inheritors of the Constitution tear themselves apart over the meaning of that very inheritance.

In Arendt's defence here, one could say that her goal in narrating the birth of the American republic was to provide a salutary story, a reinvigorating tale to stir and empower present and future generations.[74] The problematic effect of this

[69] Admittedly, she does approach this insight when observing, in relation to acts of civil disobedience, that '"the law cannot justify the violation of the law," even if this violation aims at preventing the violation of another law' (CR 99). The law, in other words, must, because *law*, oppose all extra-legal challenges to its authority and existing 'unity'.

[70] OR 214; HC 245.

[71] OR 157, 171.

[72] J Frank, *Constituent Moments: Enacting the People in Postrevolutionary America* (Durham, NC, Duke University Press, 2010) 52–61. See also Wolin, above n 54, 298–99.

[73] Arendt does, in passing, note the 'primordial crime' of slavery and the 'fact that these people [the native Americans and Blacks] had never been included in the original *consensus universalis* of the American republic' (OR 71; CR 90). However, neither truth impinges upon her celebration of the American Revolution.

[74] This is how Murphy reads her treatment of the American Revolution (P Murphy, 'Power and Paradox: Hannah Arendt's America' in A Schaap *et al* (eds), *Power, Judgment and Political Evil: In Conversation with Hannah Arendt* (Farnham, Ashgate, 2010)). It also underpins McGowan's claim that

'fable', however, is the same as 'that of all legitimating fables: to prohibit further inquiry into the origins of the system and protect its center of illegitimacy from the scrutiny of prying eyes'.[75] For in recounting the origins of the American republic, Arendt not only masks the gross injustices associated with that particular foundation—as she does with other political beginnings, notably Rome—but also blinds us to the quandaries faced in that act of founding. As the above historical observations suggest, it was and remains the case that American political history is one of continual contest over constituent power and thus sovereignty, over who could claim genuinely to represent 'the people'. Moreover, far from being separate, law and power were and are fundamentally interwoven, contested visions of and struggles over the nature of the polity—its scope and purpose, those who may claim to be citizens and those who may not—feeding into and transforming law, both statutory and constitutional.[76] In this and other respects, therefore, the American revolutionaries were not very dissimilar to the French. Neither conclusively solved the aporias of foundation, since in each case the authority of the new laws and the constitutionality of those establishing them remained in question. Yet the most serious issue here is not Arendt's suspect contrast of the Americans and French, but instead her account of political foundation, of constitutional promising, in general. For such promising is hardly ever a simple result of cooperative deliberation and consensual agreement by those party to it.[77] Instead, it is just as frequently marked by discord, distrust and mutual suspicion on the part of those contracting, their promise being sworn to through gritted teeth and often for different, even opposed, ends.[78] More than such agonism, however, there is also the ubiquitous potential for antagonism, for *hostility* towards and from those who are knowingly or unwittingly placed outside the terms of a foundational compact.

an emancipatory utopianism motivates her work throughout (J McGowan, 'Must Politics be Violent? Arendt's Utopian Vision' in C Calhoun and J McGowan (eds), *Hannah Arendt and the Meaning of Politics* (Minneapolis, University of Minnesota Press, 1997)).

[75] B Honig, 'Declarations of Independence: Arendt and Derrida on the Problem of Founding a Republic' (1991) 85 *American Political Science Review* 97, 107.

[76] Frank, above n 72, 53. Arendt herself points to the interwovenness of law and power when she remarks that the law can 'stabilize and legalize change once it has occurred, but the change itself is always the result of extra-legal action', that is, action-in-concert and power (CR 80).

[77] Think, for instance, of the Dayton Agreement of 1995, the 1998 Good Friday Agreement, the Iraqi Constitution of 2005, or, indeed, of any recent treaty arising from a major self-determination dispute. These compacts were born not of solidarity, mutual 'joy' or 'gratification' at being in the company of one's peers, but of military stalemate and a grudging recognition that strategic goals could be realised only through compromise and concession. See, eg, J McGarry and B O'Leary, 'Consociation and Self-Determination Disputes: The Evidence from Northern Ireland and Other Recent Cases' in K Breen and S O'Neill (eds), *After the Nation? Critical Reflections on Nationalism and Postnationalism* (Basingstoke, Palgrave Macmillan, 2010).

[78] Arendt glosses over the reality that collective endeavours are distinguished less by an 'agreed purpose' than by a confluence of many purposes, some of which are bound to conflict. And even when there is an 'agreed purpose', such can be subject to wildly dissimilar interpretations, giving rise to further dissension and conflict.

Arendt's consensual reading of foundational moments and wish to see in these events—at least in the American case—unproblematic instances of self-authorisation efface this potential for hostility. Of course, recognising the fact of agonism and even antagonism in founding moments does not mean affirming past instances of such conflict. No political conflict is preordained or fated to be, and each can be judged only within its specific context. Rather, it is to see in *lex* and the establishment of 'lasting ties' a further inevitable imperative element to law. As Arendt understands them, *nomos* and *lex* have contrary referents and connotations. Pre-political and a product of fabrication, *nomos* involves setting boundaries, inscribing limits and closing down spaces; directly political and the result of *praxis* proper, *lex* implies opening up, reaching out and instituting new relationships. Yet despite these differences, *lex* like *nomos* also entails limits and thus exclusions, although ones which relate less to space than to permitted modes of intersubjectivity. This is so because every promise is a particular promise that brings into being specific and determinate relationships. Thus, in arriving at an agreement, actors not only create new relationships, but also renounce alternative promises and bonds.[79] This is so on account of the nature of action itself, insofar as every deed sets in train processes that could have been otherwise and that necessarily deny and cut short rival futures. And just as with *nomos*'s creation of the polity and its unitary identity, so too is there the pervasive risk that there will be those who reject specific promises, who deem the relationships instituted arbitrary, illegitimate or unjust. The practice of augmentation, of allowing for ongoing adjustment and adaptation, alleviates this possibility without resolving it, for every subsequent revision is itself particular, one among a limitless number of possible changes.

Here once again the spectre of violence and command asserts itself. Whether concluded so as to shore up established interests or to challenge them, every promise has an outside, a remainder or surplus that is shut out from its terms and silenced. But for there to be movement, a politics *at all*, each promise must insist upon its terms and aver constraint, the compelling demand that all abide by the provisions of the agreement, even if a minority rejects certain terms or is hostile overall. And such compelling demand can succeed only if there are sufficient numbers with sufficient force to carry it through, that is, to imprint upon the polity a distinct system of rule. Always contingent, transient and never entirely reliable, this sufficient force imposes absolutes, themselves paradoxically contingent and transient but nonetheless *decisive* at the moment of contention, and thus cannot but assume the guise of sovereign. In politics, as in other areas of life where we deal with collectivities and not merely individuals, a promise is worthy of the name only when there is the will and the means to carry it through and make it a living reality despite resistance. Far from being the antithesis of the traditional

[79] A Keenan, 'Promises, Promises: The Abyss of Freedom and the Loss of the Political in the Work of Hannah Arendt' (1994) 22 *Political Theory* 297, 315.

paradigm of law, then, law as *lex* remains caught within that paradigm, since it, like *nomos*, cannot in the end avoid the resort to command and hence the violence inherent in all commandments.

V. CONCLUSION

The upshot of these reflections is that Arendt's attempt to free politics and law from the shackles of rulership and coercion ultimately fails. Certainly, neither politics nor law can be reduced to relations of command and obedience, the enforcement of an imperious will. However, neither can they be divorced from these. To the extent that she does try to divorce them, Arendt shies away from driving home the unsettling implications of both *nomos* and *lex*, misrepresents the course of historical events and hides realities that ought to, indeed must, be acknowledged. We can agree with her claim that compliance with the law is 'never unquestioning', that it admits of criticism and opposition, and yet also accept that under the sign of temporal urgency which constrains all human beings there must be limits to such questioning, critical junctures when the spade turns against bedrock and a decision, well- or ill-judged, has to be made and enforced.[80] We can agree, too, that the monotheistic appeal to an omnipotent 'immortal legislator' offends against the relativity of the human realm and the truth that mortal men and women are the originators of law, but nonetheless admit that there must be a mundane legislator—not a single, immutable agent, but a contingent group or coalition of groups—who enjoys effective sovereignty, the ability successfully to determine boundaries and relationships at particular moments, and, in that precise sense, to rule.

Arendt, then, cannot be said to have escaped the 'common dilemma' she attributes to the 'Great Tradition' insofar as her notions of law themselves give rise to absolutes and the attendant possibility of violent closure. It is noteworthy here that despite rejecting theologically-inspired conceptions of law, Arendt in describing *nomos* and *lex* herself falls back on theological tropes. Even though *nomos* is said to have required 'no transcendent source of authority', the limits of law are described as 'sacred', invested with the authority of 'Zeus, the guardian of borders and border stones'.[81] Lawgivers are said to be merely men, and yet the 'Founding Fathers' are viewed as undeniably exceptional, enjoying, by virtue of their act of foundation, a charisma appropriate to 'the Roman *maiores*, those ancestors who by definition were "the greater ones"'. As seen above, the very success of the American Constitution depended on its swiftly becoming an object of 'worship', of *pietas* and 'reverent awe'.[82] There is, admittedly, a real distinction between a religiosity informed by submission to an omnipotent deity and one

[80] CR 140.
[81] OR 187; HC 64; IP 181. See also OT 467; GTI 716–17.
[82] OR 203–04.

defined by veneration of, binding oneself back to, a civic origin and beginning.[83] However, what Arendt underplays is the truth that both forms of religious sentiment presume and depend upon an absolute that must not be transgressed and which, when transgressed, frequently prompts outraged reaction. Indeed, questioning the figure of the divine and disputing 'authentic' origins are very similar in that both, historically, have given rise to the most dangerous and intractable of conflicts.

There is no space here to explore the issue of religion in Arendt's work, or of the varieties of the absolute that impinge upon politics. I shall instead conclude with a reflection on the consequence for Arendt's thought generally of emphasising the violence in law. As I see it, this emphasis speaks to an important feature of her political theory, the ideal of *amor mundi*.[84] This ideal or ethic of care arose from her insight that the human realm as an objective and intersubjective in-between is inherently fragile, and this on account of *praxis* itself. Because spontaneous, boundless and irreversible, human action continually threatens to destroy the limits and relationships that are the very condition of its becoming. Hence Arendt's repeated insistence on the virtue of moderation, of resisting hubristic urges, and her sense of the tragedy of politics, that time and again this virtue has been lacking. To see the violence in law is, in my view, not to feed anti-political tendencies but instead to heighten the significance of Arendt's ethic of care and moderation. For only by acknowledging the exclusions and antagonisms necessarily wrought by law can the impact and scope of these exclusions and antagonisms be minimised. Yet such acknowledgement does necessitate a departure from Arendt's understanding of the tragic course of Western politics. That she offers a tragic history few can sensibly doubt: it shines through with intensity in her account of totalitarianism, the loss of a sense of the world, the disavowal of the revolutionary spirit and the rise of the 'jobholding society', to name just a few recurrent themes. But this tragic view is essentially Aristotelian in character. We, like Oedipus or Lear, have gone wrong on account of fateful misunderstandings, momentous yet corrigible errors in our perception of what the world is and could be. Arendt is, of course, right to an extent here. Western thought has perpetuated pernicious views, among these the simplistic reduction of politics to violence and of law to command. However, a more convincing vision of our tragic condition is perhaps a more genuinely Sophoclean one.[85] It is not just because we, following Plato, have misunderstood

[83] *Ibid* 198.

[84] See H Arendt, 'Epilogue' in Arendt, *The Promise of Politics*, above n 5, 201–03. For discussions of this ideal, see J Bernauer (ed), *Amor Mundi: Explorations in the Faith and Thought of Hannah Arendt* (Dordrecht, Martinus Nijhoff, 1987); K Breen, 'Agonism, Antagonism and the Necessity of Care' in A Schaap (ed), *Law and Agonistic Politics* (Farnham, Ashgate, 2009); M Canovan, 'Hannah Arendt as a Conservative Thinker' in L May and J Kohn (eds), *Hannah Arendt: Twenty Years Later* (Cambridge, Mass, MIT Press, 1997); and G Williams, 'Love and Responsibility: A Political Ethic for Hannah Arendt' (1998) 46 *Political Studies* 937.

[85] See A MacIntyre, *After Virtue: A Study in Moral Theory*, 2nd edn (London, Duckworth, 1985) 157, 163.

the true nature of politics or law that violence abounds in the world and human relations. Instead, it is because the world itself is awry, at odds with itself, that politics and law contain irreducible coercive elements. The exigencies thrown up by unforeseeable events and circumstances are what frequently force us under the oppressive shadow of violence and antagonism, and not just mistakes in our reaction to such circumstances. This view of the human condition is a starting point, I believe, for any defensible ethics, or at least an ethics that wishes to say something serious about political life. It is not to dismiss the human realm as a vale of tears, or to say that we are doomed to live with bloodied hands. Rather, it simply is to acknowledge one aspect of the predicament with which we must begin. Our duty in such a world is to limit the resort to violence and command where possible. But resorted to, as Arendt has to concede, they sometimes must be, and this through the medium of law as much as through that of politics.

2

Between Freedom and Law: Hannah Arendt on the Promise of Modern Revolution and the Burden of 'The Tradition'

MICHAEL A WILKINSON[1]

I. INTRODUCTION

'In principle, all modern constitutions begin with "We the People" '.[2]

FROM ARENDT'S REFLECTIONS on modernity an ambiguous account of the relationship between freedom and modern law emerges. On the one hand, the revolutionary events in America and France in the late eighteenth century mark the appearance of a strong sense of 'political freedom' in the world, with the novelty that subjects now consider themselves rulers.[3] 'We, the people' are the new foundations of political and constitutional authority. We become aware of our potential to authorise new institutions and new basic laws; in Habermasian terminology, the modern State is marked by the idea that subjects are citizens, not merely the 'addressees' of law but also its 'co-authors'. Exemplified in those modern revolutionary moments on either side of the Atlantic, Arendt suggests, is a radical sense of freedom as collective action in the circumstances of plurality. This signals a break with 'the great tradition'[4] of philosophy that had prioritised isolated contemplation over the plurality of politics and divorced freedom from the experience of action. And since our conception

[1] Earlier versions of this essay were presented in conferences at Antwerp University and Tilburg University. I would like to thank Chris McCorkindale and Marco Goldoni for inviting me to take part in their project, the participants in both conferences for valuable discussion, and Martin Loughlin for comments on an earlier draft.

[2] S Chambers, 'Democracy, Popular Sovereignty and Constitutional Legitimacy' (2004) 11 *Constellations* 153.

[3] H Arendt, *On Revolution* (New York/London, Penguin, 1963) (henceforth 'OR') 31.

[4] For Arendt, the 'tradition', or what she sometimes calls the 'great tradition', of political philosophy begins with Plato and ends with Marx, see ch 1 of *Between Past and Future* (New York/London, Penguin, 1968) (henceforth 'BPAF').

of law is a reflection of our self-understanding as social and political animals,[5] the new sense of political freedom that emerges with the birth of our constitutional *potentia* also implies a shift in the modern juridical consciousness.[6]

And yet, from the outset, two features of this juridical consciousness, which survive and are even reinforced by modern revolution, undermine our constitutional *potentia*. First, there is the puzzling persistence of a traditional conception of law as *command*, which assumes rulers and ruled, sovereign and subject, and an 'absolute' source of law's authority (whether 'nature's God', the 'sovereign nation' or 'self-evident truths'). Secondly, modern constitutionalism suggests the priority of *fabrication* (in the guise of constitution-making) over political *action* (or constitutional politics), a hierarchy that was implicitly set in motion by the Platonic inauguration of 'the tradition'.[7] Although the 'imperative' conception of law combined with the turn to constitution 'making' or 'fabrication' are not solely responsible for the eventual loss of the revolutionary treasure, the decline of the public realm and the eclipse of political freedom that Arendt traces in late modernity,[8] they do represent for Arendt the *hallmarks of an escape from politics and therefore from freedom itself.*

At the heart of modern constitutionalism lies this fateful ambivalence between the promise and collective self-consciousness of political freedom, which suggests an escape from 'the tradition', and an ideology of sovereignty and constitution-making that not only remains bound to 'the tradition' but also liberates it from its ancient and yet insincere prejudices against the category of 'fabrication'. This dilemma cannot be easily resolved because Arendt does not confront head-on the tension between political freedom and law, or make any systematic attempt to uncover or develop an alternative conception of law 'beyond the tradition'. The purpose of this essay is to explore the tension more systematically by drawing together Arendt's scattered remarks on the relationship between freedom and law as it appears in modernity and in contrast to earlier traditions of law based on *nomos* and *lex*.

[5] According to Joseph Raz, 'what we study when we study the nature of law is the nature of our own self-understanding … It is part of the self-consciousness of our society to see certain institutions as legal.' See J Raz, 'Can There be a Theory of Law' in *Between Authority and Interpretation* (Oxford, Oxford University Press, 2010) 31. And we might add, as this self-consciousness changes, so does our conception of the nature of law, even if, as Raz argues, the nature of law itself cannot change.

[6] I use the term 'constitutional *potentia*' in the sense of a 'power to' constitute and reconstitute basic laws, or 'political right', as Martin Loughlin puts it. See eg M Loughlin, *Foundations of Public Law* (Oxford, Oxford University Press, 2010) 11–12.

[7] Fabrication, corresponding to 'work', is one of the three aspects of the *vita activa* in Arendt's account of the human condition, alongside 'action' and 'labour'.

[8] To explain fully the eclipse of political freedom and our modern 'world alienation' would require exploration of the late modern domination of the socio-economic sphere, the rise of instrumental rationality and the logic of functionalism and 'process', culminating in the total exclusion of the public realm in 20th-century totalitarianism. This essay deals only with the early modern substitution of action in favour of fabrication and not the late modern elevation of *labour* over fabrication. For a thorough examination of these two reversals that Arendt identifies, see M Passerin D'Entreves, *The Political Philosophy of Hannah Arendt* (London, Routledge, 1994).

After presenting Arendt's critique of the traditional understanding of freedom, and exploring her suggestion that the revolutionary events demonstrate the possibility of a genuine alternative, we examine how the tradition not only maintained its grip on the juridical consciousness in the guise of sovereign command but was actually strengthened and even 'liberated' by the modern substitution of fabrication for action. Two alternatives to the traditional imperative conception of law are then examined, the Roman *lex* and Greek *nomos*. Although both avoid the appeal to the 'absolute' associated with that tradition, only the image of law as *lex* challenges the priority of fabrication over action. By way of conclusion, a final tension that remains unresolved in the Arendtian framework is introduced, the tension between *democratic* freedom and modern constitutional authority. Put simply, how can the constitutional authority of the few be reconciled with the political freedom of the many?

II. CRITIQUE OF THE TRADITION: ARENDT'S CONCEPTION OF POLITICAL FREEDOM

Although Arendt's work is sometimes credited with contributing to the prominence of 'positive freedom' in the lexicon of contemporary political philosophy, without further qualification this would be a quite misleading claim.[9] Arendt revitalises the concept of freedom in a unique manner, forging an intimate connection between freedom and the 'political' by recovering the Aristotelian category of *praxis* and by invoking those historical moments since the French and American Revolutions when freedom has made its appearance in the world. And, most radically of all, not only does she disparage the modern liberal tradition for its role in the demise of political freedom; she extends the roots of its decline back to the Platonic turn which, in announcing the philosopher's claim to rule, announces the priority of philosophy over politics and the safety of the philosopher over the action of the citizen.[10]

To recover the sense of freedom in *praxis*—*freedom to* rather than *freedom from*—is to recover the activity and experience of politics. This in turn is essential in order to come to grips with that aspect of the human condition that makes politics fundamental, namely *plurality, the fact that men, and not Man, live on the earth and inhabit the world.*[11] As Arendt so forcefully puts it at the outset of *The Human Condition*, 'plurality is specifically the condition—not only the condition *sine qua non* but the

[9] Arendt's understanding of freedom is not, as sometimes suggested, simply a reflection of positive as opposed to negative liberty in the sense described by Isaiah Berlin in his celebrated essay. For this reason, I use the term 'political freedom' rather than 'positive freedom'.

[10] BPAF 107.

[11] *The Human Condition* (Chicago, Ill, University of Chicago, 1958) (henceforth 'HC') 7. As Jerome Kohn puts it in the introduction to BPAF, plurality, action and politics are Arendt's 'trinity' (BPAF, xiv).

condition *per quam*—of all political life'.[12] Urging the recovery of political freedom is not only a reaction to the rise of *homo faber* and then of *animal laborans* in the *modern* age, to the retreat away from political action into the fields of science and economics and the functionalism and instrumentalism of human activity that this retreat entails, but a response to older, related, but more deeply-engrained facets of our loss of freedom.

It is a response first to the Platonic turn towards isolated contemplation, the retreat from politics into philosophy represented allegorically in the parable of the cave, that begins the 'great tradition', with the philosopher seeking to escape from the darkness of the cave and the shadowy company of his fellow men to find an ideal truth in solitude. It is a response, secondly, to the Christian-theological turn inwards, epitomised by the Calvinist doctrine of internal salvation, which suggests that one can suffer from total 'unfreedom' in the 'external world' and yet still be free. Freedom, on the contrary, must enjoy a worldly reality and be meaningfully experienced in action. This is no mere idealistic pipe dream for Arendt; action is at the foundation of the human condition. It is the most significant, because most distinctively human, aspect of the *vita activa*.

The great tradition of philosophy, as well as the entire impulse of the modern age, is criticised as, in Arendt's words, a 'conscious attempt to *divorce* the notion of freedom from politics' and thereby 'to arrive at a formulation through which one may be a slave in the world and still be free'.[13] Socratic philosophy and Christian theology begin this divorce by elevating above all else the *vita contemplativa*, the outstanding characteristic of which is described by analogy to the 'motionlessness' with which the inner eye 'sees the shape of the model according to which [the craftsman] fabricates his object'.[14] The modern liberal tradition continues to pursue this divorce by explicitly undermining action, and it is only accelerated with the subsequent Marxian emphasis on labour (the second reversal in the hierarchy)[15] and Engel's transformation of politics into the 'administration of things' that prefigures modern totalitarianism.[16]

Freedom in the modern liberal tradition is construed in Hobbesian terms as both materialist and personal. Based on the principle of 'non-interference', it is secured through a rational-legal framework in which the State exists only to protect individual interests. Over time this mutates into an obsession with aggregate welfare (economic 'growth'), reflects the dominance of an instrumental rationality and ultimately succumbs to the 'iron cage' of bureaucracy. Political

[12] HC 7. See also H Arendt, *The Promise of Politics* (New York, Schoken, 2005) (henceforth 'PP') 93–95.

[13] BPAF 146.

[14] HC 302.

[15] See n 8, above.

[16] See BPAF 19. The point is made as strongly in *The Human Condition*: 'Escape from the frailty of human affairs into the solidity of quiet and order,' Arendt notes, 'has in fact so much to recommend it that the greater part of political philosophy since Plato could easily be interpreted as various attempts to find theoretical foundations and practical ways for an escape from politics altogether' (HC 222).

action, replaced first by *homo faber* in the early modern condition, is ultimately displaced by *animal laborans*, leading to modern 'world alienation' with the rise of a social sphere characterised by transience and anonymity. Only foreign affairs, because not (yet) reduced to economic factors, 'seems to be left as a purely political domain'.[17] The modernist worldview thus considers politics to be 'concerned almost exclusively with the maintenance of *life* and the safeguarding of its *interests*'.[18] For Arendt, on the contrary, politics is about more than 'mere life' and 'personal interests'; it is about the *world*, which means a public realm that outlasts each and every individual.[19]

Arendt traces the fate of an alternative and authentic conception of freedom as part of the *vita activa*, from the pre-Socratic Greeks, through its demise as a result of the 'Christian suspicion' of and hostility to the public realm (particularly in Protestant salvation), to our distrust of it in the wake of the experiences of modern totalitarianism in the twentieth century. The experience of totalitarianism seems to suggest no more than that towards which the canon of modern political theory had already led us, namely, the conclusion that freedom is assured by guaranteeing a sphere of personal liberty rather than jointly exercised in the creation and maintenance of spaces for political action.

In the urge to rescue politics from philosophy by recovering a conception of political freedom, Arendt therefore takes aims at the entire Western tradition. The category of freedom has been lost to us because the tradition prioritised a dialogue with the self (the 'dialogue' between 'me and myself' in the course of *contemplation*) over the dialogue with others (participation and speech in the course of *action*). The first 'dialogue', the inward experience of freedom, in as much as its significance cannot be denied, is derivative. It is only in the second dialogue, which comprises the field of human affairs and politics, that freedom can properly be recovered:

> [A]ction and politics, among all the capabilities and potentialities of human life, are the only things of which we could not even conceive without at least assuming that freedom exists, and we can hardly touch a single political issue without, implicitly or explicitly, touching upon an issue of man's liberty ... The raison d'être of politics is freedom, and its field of experience is action.[20]

Freedom, for Arendt, is emphatically not a phenomenon of the 'will', a question of one's personal freedom to choose from a set of already existing alternatives, 'x, y or z'. It is not about being able to manage our own strategic choices, selecting the most efficient means to ends that are predetermined. It is not even about being able to choose our ultimate goals or the absence of interference (or domination) by

[17] BPAF 154. See also OR 77, viewing this as a result of Rousseau's sovereign will and its sense of national unity or the unity of the 'social'.

[18] BPAF 154. Emphasis added.

[19] 'Courage is indispensable' for this public realm, Arendt urges, 'because in politics not life but the world is at stake' (*ibid* 155).

[20] *Ibid* 145.

others in this choice and the means to pursue it. It is the freedom to 'call something into being which did not exist before', something that is not given 'even as an object of cognition'.[21] This conception of freedom, which depends upon man's faculty to begin something new, reflects the centrality of the event of 'natality' for the human condition. 'The new beginning inherent in birth,' Arendt notes, 'can make itself felt in the world only because the newcomer possesses the capacity of beginning something anew, that is, of acting', and in so doing of performing the unexpected and even the 'infinitely improbable'.[22] It is only in the course of acting and speaking in the public realm that men reveal this potential to the world by revealing *who* they are, exercising their freedom by disclosing their 'unique personal identities'.[23]

Political freedom, which must transcend both our motives and our intended goals, is not, as the analogy with the unexpected might suggest, wholly arbitrary.[24] It springs from what Arendt somewhat enigmatically calls 'principle', and as she will later note in reference to the new beginning that is the American Revolution, 'beginning' and 'principle' have the same etymological root. Principle, in contrast to the judgement of the intellect and to the command of the will, is fully manifested only in action itself. But whatever the nature of the principle that inspires action—whether it is the love of equality, which Montesquieu called virtue, or fear and distrust—it is only in action that men can experience freedom, and only through action with others that political power is generated.[25]

This experience of action in the public realm, whether it is the creation and maintenance of political and social institutions or the promises that men make to each other in their daily lives, has no independent life outside of the continued conservation of those institutions or promises by those through whose action they were constituted and might be maintained.[26] Although it is, to be sure, both unpredictable in nature and fragile in its existence, the idea of political freedom, which can be resurrected from our neglected traditions and historical experiences, still looms large in our imagination. Despite the apparent triumph of modern liberalism and the fear of any alternatives inculcated by the experience of totalitarianism in the twentieth century, we still hold out for this more demanding sense of freedom and the juridical consciousness that accompanies it. If the

[21] *Ibid* 150.

[22] HC 9, 178. Natality, she adds, 'may be the central category of … political thought … Of the three aspects of the *vita activa*, action has the closest connection with the human condition of natality.'

[23] *Ibid* 179. 'It is in the nature of beginning that something new is started which cannot be expected from whatever may have happened before. This character of startling unexpectedness is inherent in all beginnings and in all origins … The fact that man is capable of action means that the unexpected can be expected from him, that he is able to perform what is infinitely improbable' (HC 177–78).

[24] Arendt stresses that she is not suggesting the rightness or wrongness of our goals are unimportant—only that such questions are ones of judgement, which precedes the will, and not of freedom.

[25] BPAF 151.

[26] The analogy apposite to the exercise of political freedom is not the activity of work and the product of making, eg of a work of art or a novel, but of spontaneous and improvised performance in concert with others, expressed in word and deed and arising 'in between' men (*ibid* 153).

culmination of the great tradition of philosophy is the suggestion that freedom is only experienced in isolated contemplation or the pursuit of individual interests, then the episodes of modern revolution call into question such received wisdom as well as the traditional understanding of law which accompanies it.

III. ESCAPE FROM THE TRADITION: POLITICAL FREEDOM IN THE MODERN REVOLUTIONARY IMAGINATION

> The modern conception of revolution, inextricably bound up with the notion that the course of history suddenly begins anew, that an entirely new story, a story never known or told before, is about to unfold, was unknown prior to the two great revolutions at the end of the eighteenth century.[27]

The French and American Revolutions bring us closer to this conception of political freedom as it makes its appearance (or reappearance)[28] in the world, and in doing so reveal its implications for our juridical consciousness. But it bears reiteration that the period from the late eighteenth century up to the middle of the 'American century' in which Arendt was writing is that of the triumph of a liberal worldview in which 'negative liberty' looms large and 'political freedom' has largely disappeared. These revolutionary events that Arendt recovers therefore present us with something of the *exceptional.*[29] And yet although political freedom as experienced in the course of modern revolutions is in tension with the liberal tradition, as well as the Christian tradition and the great tradition of Philosophy which preceded it,[30] at the same time it appears (in hindsight) to be an inevitable part of our modern juridical consciousness manifested most apparently in the concept of *constituent power*: 'We, the people' are the foundations of the modern constitutional settlement. The recovery of political freedom therefore trades both on the exceptionality of the revolutionary moment and on its unavoidability in hindsight; it remains with us in the way we conceive of constitutionalism in modernity—namely, in accordance with an ideology of popular sovereignty, irrespective of the extent to which it is fulfilled or betrayed in practice.

'Crucial to any understanding of revolutions in the modern age,' Arendt suggests, 'is that the idea of freedom and the experience of a new beginning should coincide'.[31] Unique about modern revolution is that freedom is conceived not as a mental category of thought, judgement and will, but as a category of action

[27] OR 28.

[28] Little here turns on whether the break itself is absolute, in the sense of utterly unprecedented. Arendt elsewhere suggests the revolutionaries are attempting to recover something lost, see BPAF 140.

[29] This is sometimes missed when focusing on the text of *On Revolution*. Arendt's pessimism is presented more starkly in *The Human Condition* and *The Origins of Totalitarianism*.

[30] Arendt argues that the Christian rejection of politics is even more radical than the Platonic one because the idea of a public space is intolerable in Christianity (PP 135–38).

[31] OR 29.

and, furthermore, in a manner that supersedes the weak sense of mere 'liberation' from the oppression of the '*ancien régime*' and the constraints of the traditions that it embodied. It emerges in the strong sense of revealing our constitutional *potentia*, the capacity to create a 'new beginning' for political freedom, as well as institutions to preserve a space in which freedom can be exercised for posterity (freedom as the experience of the 'We can' rather than the 'I will').[32] Of the self-conception of the American founders, the record of the American Revolution speaks an entirely clear, unambiguous language: it was not constitutionalism in the sense of 'limited', lawful government that preoccupied their minds.[33] The main question for them 'was not how to limit power but how to establish it, not how to limit government but how to found a new one'.[34]

> Freedom needed, in addition to mere liberation, the company of other men who were in the same state, and it needed a common public space to meet them—a politically organised world, in other words, into which each of the free men could insert himself by word and deed.[35]

To capture the modernity of revolution is to capture the sense that more than merely liberation (from monarchy, despotism or oppression) is at stake, which generally trades on a negative conception of liberty as freedom *from* interference or domination. The constitution of political freedom is at stake, and this requires the establishment of political equality among citizens in a republic who are responsible for their own laws. In other words, it is about experiencing and constituting the *freedom to* govern in concert *with* others rather than the *freedom from* oppressive government *by* those in power. The Revolutions thereby arouse passions that have been dormant for man outside of classical antiquity, absent in the centuries between the fall of the Roman Empire and the beginning of the modern age. Of the sheer extraordinariness of this experience, the startling recognition of man's capacity for beginning anew, Arendt is in little doubt. It is at the root of the enormous pathos we find in both the American and the French 'revolutionary spirit', a spirit which consists, she says, in 'the eagerness to liberate *and* to build a new house where freedom can dwell', and which is 'unprecedented and unequalled in all prior history'.[36]

The event of modern revolution connects political freedom to a legal-theoretical enquiry with the emergence of this constitutional *potentia*, an idea with real juridical significance because it suggests the ultimate foundations of constitutional authority lie with the collective power of the people to constitute their own basic laws. From a juridical perspective, whilst the original political meaning of the

[32] Arendt contrasts freedom as the 'I will' with the freedom as the 'I can' (BPAF 157–61). But since political freedom is experienced in concert with others, the notion of the 'We can' presents a more apposite contrast.

[33] OR 147.

[34] OR 148.

[35] BPAF 147.

[36] OR 35. Emphasis added. But see n 28 above.

Revolutions, was, as Arendt explains, that of demanding a return to the limited government of the past—the restoration of ancient liberties that had been slowly eroded by the monarchies in England and France—the outcome was far more radical, leading spectacularly to a whole new social imaginary, based on constituent power and popular sovereignty.[37]

It is not only that limiting government—in terms of securing guarantees against it, such as those found in a Bill of Rights, including rights of representation and voting—was historically nothing new; it is that such a conception of the constitution suggests political freedom is about procuring *safeguards against* government, when in truth it is about claiming a *share in* government.[38] The difference is captured in the observation that although the idea had already developed that the people might rebel against a particularly despotic ruler, there was simply no way of describing 'a change so radical that *subjects became rulers themselves*'.[39]

The turn towards understanding the constitution as an act of collective law-making rather than merely of liberation from the tyrannical laws made by others is irrevocably tied to the period of modern revolution. Wherever we locate the beginning of modern political thought, with Locke or Hobbes, Bodin or Machiavelli, the awareness that a new beginning could actually *occur* in historical time as a *political phenomenon*, that it could be, in Arendt's words, 'the result of what men had *done* and what they could consciously set out to *do*', emerges only in the course of the late eighteenth-century Revolutions.[40] Figures in the great tradition such as Hobbes and Locke might have been *revolutionary theorists*, in the sense of questioning dogmatic assumptions about the nature of authority and the activity of political philosophy, but they were emphatically not *theorists of revolution*. The strange pathos of novelty, 'so characteristic of the modern age,' Arendt remarks, 'needed almost two hundred years to leave the relative seclusion of scientific and philosophic thought and to reach the realm of *politics*'.[41]

To be sure, we could view the revolutionary practice of the late eighteenth century as presenting less of a radical break and more of a continuity with the earlier seventeenth-century ideas of social contract, which liberated political philosophy from its theological straitjacket in its search for scientific or quasi-scientific foundations for authority.[42] In the process of historical excavation, we

[37] On popular sovereignty as an aspect of the modern social imaginary, see C Taylor, *Modern Social Imaginaries* (Durham, NC, Duke University Press, 2004).

[38] OR 143. As Arendt puts it, 'if no more had ever been at stake in the revolutions than this kind of constitutionalism ["the liberties which the laws of constitutional government guarantee and are all of a negative character" (143)], it would be as though the revolutions has remained true to their modest beginnings when they could be understood as attempts at restoration of ancient liberties: the truth of the matter, however, is that this was not the case' (*ibid* 143–44).

[39] OR 41. A constitution, in Paine's terms, is the act of a people constituting a government, not the act of government itself. Quoted by Arendt herself, OR 145.

[40] *Ibid* 46.

[41] *Ibid.*

[42] Hobbes had compared his endeavour to Euclidian geometry. In the words of Ernst Cassirer, 'the American Declaration of Independence had been preceded by an even greater event: by the intellectual

could aim our sights back further still in the search for the decisive break from the traditionalism of the Middle Ages. According to Herman Heller, the 'immanence conception' of a *pouvoir constituant* that is actually capable of action, 'which no longer shares the belief in the politically constitutive power of a transcendent God, but believes only in the *populas*, the *universitas civium*', emerges as early as Marsilius of Padua in the late Middle Ages.[43]

But intellectual history is not our prime concern. It is only when the phenomenon of revolution makes its actual *appearance* in the world that newness is no longer considered merely the 'gift of Providence' but is 'endowed with a reality *peculiar to the political realm*'.[44] The historical examples of revolution—whether it is the American or the French, the later experience of the Paris Commune of 1871, the creation of Soviets during the Russian Revolution, the French Resistance during World War II, or the Hungarian revolt in 1956—show that individual men and women could 'step forward from their private lives in order to create a public space where freedom could appear'. In doing so, it is claimed, 'they rediscovered the truth known to the ancient Greeks that action is the supreme blessing of human life'.[45] 'Only in such revolutions,' Arendt notes, 'was there a direct link between the idea of participating in government and the idea of being free'.[46]

Once political action is perceived as a phenomenon capable of *jurisgenesis* or what might be called *constitutio-genesis*, the foundations of an immanent and mundane 'authorising authority' are firmly laid; our constitutional *potentia* is laid bare. The Arendtian notion of *potentia* is conceived

> neither as a potential for asserting one's own interests or for realizing collective goals, nor as the administrative power to implement collectively binding decisions, but rather as an *authorising* force expressed in 'jurisgenesis'—the creation of legitimate law—and in the founding of institutions.[47]

Since power for Arendt, unlike violence, is always the power to act in concert with others, *potentia* is an inherently collective notion. Never 'the property of an individual' or merely instrumental to another goal, political power necessarily 'belongs to a group and remains in existence only so long as the group keeps together'.[48]

Declarations that we find in the theoreticians of the seventeenth century.' It was there that 'reason had first declared its power … its claim to rule the social life of man [and] emancipated itself from the guardianship of theological thought': E Cassirer, *The Myth of the State* (New Haven, Conn, Yale University Press, 1961) 167.

[43] H Heller, *Staatslehre* (trans Dyzenhaus) (1996) 3 *Cardozo Law Review* 1139, at 1215.

[44] OR 46. Emphasis added.

[45] D'Entreves, above n 8, 68.

[46] PP 142–43.

[47] J Habermas, *Between Facts and Norms* (Cambridge, Mass, MIT, 1996) 148. He continues: 'It manifests itself … above all in the freedom-founding acts that bring new institutions and laws "into existence"' (*ibid* 148).

[48] H Arendt, *On Violence* (New York, Harcourt, 1969) 44.

The revolutionary notion of a 'new constitutional beginning' is, however indirectly, a *juridical* phenomenon because it expresses the idea that ultimately we are the authors of our own laws. Habermas will later develop this insight into a fully-fledged discourse theory of law and democracy. But for Arendt, and not for Habermas, this promise of political freedom, which can be glimpsed in those moments of revolutionary action, is ultimately betrayed in the course of the modern age.[49] We need not get embroiled in the more general pathologies of modernity, however, because Arendt presents us with one quite straightforward and immediate reason for the failure of the constitutional *potentia*, namely, the persistence of the 'absolute' in our juridical imagination, due to the perceived need for extra-human foundations to serve as a guarantee for the new constitutional settlement. This need for an absolute persists because of our inability to move beyond a traditional conception of law as *command*. From this perspective, the idea of a revolutionary 'new beginning' presents less of a novel and tremendous possibility, than a familiar and perplexing *problem*,[50] to square the circle of legitimacy of the new power and the legality of the new laws. In the realm of ideas, and in particular those which inform our conceptions of law, the revolutionaries on both sides of the Atlantic remained tied to the juridical tradition of the past and to the political 'unfreedom' that it entailed. It is the purpose of the next section to explain how.

IV. THE BURDEN OF 'THE TRADITION': THE PERSISTENCE OF THE ABSOLUTE IN THE JURIDICAL IMAGINATION

Commentators frequently criticise Arendt for unduly favouring the US revolutionary tradition over its French counterpart, for exaggerating in her praise of the 'political' revolution in the New World and in her condemnation of the 'social' revolution in the Old.[51] The relative success of the American Revolution *is* partly reduced by Arendt to a simple comparison of material conditions, the blunt fact, as she saw it, that 'the predicament of poverty was absent from the American scene'.[52] Arendt's claim that political freedom is undermined if contaminated by

[49] Habermas's reappropriation of 'communicative power' attempts to overcome the deeply pessimistic tone in Arendt's assessment that *praxis* has been undermined, first by *homo faber* and then by *animal labourans* in the course of the modern age.

[50] The modern revolutions, Arendt clarifies, are 'the only political events which confront us directly and inevitably with the problem of beginning' (OR 21).

[51] See eg W Scheuerman, 'Revolutions and Constitutions: Hannah Arendt's Challenge to Carl Schmitt' (1997) 10 *Canadian Journal of Law and Jurisprudence* 141. Arendt herself says that 'nothing could be less fair than to take the success of the American Revolution for granted and to sit in judgment over the failure of the men of the French Revolution' (OR 68). For a criticism of Arendt's apparent removal of the fight for social justice from the political realm, see E Christodoulidis and A Schaap, ch 5 of this volume.

[52] OR 68.

the social question has received a great deal of criticism,[53] but it can be bracketed here, because in juridical terms the burden of the tradition weighs as heavily on both revolutionary experiences. This similarity between the New and Old World Revolutions is often overlooked in the push to highlight their differences, which were not only material. Thus in historical terms, whereas the French Revolution took place against a backdrop of monarchical absolutism, the American revolutionaries already had the experience of limited government—the constitutionally limited King of the English constitution—on which to draw. Quite simply, as Arendt put it, 'the more absolute the ruler, the more absolute the revolution will be which replaces him'.[54] The men of the American Revolution avoided the pitfalls not only of an essentialist nationalism, but of any assumption that power and law are unitary, stemming from a single indivisible source, which was the 'fateful blunder of the men of the French revolution'.[55] The sources of power and authority were institutionally separated from the outset in America, with power vested in 'the people', and authority embodied in the constitution and exercised for posterity by the Supreme Court and the Senate.[56]

In contrast to the disorganised yet relatively homogeneous multitude in France, America already enjoyed constituted yet diverse *pouvoirs constituants* in the form of the self-governing bodies that preceded the Federal Constitution. Because the Declaration of Independence followed constitution-making in all of the 13 colonies, the doctrine of popular sovereignty could emerge without 'unleashing the boundless violence of the multitudes'.[57] The phenomenon of political action, as well as the distinction between power and violence, was already known to the founders.[58] The social contract had actually been practised at a *horizontal* level in the form of real covenants, alliances and mutual promises (such as the Mayflower pacts) rather than merely theorised hypothetically as the *hierarchical surrender* to a Hobbesian Leviathan.

And yet although the American Revolution represents a certain success relative to the French, Arendt laments its 'loss of the revolutionary treasure', the failure to institutionalise political freedom, so that, in conformity with Jefferson's wishes, each generation might enjoy the exhilarating experience of founding anew the constitution. Blighting the efforts of the founders *from the outset*—despite their having almost miraculously stumbled upon a way out of the revolutionary impasse and of avoiding the dangers of absolutism that so beset the French—was a failure of the juridical imagination common to *both* revolutionary traditions and

[53] For an outstanding example, see S Wolin, 'Democracy and the Political' in L Hinchman and S Hinchman (eds), *Hannah Arendt: Critical Essays* (New York, SUNY, 1994) 289, focusing on the absence of any sustained reflection on social power and social justice in Arendt's work.

[54] OR 155.

[55] *Ibid* 165.

[56] The Supreme Court, Arendt notes, citing Woodrow Wilson, exists as a kind of 'Constitutional Assembly in continuous session' (*ibid* 200).

[57] *Ibid* 166, 182.

[58] *Ibid* 181.

of a different order than any material or institutional contrasts would suggest. So even the American Revolution, which was not burdened either with political or nationalistic absolutism, or with desperate poverty, still was burdened by the philosophical-political need for an *absolute*; it 'still occurred within a tradition that was partly founded on an event in which the "word had become flesh", that is, on an absolute that had appeared in historical time as a mundane reality'.[59] That the need for a transcendent, transmundane source of religious or quasi-religious sanction to ground the new constitutional foundation persisted in America showed that 'the problem of an absolute is bound to appear in a revolution'. Indeed, that such is the case, 'we might never have known without the American revolution', since in other respects it distinguished itself so clearly from the predicament of the Old World.

The Revolutions on both sides of the Atlantic faced the task of establishing a new authority, 'unaided by custom and precedent and the halo of immemorial time'.[60] The absolute was thus invoked to break the two 'vicious circles' of the legality of the new source of law and the legitimacy of the new source of power. Sieyes 'solved' this problem by drawing his famous distinction between *pouvoir constituant* and *pouvoir constitué*, placing the *pouvoir constituant* in a perpetual state of nature and anchoring power and law in the will of the *nation*, 'which remained outside and above all government and all laws'.[61]

But substituting natural law with the mythical will of the nation, which for Arendt is 'the cheapest and most dangerous disguise the absolute ever assumed in the political realm', was no genuine solution at all to the vexed problem of foundations. Besides the nation being a 'dangerous' and 'cheap' *substitute* for popular sovereignty (rather than a genuine expression thereof), there is a problem of future stability for the new republic. Since the will of the 'multitude' is transient almost by definition, 'a structure built on it as its foundation is built on quicksand'.[62] This state of endless fluidity enabled the authoritarian manipulation of the idea of the national will, leading to Napoleon Bonaparte being able to declare: '*Je suis le pouvoir constituant*'! So the appeal to a quasi-metaphysical nationalism seems to be caught between two poles: it is inauthentic and imposed from the top-down (an 'invented' tradition), or it is a genuine reflection of the political and social reality on the ground, but, and therefore, it is inherently unstable.

America was not ready to 'invent' its nationalism, and it thus avoided that particular temptation that beset the French. And yet despite having serendipitously stumbled upon the path to avoiding 'the absolute'—the very act of founding itself—the Americans ultimately failed, like their French counterparts, to preserve the

59 *Ibid* 160.
60 *Ibid*.
61 *Ibid* 163. As Sieyes puts it in his revolutionary pamphlet, *What is the Third Estate?*, 'the nation is prior to everything. It is the source of everything. Its will is always legal; indeed it is the law itself.' See E Sieyes, *Political Writings incl. 'What is the Third Estate?'* (trans M Sonenscher) (Indianapolis, Ind, Hacket Pub Co, 2003) 136.
62 OR 13.

new constitutional *potentia*. According to Arendt, we cannot divorce this failure from the problem of 'the absolute', which persisted due to the second vicious circle of the legality of the new laws of the republic. The New World revolutionaries remained plagued by the need for a ground for law that would serve as an authority for the new constitution, the need, as it might be described, for an 'Immortal Legislator'.

> [T]he very task of laying down a new law of the land, which was to incorporate for future generations the 'higher law' that bestows validity on all man-made laws, brought to the fore, in America no less than France, the need for an absolute.[63]

Although this problem did not lead the men of the American Revolution 'into the same absurdities' as it did the French, it nevertheless betrayed the promise of political freedom. In the American no less than the French revolutionary mind, to square the circle of the legality of the new laws, to put the 'law above men', as Rousseau puts it, *il faudrait des Dieux*.[64] That the need to base their claims on foundations external to and independent of mere assertion or opinion continued to haunt the men of the American Revolution and infect their own ideas is evidenced by their appeal to 'self-evident' truths in the Declaration, an alternative, but equally ideological, absolute to Divine Right. The declaration that 'we hold these truths to be self-evident', combines the *relative*, 'an *agreement* between those who have embarked on revolution', and the *absolute*, 'a *truth* that needs no agreement since, because of its self-evidence, it compels without argumentative demonstration of political persuasion'.[65]

This need for absolute foundations for basic laws infected the Enlightenment mind more generally, whether in the form of Rousseau's theological lament or Kant's sardonic quips that man is an 'animal that needs a master' and that one 'ought to obey God rather than men'.[66] Modern constitutionalism reflects the 'Platonism of modern natural law', the Constitution becomes the new God to worship or the new myth to behold, and the revolutionary treasure of political freedom is lost in the constitutionally frozen republic.

[63] *Ibid* 182.

[64] *Ibid* 184.

[65] *Ibid* 192. 'The authority of self-evident truth may be less powerful than the authority of an "avenging God", but it certainly still bears clear signs of divine origin; such truths are, as Jefferson wrote in the original draft of the Declaration of Independence, "sacred and undeniable"' (*ibid* 194).

[66] Kant was famously ambiguous about the course of the French Revolution, maintaining a preference for the republican over the democratic form of government (democracy for Kant is despotism), because only with the former will the ruler 'reflect that he has taken over an office *which is too great for a human being*, namely that of administering God's most sacred institution of earth, the rights of man'; in H Reiss (ed), *Kant's Political Writings* (Cambridge, Cambridge University Press, 1991) 103. Although beginning from the moral principle of autonomy, the realities of the political realm are of a republican sovereign determining the general will on our behalf. Kant is ultimately unable to believe in democratic constitution-making because of his faith that 'we ought to obey God rather than men' (*ibid*, 31, fn 1). The central conviction of constitutionalism, Friedrich later argues, has a *religious* foundation; it reflects the notion of 'a divine justice that transcends the human understanding'; C Friedrich, *Philosophy of Law in a Historical Perspective* (Chicago, Ill, Chicago University Press, 1958) 19.

And yet the insight that Arendt's work on revolution brings to bear is that this reflects a problem 'inherent' in the traditional conception of law.[67] The legacy bestowed by the tradition was an image of law based on command by a superior and obedience by a subject, Hebrew in origin and represented by the Divine Commandments of the Decalogue.[68] 'Only to the extent that we understand by law a commandment by which men owe obedience regardless of their consent and mutual agreements,' Arendt argues, 'does the law require a transcendent source of authority for its validity, that is, an origin which must be beyond human power.'[69]

Because of the *apparent* 'arbitrariness' of the new beginning—after the revolutionary hiatus between a 'no-longer' and a 'not yet'—it seemed natural to seek for 'an absolute' as a foundation for the new republic. The problem of the beginning, notes Arendt, 'appears first in thought and speculation about the origin of the universe', and the Hebrew solution for its perplexities was 'the assumption of a Creator God who is outside his own creation in the same way as *the fabricator is outside the fabricated object*'.[70] The notion of the Sovereign being at the origin and outside of the 'fabricated' (or positive) law survives in Austin's theory of law as the command of the Sovereign, and reaches its apogee in Carl Schmitt's theory of the Sovereign as he who decides on the exception.[71]

This imperative view of law is built upon the tradition's fundamental misconception of freedom as the arbitrary exercise of individual will. With the association of law as a command of the will—the very essence of the 'will' is to command and be obeyed, Arendt notes—the notion of sovereignty continues to dominate our modern juristic imagination, whether it is the sovereignty of the ruler (as in the ideology of 'popular sovereignty'), or the sovereignty of a rule or set of rules (as in the expression the 'sovereignty of the constitution'). According to Arendt, this notion of sovereignty and its accompanying conception of rule are designed to *avoid* the uncertainties of political action in the conditions of human plurality. They mark the desire to *escape* from politics, and therefore from freedom, altogether. The 'hallmark' of all such escapes from politics is, says Arendt, 'the concept of rule', because it implies 'that men can lawfully and politically live together only when some are entitled to command and others forced to obey'.[72] The commonplace

[67] OR 195. Only Montesquieu manages to break from the 'tradition' of legal absolutism, see below.

[68] *Ibid* 189.

[69] *Ibid.*

[70] *Ibid* 206.

[71] For Schmitt, the sovereign decision is an 'absolute beginning' because 'it springs from normative nothingness and a concrete disorder': A Kalyvas, 'Who's afraid of Carl Schmitt?' (1999) 25 *Philosophy and Social Criticism* 87, 97. Kalyvas explains that the idea of a creation *ex nihilo* is a legacy of Schmitt's political theology, the analogy is the divine power which can create an order to which it is not itself subject just as the constitution cannot absorb the constituent subject, the people. See A Kalyvas, 'Carl Schmitt and the Three Moments of Democracy' (2000) 21 *Cardozo Law Review* 1542.

[72] HC 222.

notion that political community is necessarily constituted in this dualistic fashion rests on a *suspicion* of action and the wish for it to be displaced.

From a juridical perspective, the persistence of the 'absolute' is linked to the image of man as *homo faber*, in the sense of being a law- or constitution-*maker*, because it is a reflection of the theological image of 'God the creator'. Rules are 'fabricated' in advance in accordance with a preconceived 'idea' (the result of 'contemplation') and in order to present firm boundaries to political action and limit the contingencies of human affairs.[73] Once a substitute for action is found, politics then becomes mere administrative execution, analogous to the private economic decisions of the household, a substitution that, we shall now see, is not distinctively modern but takes its cue from the Platonic inauguration of the 'great tradition'. That the essential characteristic of all authoritarian government is a source of authority 'beyond the sphere of power' and, like the law of nature or the commands of God, not itself 'man-made', goes right back to Plato's political philosophy.[74]

V. THE LIBERATION OF THE TRADITION: THE EMERGENCE OF *HOMO FABER* FROM MODERN REVOLUTION

In modern terms, it is said, 'constitution' actually means the 'active making of a new order, as opposed to its gradual emergence in the course of a continual historical development'; it involves 'the idea of an authority and an author whose willpower is the ultimate cause of the polity'.[75] So the modern mind was not only unable to escape the traditional conception of law; it strengthened the prejudice against political action by idolising constitution-*making* or constitutional *authorship* (as well as by turning towards a Darwinian assessment of domination as an aspect of our supposedly 'natural' instincts of command and obedience).[76]

In some respects, it is no surprise that fabrication rather than action, constitution-making rather than political freedom, comes to dominate the juridical imagination. The idea emerges in modernity that even newness itself can be 'man-made', with the revolutionary beginnings of the autonomy of the political coinciding with the emerging consciousness that man can make his own *history*.[77]

[73] HC 222.

[74] BPAF 110.

[75] U Preuss, 'Constitutional Power-Making for the New Polity: Some Deliberations on the Relations Between the Constituent Power and the Constitution' (1993) 14 *Cardozo Law Review* 639.

[76] Arendt's critique of fabrication extends to authorship: 'Neither the individual life story nor the mundane social reality of historical events have an identifiable author, action being entangled in the web of human relationships. Real stories, in distinction from those we invent, have no author.' (HC 185).

[77] Loughlin connects this process to the birth of modern public law: 'The era of religion thus comes to a close only when law is acknowledged to be a human construct, devised by humans according to their own self-defined purposes. Only under conditions of secularisation and positivisation is the medieval idea of fundamental law transformed into the modern discipline of public law.' (Loughlin, above n 6, 7).

It is then a short step to conceiving man's ability to make his own laws, a precursor, in later modernity, and even more spectacularly, as Arendt puts it, to his ability to make 'nature', culminating with his potential escape from the physical and social-psychological confines of the Earth itself.[78]

Constitution-making becomes something of an obsession in modernity, with the commonplace metaphor that constitution-makers are the 'architects' of a pre-political artifice, making constitutions like 'puddings to a recipe'. The escape from politics suggested by the traditional conception of law as command is thus accompanied by the rise of *homo faber* 'from the great revolution of modernity', the burden of the tradition compounded with the anti-political substitution of making for acting. This paradigmatically modern notion of constitutional design has come under sustained attack by those for whom it represents the top-down imposition of a planned order rather than the recognition of the customs or conventions of a relatively homogeneous community that evolves gradually through time.[79]

And yet Arendt's critique of constitution-making depends not upon any relatively homogeneous community or communal identity but, conversely, upon the *plurality* of men that characterises the human condition. For Arendt, to state it bluntly, making is not equivalent to acting, and fabrication does not amount to the exercise of political freedom. On the contrary, the rise of *homo faber* takes place at the expense of political freedom; it is because of the fundamental condition of plurality on which politics is based that *homo faber*, implying the idea of *one* man making something out of other men, is an anti-political category. And Arendt's critique is radical because she deems the idealisation of fabrication to have been set implicitly in motion by the Platonic inauguration of the great tradition, and only liberated, but not fundamentally transformed, by the modern worldview.

So although modern constitutionalism is in danger of suppressing political action, 'the modern age … was *not the first* to denounce the idle uselessness of action and speech in particular and of politics in general'.[80] Exasperation with political action—its unpredictability, irreversibility and anonymity—is in fact 'almost as old as recorded history'.[81] It reflects Plato's foundational hierarchy of the *vita*

[78] *The Human Condition* begins with the space race, the 'first step towards escape from men's imprisonment to the earth' (HC 1). According to Arendt, it is Hobbes who introduces the new concepts of 'making' into political philosophy, evident in his metaphor of that '*artificial* man' who is the 'Great Leviathan' (*ibid* 300).

[79] Charles Taylor, for example, expresses this criticism in his work on Hegel: 'The idea of just designing a constitution and then putting it into practice is an Enlightenment idea. It treats the whole affair as an engineering problem, an external matter of means and design. But a constitution requires certain conditions in men's identity, how they understand self; and hence this enlightenment idea is radically shallow. To try in philosophy to transcend one's age is like trying to jump over Rhodes.'; C Taylor, *Hegel* (Cambridge, Cambridge University Press, 1975) 421.

[80] HC 220. Emphasis added.

[81] Ibid. The difference between action and fabrication is given explicit articulation by Aristotle in his Nichomachian ethics: '[D]oing and making are generically different, since making aims at an end distinct from the act of making, whereas in doing the end cannot be other than the act itself: doing well is itself the end.' Quoted in J Taminaux, 'Athens and Rome' in D Villa (ed), *Cambridge Companion to Hannah Arendt* (Cambridge, Cambridge University Press, 2000) 168.

11112511752

contemplativa over the *vita activa*, the priority of philosophy over politics,[82] a story which begins with the Platonic identification of the division between thought and action 'with the gulf that separates rulers from those over whom they rule'. Although the basis for this separation is the experience of the household and the master–slave relationship,[83] it plays 'its most decisive part in the organisation of public matters' and becomes intimately connected with our understanding of politics.[84] In the master–slave relationship, there is a clear separation between contemplation and action: '[H]e who knows does not have to do and he who does needs no thought or knowledge.'[85] And as the philosopher-king commands the city, Arendt notes, 'the soul commands the body and reason commands the passions'.[86]

This identification of knowledge with command and rule and of action with mere obedience and execution was so powerful that it not only 'overruled all earlier articulations in the political realm', it also 'became authoritative for the whole tradition of political thought'.[87] The domination of rulership over action was attained and given extended longevity because of the interpretation of 'rule' in terms of fabrication. Even the key word of Plato's philosophy, 'idea', is taken from experiences in the realm of fabrication, from the division between the perception of an image of the 'product-to-be' and the 'means' of making it. According to the parable of the cave, it is only in returning to the shadowy company of his fellow men that the philosopher needs 'the idea'—the true essence of being—for guidance, to act as a standard or rule 'by which to measure … the varied multitude of human deeds and words with the same absolute, "objective" certainty with which the craftsman can be guided in making'.[88]

Since Plato's analogies of household life and the private sphere, such as master–slave or shepherd–flock, would, when applied to the public sphere, suggest the quasi-divine quality of rulership (to distinguish the ruler 'as sharply from his subjects as the slaves are distinguished from the master or the sheep from the shepherd'), Plato instead constructs the public space in the image of a fabricated object, which 'carried with it only the implication of ordinary mastership'.[89] With this image, the concept of the 'expert' enters the realm of political action for the first time, and the competence of the statesman in human affairs is understood

[82] The hierarchy of action over fabrication 'had in fact, though not expressly already been overruled in the beginnings of political philosophy by the philosophers' deep-rooted suspicion of politics in general and action in particular'. Arendt continues by arguing that for Plato there is an 'inner affinity' between contemplation and fabrication, *theoria* and *poiesis* (HC 301).

[83] HC 223.

[84] *Ibid* 224.

[85] *Ibid* 223.

[86] *Ibid* 224.

[87] *Ibid* 225.

[88] *Ibid* 226.

[89] *Ibid* 227. The analogy of the 'idea' that the craftsman has, visualised by his 'inner eye' and which transcends the product and lies 'beyond the fabrication process it guides', suggests that there are ideal standards for failure or success. 'The ideas become the unwavering "absolute" standards for political and moral behaviour and judgment in the same sense that the "idea" of a bed in general is the standard for making and judging the fitness of all particular manufactured beds' (BPAF 110).

in the same sense as that of the 'carpenter to make furniture or the physician to heal the sick'.[90]

The substitution of acting for making and the concomitant degradation of politics into a means to obtain a 'higher' end, whether the safety of the philosopher, the salvation of souls, or the modern belief in the 'progress' of society, is therefore as old as the 'great tradition' of philosophy.[91] Although only the modern worldview defined man as *homo faber* and finally overcame the suspicion of fabrication, this did not constitute a reversal but rather a liberation from prejudices which had prevented the tradition 'from openly declaring that the work of the craftsman should rank higher than the "idle" opinions and actions that constitute the public realm'.[92]

This displacement of action is associated by Arendt 'with the whole body of argument against *democracy*', and, she continues, it is ultimately an argument against the essentials of politics itself because it tramples over the human condition of plurality, 'the condition *sine qua non* for that space of appearance which is the public realm'.[93] The attempt to do away with this plurality, whether through monarchy, tyranny, the benevolent Platonic philosopher-king or those forms of democracy that assume the body politic to constitute an unproblematic unity, 'is always tantamount to the abolition of the public realm', banishing the citizen to the private sphere of personal and material interests. In the Platonic Republic, Arendt notes, 'the philosopher-king applies the ideas as the craftsman applies his rules and standards; he "makes" his City as the sculptor makes a statue; and in the final Platonic work these same ideas have even become laws which need only be executed'.[94] Politics then becomes about mastering the techniques of human affairs according to a predetermined plan, based on a constitutional blueprint for a utopia. In the modern age, this is reflected in our valuing the work of the politician as a technician or craftsman, rather than the opinions of those acting and speaking with each other in the public realm.[95]

VI. CONCEPTUALISING LAW BEYOND 'THE TRADITION': *NOMOS* OR *LEX*?

Was there any alternative to the traditional conception of law, which assumed rulers and ruled, sovereign and subject and an absolute source of authority, and

[90] BPAF 111.

[91] HC 229.

[92] Plato and, albeit to a lesser degree, Aristotle, who deemed craftsmen not even worthy of full citizenship status, nevertheless 'were the first to propose handling political matters and ruling political bodies in the mode of fabrication' (*ibid* 230).

[93] *Ibid* 220.

[94] *Ibid* 227.

[95] *Ibid* 229. This turns the evaluation of law and politics into an assessment of means and ends, and it therefore prefigures the domination of instrumental rationality that Max Weber documented.

which retained such a tight grip on the modern juridical consciousness? Was there any alternative to the idealisation of the constitution-maker as *homo faber* at the expense of genuine political action and freedom? Arendt insists that there were other juridical traditions and experiences on which the revolutionary imagination could have drawn:

> When the Athenian city-state called its constitution an isonomy, or the Romans spoke of the *civitas* as their form of government, they had in mind a concept of power and law whose essence did not rely on the command–obedience relationship and which did not identify power and rule or law and command.[96]

Although the revolutionaries of the late eighteenth century did partly turn to antiquity in attempting to construct a new republic that would rest on the principle of the consent of the governed, they were ultimately unable to escape the shackles of the tradition. They overlooked the potential of two alternative conceptions of law, the Greek *nomos* and the Roman *lex*, both of which could have mitigated the burden of the tradition and its problem of the absolute, which 'neither Roman nor Greek antiquity was ever perplexed by'.[97] Neither the Greek *nomos* nor the Roman *lex* was of divine origin, and neither the Greek nor the Roman concept of legislation needed divine inspiration or a legislator who was outside of and above his own laws. Although it was true that the Greeks thought the law-giver could be a stranger called from abroad, 'this meant no more than that the laying down of the law was pre-political … just as building the walls around the city was prior to the coming into existence of the city itself'.[98] The very word, *nomos*, which 'received its full meaning as the opposite of … things that are natural', stresses the '"artificial", conventional and man-made nature of the law'.[99] Although the Roman *lex* was in an important sense different from Greek *nomos*, neither *lex* nor *nomos* required a transcendent source of authority.

The metaphor of 'building the walls around the city' of course recalls the modern category of constitution-*making* and signals an important difference between the twin conceptions of antiquity, which Arendt only hints at in her analysis of their influence on the men of the eighteenth-century Revolutions. In examining the contrast, rather than the similarity, between these two conceptions, the Roman *lex* suggests a path beyond the tradition, albeit one which was not ultimately followed, whilst the Greek *nomos* reveals the pitfalls characteristic of the category of fabrication and the idealisation of *homo faber*.[100]

[96] Arendt, above n 48, 40.

[97] Arendt insists that John Adams was wrong in claiming that 'the general opinion of ancient nations' was that 'the Divinity alone was adequate to the important office of giving laws to men' (OR 186).

[98] *Ibid*.

[99] *Ibid*.

[100] In the posthumously published 'Introduction *into* Politics', Arendt presents the contrast between *nomos* and *lex* in a stark fashion. The contrast is introduced after a discussion of the political significance of the Trojan war of annihilation, significant not only because of the threat of a contemporary war of annihilation in the wake of the Second World War and the bombing of Hiroshima, but because

The Roman *lex*, construed by Arendt as meaning 'lasting tie' and eventually 'contract', can be understood as linking human beings together through mutual agreements,[101] and hence through the faculty of *promising*, to which Arendt gives great weight in *The Human Condition* and claims to have influenced the American (as opposed to the French) revolutionaries via the writings of Montesquieu. The great variety of contract theories to which Roman *lex* gave birth 'attests to the fact that the power of making promises has occupied the center of political thought over the centuries'.[102] We shall return to the faculty of promising as central to political action in our concluding remarks, but it is important to note that this potential is one that is revealed uniquely through the Roman *lex*, because although the Greeks, like the Romans, tied law to the activity of speech that was central to all politics, only for the Romans did legislative activity, and the laws themselves, belong to the realm of politics. For the Greeks, on the other hand, 'the legislator's activity was so radically disconnected from the truly political activities and affairs of the citizens within the polis that the law-giver did not even have to be a citizen of the city'. On the contrary, he could be engaged from outside to perform his task, Arendt continues, 'much like a sculptor or architect commissioned to supply what the city required'.[103]

Since the Greek concept of *nomos* is *pre-political*, it is associated, like the activities of Plato's philosopher-king and modern constitution makers, with an isolated and even singular task of contemplation that is followed, like the work of 'sculpture' or 'architecture', by a process of fabrication in accordance with a preconceived plan:

> For the Greeks, law … is essentially conceived by a law-giver and must first exist before it can ever enter into the political realm. As such it is pre-political, but in the sense that it is constitutive for all further political action and interaction. Just as the walls of the city … must first be built before there can be a city identifiable by its shape and borders, the law determines the character of its inhabitants … The law is a city wall that is instituted and erected by one man, inside of which is created the political realm where many men move about freely.[104]

in interrogating 'the solution to the question of war' Arendt reflects, 'we might discover the origin of the concept of law'. For the Greeks, the 'grand impartiality' of Homer's account of the Trojan war suggested the complete exclusion of war and the brute force it entailed 'from what was truly political', namely that which arose between and belonged to the citizens of the *polis*. To the Greek way of thinking, she adds, 'freedom was rooted in place, bound to one spot and limited in its dimensions and the limits of freedom's space were congruent with the walls of the city, of the polis, or, more precisely, the agora contained within it' (PP 170). Cf K Breen, ch 1 of this volume.

[101] PP 179.

[102] HC 244.

[103] PP 179.

[104] *Ibid* 180. See also OR 186–87. Also HC 194: for the Greeks already, 'the law-maker was like the builder of the city wall, someone who had to do and finish his work before political activity could begin' and was therefore to be treated 'like any other craftsman or architect'.

There can be little doubt that Arendt reconstructs this conception of law in order to challenge it.[105] If reconstructed in the manner of *nomos*, law is associated with precisely those aspects of the human condition that are not merely pre-political but in an important sense *anti*-political: violence, singularity and fabrication, as opposed to power, plurality and action. The crucial point, Arendt stresses, is that the law in terms of *nomos* has something violent about it because it comes into being 'by means of production, not of action'. The law-giver in Greece 'resembles the architect of the city and its builder, not the *politikos* and citizen'.[106] This conception of law as an aspect the human artifice is echoed by modern man's conviction that he 'can know only what he makes' and that he is therefore primarily *homo faber* rather than *animal rationale*. The apparent necessity and in some cases glorification of violence has been particularly striking in the series of modern revolutions, Arendt notes, with the 'exception of the American'.[107]

And yet the 'singularity' inherent in the category of fabrication and characteristic of the Greek conception of law-making did have a telling influence on the founders.[108] The Platonic understanding of rule, through which 'the many become one in every respect', is of course reflected in the American founding motto, *e pluribus unum*. It was fear of plurality and of the unpredictability and spontaneity of political action (the entanglement in a complex web of human relationships that it entails) which had inspired the Greeks to *set limits* by means of *nomos* and 'to interpret the law not as a link and a relationship, but rather as an enclosing border than no one should overstep',[109] just as a similar fear might be thought to underline Madison's concern as expressed in Federalist Number 10 to guard against political factions.

This assumption that the purpose of constitutional law is to place limits on political action is ultimately tied up with the same erroneous and reductive conception of politics and of freedom that plagued the traditional conception of law as command. So although the Greek conception of *nomos* does not fall prey to the

[105] More than once, Arendt expresses her allegiance to the Roman notion of *lex*. After the passage just cited, Arendt speaks of the Roman conception as 'extraordinarily fruitful' (PP 180). In HC, she speaks of the 'true genius' of Rome; and in OR, of the 'great Roman model'. On the influence of Roman thought in Arendt, see D Hammer, 'Hannah Arendt and Roman Political Thought' (2002) 30 *Political Theory* 124–49.

[106] PP 181. For Arendt, the architectural metaphor of fabrication *always* suggests a certain violence; without the violence of the maker, 'no fabrication could ever come to pass' (HC 228). See also PP 111.

[107] HC 228. Although misleading as a broader historical point, this is conceptually significant in that it suggests not only that violence is distinguishable from power, but also that it is avoidable in constitutional politics. See also BPAF 140.

[108] Madison, for example, noted that the task of framing the constitution of government has in history 'been performed by some individual citizen, of pre-eminent wisdom' in Federalist #38, in C Rositer (ed) *The Federalist Papers* (New York, New American Library, 1961) quoted by Arendt, OR 312. The revolutionaries on both sides of the Atlantic were influenced by the Machiavellian idea that 'to found a new republic must be the work of one man only' (OR 207). Contributing to the failure of the French case was Robespierre's self-perception as the 'architect' who will build out of 'human material a new house for human beings' (OR 208).

[109] PP 186.

absolutism of the Hebrew-Christian tradition, it does, like *command*, ultimately reflect the same attempt to *escape* from political freedom, where freedom is understood as the ability 'to call something into being that did not exist before', to bring something new into the world in concert with others and in the context of plurality. The upshot of *nomos* is that freedom is secured by ensuring restraints, even if these are understood in modern constitutional language as 'enabling restraints'; in both cases freedom is that which *remains* after the city wall has been built. As in the 'housing' metaphor that Arendt herself employs, freedom is left to 'dwell' after the house has been constructed rather than exercised in the construction (and reconstruction) of the house itself. If freedom is left merely to 'dwell', it might not be long before it dissipates altogether.

The basic error of the tradition, Arendt notes, lies in its identification of freedom with sovereignty, something that 'has always been taken for granted in political as well as philosophic thought'.[110] But 'no man,' Arendt admonishes, 'can be sovereign because not one man, but men, inhabit the earth'[111]; sovereignty as an idea simply makes no sense in the human condition of plurality. The notion that constitutional law is a *pre-political* construction, presenting a space that 'houses' (by regulating and limiting) freedom *qua* personal sovereignty is therefore paradoxically a mirror image of the erroneous conception of law as command. It is the wholesale rejection of freedom as personal sovereignty—*freedom from* undue interference by others—that suggests the alternative conception of *freedom to* constitute and reconstitute our basic laws. This constitutional *potentia* exemplified by episodes of modern revolution demonstrates not only that political freedom is experienced as the exercise of power in common with others, but also that law and politics are thoroughly and foundationally intertwined.

Ironically, although the founders of the American republic could not escape the traditional imperative conception of law, they had stumbled on the answer to the vicious circle of law's foundations. The act of engaging with one another through promises and mutual ties, reminiscent of the Roman *lex*, and which constituted the 'new beginning' of the republic, carries its own *principle* with it. It had, moreover, in Montesquieu and his theory of the separation of powers, the only philosopher of the Enlightenment who consistently avoided the absolute and the basic conflation of freedom and sovereign will:

> [A]mong the pre-revolutionary theorists only Montesquieu never thought it necessary to introduce an absolute ... into the political realm. This is closely connected with the fact that ... only Montesquieu ever used the word 'law' in its strictly Roman sense ... as the relation subsisting between different entities ... Neither religious nor natural laws, therefore, constitute for Montesquieu a 'higher law', strictly speaking ... And since, for Montesquieu, as for the Romans, a law is merely what relates two things and therefore is relative by definition, he needed no absolute source of authority and could describe

110 HC 234.
111 *Ibid.*

the 'spirit of the laws' without ever posing the troublesome question of their absolute validity.[112]

The contrast with Rousseau is telling.[113] Rousseau's 'General Will' is still *God-like*, it is 'still a divine Will which needs only to will in order to produce a "law"'.[114] His substitution, as Arendt sees it, of consent and opinion with this category of the 'will', 'essentially excludes all processes of exchange of opinions and an eventual agreement between them'.[115] For Arendt this speaks of a complete absence of freedom: the difference is fundamental, for Arendt, as explained in her critique of 'the tradition', freedom dwells in the 'We can', not the 'I will' (or even 'We will'). Freedom is experienced as the capacity to perform the 'infinitely improbable', to act in concert with others in the public realm and to bring something new into the world. It is expressed politically through the 'framework of ties and bonds, such as laws and constitutions', which ultimately derive their legitimacy 'from the faculty of promising with one another in the face of the essential uncertainties of the future'.[116]

VII. CONCLUDING REMARKS: RECONCILING POLITICAL FREEDOM AND CONSTITUTIONAL AUTHORITY?

Does the image of law as *lex* therefore suggest an alternative path towards the reconciliation of political freedom and law, so that we need not confront constitutionalism as presenting a fateful ambivalence between them? To be sure, *lex* avoids the image of fabrication and its concomitant suppression of political freedom, with its rejection, as Jeremy Waldron has recently reminded us, of the *singularity* of the constitutional framer—one man *making* something out of other men. It presents instead an image of constitutionalism as political freedom, 'as an activity that arises among men acting and speaking together'.[117] An exploration of this image will invite further reflection on the tension between the authority of the constitution and *democratic* political freedom.[118]

112 OR 188–89.

113 '[J]ust as Montesquieu's theory of the separation of powers had become axiomatic for American political thought … , so Rousseau's notion of a General Will … became axiomatic for all factions and parties of the French revolution, because it was indeed the theoretical substitute for the sovereign will of an absolute monarch.' (*ibid* 155)

114 *Ibid* 183.

115 *Ibid* 76. She continues by criticising the inherent *instability* of the General Will, most evident in Robespierre's revolutionary appropriation of Rousseau's idea, but which Rousseau himself concedes with his famous line, '*il est absurde que la volonte se donne des chaines pour l'avenir*'. As such the general will is built, like Robbespierre's *pouvoir constituant*, on 'quicksand'. The very idea of a unity of wills upon which Rousseau relies, Arendt says, comes from the basic proposition that two antagonistic wills are united in the presence of a third that opposes them both, and thus leads to the presupposition of a common national enemy (and of course show us the relatively direct route towards Carl Schmitt) (*ibid* 78).

116 BPAF 162.

117 J Waldron, 'Arendt's Constitutional Politics' in Villa (ed), above n 81, 204.

118 On the relationship between democracy and the political in Arendt's work, see Wolin, above n 53. He suggests that the 'antidemocratic strain', most evident in Arendt's earlier work, is tempered in her later writings as a result of her political experiences in the 1960s.

The constitutive activity suggested by *lex* is conducive to political freedom because it is about calling forth something intangible and improbable through the joint exercise of power, the mutual pledges and collective acts of promising, on the basic principle of *pacta sunt servanda*. So the tragic irony of the lost revolutionary tradition in America is, for Arendt, that the founders had actually stumbled across the method of avoiding the descent into the absolutism of the tradition, through the mutual promises and covenants based in the reciprocal trust of the early settlers: this foretold the creation of the political beginning which was to be the new republic. The act of foundation could operate as a 'fountain of authority', just as the word 'constitution' carries a twofold meaning—it is both the act of constituting and the result of what is constituted:

> The very fact that the men of the American revolution thought of themselves as founders indicated the extent to which they must have known that it would be the act of foundation itself, rather than an Immortal Legislator ... or self-evident truth or any other transcendent ... source, which eventually would become the fountain of authority in the new body politic ... It is futile to search for an absolute to break the vicious circle in which all beginning is inevitably caught, because this absolute lies in the very act of beginning itself.[119]

The vicious circle of the legality of the new law and the legitimacy of the new power is tamed not by positing an *absolute*, but by developing a *principle* from the act of beginning itself, which, Arendt notes, for the first time in history occurs in America 'in broad daylight'.[120] This event, breaking into the continuous sequence of historical time, manifests the constitutional *potentia* and reveals the possibility of political freedom without the absolutism of a *creatio ex nihilo*. What saves the act of beginning from arbitrariness 'is that it carries its own principle with itself, or to be more precise, that beginning and principle are not only related to each other but are coeval'.[121] The political relevance of these insights, Arendt argues, is that they stand in opposition to the claim that violence is necessary for all foundations and unavoidable in all revolutions, a claim that she (misleadingly) suggests is refuted by the American revolutionary experience.[122] What the experience does genuinely point to is the possibility of a distinction between the beginning as 'absolute'—as in the case of fabrication in accordance with a fixed ideal—and the beginning as a 'principle' of joint political action, which is always dynamic, temporal and contingent:

> [A] terminological distinction between the word 'principium' (beginning of the world) and 'initium' (the beginning which is a man), underlin[es] that, by contrast with the absolute beginning (principium) that can only be the work of God, the human beginning

119 OR 205.

120 When the element of 'beginning', which was initially co-joined with the entitlement to rule, disappeared from the concept of rulership, 'the most elementary and authentic understanding of human freedom disappeared from philosophy' (HC 224–25).

121 OR 213.

122 HC 228. Arendt's claim is historically dubious, but still conceptually relevant.

(initium) is always inserted within the continuum of time and thus necessarily amounts to a re-beginning.[123]

And yet what is distinctive about the escape from tradition is not only the novelty and exhilaration of political freedom, but also the fact that the revolutionary events 'concern the many and not the few'.[124] In this sense, modern revolution is not only about freedom, but also about *equality* as a 'birthright', which 'was utterly unknown prior to the modern age'.[125] Newness, as Arendt puts it, 'reaches the market place' in the wake of modern revolution.[126] It is, in other words, although Arendt fails to develop the point, the birth (or rebirth) of *democratic* political freedom that is signalled by the late eighteenth-century Revolutions. Constitutional *potentia* must be understood as a democratic *potentia* if it is to remain faithful to the promise of modernity.

Although the revolutionaries still, unhappily, talked about 'obedience' to law, because of their inability to transcend the tradition, what they meant, according to Arendt, was rather the support of the laws through the consent of the citizen. This understanding of power based on consent recalls another aspect of Arendt's distinction between power and violence. Whereas violence can manage without the many, power always stands in need of numbers.[127] After the modern democratic revolutions, constitutionalism must therefore stand against the Platonic understanding of it as that part of theology which 'taught the few how to rule the many', as well the liberal understanding of it as a 'counter-majoritarian' device based on the 'fear of the many'. It should instead approximate to the Greek *isonomy* (the notion of 'no-rule'), which conceives equality not on any naturalistic basis or self-evident truths, but in virtue of the social and political equality of citizenship.[128]

But how can 'the many' act in concert when it comes to constitutional politics? Or, to reverse the question, how can mere 'consent' be sufficient for the generation of political power and expression of political freedom? The choice we seem to be faced with is the following: Restrict political freedom to the freedom-founding actions of those who actually engage in the constitutive activity associated with *lex*, thereby rendering freedom elusive and elitist, sporadic and fleeting; or generalise and dilute political freedom and risk that it becomes little more than the pallid

[123] S Delacroix, 'Schmitt on Kelsenian Normativism' (2005) 18 *Ratio Juris*, 40, fn 25, paraphrasing from HC 177, fn 3.

[124] See OR 39.

[125] *Ibid* 40. She continues: 'Liberation in the revolutionary sense came to mean … that all those who always lived in darkness and subjection to whatever powers there were, should rise and become the supreme sovereign of the law.' The problem is that rather than overcoming the concept of sovereignty, this suggests that the sovereign had merely been replaced; it was now a popular sovereignty that lay at the foundations of the constitution.

[126] *Ibid* 47.

[127] Arendt, above n 48, 42. 'It's the people's support that lends power to the institutions of a country, and this support is but the continuation of the consent that brought the laws into existence to begin with': (*ibid* 41).

[128] OR 30–31. Arendt suggests elsewhere that 'isonomia' is merely the equal right to speak in the *polis* and that it is a mistake to associate equality with justice, as is the modern inclination (PP 118).

acquiescence in the structure of constitutional authority.[129] A similar problem is often reconstructed in constitutional theory with regard to future generations: how are they in practice to re-live the mutual constitution of the body politic, as Jefferson wished, without descending into chaos, as Madison feared?

There is thus a final dilemma, an examination of which brings us closer to the tension between political freedom and law. The lost spirit of revolution seems to be the inevitable result of a paradoxical problem of foundations, since it contains two elements that appear to be irreconcilable: modern constitutionalism must exhibit a concern for *both* the stability and authority of the new structure *and* the 'exhilarating awareness of the human capacity of beginning'.[130] Arendt argues persuasively that the institutions of the post-revolutionary era that gave stability to the new polity, the Senate and the Supreme Court, and answered the early preoccupation with permanence and the 'augmentation' of the foundations of the republic, were precisely those same institutions which destroyed the spirit of revolution itself and undermined the possibility of maintaining political freedom in terms of the democratic constitutional *potentia* of 'We, the people'. But how, if at all, can the political freedom of the many be reconciled with the constitutional authority of the few, without reintroducing a problematic foundationalism of popular origins?

Although this is a dilemma that Arendt never directly confronts, she does suggest an analogy that is more apposite to its resolution than that of 'fabrication' (or even of 'promising'). More apt to capture the 'immanence and plurality' of democratic constitutionalism than the metaphor of building, housing or erecting walls and structures is that of constitutional law as 'political grammar or syntax'.[131] Rather than suggesting a one-off activity or constitutional moment when the 'house' wherein freedom can dwell is constructed or reconstructed in one go, it suggests a dynamic and ongoing narrative in the changing circumstances of plurality, and in which freedom is negotiated and renegotiated in the public realm. Constitutionalism as *political grammar* represents the idea that even our most fundamental law is *relational and dynamic*, developing symbiotically with politics and the exercise of political freedom rather than being fabricated or constructed 'up front' as a timeless container for the vicissitudes of political action.[132]

129 In contrast to her assessment of revolutionary political freedom, Arendt suggests that the Greek concept of freedom 'does not require an egalitarian democracy' but rather 'a quite narrowly limited oligarchy or aristocracy' (PP 118). This tension between a revolutionary and an aristocratic sense of freedom is pervasive in Arendt's work.

130 Cohen and Arato argue that this problem is due to Arendt's failure to draw on the concept of civil society as a mediator between law and power; see J Cohen and A Arato *Civil Society and Political Theory* (Cambridge, Mass, MIT, 1992) 193.

131 Waldron, above n 116, 204. See OR 175.

132 As Martin Loughlin has put it: 'Public law is neither a code of rules or a set of principles but a practice. Understood as the law relating to the activity of governing, public law can be defined as that assemblage of rules, principles, canons, maxims, customs, usages, and manners that condition, sustain and regulate the activity of governing. These practices comprise conventions and rules of speech—a vocabulary and a syntax—which are being continuously developed.' M Loughlin, *The Idea of Public Law* (Oxford, Oxford University Press, 2003) 155.

3

Law and the Space of Appearance in Arendt's Thought

JOHAN VAN DER WALT*

I. INTRODUCTION

> A life spent entirely in public, in the presence of others, becomes, as we would say, shallow. While it retains its visibility, it loses the quality of rising into sight from some darker ground which must remain hidden if it is not to lose its depth in a very real, non-subjective sense. The only efficient way to guarantee the darkness of what needs to be hidden against the light of publicity is private property, a privately owned place to hide in.[1]

THE CONCERN WITH the appearance of the world in human consciousness, the fundamental concern of the tradition of European philosophical inquiry that came to be called *phenomenology*, runs like a constant thread through Hannah Arendt's work. But this passage from *The Human Condition* marks the specificity of her place within the phenomenological tradition like no other. It marks the way she focused the phenomenological concern with the appearance of the world on the way the world comes to light when political action sets forth and leaves behind the private concerns of the home. The central aim of this essay will be to illuminate this specificity of Arendt's contribution to phenomenology in terms of a fundamental phenomenology of law. In pursuit of this aim it will also highlight the resonances in Arendt's work with two other major phenomenologists of her time, namely, Martin Heidegger and Maurice Merleau-Ponty.[2]

* I am grateful to everyone who participated in the workshop on *Arendt and the Law* in Antwerp, June 2010. Many helpful comments during the workshop helped me to improve the original draft of this essay substantially. I also wish to note my indebtedness to a reading group with Henk Botha, Wessel le Roux, André van der Walt and Karin van Marle with whom I first started reading Arendt in the course of 1995–96. Many of the thoughts I articulate in this essay already started taking shape then. Responsibility for errors and misunderstandings of course remain strictly mine.

[1] H Arendt, *The Human Condition* (Chicago, Ill, University of Chicago Press, 1989) 71.

[2] Heidegger's influence on Arendt is well-known and visible in almost all her works, notwithstanding the very different and quite opposite positions she takes in with regard to many common concerns in their respective oeuvres. As a fascinating letter from Arendt to Heidegger reveals, she discovered

The reading of Arendt that will be expounded in this essay will go through a number of phases. The first phase responds to the need to understand clearly what is at stake when phenomenology turns its attention to the phenomenon, to *that which appears*. This is the focus of section II. ('Appearance, Reality, Truth'). The second phase of the reading illuminates the kinetic trajectory that informs the word 'appearance'. Appearance concerns the *transitory*, *intransitive* or *in-transit* interim of a (this or that) *coming* to light of the world from the dark margins of consciousness into the illuminated centre of human intentionality. The dark margins of consciousness continue to haunt and circumscribe enlightened or illuminated intentionality. These margins require phenomenology to retrace its own steps again and again so as to capture or recapture that which has again eluded and will ever again have eluded intentionality. This is the point of Husserl's obsessive phenomenological reductions. Husserlian phenomenology, argues Maurice Merleau-Ponty, thus became a Sisyphean concern of consciousness with its own constituting boundaries, with that which always remains overlooked so as to constitute intention. Martin Heidegger would emphasise in comparable regard the irreducible *lethé* that marks the *aletheia* or *aletheuein* of *phainesthai*, the sombre concealment from which the disclosure at issue in any coming to light cannot extract itself. These Husserlian and Heideggerian themes are clearly evident in the passage from *The Human Condition* with which we began. They are expounded in more detail in section III. ('Appearing: The *Phainesthai* of the Phenomenon').

Section IV. ('Her Shadow and its Shade') turns to Arendt's engagement with the phenomenon of poverty. Arendt understood well that poverty contaminates the space of appearance. That she did not perceive this contamination as a political concern, perhaps the fundamental concern in modern politics, constitutes, phenomenologically speaking, a remarkable failure. She was well aware of the way poverty *appeared* on the public scene of modernity, but she wilfully lamented and resisted this phenomenon for reasons of a nostalgic attachment to an earlier politics that was unconcerned with poverty, a politics that according to her was evident in classical Greece. This nostalgia moved her to confine concerns with bodily needs to the private sphere. This nostalgic move was shockingly out of touch with the times in which she lived, but it also went hand in hand with a profound insight, the insight that the private domain shields and must shield from politics the existential concerns of the human heart. Humans do not just live, they exist emphatically concerned with the ultimate worth and worthiness of their lives. This libidinal concern with worth and worthiness not only needs protection from public scrutiny. It exists as such by virtue of the desire to withdraw from everything that has become public. It therefore cannot and should not be the

Merleau-Ponty very late in her life (cf H Arendt and M Heidegger, *Hannah Arendt Martin Heidegger Briefe 1925–1975* (Frankfurt am Main, Vittorio Klostermann, 1999) 225), but from that moment on she relied substantially on his thinking and clearly recognised the phenomenological roots which they shared.

concern of politics. This is the profound counter-side of her spurious thought that poverty is not a political concern.

Section V. ('The Literary Exception') turns to the place of the law in Arendt's thought. The law would seem to be an endpoint for Arendt, a culmination of self-evidence, a termination of appearance. She seems to espouse an understanding of natural law and natural legal principles that already govern polities prior to the positive political articulation of the law. Nothing new can appear from the dark recesses of human existentiality as far as the law is concerned. This is evident from her insistence that political revolution is fundamentally a matter of restoring timeless principles of law that exist prior to their revolutionary enactments. Law thus seems to be exempted from the space of appearance. It is not a phenomenon. The law does not appear. It always exists already fully apparent. Considered in terms of the opening quotation from *The Human Condition* above, the law thus conceived cannot but be shallow. The law is or must be assumed to be 'entirely ... public' and therefore shallow. The apparent shallowness of the law is recognised by no one less than Rawls.[3] Section VI. ('Literary Depths and the "Shallowness" of Law') nevertheless goes on to argue that the law is not shallow. The apparent shallowness of the law concerns, in fact, the inverse or negative depth of the law. The inverse depth of the law consists in the way it deliberately takes leave of or withdraws from the existential depths explored in literature. Law and politics are not and should not be concerned with compassion, but literature is and can be so at heart's desire, Arendt contends. Section VI. reads this distinction between literature and politics as an invitation to explore a relation between law, politics and literature that takes leave of the edifying view of this relationship currently on offer in 'law and literature' circles, the edifying view in terms of which law can gain insights from literature.

The completely different understanding of the relation between law and literature that comes to the fore in Arendt's thought illuminates the directly opposite trajectories of appearance evident in literature, on the one hand, and law, on the other. Law and literature may traverse the same space of appearance, but they do so in directly opposite directions. The inverse trajectories of law and literature do not render the one profound and the other shallow. They render the one positively and the other negatively profound. At issue here is not the shallowness of law when compared to literature, but the inverse or negative depth of law.

Section VII. ('The Inverse or Negative Depth of the Law') illuminates the legal theoretical gains evident in the Arendtian regard for the negative or inverse depth of the law. It shows how this understanding of the law helps us to come to terms with the legal theoretical and doctrinal puzzles that Arendt raises in response to the Eichmann trial. Section VIII. ('Back to the Beginning') briefly returns to reflect on the passage from *The Human Condition* with which we began, in view of the thoughts expounded in its wake.

[3] J Rawls, *Political Liberalism* (New York, Columbia University Press, 1996) 243.

II. APPEARANCE, REALITY, TRUTH

A number of key passages in *On Revolution* show how much Arendt's political thought pivoted on key concerns of phenomenology. Close to the beginning of the work she makes an almost programmatic enunciation in this regard:

> For political thought can only follow the articulations of the political phenomena themselves, it remains bound to what appears in the domain of human affairs; and these appearances, in contradistinction to physical matters, need speech and articulation, that is, something which transcends mere physical visibility as well as sheer audibility, in order to be manifest at all.[4]

Arendt clearly moves very close to Heidegger here. At issue in this passage is not only the phenomenological concern with phenomena, but more specifically the hermeneutic turn in phenomenology that Heidegger would bring about in *Sein und Zeit*.[5] The result of this hermeneutic turn was a heightened regard for linguistic disclosure rather than empirical observation (mere visibility/sheer audibility) as the source of appearing and appearance in human concerns. Appearing or appearance, *phainesthai*, would become for Heidegger a matter of *coming to language* or being *on the way to language*, as the title of one of his later works suggests.[6]

What the phenomenologists, hermeneutic or epistemological, had in common was the conviction that truth, Being or reality was not a fixed object beyond the empirical observations or interpretive understanding of the subject, but only and exactly that which *comes to the fore* in the intentional observation or understanding of the subject. Arendt undoubtedly shared this frame of mind, and she invoked it in poignant fashion to analyse the cause of the interminable suspicions that informed Robespierre's 'terror of virtue' during the French Revolution. As she puts it:

> Theoretically, the answers to these questions may ultimately lie within the range of one of the oldest metaphysical problems in our tradition, the problem of the relationship between being and appearance, whose implications and perplexities with respect to the political realm have been manifest and caused reflection at least from Socrates to Machiavelli. The core of the problem can be stated briefly and, for our purpose, exhaustively by recalling the two diametrically opposed positions which we connect with these two thinkers.[7]

For Socrates, contends Arendt, appearance *is* the truth in human affairs. There is nothing behind appearance which politics can or ought to pursue. Machiavelli's thought, in clear contrast, is informed by the assumption of transcendent Being, the assumption of a transcendent reality beyond the worldly realm of mere appearance. For Machiavelli, the wordly realm is all that counts in politics. The Christian

[4] H Arendt, *On Revolution* (New York, Penguin Books, 1990) 19.
[5] M Heidegger, *Sein und Zeit* (Tübingen, Max Niemeyer Verlag, 1979) 37.
[6] M Heidegger, *Unterwegs zur Sprache* (Pfullingen, Günther Neske, 1986).
[7] Arendt, above n 4, 101.

doctrine of two worlds, the heavenly and earthly, thus released the earthly from the constraints of truth and freed it up for the strategic pursuit and maintenance of secular power. This Christian understanding did not make truth irrelevant for politics. As Arendt, points out, Machiavelli was as concerned as Socrates with 'hidden crimes', but for him such crimes were known and punished by God, not by men. The acts of the sovereign rulers were therefore not to be judged on earth.[8] Socrates, argues Arendt, believed in the inevitability of the *disclosure* of truth in politics. For him, the *truth* of politics could not *but appear*. This was so because the political actor already and inevitably appears to himself. There was an internal division in the political self between 'the agent and onlooker'. In order to deceive others, the agent also had to deceive himself. That is why, contends Arendt, the Greek *polis* necessarily was a world of *phainomena*, of true appearances:

> [T]he polis, and the whole of the political realm, was a man-made space of appearances where human deeds and words were exposed to the public that testified to their reality and judged their worthiness. In this sphere, treachery and deceit and lying were possible, as though men, instead of 'appearing' and exposing themselves, created phantoms and apparitions with which to fool others; these self-made illusions only covered up the true phenomena (the true appearances or *phainomena*), just as an optical illusion might spread over the object, as it were, and prevent it from appearing.[9]

Arendt's argument is ultimately that deception was a hard feat to pull off in this world so intent on letting the truth come out, on letting it appear. It was 'too ambitious', she says, for in order to deceive others effectively, the agent first had to deceive himself, his inner onlooker, just as we still say today that an actor must make a role his own to make his acting convincing to others.[10] Her argument is compelling to the extent that it surely must have been more difficult to deceive in the close-knit political community of the Greek *polis* where public scrutiny was a matter of daily routine, than it is in the endless bureaucratic corridors of power of modern societies. It must surely have been much more difficult in the former, constantly and coherently to maintain a facade in which the actor did not and could not believe himself, than it is in the latter. But the argument surely cannot claim to deal comprehensively or conclusively with the problem of treachery and deception. It does not deal with the fact that pathological deception—the hidden crime—remains a problem with which the phenomenological concern with appearance, in the whole phenomenological tradition, has yet to/will always have to come to terms. Was the Greek *polis* really so innocent, so thoroughly candid, so thoroughly disclosing, so thoroughly phenomenological, one might say, as to render 'the phenomenon of deception' an insignificant question? Arendt and the phenomenological tradition would seem to assume the fundamental innocence of appearance. For them 'the phenomenon of deception' would seem to be an

8 *Ibid* 101–02.
9 *Ibid* 103.
10 *Ibid.*

oxymoron that need not detain us for long. This is the weak side of her argument, and the weak point that must always haunt the phenomenological tradition. It is a weak point, however, that will and must also continue to haunt earthly existence as such. It can only be overcome, rendered a non-problem, by the religious assumption of an omniscient God that really knows the hearts of men and will ultimately punish the wicked. It is only realistic to assume that many hidden crimes and treacheries have indeed gone down in history completely undetected; hence perhaps the ultimate allure of faith, religion and God.

Phenomenology cannot play God. It accepts the irreducibly and irredeemably finite and perspectival nature of human cognition. But it can claim confidently enough that the inescapable and vast variety of perspectives among humans, conditioned as it is by the irreducible plurality of human existence, affords humans at least provisionally reliable cognitions of epistemological and political essentials—that which everyone from their varying perspectives can consider as *incircumventible perspectives* and therefore incircumventible 'truths' of human co-existence. These essentials never attain to the conclusive stability of Platonic ideas, but the loss of this Platonic certainty also rids cognition of the equally Platonic idea of a false world of mere opinions, as Arendt noted well with reference to Nietzsche's famous observation in this regard: 'We have abolished the true world. What has remained? The apparent one perhaps? Oh no! With the true world we have also abolished the apparent one.'[11] Once rid of the impulse to purchase the burdensome insurance policy of absolute truth, humans may regain the simple experience of the world, the simple experience of the 'there is' of the world, as Merleau-Ponty wrote.[12] Phenomenology clearly anticipated the Rawlsian insight that public reason offers us a common world even though and exactly because it does not seek to offer us the ultimate truth of things.[13] I shall return to this point below.

Arendt makes her point regarding the political and phenomenological truth of the world of appearance against the background of the French Revolution and Robespierre's 'terror of virtue'. If there is a lesson to be learnt from Robespierre's 'terror of virtue', she maintains, it is this: An undue concern with truth and truthfulness in politics cannot avoid becoming murderous, and cannot hope to create and maintain anything like a lasting and stable polity. For there is no way that the best of human hearts can prove itself to be fully virtuous; there is no way that any political institution can claim to reflect the full truth of human existence. If politics is to pursue perfect virtue and conclusive truth, it must turn into the constant elimination of suspected vice and the constant destruction of ever-imperfect

[11] H Arendt, *The Life of the Mind* (New York/London, Harcourt Inc, 1978) 11.

[12] *Ibid* 49: 'What Merleau-Ponty had to say against Descartes is brilliantly right: "To reduce perception to the thought of perceiving … is to take out an insurance against doubt whose premiums are more onerous than the loss for which it is to indemnify us: for it is to … move to a type of certitude that will never restore to us the "there is" of the world.'

[13] Rawls, above n 3, 212–14 (the lecture on 'Public Reason').

institutions. Thus did the French Revolution come to devour its children and fail to produce lasting legal institutions. The American Revolution was relatively bloodless and produced a lasting polity with a lasting constitution exactly because the American founders made peace with the vice of men and believed it could be contained adequately enough through political participation and the varying perspectives afforded by the free competition of multiple opinions. As Arendt puts it, 'their common sense was never exposed to the absurd hope that man, whom Christianity had held to be sinful and corrupt in its nature, might still be revealed to be an angel'.[14] Phrased in phenomenological terms, one can say they trusted that an on-going exchange of admittedly finite perspectives would safeguard the minimum levels of essential knowledge and essential virtues required for durable human co-existence, notwithstanding the possibility, likelihood or inevitability of less than virtuous and less than truthful perspectives also taking part in these exchanges.

The times through which Arendt lived would not spare her an awareness of vicious political crimes and radical evil in politics. She was duly conscious that such crimes and evil can also 'make their appearance'. '[W]herever they make their appearance,' she observed, 'they transcend' and 'radically destroy' the 'realm of human affairs and the potentialities of human power'.[15] She can perhaps be read to have phrased this view more rigorously when she earlier contended that the power of totalitarian movements consisted exactly in *not appearing*, that is, in not showing or revealing itself, in remaining secret and secretive, in consistently avoiding any recognisable shape.[16] The latter position is more consistent with the phenomenological politics that we are distilling from her work in this essay; more consistent with her own analysis of deception as non-appearance or an obstruction of appearance. Totalitarian movements are indeed fundamentally 'anti-phenomenological' in the way they destroy the interaction and inter-interrogation of multiple political perspectives; in the way they refuse contestation. They reduce the human condition of plurality to a oneness that monopolises interrogation murderously, if not indeed to a oneness achieved through murder; a oneness by murder that neither bothers nor needs to interrogate, but simply annihilates otherness.[17] Claude Lefort, life-long friend of Merleau-Ponty and editor of *L'Visible et l'invisible*, may well have taken much inspiration also from this work when he later defined totalitarianism in terms of its suppression of plurality and fundamental assumption of the oneness of the people.[18] The most consistent way of describing such totalitarian destructions of plurality *phenomenologically* would be to invoke not the *appearance* of some or other pathological variety of the political,

[14] Arendt, above n 4, 95.

[15] Arendt, above n 1, 241.

[16] H Arendt, *The Origins of Totalitarianism* (New York/London, Harcourt Inc, 1976) 403.

[17] Cf H Arendt, *Eichmann in Jerusalem* (New York, Penguin Books, 1994).

[18] Cf Lefort's analysis of the logic of totalitarianism in terms of '*du peuple-Un*' and '*d'un pouvoir-Un*' that allows for no differentiation in C Lefort, *L'invention démocratique* (Paris, Fayard, 1994) 101.

but the complete *dis-appearance of the political* as such. The Arendtian concern with the *appearance of the political* must therefore endorse a constant multiplicity of political opinions and factions.[19] Her concerns with appearance and plurality go hand in hand.

Be that as it may, Arendt did not entertain the notion of the innocence of 'normal' or 'healthy' democratic politics, the innocence of appearance. Getting rid of the burdensome insurance policy of absolute truth, according to her, was not going to eliminate the risk of serious political harm that might well have spawned the quest for that policy in the first place. It might at best spare us the excess harm to which that policy itself often gave and gives rise. Arendt was well aware that the finite perspectives that inform all political action invariably doom politics to cause unforeseen harm, however much it might have been contemplated and executed in good faith; hence her regard for the crucial role of forgiveness in human politics. Nothing new would ever appear in the world without forgiveness, for no new action can ever be taken again without an act of forgiveness:

> Without being forgiven, released from the consequences of what we have done, our capacity to act would, as it were, be confined to one single deed from which we could never recover; we would remain the victims of its consequences forever.[20]

One could tie up this thought by contending that appearance requires forgiveness; forgiveness conditions appearance. There is thus an intrinsic relation between appearance, forgiveness and *giving*. A certain civility and generosity sustain the world and the possibility of new worlds. Appearance gives and forgives the world.

III. APPEARING: THE *PHAINESTHAI* OF THE PHENOMENON

Appearance nevertheless does not always give us our daily bread, as the pervasive appearance of poverty makes all too clear. Arendt was remarkably cavalier about this, as we shall soon see. But appearance *does* give us whatever existence we have. It does so by way of an emergence, an event of disclosure that draws or redraws the line between the disclosed and the undisclosed, the visible and the invisible, the known and the unknown, the comprehensible and the incomprehensible. Natural human consciousness, a pervasive aspect of the human condition, consists in an act of overlooking that allows for vision or sight. *Within* the window of vision opened by this act of overlooking, modern science and epistemology constructed a paradigm of knowledge that pivoted on a subject–object relationship and the endeavour to ensure the subject mirrors the object adequately if not perfectly. But the windows of vision that open by acts of overlooking precede the subject–object-oriented paradigm of science. The subject–object paradigm of science comes later.

[19] Arendt, above n 4, 93, 225.
[20] Arendt, above n 1, 237.

It articulates itself within a space already opened by the fundamental act and fact of human intentionality, already opened by the window of intentional looking and overlooking.

Science is thus already far removed from the human being's initial encounter with the world. It is far removed from the way things appear to humans, far removed from the thing itself, *die Sache selbst*. This was Husserl's opening gambit with which he launched a mode of philosophical inquiry that would first become known as *phenomenology*, as he himself called it, then as *hermeneutics*, due to Heidegger's intervention, and still later as *deconstruction*, as Derrida would have it. *Zurück zu den Sachen selbst* ('back to the things themselves') was Husserl's call in response to his perception that modern science was increasingly losing touch with human existence, that is, with the lived world or life-world of humans.[21]

The phenomenological return to the things themselves and the method through which it seeks to capture the essences of things are ever-incomplete and interminable, contends Merleau-Ponty. Phenomenology seeks to say what remains unsaid, it is an eternal recommencement—'*[l]e philosophie dit encore les inédits, est un commençant perpetuel*'.[22] Husserl's transcendental consciousness, claims Merleau-Ponty, was not Kant's time-proof transcendental set of categories and forms of perception, but a historically contingent and precarious undertaking that had to retrace its own steps continuously. In his own work Merleau-Ponty invokes the notion of a bodily existence that precipitates a now errant, now re-assembled visibility—'*la visibilité tantôt errante et tantôt rassemblée*'.[23] And this incessant errancy and re-commencement, Merleau-Ponty points out, phenomenology shares with literature and art. He also invokes in this regard a thought that is central to Arendt's work, namely, the natality of history, '*l'histoire à l'état naissant*'.[24] Arendt can nevertheless be said to have added something unique to this regard for the natality of history that is crucial for her understanding of law and literature and the difference between them. It is tempting to say that she exempted law from the exploratory phenomenology of literature and art that Merleau-Ponty points out here. But this would not be the full story, as we shall soon see. Law indeed comes forth from the nascent state of things by taking leave of literature, by splitting off from it. As will become clear below, the birth of both law and literature consists for her in their splitting up and veering off into different and quite opposite directions. This is a crucial move in her thinking that guides one towards a profound phenomenology of law, that is, to a profound understanding of the way the law first appears in the world.

On the basis of this phenomenology of law, resolutions of some of the oldest conundrums in legal theory—notably those that came to the fore in the Eichmann

[21] Cf E Husserl, *Die Krisis der europäischen Wissenschaften und die transzendentale Phänomenologie*, Husserliana Bd XXIX (Dordrecht/Boston/London, Kluwer Academic Publishers, 1993) 167–245.

[22] M Merleau-Ponty, *Phénoménologie de la Perception* (Paris, Gallimard, 1945) 14.

[23] M Merleau-Ponty, *Le visible et l'invisible* (Paris, Gallimard, 1964) 181.

[24] Merleau-Ponty, above n 22, 22.

case—suddenly become plainly visible, as we shall see below. But the splitting-off that takes place between law and literature does not mean that they no longer share the space of appearance. They continue to do so, but they do so differently. An incisive phenomenology of law must mark both its abyssal difference from and its intimate proximity to literature and art. The law is fundamentally different from art and literature and does not tolerate facile translations of literature into law, as Richard Posner notes well,[25] but it remains close to literature because of the way it shares with literature the same space of appearance.

Legal theory's prolonged struggles with the conundrums in the Eichmann case may well relate to the fact that it has all along been addressing them from too far, that is, from within the confines of a positivist legal scientific discourse that is already miles away from the way the law appears in the world, miles away from the things at issue when the law first appears. Arendt's phenomenology of law casts light on these conundrums by affording legal theory a return to the fundamental thing that takes place when we begin to call something law, that is, by affording legal theory a return to the thing [of law] itself. But in the same move that would come to cast so much light on the law, she would also allow a shadow to fall over her work. We need to retrace our steps and address this shadow, this blind spot in her phenomenology of law.

IV. HER SHADOW AND ITS SHADE

Arendt's diagnosis of the Jacobin terror in *On Revolution* highlights the spurious link it effected between politics and compassion, and more specifically, the link between politics and compassion with the poor.[26] The diagnosis is, on the one hand, informed by a strong and accurate intuition regarding the need to sever politics from passion of whatever kind, compassion included. It is nevertheless also deeply misguided in the way it appears to equate or at least conflate the self-evidently legitimate *rational* political concern with poverty, on the one hand, and compassion with poverty, on the other. A critical engagement with Arendt's thought on this count must show up her failure to distinguish clearly and more thematically between the rational political concern with poverty and compassion with poverty. Her contention that poverty is not a political concern is scandalous, as I have averred above, because of the way it nostalgically reduces the political to a romantic, nostalgic and misguided concern with *pure* political freedom as such, as if politics, like art, is nothing but a concern with creative freedom and the pursuit of excellence, and not more fundamentally a concern with the freedom

[25] R Posner, *Law and Literature* (Cambridge, Mass/London, Harvard University Press, 1998) 324–32. For a further discussion of Posner's views in this regard, cf J Van der Walt, 'Agaat's Law—Reflections on Law and Literature with Reference to Marlene van Niekerk's Novel *Agaat*' (2009) 126 *South African Law Journal* 695, 699.

[26] Arendt, above n 4, 59–114.

to establish the most reasonable and enduring forms of communal life that circumstances would allow.

Poverty is not just a question with regard to which some of us personally are as passionate or compassionate as others are dispassionate or compassionless (as the average Democrat/Republican or Labour/Tory split might prompt one to conclude). It is a concern which everyone could and should rationally acknowledge as central to the broader political concern with stable and enduring polities. It was in the wake of a *fatal dis-appearance of the political* that the writers of the German *Grundgesetz* of 1949 insisted that the Federal Republic of Germany would henceforth be a social State. Never again, was the idea and aspiration, would masses of disempowered and desperate people become the essential energy of totalitarian imaginations. The social State clause—article 20(1)—in the German *Grundgesetz* is an embodiment of the insight that a critical minimum of social politics is a precondition for sustaining the appearance of the political.

The political concern with founding and maintaining stable polities surely allows for and requires a good deal of creativity and imagination, but it is not principally or purposefully concerned with this creativity. Arendt's mistake was to turn one of the conditions for and means of politics—creative imagination—into its end. Thus does she end up with an understanding of politics as political theatre that is scandalously out of touch with the exigencies and democratic consciousness of her time, and which smacks more of the politics of grandeur of pre- and post-revolutionary Europe, feudal and restoration-era Europe, than the revolutionary spirit that she claims to celebrate. As such her political thought was remarkably out of touch with the *appearance* of her own time, that is, with the way human concerns showed themselves in the time she lived. She was clearly out of touch with the fundamental *phenomenological* awareness of how different historical times demand different responses and responsibilities from humans—indeed creative and imaginative responses and responsibilities. Arendt would not accept that the social question had become a major *political* concern in the wake of *the great transformation* of society wrought by modern capitalism. She was aware of this transformation. That the poor had 'appeared' irrevocably on the political scene of modernity, was something she knew and sometimes articulated in inimitable fashion. Referring to the multitude on the march during the French Revolution, she wrote that

> this multitude, *appearing for the first time in broad daylight*, was actually the multitude of the poor and the downtrodden, who every century before had hidden in darkness and shame. What from then on has been irrevocable, and what the agents and spectators of revolution immediately recognized as such, was that the public realm—reserved, as far as memory could reach, to those who *were* free, namely carefree of all the worries that are connected with life's necessity, with bodily needs—should offer its space and its light to this immense majority who are not free because they are driven by daily needs.[27]

[27] Arendt, above n 4, 48, emphasis added.

Arendt's work is fundamentally informed by this observation. It is driven by it. Her work is driven by the regretful perception that the appearance of poverty on the stage of politics ruined this stage. Her regret in this regard stemmed from a *wilfully romanticising* and deeply melancholic interpretation of ancient Aegean politics. Her romanticism and melancholy—and its almost obsessive fascination with excellence—committed her to a political position that can easily be confused if not compellingly associated with the passionate lack of compassion that progressive political thought associates today with the libertarian right. That the same thought *appears* differently in different times was not one of her eminent concerns.[28]

This is the shadow that hangs over her work, one that may well relate in complex ways to a larger shadow that cast a whole generation of especially German but also broader European politics into darkness.[29] But shadows do cast shades, and in the shadow of Arendt's thought also looms a crucial insight under which contemporary political thought may yet find shelter against the allure of darker nights. At issue here are her reflections on the source of darkness in politics, namely, the darkness of the human heart. In a passage that resonates deeply with our opening quotation above, she writes:

> Whatever the passions and the emotions may be, and whatever their true connection with thought and reason, they certainly are located in the human heart. And not only is the human heart a place of darkness which, with certainty, no human eye can penetrate; the qualities of the heart need darkness and protection against the light of the public to grow and to remain what they are meant to be, innermost motives which are not for public display. However deeply heartfelt a motive may be, once it is brought out and exposed for public inspection it becomes an object of suspicion rather than insight; when the light of the public falls upon it, it appears and even shines, but, unlike deeds and words which are meant to appear, whose very existence hinges on appearance, the motives behind such deed and words are destroyed in their essence through appearance; when they appear they become 'mere appearances' behind which again other, ulterior motives may lurk, such as hypocrisy and deceit.[30]

This, then, was the unforgiving logic that doomed Robespierre and the Jacobins, once committed to a politics of the heart and heart-felt compassion they inevitably fell prey to interminable suspicions regarding the pureness of their hearts.[31]

[28] Arendt famously explained Heidegger's involvement with the National Socialist Party in terms of the political idiocy typical of philosophers like Thales, who, with their gaze fixed in wonderment on the stars, stumble into holes. Cf Arendt and Heidegger, above n 2, 179–92. Her failure to respond to something so central to the politics of her own time surely smacks of the same political idiocy. Fixated on the 'purely political nature' of the first American Revolution of 1776, she appeared to be completely oblivious to the second American Revolution, the New Deal Revolution of 1937, literally in the wake of which she was writing and of which poverty and social equality were the exclusive concerns.

[29] Compare J Derrida, *Of Spirit. Heidegger and the Question* (Chicago, Ill, University of Chicago Press, 1987) 109.

[30] Arendt, above n 4, 96.

[31] *Ibid.*

If the secrets of the heart are to be fathomed in human affairs, contends Arendt, it is not in politics that this should be done, but in poetry and literature:

> If we want to know what absolute goodness would signify for the course of human affairs (as distinguished from the course of divine matters), we had better turn to the poets, and we can do it safely enough as long as we remember that 'the poet but embodies in verse those exaltations of sentiment that a nature like Nelson's, the opportunity being given, vitalizes into acts' (Melville). At least we can learn from them that absolute goodness is hardly any less dangerous than absolute evil.[32]

The crucial move that Arendt makes here is to extract the exultations of sentiment from the concerns of politics and to reserve them for the domain of literature. Exultations being exultations do not come in half measures. They are absolute, and for this reason not fit for translation into politics. They are as dangerous for the political when they are good as they are when they are bad; hence the need to separate politics from sentiment and the secrets of the heart, that is, from the dark concerns of life. She confines the former to the demanding light of reason. The latter she reserves for literary explorations that not only render them safe to explore ('we can do it safely enough'), but also guard them safely. Following a suggestion of Italo Calvino, one can say that Arendt recognises the *apocryphal* origins and nature of literature, its emanation from (*apo*) the secret (*kryphos*).[33]

The significance of this move—this separation of politics from passion—becomes clear when one brings to bear on Arendt's thought Giorgio Agamben's engagement with the relation between life and politics and life and law. Central to Agamben's thoughts in this regard is the endeavour to stabilise the distinction between the state of exception and the regular rule of law. His earlier work *Homo Sacer* already announced the need for an alternative to the politics of the *ban* and the constant risk of totalitarian slippages between states of exception and the regular rule of law that this politics always runs (slippages during which the state of exception becomes the rule and *auctoritas* and *potestas* become one). In his recent work on St Paul he finally finds this alternative in the notion of messianic time of the Christian *ekklesia*. The Christian community lives under the rule of earthly law *as if not* (*hos me*) living under it, as if living already now under the reign of the Messiah and the final redemption by and reckoning of God.[34] The real state of exception, the realisation of the full potentiality of existence, is thus postponed to the day of final reckoning to which God has the sole prerogative.

At issue in this Christian thought is indeed the prerogative of God to unite *auctoritas* and *potestas* and life and law. God alone can make law that redeems life. The only redemption possible in the meantime, suggests Agamben, is the literary redemption offered by literature. The task of literature, he contends

[32] *Ibid* 81.

[33] Cf I Calvino, *If on a winter's night a traveller* (London, Vintage Paper Back, 1988) 72; Van der Walt, above n 25, 713.

[34] G Agamben, *The Time that Remains* (Stanford, Cal, Stanford University Press, 2005) 19–26.

with reference to Dostoyevsky, is to remember unforgettable life, to remember unredeemed singular life, to remember the secrets of the heart, we can say with reference to Arendt. Literature is thus to effect some measure of the redemption for which earthly politics is not destined.[35] A similar delegation of redemption and the state of exception to the domain of literature is evident in Arendt's thinking. By reserving the dark secrets of the human heart for literary explorations, she confines them to a domain beyond the regular rule of law and prevents them from contaminating the law with apocalyptic visions. Literature, we shall see, constitutes the only real state of exception in her thought.

V. THE LITERARY EXCEPTION

Does Arendt really reserve the state of exception for literature? Is she not the one who, with reference to Jefferson, endorsed every generation's right to rebel?[36]

Not quite, or in any case, not simplistically so. Her ultimate concern was surely the ability of political action to found lasting political institutions; institutions, moreover, that are founded on pre-existing principles of positive natural law that are not the product of revolutionary creation. Revolutions, she maintained, are acts of 'restoration and re-establishment'.[37] In this regard, she can be said to have been concerned, like Agamben, with the stabilisation of the distinction between constituent and constituted power, and between potentiality and actuality. With regard to both of these pairs of concepts, her concern clearly prioritised the latter over the former. For Arendt, the primary task of revolutions can ultimately only be to re-enact the eternal and unchangeable principles of natural law. Revolutions do not create or bring to the fore new principles of justice; they rely on and re-enact the ever-present and already-disclosed principles of natural law, 'the laws of nature and nature's God', 'truths' that could be held as 'self-evident'.[38] In this regard Arendt's thought *appears to erase* the concern with states of exception from her contemplation of worldly politics. She seems to remove the sovereign and the state of exception from the scene of revolution. The fundamental principles of law are always in place. Revolutions do not challenge them, they rely on them. If there remains an element of a real state of exception in her thought, a real sovereign encounter with bare life, it is the literary state of exception. It is for literature that she reserves the exploration of the secrets of the heart and of life, and the ultimate concerns of life with questions of good and evil.

[35] For a more extensive discussion of Agamben on this point, cf J Van der Walt 'The Shadow and its Shade' (2009) 24(2) *South African Public Law* 269–96; J Van der Walt, *Law and Sacrifice* (London, Cavendish, 2005) 197–204.

[36] Arendt, above n 4, 232–33.

[37] *Ibid* 208–11.

[38] *Ibid* 192–93.

In this regard Arendt also seems to have exempted the fundamental principles of law from the trajectory of appearance outlined in the passage from *The Human Condition* with which we opened our inquiry into her thought at the beginning of this essay. The law ultimately does not emanate from some dark private mystery so as to appear in the broad daylight of the public. The law is for her that aspect of public life that is always already and therefore exclusively public. It does not come forth from the darkness of the private into the light of the public. Or so it seems. And this leaves us with the question whether the law, like a life spent entirely in public, is shallow. Does Arendt ultimately leave us with a concept of law that is necessarily shallow, especially when compared with the depths explored by literature? If so, she is surely not the only prominent thinker of our time to have done so. John Rawls also argued for fundamental principles of law that would exclude from their scope comprehensive convictions regarding good and evil and the deeper concerns of the heart. He referred to the principles of *public reason* in this regard and expressly acknowledged their apparent shallowness:

> As institutions and laws are always imperfect, we may view that form of discourse as imperfect and in any case as falling short of the whole truth set out by our comprehensive doctrine. Also, that discourse can seem shallow because it does not set out the most basic grounds on which we believe our view rests.[39]

VI. LITERARY DEPTHS AND THE 'SHALLOWNESS' OF LAW

Prominent conceptions of the relationship between law and literature current today understand the private/public divide in terms of a facile trajectory of private truths from the dark secrets of the heart into the daylight of law, into the daylight of the public. The literary regard for the secrets of the heart improves the law. It teaches the law mercy. Thus can the law—literary informed law—increasingly accommodate the private in the public sphere.[40] The phenomenological experience of the private/public divide evident in Arendt's work contradicts and rejects these conceptions of law and literature fundamentally. At issue in them is a *metaphorical* understanding of the relation between law and literature in terms of which the insights of the former can simply be carried over (*meta-pherein*) from literature to law. Thus does literature become a source of useful metaphors for legal reasoning. This understanding of law and literature cannot but leave both doomed to shallowness.

The phenomenological understanding of the relation between law and literature, to the contrary, experiences invariably how literature and law split off into different directions, the one into the direction of the dark, unique, intimate, uncommunicative and incommunicable secrets of the human heart, the other into

[39] Rawls, above n 3, 243.

[40] For a critical engagement with this understanding of law and literature, cf again Van der Walt, above n 25, 695–739.

the need for transparency and rules of common understanding. Borrowing from Heidegger, one can call this experience of an originary splitting between literature and law *diaphorical*. Central to this experience is the observation of an event of splitting that carries human experience off into two different or differing (*dia-pherein*) trajectories.[41] With Merleau-Ponty, one can call this a *chiasmic* experience of the relation between law and literature.[42] It is an experience that invariably sees literature veering off into the invisible and the obscure, law into the visible and the transparent. This is how the law appears. It appears by withdrawing from all literary concerns with the secrets of human heart. Thus *does* it attain a quality of having appeared; of having emerged from the dark secrets of the private and the heart, if only by having taken leave of them. Thus *does* it attain a unique depth.

Law and literature come to the fore from the same event, from the same diaphoric or chiasmic *splitting* (*Zwiefalt*) that sends them off into different directions. Having *event-ually*, that is, through the event of their splitting, become literature, on the one hand, and law on the other, they relate differently to this originating event. Literature, especially poetry, incessantly and obsessively harks back to its origin, that is, to the event from which it originates. In order to do so it cannot but risk the obscurity of its origin, and therefore must claim for itself the exceptional sovereignty and licence to risk this obscurity. The law, on the other hand, by definition forfeits this licence and sovereignty. The law is by definition that which must *come clear*, that which must take leave of its origins in order to *become clear*, in order to become transparent enough to establish common rules of mutual understanding and civility.

The law's forfeiture of artistic sovereignty nevertheless does not happen instantaneously and never happens conclusively. This is the profound insight that Kelsen articulates when he states that *pure law* never exists. Pure law, the law contemplated by a pure theory of law, is never positive or posited—*nie gesetzt*. Pure law is always only presupposed (*vorausgesetzt*) by a pure theory of law.[43] The reality of law always retains the imprint of its sociological and existential origins. It never sheds the shadows of the shades whence it commenced. To be sure, it by definition resists these shadows. Its negative or negating relation to its origins defines it. But the very definitional nature of this negation and resistance means the negated and resisted origin cannot be erased. Law cannot shed its shadow. The shadow cannot be shed. The law, too, is irreducibly apocryphal.[44]

The law *does* therefore *appear*, *does* come forth from darkness, is therefore not shallow but profound for the very reason of its on-going denial of depth, for the very reason of its insistence to move towards the light and become fully illumi-

[41] Heidegger, above n 6, 25.

[42] Merleau-Ponty, above n 23, 172–204, 268–70.

[43] H Kelsen, *Reine Rechtslehre. Einleitung in die rechtswissenschaftlcihe Problematik* (Leipzig, Deuticke, 1934) 66–67.

[44] Cf Van der Walt, above n 25, 739. The law, too, is apocryphal, I argued already here, but it is so 'in a state of denial', that is, negatively so.

nated, fully transparent and therefore apparently shallow. The law is as profound as literature, only *differently* so, negatively or inversely so. Those who do not sense this unique depth behind Rawls's acknowledgement of the shallowness of law and public reason, fail to do so for reasons of lacking an essential phenomenological consciousness. Those who fail to sense the depth in Arendt's paradoxical concern with a revolutionary natality that is 'sheltered by the *transparent* virtues with which our ancestors have at least sometimes set the world at peace',[45] do so for reasons of failing or refusing to observe how things have come and still come to appear to humans. Human reality shows itself by the way law and literature (and art) split off into opposite directions and contrasting relations to their common origins.

Arendt sometimes leaves one with the impression that the law does not appear. Law-making, she writes in *The Human Condition*, was not considered by the ancients to be *action* in the political sense of the word and thus did not figure within the 'space of appearance'. Law-making was a form of manufacturing, the work of *homo faber*. *Homo faber*, she argues, appeared only by virtue of his artefacts, and this appearance was inferior to political action through which the actor appeared by showing himself.[46] The ancients likened the work of law-making to the building of the city walls, that is, to work that had to be done and finished 'before political action could begin'.[47] The conception of constitution-making that she expounds in *On Revolution* differs radically from the view of law-making expounded in *The Human Condition*. Had she left matters with 'the laws of nature and nature's God', and with John Adams's 'great Legislator of the Universe',[48] she surely would have been stuck in an understanding of law-making as an activity that precedes politics and is already accomplished before political action commences. She would have been stuck in a conception of law as a pre-existing and eternal presence that is always already self-evident and requires no appearance, no disclosure. Her phenomenological background, however, would not have allowed her to tolerate this metaphysics of presence, a metaphysics which here makes particularly clear its *onto-theological* trappings,[49] its assumption of a 'great Legislator of the Universe' whose eternal laws underpin and secure the finite worlds of humans.

Arendt's first 'destructive' or 'deconstructive' step away from this metaphysics of eternal presence consisted in highlighting the incongruity evident in Jefferson's notion that constitutional provisions were 'truths' that *had to be held* as 'self-evident':

> Jefferson must have been dimly aware of [the fallacy of this position that ... mathematical 'laws' were of the same nature as the laws of a community, or that the former could

[45] Arendt, above n 4, 211.

[46] Arendt, above n 1, 207–12.

[47] *Ibid* 194.

[48] Arendt, above n 4, 185.

[49] M Heidegger, 'Einleitung zu Was ist Metaphysik' in M Heidegger, *Wegmarken* (Frankfurt am Main, Vittorio Klostermann, 1978) 373–74; M Heidegger, *Identität und Diferenz* (Pfullingen, Günther Neske, 1986) 50–51.

> somehow inspire the latter], for otherwise he would not have indulged in the somewhat incongruous phrase, '*We hold* these truths to be self-evident', but would have said: These truths are self-evident.[50]

One clearly discerns here—in this indispensable *holding* of truths as self-evident—an echo of the performative *presupposition* which Kelsen recognised as a condition for the notion of pure law, of law that is not just a matter of power but authoritatively and self-evidently law, and which can therefore claim respect and obedience. Arendt highlights this performativity further by emphasising *the promise* or *act of promising* that informs this 'holding as self-evident'. And now, quite in contrast to *The Human Condition*, she views this action to consist in world-building in the full political sense of the world. She no longer views it as the merely pre-political manufacturing of city walls:

> Hence binding and promising, combining and covenanting are the means by which power is kept in existence; where and when men succeed in keeping intact the power which sprang up between them during the course of any particular act or deed, they are already in the process of foundation, of constituting a stable worldly structure to house, as it were, their combined power of action. There is an element of world-building capacity of man in the human faculty of making and keeping promises. Just as promises and agreements deal with the future and provide stability in the ocean of future uncertainty where the unpredictable may break in from all sides, so the constituting, founding, and world-building capacities of man concern always not so much ourselves and our own time on earth as our 'successor' and 'posterities'.[51]

The law-making and constitution-making promise to hold as self-evident now not only qualifies as action; it qualifies, with reference to Cicero, *en plus* as the most excellent form of political action:

> No man is so much raised on high by any of his acts as are those who have reformed republics and kingdoms with new laws and institutions ... After those who have been gods, such men get the first praises.[52]

And what also becomes evident here—in this praise for the acts of founders and law-makers—is the turn away from the worship of a Supreme Being to a worshipping of founding itself and a 'blind worshipping'—in the words of Woodrow Wilson—of the constitution itself. This worshipping of the act of founding, argues Arendt, saved the American Constitution from the crumbling of religious authority in the modern age: '[W]hat saved the American Revolution from this fate was neither "nature's God" nor self-evident truth, but the fact of foundation itself.'[53] At issue here for Arendt is a thought that Heidegger pursued painstakingly in *Der Satz vom Grund*, namely, the notion of a ground or beginning that need not take its foundation from elsewhere but carries it within itself. Heidegger invoked in

[50] Arendt, above n 4, 193.
[51] *Ibid* 175.
[52] *Ibid* 202.
[53] *Ibid* 196.

this regard Angelus Silesius' rose that 'exists because it exists'; it has its ground in itself and does not obtain it from elsewhere.[54] Arendt turns to etymology. She invokes 'the beginning and principle, *principium* and principle [that] are not only related to each other, but are coeval', as is suggested clearly by the Greek word *arche* which 'means both beginning and principle'.[55]

The Heideggerian influence does not stop here, it only becomes more and more evident. The legends of founding, relates Arendt, 'unanimously tell us of great leaders who appear on the stage of history precisely in [the] gaps of historical time':

> With respect to revolution, these tales ... insist on a hiatus between the end of the old order and the beginning of the new, whether it is of no great importance in this context whether the hiatus is being filled by the desolate aimless wanderings of Israeli tribes in the wilderness or by the adventures and dangers which befell Aeneas before he reached the Italian shore ... [T]his hiatus obviously creeps into all time speculations which deviate from the currently accepted notion of time as a continuous flow; it was therefore an almost natural object of human imagination and speculation, in so far as these touched the problem of beginning at all.[56]

This passage evidently relies fundamentally on Heidegger's critique of linear conceptions of time. Heidegger articulated this critique for the sake of opening a different contemplation of time in terms of the event, the *Ereignis*.[57] Heidegger understood the event in terms of a splitting, a *Zwiefalt*, a diaphorical opening of a rent or *Riss*.[58] Merleau-Ponty would invoke in this regard *le chiasme*, *la fission fondamentale*.[59] *Le chiasme* is the birth of history, or history in the state of its birth—'*l'histoire à l'état naissant*';[60] the earliest moment or not-yet moment in which the difference between the visible and invisible becomes manifest *for* and *before* the first time. Arendt's invocation of the *hiatus* clearly belongs to these phenomenological contemplations of the *Ereignis* and the *chiasme*. And it is from the vantage point of this *hiatus*, *Riss*, *Zwiefalt* or *chiasme* that the significance of Arendt's thought for our understanding of law becomes clear. For it is crucial for our understanding of law to understand the arrival of the visible, the arrival of evidence and self-evidence, the arrival of law. We need to understand the nature and trajectory of this arrival.

54 M Heidegger, *Der Satz vom Grund* (Pfullingen, Günther Neske, 1986) 101–02.
55 Arendt, above n 4, 212, 213.
56 *Ibid* 205.
57 Heidegger, above n 5, 372–437. Cf also M Heidegger, *Zur Sache des Denkens* (Tübingen, Max Niemeyer Verlag, 1976) 1–25.
58 M Heidegger, above n 6, 24–33.
59 Merleau-Ponty, above n 23, 172–204, 268–70.
60 Merleau-Ponty, above n 22, 22.

VII. THE INVERSE OR NEGATIVE DEPTH OF THE LAW[61]

The law, then, is not shallow. It is *brought* forth by a profound commitment to hold certain truths as self-evident and transparent; self-evident or transparent to the extent of risking the *appearance* of shallowness. The law's profound commitment, we have seen, turns on two acts of giving: the act of promising and the act of forgiving. Perhaps we should begin to re-read the 'civility' with which Rawls seeks to vault us past the apparent 'shallowness of the law' in terms of this promise and forgiveness that Arendt brings to bear on legal and political thought.[62]

The law is as deep as literature, only inversely so. The law's depth is a negative depth. Unlike literature, it cannot affirm but must deny its own depth. It is nevertheless as deep and as *apocryphal* (a mere presupposition, not real, says Kelsen) as literature. This is so because they both come forth from the secret gaps in time for which historiography cannot account—the counter-time of a counter-day (*contre-temps du contre-jour*) a later phenomenologist would say.[63] At issue is the heart of time that only literature has the licence to explore affirmatively; hence the need to grasp the inverse relation between the sovereignty of literature and the literary state of exception, on the one hand, and the regular rule of law, on the other.

The law is not shallow then. What comes across or appears as shallow legality is merely the end result of the constructive Kelsenian purification through which law keeps the literary depths of life at bay. In other words, what comes across as shallow legality is the outward manifestation of its inverse depth. The law deals with life and death and the depths of life and death from the purified vantage point of its legalistic end results or end phases. This purified vantage point also allows the law to deal with life that manifestly lacks depth. For life can indeed also be banal and shallow, as Arendt observed with reference to Adolf Eichmann.[64] In fact, the purified vantage point of constructed law is exactly what allows law to deal with the apparent puzzles that Arendt raises in response to the Eichmann trial. Three apparent puzzles are at stake here, none of which poses a real dilemma for the Arendtian/Kelsenian conception of law that we are developing here. The first concerns the observation that the law is not equipped to deal with

[61] I am thankful to Lawrence Douglas for probing questions that prompted me to rethink and rewrite this part of the paper substantially after the Antwerp workshop on *Arendt and the Law*, June 2010.

[62] Compare Frank Michelman's take on Rawls in this regard: '[Constitutionalism] hopes to vault people past their real, unliquidated disagreements and uncertainties regarding the actual, substantial merits—the all things considered rightness, goodness, or prudence of ... laws and other legal acts. ... It invites the parties to such disagreements and uncertainties to slide past them, "get over" them'. Cf F Michelman, 'Constitutional Legitimation for Political Acts' (2003) 66 *MLR* 1, 6–8.

[63] J Derrida, *Politiques de l'amitié* (Paris, Éditions Galilée, 1994) 31.

[64] Cf Arendt, above n 17, 49, 252, 287–88. On these pages Arendt refers to Eichmann's sheer inability to think and the banal thoughtlessness of his evil deeds. She does not use the word 'shallow' here, but she does so when she returns to her experience of Eichmann in *The Life of the Mind*, above n 11, 4: 'I was struck by a manifest shallowness in the doer that made it impossible to trace the incontestable evil of his deeds to any deeper level of roots or motives.'

crimes of the scale of the Holocaust, 'that it was pointless to impose the death sentence for crimes of such magnitude'.[65] The second concerns the manifest absence of *mens rea* in the case of Eichmann. The third concerns the problem of retroactivity, the problem of convicting someone of a crime that had no positive legal existence at the time it was committed.

Arendt credits the first puzzle with some merit: '[It is] true in a sense, except that it could not conceivably mean that he who had murdered millions should for this very reason escape punishment.'[66] Quite in contrast to Arendt, the understanding of law that emerges from the phenomenological reflection on her thought above credits the argument with no such merit. The negative or inverse depth of the law demands that it view the parity between crime and punishment as a secondary concern in the case of all serious or 'capital' crimes. From the vantage point of its inverse depth, it knows well that it cannot fathom the crime and should therefore not endeavour to meet it with 'adequate punishment'. Effective punishment suffices. Effective punishment could consist in any significant degree of sacrificial relief (vengeance) offered to victims and those connected to them,[67] any significant degree of deterrence offered to future criminals and any degree of rehabilitation that it may bring about. And the question from this point of view would of course always be whether long-term or life imprisonment would not have been more effective on all counts in Eichmann's case. Who knows whether even this man, according to Arendt so completely incapable of thought, might not have come to have 'some thoughts' after 10 or 20 years in jail? Concerns of rehabilitation will of course have always been outweighed exponentially by the massive sacrificial yearning that burdened this case, but one should at least ask whether the possibility of some startled thought flashing through this mindless mind would not have been raised significantly on hearing that, after having been duly convicted, that he is free to walk out of court, and will be escorted back to Argentina should he so wish?

The second puzzle concerns Eichmann's apparent lack of *mens rea*. Arendt makes mention of the subjective element—the intent to do wrong—of the crime that all modern legal systems take as a precondition for criminal conviction, and suggests that it was absent in Eichmann's case.[68] She was not a lawyer or legal theorist, and it is understandable that she would not have engaged with the finer aspects of the legal debates of her time on *mens rea*. That is probably why she failed to observe that the 'subjective element' of *mens rea* was no longer understood to be that 'subjective' by the time Eichmann stood trial. The theory of criminal law had by that time largely moved away from the 'psychological' approach to *mens*

[65] Arendt, above n 17, 250.

[66] *Ibid.*

[67] Vengeance should of course play no role in punishment according to contemporary theories of sentencing, but a phenomenology of law would probably doubt whether such a completely non-sacrificial conception of law is realistic.

[68] Arendt, above n 17, 277.

rea that was current in the nineteenth century. The 'normative' approach to *mens rea* that became dominant in the twentieth century, quite expressly gave up on the idea that the state of mind of the accused could be proved. Sufficient for a finding of *mens rea*, the new approach held, was the application of norms of assessment or presumptions regarding the criminal state of mind. Central to these was the presumption that the accused willed the natural consequences of his actions.[69] This was of course not the problem in the Eichmann trial: Eichmann's defence was not that he did not intend to murder or did not know that killing would ensue from his actions; his defence was that he had no consciousness of doing wrong. He merely and dutifully executed decisions taken and orders issued by others. But here too does contemporary criminal law resort to constructions. Mere obedience to a manifestly unlawful command does not count as a defence in law, postulates the applicable rule. As to the question what constitutes a 'manifestly unlawful command', the rule states further: Manifestly unlawful is that which a reasonable person would deem manifestly unlawful. The law, in other words, was not at all concerned with Eichmann's subjective assessment of the lawfulness of the murderous commands that he obeyed. It was concerned with an objective standard: How would reasonable persons generally assess commands like those Eichmann executed?

Thus does the law deal with crime without having to probe either its hidden depths or its sheer banality. In a profound sense, or negatively or inversely profound sense, it judges only acts perpetrated and not the perpetrators of acts. From the perspective of the law, it matters little whether Eichmann's motivation was sublime or banal. From the perspective of law, it also matters little whether he really had knowledge of wrongfulness or not. The law simply subjected him to an objective standard regarding the state of mind he should have had. But the troublesome questions are not yet fully solved. What if the whole context of action was so corrupt that this objective standard of the reasonable person could not be applied? What if that which we today deem to be utterly and atrociously unreasonable was generally deemed reasonable at the time? This is the deep end of Arendt's concern with the legal coherence of the Eichmann trial:

> If we are to apply this whole reasoning to the Eichmann case in a meaningful way, we are forced to conclude that Eichmann acted fully within the framework of the kind of judgment required of him: he acted in accordance with the rule, examined the order issued to him for its 'manifest' legality, namely regularity; he did not have to fall back on his 'conscience', since he was not one of those who were unfamiliar with the laws of his country.[70]

In other words, there was no discrepancy between the commands Eichmann executed and the law he knew and took for granted. One can see now how the question regarding Eichmann's state of mind leads straight into the question of

[69] For textual references to this development in criminal theory, cf Van der Walt, above n 25, 721.
[70] Arendt, above n 17, 293.

the non-retroactivity of criminal legislation—*nullum crimen, nulla poena sine lege*, as it must. But the phenomenological reflection on Arendt and the law must remain puzzled by Arendt's concern in this regard.[71] She pays considerable attention to the problem of non-retroactivity. She cites extensively in this regard the reflections of the court on the retroactivity of the Israeli legislation applied during the Eichmann trial—the Nazis and Nazi Collaborators (Punishment) Law of 1950—and the London Agreement of 1945 that was applied during the Nuremberg Trials:

> 'This particular legislation', the judgment pointed out, 'is totally different from any other legislation usual in criminal codes,' and the reason for its difference lies in the nature of the crimes it deals with. Its retroactivity, one may add, violates only formally, not substantially, the principle *nullum crimen, nulla poena sine lege*, since this applies meaningfully only to acts known to the legislator; if a crime unknown before, such as genocide, suddenly makes its appearance, justice itself demands a judgment according to new law.[72]

One should not be mislead by the spurious logic of this reasoning. Why, might one ask, would this reasoning not be applicable to just about every instance in which one might want to invoke the principle of *nullum crimen, nulla poena sine lege*? On what basis can it be said that the principle applies only to acts that are pervasively and enduringly known before they are criminalised? The problem of new crimes surely does not always relate to acts that have existed conspicuously and enduringly. It often relates to new manifestations of human deviousness with which legislators have not been confronted before. The fact that they also sometimes concern the criminalisation of long-existing social practices as a result of changing moralities surely does not warrant the rule the court invoked in the Eichmann trial. Arendt quite understandably observes that 'the discussion of these matters has remained somewhat confused'.[73] Remarkable, however, is her failure to invoke in this regard a more forceful explanation why the principle of non-retroactivity should not apply to crimes such as those committed by Eichmann. For central to her thinking about law and the foundations of law, as we have seen above, is a principle that goes to the heart of the matter at issue here. The foundations of law may be eclipsed in dark times. They may not always be self-evident. They may require revolutionary re-founding from time to time. But when they are

[71] As it also cannot but be puzzled by the exuberant and self-indulgent moral lesson she contrived for the 'proper sentencing' of Adolf Eichmann—why on earth should one endeavour to expound 'profound' considerations of 'sharing the earth' for the conviction of one whom one has already considered to be irredeemably banal and shallow? Would the inverse or negative depth of the law not have required that the sentencing of Eichmann be accompanied by nothing more than a silent gesture of sheer disbelief and dismay, perhaps nothing more than a barely noticeable shrug of a shoulder? Is it because Arendt seeks to express and make manifest here what should not be expressed and made manifest; is it because she is expressing her own heart here, that her sentencing of Eichmann itself comes across as painfully shallow? Cf Arendt, above n 17, 277–79.

[72] Arendt, above n 17, 254. Cf also *ibid* 272–73.

[73] *Ibid* 255.

thus re-founded, they are again *held* to be self-evident, however much we realise increasingly as history progresses that they *are not* always self-evident. We saw above how central this point is to her argument in *On Revolution*. Consider now the way she had already phrased it eight years earlier in *Men in Dark Times*:

> The most frightful errors have replaced the 'best-known truths', and the error of these doctrines constitutes no proof, no new pillar for the old truths … [And] it is likewise inevitable that … people's mistrust of the world and all aspects of the public realm should grow steadily. For the fragility of these repeatedly restored props of the public order is bound to become more apparent after every collapse, so that ultimately the public order is based on people's holding as self-evident precisely those 'best known truths' which secretly scarcely anyone still believes in.[74]

The regard for the sheer performativity of law, the Kelsenian move of acting *as if there is law*, the act of faith that founds the law, can hardly be articulated more forcefully than Arendt does it here. But this is the remarkable thing about this Kelsenian move: the universality and timelessness that it demands despite its fragile and contingent origins. One cannot *hold* truths as self-evident and concede at the same time, perhaps because of empirical pressures, that others did not see them as self-evident. One either holds them as self-evident or one does not. And when one truly does so, one quite simply cannot at the same time exempt others from this self-evidence without contradicting oneself. *Holding* a truth as self-evident demands imposing this *assumed* self-evidence on others. In fact, as we saw from this passage from *Men in Dark Times*, holding a truth as self-evident may even require *imposing it on ourselves*, for we too may not always see it as self-evident. That is also why, for our own sake and the sake of others, as Rawls teaches us, we should not hold too many truths as self-evident. But this is another issue. The important thing to grasp here is this: If *we* hold it as self-evident that Eichmann's acts constituted the gravest of crimes, we hold it as self-evident *for everyone*, also for Eichmann and his generation of Germans. That is the meaning of self-evidence. It cannot have another meaning. Once one has grasped this point, the principle of non-retroactivity should no longer concern us in cases such as Eichmann's.[75]

This is what is ultimately at issue in the concept of commonsense judgement about right and wrong that Arendt develops with reference to Kant's theory of judgement. At issue in judgement is never just a question of what 'I think', but always a matter of thinking or imagining what others also think or would think. In other words, judgement is indeed about *common* sense.[76] As such, it turns on the same communality that informs, according to Merleau-Ponty, basic acts of perception and the faith that we invest in our basic perceptions, the faith that

[74] Cf H Arendt, *Men in Dark Times* (Middlesex, Penguin Books, 1973) 19.

[75] It is in this respect that not only Americans, but all of humanity *must* understand themselves to be 'always under law' as Michelman contends, even when they are not. Cf F Michelman, 'Always under law? (Constitutional Democracy)' (1995) 12 *Constitutional Commentary* 227; F Michelman, 'Can Constitutional Democrats be Legal Positivists? Or why Constitutionalism' (1996) 2 *Constellations* 292.

[76] Cf H Arendt, *Responsibility and Judgment* (New York, Schocken Books, 2003) 137–43.

we share the same world. Merleau-Ponty insists, with reference to Husserl, on the condition of the self as 'precluded from becoming an absolute individual' ('*qui m'empêche d'être absolument individu*'), as 'exposed to the regard of others as a man among men' ('*m'expose au regard des autres comme un homme parmi les hommes*'), as 'one consciousness among many' ('*une conscience parmi les consciences*').[77] The conviction that we are not nothing ('*de n'être rien*'), and indeed exist in the world in the way we do ('*de ne vivre qu'en parasite du monde, d'habiter un corps et une situation*'), turns on this fundamental communality of perception and on the experience of being perceived by others ('*l'expérience du regard d'autrui sur moi*').[78]

Arendt endorsed this communality of experience expressly:

> Our 'perceptual faith', as Merleau-Ponty has called it, our certainty that what we perceive has an existence independent of the act of perceiving, depends entirely on the object's also appearing as such to others and being acknowledged by them. Without this tacit acknowledgment by others we would not even be able to put faith in the way we appear to ourselves.[79]

The historical or empirical encounter with some individuals, even a generation of individuals, who made a mad mockery of the basic precepts of common experience and common judgement surely served to shake these precepts to their roots. 'Do we all still live in the same world?' is a question one may well be inclined to ask after Auschwitz. But those who survived unscathed enough to re-invest faith in a common world can only do so with resort to commonsense judgements regarding common humanity, common decency and common criminality, on the one hand, and literary explorations of the depths of depravity, on the other. In fact, the latter explorations were clearly better left to those who did not survive unscathed enough, who never quite returned to a common world of self-evidence. It was up to Celan, amongst others, not the law, to probe the black holes of and before time that haunted the Nuremburg and Eichmann trials; the black milk of the dawn—*schwarze Milch der Fruhe*—that spawned the post-Auschwitz times that are ours.[80]

VIII. BACK TO THE BEGINNING

The gap in time, the heart of time, the hiatus; this is the darkness or the source of darkness that Arendt brings to bear in the passage with which our inquiry into Arendt and the law commenced above; the passage in which she describes the relation between the private and the public, indeed, as a *passage*. The relation between the private and the public, we saw there, consists in the passage from the darkness of the private to the light of the public. This darkness of the hiatus, the

77 Merleau-Ponty, above n 22, 12–13.
78 Merleau-Ponty, above n 23, 89.
79 Arendt, above n 11, 46.
80 Cf P Celan, *Gesammelte Werke I* (Frankfurt am Main, Suhrkamp, 1983) 41.

heart of time, does it also refer to the *darkness of the human heart* that Arendt reserves for the explorations of literary narratives? Is the human heart the hiatus? Perhaps. Perhaps it was his own heart that Aeneas was pursuing during his wanderings; his own heart that Virgil was exploring through Aeneas. Perhaps it is their own hearts that the Israelis were pursuing in the desert, are still pursuing today, often at the expense of illuminated or enlightened law and order. Is it accurate to associate these chiasmic pursuits of the heart with the 'private' and 'private property', as Arendt does? One should note how close she comes to echoing Heidegger's invocation of *Eigentlichkeit* and, by implication, *Eigentum* (property) for these authentic pursuits of the heart.

Perhaps it is, from a perspective of law and the legal, not inappropriate to refer to the dark domains of the heart as 'the private' that needs to be shielded by property rights—in any case, up to the point that we wish to protect and not prosecute this privacy by law. But considering what is really at stake here, it is a rather un-poetic and shallow way of putting it. One should always remain alert to the way the profoundest of thinkers, and here specifically Arendt and Heidegger, sometimes rush in like lawyers where poets would fear to tread.

4

A Lawless Legacy: Hannah Arendt and Giorgio Agamben

VIVIAN LISKA

'*NOTRE HÉRITAGE N'EST précédé d'aucun testament*' ('Our inheritance was left to us by no testament').[1] These words by René Char, which Hannah Arendt places at the beginning of her foreword 'The Gap between Past and Future', also hold in a figurative sense for Arendt herself. Since Arendt's legacy is likewise not provided with a testament, its afterlife can be measured by the claims of those who appeal to her in their work. In a letter to Arendt dated 1970, Giorgio Agamben writes:

> I am a young writer and essayist for whom discovering your books last year has represented a decisive experience. May I express here my gratitude to you, and that of those who, along with me, in the gap between past and future, feel all the urgency of working in the direction you pointed out.[2]

The letter, in which the then 26-year-old Agamben emphatically assures Arendt of his intention of continuing to work in the direction she has shown, situates its author and those who think like him in a 'gap between past and future'. He is clearly referring to Arendt's foreword to *Between Past and Future*, whose original title 'The Gap between Past and Future' announces the space of thought which the ensuing 'exercises in political thinking' occupy. Arendt's 'gap in time' designates a break in the linear, chronological flow as an intermediate period, an interval, 'which is altogether determined by things that are no longer and by things that are not yet', and which, Arendt continues, has repeatedly been shown to contain 'the moment of truth'.[3] The differences in their respective understanding of this gap, in both its temporal and its spatial meaning, have major implications for their approaches to many different aspects of their thinking. These differences can

[1] H Arendt, 'The Gap between Past and Future' in *Between Past and Future* (New York, Viking Press, 1968) 3.

[2] Arendt Archive, Manuscript Division Library of Congress, Letter of 21 February 1970 from Agamben to Arendt. Quoted in M Siegelberg, 'Arendt's Legacy Usurped. In Defense of the (Limited) Nation State' (Fall 2005) *Columbia Current*, 38.

[3] Arendt, *Between Past and Future*, above n 1, 9.

be shown also to contain 'the moment of truth' about the relationship between Arendt's and Agamben's approaches to the law.

Giorgio Agamben is known as one of the most radical critics of the political state of the world in our times. More forcefully than any other thinker today, he proclaims that sovereign tyranny, supported by the legal system of modern democracies, holds us in the thrall of an all-pervasive domination, subjecting us to an omnipresent 'state of exception'. He describes this state as a condition in which the law has defied all boundaries and infiltrated every aspect of life, to the point where life and law can no longer be distinguished. While Agamben's diagnosis, though arguably excessive, is defensible, the cure he proposes is another, far more contentious matter. Agamben lets the wretchedness of the present swell before our eyes to the point where only a Messiah can save us, suspend the rule of law and redeem our planet.

Given the radicalism of Agamben's antagonistic approach to the law, which contrasts with the equivocal one taken by Arendt, the pairing of these two thinkers may seem surprising. However, from his early essays in *The Man without Content* to his more recent work, notably his most famous volumes of *Homo Sacer* and beyond, Agamben considers himself an heir of Arendt. In what follows I shall explore this claim. I shall, however, refrain from a comparison between Arendt's and Agamben's numerous concrete common concerns: a preoccupation with biopolitical issues; a critique of Human Rights in relation to the Nation State; a special attention for the excluded from society—*paria* or *homo sacer*—or the plights and 'privileges' of refugees. Instead, I intend to compare and contrast the very structure of thinking underlying these and other aspects of their work, most significantly their respective search for an alternative to a strictly legalistic understanding of politics and its relation to sovereignty. This approach will allow me to probe the conclusion of a recent article on Arendt and Agamben, 'that neither the problem of violence nor the problem of origins and new beginnings should stand in the center of an imaginary controversy between Agamben and Arendt, but the problem of the law'.[4] I hope to provide evidence for this insight, as well as to show how the two thinkers' respective approach to violence, to origins and new beginnings is inextricably intertwined with the problem of the law.

For both Arendt and Agamben, the 'gap in time' is a major figure in their political thinking that rests on the idea of an interruption of the course of events correlated with the advent of a new beginning. In his early writings, Agamben explicitly claims to embrace Arendt's 'exercises in political thinking' as a model for his own thought, and uses the vocabulary of Arendt's 'The Gap between Past and Future' when describing this interruption. Like Arendt, Agamben speaks of a

[4] E Geulen, 'Gründung und Gesetzgebung bei Badiou, Agamben und Arendt' in E Geulen, K Kaufmann and G Mein (eds), *Hannah Arendt und Giorgio Agamben. Parallelen, Perspektiven, Kontroversen* (München, Fink Verlag, 2008) 74.

'space between past and future',[5] a state 'suspended in the inter-world between old and new',[6] an 'interval between what is no longer and what is not yet'.[7] Both Arendt and Agamben describe the place where past and future meet as a crisis that charges the present with urgency. For both, the interval is a battlefield where the antagonistic forces of past and future clash in the present. Arendt speaks of a 'kind of warfare',[8] Agamben of 'struggle' and, repeatedly, of a 'conflict between old and new, past and future'.[9] For both, it is also the place where the new can emerge. The similarity in the wording of Arendt's and Agamben's description of this interval simultaneously reveals significant differences that point to their divergent and occasionally even contrary configurations of this interruption: As I have shown in other contexts elsewhere[10] and will try to show here in relation to the law, Arendt's gap is a space, a temporal interval, a three-dimensional place; Agamben's is a line, a spot or a threshold devoid of spatial extension and belonging to neither side of the divide.

This contrast manifests itself at different levels, both in the chronological and the spatial meaning of the gap-metaphor. Spaces are omnipresent in Arendt's political thought, be it in her description of the public sphere, the sequence constituting the successful revolution, or the condition of thinking itself. By contrast, liminality dominates Agamben's political and philosophical vocabulary: From the *infans* on the threshold between silence and speech to the *muselman* on the border between life and death, from the *enjambement* between poetic verses to the *caesura* interrupting the metric rhythm in Hölderlin's hymns, these instances of division constitute 'zones' or 'points of indistinction'. These thresholds, which are, in themselves, without ground or foundation, constitute a 'pure' and empty interruption that escapes all mediation, preconception and precondition. Belonging to neither side of the partition, they contain a potential to blur distinctions and counteract division and exclusion—an inevitable consequence of spaces—but they also remain untouched by the concrete particulars of the phenomenal world. There is undoubtedly a certain similarity with Arendt's conception of new beginning as an absolute that cannot be constructed or derived, and that escapes will and intention: 'Not only is it not bound into a reliable chain of cause and effect,' but 'the beginning has, as it were, nothing whatsoever to hold on to; it is as though it came out of nowhere in either time or space'.[11]

However, her *incipits* in themselves are not political yet. Arendt's insistence on spaces constitutes her attempt to make room for the impact and elaboration

[5] G Agamben, *The Man without Content* (trans Georgia Albert) (Stanford, Cal, Stanford University Press, 1999) 10.

[6] *Ibid* 114.

[7] *Ibid* 112.

[8] Arendt, *Between Past and Future*, above n 1, 8.

[9] Agamben, above n 5, 110, 112.

[10] Cf V Liska, 'Die Tradierbarkeit der Lücke in der Zeit. Arendt, Agamben und Kafka' in Geulen, above n 4, 74.

[11] H Arendt, *On Revolution* (London, Penguin, 1991) 206.

of these ineffable phenomena, to introduce and preserve them in a concrete, historical realm and make their potential available to the intervention of man. By contrast, Agamben's political critique rests on a thinking that is concerned with cuts, thresholds and empty spots that escape manipulation, avoid new foundations and instead perform the theoretical enthronement of discontinuity as such.

These differences between Arendt's and Agamben's metaphorical figuration of interruptions have far-reaching philosophical and political consequences. In her descriptions of the gap, Arendt stresses the *duality* of ending and beginning as two separate moments. Agamben instead performs a *dialectic* reversal—however impure, because leaving a 'rest'—in which the ending of the old *is* the beginning of the new. Arendt precisely rejects such 'dialectical subtleties' and disparages them as a trick '*bei dem immer das Eine in das Andere umschlägt und es erzeugt*' ('where one thing always reverses into its other and produces it').[12] Antitheses which in Arendt are left to stand in juxtaposition or in succession, for Agamben consistently turn into one another: His view that the new can *only* appear in the destruction of the old, indeed that it occurs *out* of the destruction,[13] contrasts with Arendt's ideas of a new beginning. Hence Arendt emphasises the 'hiatus between the end of the old order and the beginning of the new', and insists that 'freedom is no more the automatic result of liberation than the new beginning is the automatic consequence of the end'.[14] It can be achieved only with the constitution of a new political community. Arendt's description of the two phases of revolutions, where the initially arbitrary and quasi-miraculously initiated upheaval must, in a second moment, be preserved and consolidated by a founding constitution, is the most significant case in point. Agamben, by contrast, sees in the legal foundation of a new order a betrayal of the interruption and, inevitably, the origin of a new oppressive regime. For Arendt, the 'hiatus' between the old and the new order, which she describes as the interval between the 'no longer' and the 'not yet', interrupts the 'omnipotent continuum of time'[15] and opens up the space in which thought, politics and freedom can occur. About the interface between old and new Agamben writes: 'The continuum of linear time is interrupted, but does not create an opening beyond itself'.[16] For him, every space implies exclusion, just as every founding moment rests on a sacrificial structure. While his implicit critique of Arendt may be justified, the price implied in his alternative is high.

[12] H Arendt, *Zwischen Vergangenheit und Zukunft. Übungen im politischen Denken I* (München, Piper, 2000). 33. This reference is to the German edition of *Between Past and Future* where this sentence differs from the English version. The German text was written or translated by Arendt herself. See the afterword in this edition, 373–74.

[13] G Agamben, *Potentialities. Collected Essays in Philosophy* (ed and trans D Heller-Roazen) (Stanford, Cal, Stanford University Press, 1999) 151–57.

[14] Arendt, above n 11, 205.

[15] *Ibid.*

[16] Agamben, above n 5, 113.

Arendt's space allows for a freedom of movement that hands the enigma of new beginnings over to human agency. Agamben presents his diagnosis of modernity in words that in part unmistakably echo Arendt's:

> Man is deprived of reference points and finds himself wedged between, on the one hand, a past that incessantly accumulates behind him and oppresses him with the multiplicity of its now indecipherable contents, and on the other hand a future that he does not yet possess and that does not throw any light on his struggle with the past.[17]

However, Agamben does not follow Arendt where she insists that the gap in time and the freedom it provides result from man's own 'constant fighting, his making a stand against past and future'. For Arendt, it is 'only because man is inserted into time and only to the extent to which he stands his ground [that] the flow of indifferent time'[18] is interrupted. For Agamben, by contrast, there remains only the interface of a rupture and no other possibility of moving than a conjuration of a reversal on the spot itself. Where Arendt creates a space, Agamben sees a break; where she opens up a realm, he turns to divisions; where she inserts an opening for the possibilities of human action upon worldly reality, he conjures up a reversal that risks undoing not only time and space, but the reality of the lived world itself. For Arendt, the interruption of the omnipotent continuum of time is the place of human intervention. For Agamben, no man stands at the point where past and future meet. There is no longer a ground for him to stand on, and certainly none where the concerted action of many can take place. Instead of imagining a free space *within* history, where, as for Arendt, a 'stable worldly structure' can be built and man's 'world-building capacities'[19] can be deployed, Agamben collapses end and beginning into a single, spaceless spot and becomes a herald of history's end.

In *The Time that Remains,* his reading of Paul's 'Letter to the Romans', Agamben conjures up this end. He sees in Paul's epistle the 'oldest and most demanding messianic texts of the Jewish tradition',[20] and in this tradition the model, if not the prefiguration, of an anarchist demise of legalism. Paul's suspension of the law is, for Agamben, the ultimate messianic gesture: It transforms an oppressive 'state of indistinction', a condition in which the law has become indistinguishable from life, into a redemptive one in which the law's oppressive power is undone. This figure, which is bent on the vanishing of the world in its present state and rests on the belief that all divisions will eventually disappear, underlies Agamben's entire structure of the messianic. The conflation of State law and Jewish religious law, or

[17] *Ibid* 108.
[18] Arendt, *Between Past and Future*, above n 1, 11.
[19] *Ibid* 175.
[20] G Agamben, *The Time That Remains. A Commentary on the Letter to the Romans* (trans P Dailey) (Stanford, Cal, Stanford University Press, 2005) 3.

Halacha, presupposed by this construction is, however, far from self-evident, and certainly runs counter to Arendt's views.[21]

'From a political-juridical perspective,' Agamben writes in *Homo Sacer*, 'messianism is a theory of the state of exception—except for the fact that in messianism there is no authority in force to proclaim the state of exception; instead there is the Messiah to subvert its power'.[22] In keeping with the antinomies of messianic precepts, Agamben equates the conditions of redemption with the structures governing oppression: Both the state of exception and the state of redemption rely on the suspension of the law. However, while the state of exception proclaimed by the sovereign spills over into every aspect of life and puts the entire planet under the ban of an oppressive law, the 'real', messianic 'state of exception'—a notion Agamben borrows from Walter Benjamin[23]—suspends the validity of the law and releases bare life into a new freedom. Only when life has absorbed the law to the point of suspending it, rather than letting the law rule over life, will the ban be abolished and humanity redeemed. Agamben himself calls the path to redemption—the question as to *how* this reversal at the 'point of indistinction' is to occur—'a Gordian knot, not so much the solution of a logical or mathematical problem [but] an enigma'.[24] In the absence of a space, the enigma of the new beginning remains, in Agamben's scheme, a proverbial knot upon which no human action except for violent destruction is possible.

The possibility of human action is, by contrast, precisely what Arendt affirms, even in her treatment of both the Apostle Paul and Jewish antinomian messianism. For her, the importance of Paul—somewhat implausibly—lies less in his being the harbinger of a suspension of the law than in his being the inventor of human will. Arendt does indeed affirm Paul's creed that the law, given as a command as in the Old Testament's 'thou shalt do', incites to sin, and distinguishes this call to submission from 'the New Law' that says 'thou shalt *will*',[25] but insists that the Law, for Paul, remains equivocal, that it *also* is '"good, in order that sin might be shown to be sin," (Rom 7:13) but since it speaks in the voice of command, it

[21] The main inspiration behind Agamben's reading of Paul as a Jewish messianic figure is the idiosyncratic rabbi-intellectual Jacob Taubes. Significantly, Taubes writes: 'I am not authorized (I don't think this is so simple) to unravel what Paul means when he says "the law": Does he mean the Torah, does he mean worldly law, does he mean natural law? It is all of these together'. See especially J Taubes, *Die politische Theologie des Paulus* (Munich, Fink Verlag, 2003) 37.

[22] G Agamben, *Homo Sacer: Sovereign Power and Bare Life* (trans D Heller-Roazen) (Stanford, Cal, Stanford University Press, 1998) 57f.

[23] Cf W Benjamin, 'On the Concept of History' in M Bullock and MW Jennings (eds), *Selected Writings* (Cambridge, Mass, Harvard University Press, 2006) 394.

[24] Agamben, above n 22, 48.

[25] 'It was,' Arendt explains, 'the experience of an imperative demanding voluntary submission that led to the discovery of the Will, and inherent in this experience was the wondrous fact of a freedom that none of the ancient peoples—Greek, Roman, Hebrew—had been aware of'. Arguably, the Hebrew Bible's story of the Expulsion from Paradise already opens up the path to free choice. Arendt indeed concludes that Paul 'remained a Jew', and that Paul's discovery of inwardness can already be found in the Old Testament, notably in Job. See H Arendt, *The Life of the Mind* (San Diego, Cal, Harcourt, 1978) 71.

"arouses the passions and revives sin"'.[26] More importantly, Arendt sees in Paul the inventor of free will: In insisting on the significance of intention in questions of good and evil, he shifts the weight of the decision from a matter of submission to an act of choice. For Arendt, this discovery of the will and its internal conflict is 'radical human freedom, the ability to dissent from what is given to man'[27] and to intervene in the world.

Similarly, for Arendt, the political importance of Jewish antinomian messianism does not lie primarily and directly in its deactivation of the Law. In her at times astonishing response to Gershom Scholem's studies of Jewish mysticism, particularly his work on the seventeenth-century cabbalist and self-declared Messiah Sabbatai Zevi, Arendt shares Scholem's sympathies for this antinomian cabbalist movement. What attracts her to these Jewish mystical ideas is their resistance to 'modern doctrines asserting that man is but a part of matter, subject to physical laws and without freedom of action'.[28] Instead, the Jewish cabbala provided its practitioners with 'secret means for gaining power for participating "in the drama of the world"'. The confidence that they could partake 'in the power which rules the world' liberated them from being mere victims of incomprehensible forces, made them discover 'a working knowledge of reality'[29] and, unlike Christian mystics, for whom salvation had already taken place, encouraged them to action. Although the Sabbatian movement endowed Jewish mysticism, which, until then, had 'kept itself within the Law', with antinomian forces, the source of the movement's political impact did not derive from this demise of the law. Instead, it was the collective drive to action instilled by the cabbala that made them turn away from 'the mere interpretation of the Law', which had, for centuries, kept the rabbis outside the sphere of history and politics. Furthermore, the new collective political action created a bond that could replace the *Halacha*, religious Law, which had formerly been 'the only tie of the people in the Diaspora'.[30]

Unlike Agamben, Arendt avoids conflating religious law and political action. What matters to her in her discussion of antinomian messianism is not the transgression or deactivation of the Law but the empowerment of man on the 'public scene of history'. For Arendt, the danger of the *Halacha*, which was suspended by Paul and transgressed by the antinomian sects, lies neither primarily in its sovereign origin nor in its oppressive authority, but in its power to distract from

[26] *Ibid* 71.

[27] S Jacobitti, 'Hannah Arendt and the Will' (1988) 1 *Political Theory* 16, 53–76.

[28] H Arendt, *The Jewish Writings* (eds J Kohn and RH Feldman) (New York, Schocken Books, 2007) 306.

[29] *Ibid* 306–07.

[30] *Ibid* 309. Arendt's depiction of the Sabbatians as an authentic political movement is, to say the least, questionable, and, as Richard J Bernstein has pointed out, says more about Arendt's political convictions and her attraction to spontaneous beginnings emerging in popular movements than about these 17th-century Jewish mystics. Cf RJ Bernstein, *Hannah Arendt and the Jewish Question* (Cambridge, Mass, MIT Press, 1996) 57–58.

political action.[31] Interestingly, 'the mere interpretation of the Law' to which Arendt objects is, for Agamben, the only mode in which the Law may subsist. Quoting Benjamin, he writes: 'The law which is studied and not practiced any longer is the gate to justice.'[32] In keeping with Walter Benjamin, and in terms that most dubiously correlate *Halacha* and the secular order, Agamben considers the study of the law a beneficial replacement for its practice and a subversive assault on its power. Again, Arendt's idea of antinomian liberation requires several distinct moves and a space of action, while Agamben's rests on a deactivating reversal from practice to study that occurs on the very spot of the oppressive power itself.

This distinction between Arendt's space and Agamben's spot or line of division clearly goes beyond differences in their views on time and history. It also explicitly determines the topographical structure of their respective approaches to the law, both in its secular and religious meaning, whereby this distinction is itself at stake. Agamben indeed adopts Carl Schmitt's contention that 'all the concepts of modern theory are secularized theological concepts',[33] particularly the political concepts of decision, exception and sovereignty. The sovereign is for Schmitt—and, in some crucial ways for Agamben—a 'mundane factor that has taken the place of God'.[34] It is this power of the sovereign—according to Schmitt the one who proclaims the state of exception—that turns the radical reversal of this state into messianic redemption. If the state of exception is determined by a ubiquitous law and its reversal is correlated with the demise of the law, then the law clearly conflates religious and secular law. In Arendt's search for a law divested of sovereignty, it is precisely this conflation that is to be put into question.

In *The Human Condition* Arendt, again evoking the distinction between space and boundary, evokes the concept of the law in the Greek *polis*:

> The law originally was identified with [a] boundary line, which in ancient times was still actually a space … The law of the *polis*, to be sure transcended this ancient understanding from which, however, it retained its original spatial significance. The law of the city-state was neither the content of political action … nor was it a catalogue of prohibitions, resting, as all modern laws still do, upon the Thou Shalt Nots of the Decalogue. It was

[31] It would be worth pursuing a critical appraisal of Arendt's understanding of Jewish Law, which she associates with the Decalogue and the 'Thou Shalt Not' imposed by a divine sovereign. Another understanding of the *Halacha* is possible, one that would certainly have a greater appeal to Arendt. Such an alternative view would consider Jewish religious law as it manifests itself in the Talmud, where it is intertwined with the narrative commentary of the *Haggada* that often serves as a corrective of the Law itself and thereby exceeds the rigidity of the 'Thou Shalt Not'. In this form it takes the concreteness of human affairs into account and remains open to manifold interpretations that are not once and for all to be decided upon by a sovereign authority. Cf M Halbertal, 'At the Threshold of Forgiveness: A Study of Law and Narrative in the Talmud' (2011) 2 *The Jewish Review of Books* 3, 33–34.

[32] W Benjamin, 'Franz Kafka: On the Tenth Anniversary of His Death' in *Illuminations* (ed H Arendt) (New York, Schocken Books, 2007) 139.

[33] C Schmitt, *Political Theology* (trans G Schwab) (Chicago, Ill, The University of Chicago Press, 1986) 36.

[34] C Schmitt, *Political Romanticism* (trans G Oakes) (Cambridge, Mass, MIT Press, 1991) 17.

> quite literally a wall without which … there could not be a political community. This wall-like law was sacred but only the enclosure was political.[35]

Arendt, in her attempt to protect the political space from legislation, her search for a model to think the law devoid of a detached sovereign power ruling over others, ultimately does not fully embrace the Greek model because it still retains the act of an external sovereign legislator.[36] However, she affirms the distinction between the law as the enclosure of a space and this space itself, whereby the space alone is political and the law a mere fence surrounding and protecting it. She thereby divests the enclosure, and with it the political itself, of the dimension of the sacred and its association with sovereignty, which then remain with the walls alone. This stands in contradistinction to Agamben's concern with the law, the division, the wall itself. For him, this very wall constitutes the 'zone of indistinction', which is responsible for the 'inclusive exclusion' of what has to remain outside—an exclusion that nevertheless keeps the excluded one in thrall of the power that excludes him—but which is also the place where redemption occurs. Defining the law as the very principle of division, the 'division of the division' that occurs in this very 'zone of indistinction' suspends the law, which is, for Agamben, the political gesture per se. For Arendt it is within the political space created and sheltered by the wall-like law that the new beginning becomes political. For Agamben, the new arises through the crossing of this wall—a boundary that retains its sacred, theological dimension. Contrary to Arendt's distinction between the wall and the enclosure—the division and the space, the sacred and the political—Agamben's conflation of these realms underlies his messianic idea of a reversal of the state of exception in which we live. In making the wall and the enclosure indistinguishable, and in substituting the sovereign with the Messiah, Agamben remains—be it *ex negativo*—within the logic of sovereignty. In his implicit critique of enclosures—their continuing and inescapable structure of exclusion and their tendency of conservation and fixity—Agamben implicitly points to certain limitations of Arendt's attempt to think a space of freedom. However, his own alternative performs a radical reversal of her legacy: In divesting the scene of new beginnings of a space for human intervention and concerted action, he discards what is arguably most valuable in Arendt's own intervention in the debate about the status of the law and its relation to the political in the modern age.

[35] H Arendt, *The Human Condition* (Chicago, Ill, The University of Chicago Press, 1958) 64.
[36] Cf M Twellmann, 'Lex, nicht nomos. Hannah Arendts Kontraktualismus' in Geulen, above n 4, 84.

Part II

On Constitutionalism and Institutions

5

Arendt's Constitutional Question

EMILIOS CHRISTODOULIDIS AND ANDREW SCHAAP

ONE ALWAYS BEGINS by 'drawing a distinction', Niklas Luhmann was fond of reminding us, and Arendt begins *On Revolution* by drawing a distinction that throughout the treatise remains stark, pivotal, resistant, insubordinate to mediation, synthesis and sublation. It is the distinction between the social and the political. It lies at the basis of the constitutional question, and as foundational informs not just the remit of the constitutional *but its very possibility*: because it does not allow us to step behind it, the foundation that is, and to put it to question *politically*.

The departure is significant and the endurance of the distinction remarkable. We find the quasi-normative function that the distinction performs replicated later and in different forms, but invariably working at the deep level of context-setting. It is, for example, famously articulated in Agamben's 'bio-political fracture'. Agamben's *bios/zoe* distinction mirrors Arendt's, in his insistent return to the 'zone of indistinction' between the two terms that mirrors her resistance to any kind of dialectical overcoming of the social and the political. And for him, all too impatiently, it is the endurance of the distinction that explains the travesty of 'political' projects launched to tackle need abroad: '[T]oday's democratico-capitalist project of eliminating the poor classes through development not only reproduces within itself the people that is excluded but also transforms the entire population of the Third World into bare life.'[1]

What makes the distinction between the political and the social so fundamental and, we shall argue, fundamentally problematic? Let us take this gradually.

I. UNBURDENING THE CONSTITUTION

The second chapter of Arendt's famous book is dedicated to the 'social question', or what 'we may better and more simply call the existence of poverty'.[2] When

[1] G Agamben, *Homo Sacer: Sovereign Power and Bare Life* (Stanford, Cal, Stanford University Press, 1998) 179. See JG Finalyson, '"Bare Life" and Politics in Agamben's Reading of Aristotle' (2010) 72 *The Review of Politics*, 97–126.

[2] H Arendt, *On Revolution* (Harmondsworth, Penguin, 1990 [1963]) 60.

Robespierre declared that everything which is necessary to maintain life must be common good and only the surplus can be recognised as private property, for Arendt 'he was, in his own words, "subjecting revolutionary government to the most sacred of laws, the welfare of the people, the most irrefragable of all titles, necessity."'[3] For her it was necessity, the urgent needs of the people, that unleashed the terror and sent the Revolution to its doom. She cites Jefferson approvingly, when he declared that a people 'so loaded with misery would [not] be able to achieve what had been achieved in America'. And about John Adams's 'conviction' that a free republican government 'was as unnatural … as it would be over elephants, lions, wolves [etc] in the royal menagerie at Versailles', she proclaims, rather disturbingly, that 'years later, events to an extent proved him right'.[4]

Why do the cries of the dispossessed masses not resonate politically? What is it about their movement that 'sent the revolution to its doom'? The 'transformation of the Rights of Man into the Rights of the Sans-Culottes', Arendt argues, abandons the foundation of freedom to the 'powerful conspiracy of necessity and poverty', Robespierre's relentless insistence on the latter forcing him to miss the 'historical moment' to 'found freedom'.[5] Arendt's unreserved admiration for the American Revolution is nowhere thrown into starker contrast with her misgivings about the French Revolution than in these pages on the 'social question', and this in the context of the acutest of analyses of Robespierre's claim to speak on behalf of the dispossessed. The guiding distinction operates here to set up freedom against necessity as involving contrasting logics, a contrast that Arendt is keen to map on to the distinction between the social, as sphere of necessity, and the political, as sphere of freedom.

Marx is the obvious counter-point, and Arendt takes the challenge head on. 'It took more than half a century before the transformation of the Rights of Man into the Rights of the Sans-Culottes, the abdication of freedom before the dictate of necessity, had found its theorist' in Marx.[6] What a strange formulation this is, couched in a vocabulary of abdication, and thus of a certain refusal of a different route. What, one might pause to ask, does 'abdication of freedom' mean for the sans-culottes? What possibility of freedom did the Parisian mob really forgo in bringing the 'needs of the body' into the streets? What makes this simple question so difficult for Arendt to ask? Nothing but her unwavering reassertion of the founding disjuncture. Notwithstanding the lip service to his greatness ('the greatest theorist the revolutions ever had'), a kind of knee-jerk anti-Marxism dominates her thinking here, most tellingly in the extraordinary reversal that she attributes to Marx in the 'social question'.

[3] *Ibid* 60.
[4] *Ibid* 68.
[5] *Ibid* 60–61.
[6] *Ibid* 61.

Marx's genius and ultimately his theoretical error, for Arendt, is that he *read the social question in political terms*. That means that he read the question of *poverty* as a question of the suppression of *freedom*, and the way he achieved this was through the theory of exploitation. This allows the connection between the two spheres to be 'mediated':

> Marx's transformation of the social question into a political force is contained in the term 'exploiation', that is in the notion that poverty is the result of exploitation through a 'ruling class' which is in the possession of the means of violence … His most explosive and indeed most original contribution … was that he interpreted the compelling needs of mass poverty in political terms as an uprising, not for the sake of bread or wealth, but for the sake of freedom as well.[7]

Thus, asserts Arendt, in order to conjure up a 'spirit of rebelliousness that can spring only from being violated, not from being under the sway of necessity' Marx helped to persuade the poor 'that poverty itself is a political not a natural phenomenon, the result of violence and violation rather than scarcity'.[8]

Arendt sets out to prove Marx wrong to interpret the 'predicament of poverty in categories of oppression and exploitation', by returning to the embeddedness of her founding distinction, the foundational character of the disconnect.[9] This involves a striking reversal that puts the burden on her interlocutor to defend the attempted 'synthesis' through exploitation. Her argument involves as ever the restatement of the obviousness of her premises and the foundational nature of the organising disjuncture. The recovery of the ability to act cannot spring from necessity since the logic of 'emancipation' is too rooted in the release of a natural propensity. *Becoming-political* is thus a problem for Arendt in the absence of the preconditions of such action in freedom. It is this absence that drives Marx to attach himself to the Hegelian dialectic in which 'freedom would directly rise out of necessity', a dialectic and a coincidence that Arendt has earlier characterised as 'perhaps the most terrible and, humanly speaking, least bearable paradox in the body of modern thought'.[10] But for Arendt the two spheres are not and cannot be tied dialectically—necessity never gets a foothold in a dialectic of action.

Having repeated her premises, Arendt's rebuttal of Marx becomes fairly cursory. Her first criticism is that he abandons 'the revolutionary élan of his youth' to redefine it in economic terms, which means also the 'iron laws of historical necessity'[11]; 'necessity' again serving to fold the revolutionary moment back into the binarism from which it seemingly never can depart. Her second criticism is that he 'strengthened more than anybody else the politically most pernicious doctrine

[7] *Ibid.*
[8] *Ibid* 62–63.
[9] *Ibid* 63.
[10] *Ibid* 54.
[11] *Ibid* 64.

of the modern age, namely that life is the highest good and that the life process of society is the very centre of human endeavour.'[12] With this new emphasis,

> the role of revolution is no longer to liberate men from the oppression of their fellow men, let alone to found freedom, but to liberate the life process of society itself from the fetters of scarcity so that it would swell into a stream of abundance. Not freedom but abundance became the new aim of revolution.[13]

A displacement thus of the very aspiration of political action, a falling short that turns out to be a radical undercutting of the logic of political action.

If this appears a rather odd rendering of Marx, or at least a rather facile turning of the later Marx against his earlier, better self, it is because it is that, both odd and facile, based on an impatient misreading that identifies in Marx the 'ambition to raise his science to the rank of a natural science' at the expense of the political, 'a surrender of freedom to necessity'.[14] 'The trouble,' Arendt will tell us, 'is of a theoretical nature'.[15] Marx's economic explanations simply merge violence and necessity together back into the sphere that, properly understood, is on the other side of the political, the concept itself of a 'political economy' an impossible merger of two domains.

Antonio Negri, who in *Insurgencies* initially reserves some praise for Arendt's 'very rich and fierce phenomenological exercise', is left 'ill at ease' at this point by her 'definition of constituent power'.[16] 'The constitutive phenomenology of the principle reveals itself as perfectly conservative' and she thus 'bears the responsibility of the contempt towards the multitude that does not want to be the people, of a constituent power that does not want to be the bourgeoisie'.[17]

We shall return to Negri's careful rebuttal of Arendt's take on constituent power later. For now we join him in feeling somewhat 'ill at ease' with what in fact confronts us here: an astounding 'partage of the sensible', a carving up and separating-off of the question of human welfare from politics, and the redress of misery from what is properly the political aspiration of freedom. To claim that the masses that storm revolutionary Paris in 1789, and then in 1848 and in July 1871, raise the 'social' rather than the political question, is to sever the question of distribution from the political means of redressing asymmetries in access to the means of production and the distribution of its products. In Arendt, this severing underwrites nothing less than the understanding itself of the political and the possibility itself of freedom.

We have seen how the social/political distinction is mapped onto that between necessity and freedom, and Marxism rejected as suggesting an unsustainable bridging of both sets through the notion of exploitation, a move that in Arendt

[12] *Ibid* 64.
[13] *Ibid* 64.
[14] *Ibid* 65.
[15] *Ibid* 64.
[16] A Negri, *Insurgencies* (Minneapolis, University of Minnesota Press, 1998) 16.
[17] *Ibid* 17, 206.

becomes something akin to a categorical mistake. This constitutive severing is buttressed through a second one, and the distinction between compassion and solidarity deployed to qualify further the political proper. With Marx, she has expelled 'exploitation' from the political; with Rousseau she is now poised to expel 'compassion'.

One of the many striking features of the analysis of the 'social question' in *On Revolution* is that it relegates Rousseau to a theorist of 'compassion' in the first place, in taking as fundamental Rousseau's near-axiomatic 'innate repugnance at seeing a fellow human suffer'.[18] Rousseau found compassion to be the most natural human reaction to the suffering of others, and therefore the very foundation of all authentic 'natural' human intercourse':[19]

> It was this capacity for suffering that Rousseau had pitted against the selfishness of society on the one hand, against the undisturbed solitude of the mind, on the other. And it was to this emphasis on suffering, more than to any other part of his teachings, that he owed the enormous, predominant influence over the minds of the men who were to make the Revolution, and who found themselves confronted with the overwhelming sufferings of the poor to whom they had opened the doors to the public realm and its light for the first time in history.[20]

What Rousseau had introduced to political thought, Robespierre carried over into revolutionary practice.

To see what Arendt sees wrong in compassion we must take a step back, to return to the idea of representation and what it means to speak 'on behalf of':

> The men of the [French] Revolution and the people whom they represented were no longer united by objective bonds in a common cause; a special effort was required of the representatives, an effort of *solidarization* [emphasis added] which Robespierre called virtue, and this virtue … did not aim at the *res publica* and had nothing to do with freedom. Virtue meant to have the welfare of the people in mind, to identify one's own will with the will of the people—and this effort was directed primarily toward the happiness of the many.[21]

The very definition of the term '*le peuple*' that designates those who were spoken for and on behalf of, is 'born out of compassion',[22] and the 'term became equivalent for misfortune ('*le people, les malheureux m'appaudissent*' Robespierre would claim). In the absence of political mediation as such, the legitimacy of the representatives of the people could reside only in the 'compassionate zeal' of those who were prepared to raise it to 'the rank of the supreme political passion and highest political virtue'.[23] They came to express the 'will' of the people, and the cue they took from Rousseau was that the general will was what bound the many into one,

[18] Arendt, above n 2, 71.
[19] *Ibid* 80.
[20] *Ibid* 80–81.
[21] *Ibid* 74–75.
[22] *Ibid* 75.
[23] *Ibid.*

and thus had to be one (‘*Il faut une volonte UNE*’, Robespierre insisted) or not at all. This ‘speaking on behalf of’ came to supplant ‘all processes of exchange of opinions and an eventual agreement between them’.[24] Arendt insists on an important point here: that in the zeal and impetus of this supplanting, the will is uprooted from the worldly institutions which alone underwrote what they had in common, and thus cancelled it out.

It is on these grounds that Arendt will condemn the colonisation of public space by the ideals of compassion and virtue, and a misconception of solidarity that stems from the latter to inform the former (solidarity will be restored later to its proper political-institutional understanding): ‘Robespierre’s “terror of virtue” cannot be understood without taking into account the crucial role compassion had come to play in the minds and hearts of those who acted in the course of the French Revolution.’[25] Compassion, with its gaze on concreteness and particularity, is both inappropriate institutionally and destructive when it informs the acts of the ‘virtuous’, because it collapses the space in-between that commonality demands as constitutive of what it means to share a world:

> Because compassion abolishes the distance, the worldly space between men where political matters, the whole realm of human affairs, are located, it remains, politically speaking, irrelevant and without consequence … As a rule it is not compassion which sets out to change worldly conditions in order to ease human suffering, but if it does, it will shun the drawn-out wearisome processes of persuasion, negotiation and compromise, which are the processes of law and politics, and lend its voice to the suffering itself, which must claim for swift and direct action, that is, for action with the means of violence.[26]

By the time we reach section 4 of Arendt’s chapter, ‘compassion’ has given way to ‘pity’, and its objects, ‘*les malheureux*’, have respectively given way to ‘*les faibles*’ in order for the ‘alternative’ to be designated as ‘solidarity’:[27]

> ‘Solidarity’ allows men to establish deliberately and, as it were, dispassionately a community of interest with the oppressed and the exploited. The common interest would then be the ‘grandeur of man’, or the ‘honour of the human race’, or the dignity of man. For solidarity, because it partakes of reason, and hence of generality, is able to comprehend a multitude conceptually, not only the multitude of a class or a nation, or a people, but eventually all mankind. But this solidarity, though it may be aroused by suffering, is not guided by it, and it comprehends the strong and the rich no less than the weak and the poor; compared with the sentiment of pity, it may appear cold and abstract, for it remains committed to ideas—to greatness or honour, or dignity—rather than to any ‘love’ of men.[28]

[24] *Ibid* 76.
[25] *Ibid* 79.
[26] *Ibid* 86–87. From Herman Melville she takes this: ‘[T]hat goodness … shares with elemental evil the elementary violence inherent in all strength and detrimental to all forms of political organisation’ (*ibid* 87).
[27] *Ibid* 88.
[28] *Ibid* 88–89.

Notwithstanding the perhaps underhand dig at Robespierre—that 'pity' has a 'vested interest in the existence of the unhappy'[29]—it has also 'proved to possess a greater capacity for cruelty than cruelty itself'. 'Proved' is an odd word here in the midst of a conceptual analysis, but it does reveal something interesting about a certain bias that returns and returns again to colour the mapping of distinctions. But there is something even more disquieting about the direction that Arendt's analysis now takes. She aims it, again, at the Jacobins: since the Revolution had opened the gates of the political realm to the poor, this realm had indeed become 'social'. It was overwhelmed by the cares and worries which actually belonged in the sphere of the household and which, even if they were permitted to enter the public realm, could not be solved by political means, since they were matters of administration, to be put into the hands of experts, rather than issues which could be settled by the twofold process of decision and persuasion.'[30] And further: 'Their [the revolutionaries'] need was violent, and as it were, pre-political; it seemed that only violence could be strong and swift enough to help them.' This dire section of the chapter on the 'social question' finds its disturbing culmination in the concluding paragraph where Arendt asserts: 'Nothing we might say today, could be more obsolete than to attempt to liberate mankind from poverty by political means; nothing could be more futile and more dangerous.'[31]

What began as an extraordinary analysis of the phenomenology of the revolutionary event, of the constituent and of the novelty of the concept of beginning, thus winds up as bourgeois alarmism. And Negri is surely right to express his unease about a move that 'at the very moment when she illuminates the nature of constituent power Arendt renders it indifferent in its ideality or equivocal in its historical exemplification.'[32] His critique is twofold: her account of the formation of political space 'becomes the key to a historicist hermeneutics that systematically flattens down, or deforms, the novelty of the event and limits it to the American example'; and the 'ambiguity of the beginning … [is] resolved in formal terms, according to the demands of an idealism content to find a correspondence in institutions'.[33]

Both points are well taken and developed in *Insurgencies*. But there is also something else important to observe about the trajectory, that has nothing to do with Arendt's political sympathies or failings, or her admiration for the constitutional arrangement of the US, but more with a process where the drawing of distinctions has selectively opened up and simultaneously foreclosed a space for the appearance of the political. What is at stake is the withdrawal of that space of appearance, as in the case where the social demands of recognition and distribution

[29] *Ibid* 89.
[30] *Ibid* 91.
[31] *Ibid* 114.
[32] Negri, *Insurgencies*, n 13 above, 17.
[33] *Ibid* 17.

are denied a political register. The denial is then effaced, doubly forgotten or rendered 'immemorial' in Lyotard's precise meaning, when the very purity of the constitutional question demands that its statement in political terms proper—as condition of freedom—is *its unburdening from the social question.*

II. DOMESTICATING THE AGON

Arendt's fundamental distinction between the social and the political thus effectively domesticates the agonism that she valorises, evacuating any transformative potential that it might otherwise promise. Arendt offers a powerful image of constituent power as pertaining not only to the act of constituting the laws of government but to the constitution of the common, the disclosure of a common world.[34] For her, a revolution is properly political to the extent that it aims at constituting and preserving a space of appearances within which citizens can continue to engage in a striving for distinction and recognition. From the agonistic interplay of a plurality of perspectives brought to bear within the public sphere, the commonness of the world that lies between citizens is constantly disclosed and reconstituted. While *liberation* from domination by men and the necessities of nature is a condition of possibility for the establishment of such a space of appearances, this space, she insists, emerges only through the enactment and enjoyment of *freedom* as an end in itself.

In contrast to her characterisation of the necessity, hierarchy, obscurity and conformity of the social, her conception of the political in terms of spontaneity, equality, publicity and plurality presents an inspiring image of constituent power. Indeed, Negri admires Arendt for having 'given us the clearest image of constituent power in its radicalness and strength'.[35] Constituent power inheres in the exhilarating experience of initiatory action, but ultimately also in the production of the common. For Arendt, as Negri puts it, freedom 'becomes public space, constituting a communicative relation, its own conditions of possibility and therefore its own strength. It is the polis. Freedom is a beginning that poses its own conditions'.[36]

Scholars of Arendt have been tempted to bracket the reactionary or 'elitist' element of her thought that is encapsulated in her conception of the social, in order to appropriate the 'democratic' strain, which celebrates the creative, world-disclosing essence of the political.[37] But such a selective reading of Arendt

[34] Arendt, above n 2, 145.
[35] Negri, above n 13, 19.
[36] *Ibid* 15.
[37] See, eg, M Canovan, 'The Contradictions in Hannah Arendt's Thought' (1978) 6 *Political Theory* 5; and J Habermas, 'Hannah Arendt's Communications Concept of Power' (1976) 4 *Social Research* 3, 15: 'I want only to indicate the curious perspective that Hannah Arendt adopts: a state which is relieved of the administrative processing of social problems; a politics which is cleansed of socio-economic issues … The path is unimaginable for any modern society.'

is limited because her political ontology is underpinned by a dichotomy between necessity and freedom. One cannot bracket here without undoing, or at least leaving the political fundamentally under-determined. Indeed, for Arendt, the achievement of action is precisely the transcendence of necessity: the causal relations to which the natural world is subject. It is through this transcendence that actors distinguish themselves as human. Conversely, subjection to necessity is inherently dehumanising. To be subject to necessity is to be deprived of the possibility of meaningful action and the existential achievement of self-disclosure. Hence her unflattering descriptions of 'savages', stateless people, the poor and other marginalised groups.

For Arendt, human beings are capable of action by virtue of being born. She takes birth, here, not as a biological fact that humans share with animals but as a social fact, since only human beings *appear* at birth in a world that is constituted through work and action. This world is a condition of possibility for the *event* of birth because the human artifice produced through work provides a measure of durability and permanence against the cyclical futility of nature. Moreover, the web of relationships that are constituted through action provides a social context in which the event can be witnessed, commemorated and invested with meaning.

Correlatively, the established constitution of a political community is part both of the artifice of things (as *nomos*, its wall-like aspect enclosing the common) and of the web of relationships (as *lex*, its relational aspect constituting individuals as persons through mutual recognition). The purpose of the constitution is to enable the continuity of the community through time by providing a measure of permanence to human affairs, to *house* the space of appearances, making possible an organised remembrance. Moreover, it provides a measure of predictability through establishing shared expectations, that enables the polity to act into the future. The purpose of a constitution should be to commemorate the inaugural event through which the community is constituted, so that the principle of freedom it revealed can inspire and animate the public sphere of the constituted community. Through speaking and acting together within this public sphere citizens would thus enact their freedom anew, augmenting the authority of the constitution that was anticipated in its founding moment.

Arendt's thought has the merit of returning our attention to the fundamental dimension of politics as always ultimately concerned with the constitution of the common. However, it is difficult to extract from her work a conception of transformative politics precisely because her conception of action is 'ontologically rooted' in the 'fact of natality'.[38] For her, the world-disclosive possibility of action is tied to the desire for self-disclosure, which she takes to be part of the human condition. The struggle for recognition to which this gives rise and the common that it discloses emerges against the dark background of the sheer givenness of human existence in a state of nature. What this ontological grounding of agonism

[38] H Arendt, *The Human Condition*, 2nd edn (Chicago, Ill, University of Chicago Press, 1998) 247.

elides, however, is how the common itself, its stakes and its shares, can become the object of political contest.

To be sure, in the Arendtian public sphere, individuals contest the way the world appears to them through the exchange of opinions. But politicisation typically entails a struggle to represent a rival image of the common, which denaturalises our common sense of the world. Arendt's interest in the initiatory quality of praxis, however, does not arise from a concern to conceptualise acts of politicisation. Rather, her concern is with resisting the rise of mass society, which made possible totalitarianism. In particular, Arendt deplores the emergence of what Foucault would call biopolitics ('the rise of the social') in which the life process of society (or the population) becomes the primary concern of politics. Arendt blames the modern elevation of life to the highest of goods for the spread of world-alienation, loneliness, and the futility and meaningless of modern life, which created a vacuum within which totalitarianism could emerge.

In modernity, the scope for human freedom has been diminished because the activity of labour and its concern with satisfying the needs of the body—'making life easier and longer'– have come to dominate the public realm.[39] While Arendt distinguishes the political sharply from the social, then, this is not a simple opposition. Whereas, for Arendt, our political interest in actualising freedom is a properly public concern, our economic interest in sustaining life is a properly private concern. The social, in contrast, is a hybrid realm that comes about by the improper pursuit of economic concerns in public life. Society is the 'public organization of the life process itself … the form [of living together] in which the fact of mutual dependence for the sake of life and nothing else assumes public significance'.[40] The cost of elevating life as the ultimate end of political organisation is that human affairs are deprived of the reality and significance that comes from the world-disclosing activity of *praxis*.

Arendt turns to the Greek *polis* to recuperate a conception of the political that might redeem the contemporary world from this malaise. She looks to the experience of the Greek *polis* not out of nostalgia but, she claims, because 'a freedom experienced in the process of acting and nothing else—though, of course, mankind never lost this experience altogether—has never again been articulated with the same classical clarity.'[41] And it is in this context that she appropriates the Aristotelian distinction between *zoe* and *bios*: 'between activities related to a common world and those related to the maintenance of life, a division which all ancient political thought rested as self-evident and axiomatic'.[42] According to Aristotle, she observes, the good life.

[39] *Ibid* 208.
[40] *Ibid* 46.
[41] H Arendt, *Between Past and Future* (Harmondsworth, Penguin, 1993) 165.
[42] Arendt, above n 35, 28.

> was "good" to the extent that having mastered the necessities of sheer life, by being freed from labour and work, and by overcoming the innate urge of all living creatures for their own survival, it was no longer bound to the biological life process.[43]

The political ontology that she outlines in *The Human Condition* (with its threefold distinction between labour, work and action) thus accounts for the intransigence of the distinction between the social and the political that pervades her conceptual and historical analyses in *On Revolution*. Whereas the activity of labour corresponds to the human condition of life itself, the activity of *praxis* corresponds to the condition of plurality. Labour is inherently unpolitical and potentially anti-political for Arendt, since it is 'an activity in which man is neither together with the world nor with other people, but alone with his body, facing the naked necessity to keep himself alive'.[44] While labour may be organised and undertaken as a collective enterprise, it does not reveal anything of the world that lies between those engaged together in sustaining life. It 'has none of the distinctive marks of true plurality', since in labouring together human beings do not act as unique individuals but as 'mere living organisms' that are 'fundamentally all alike'.[45]

Arendt's brief but approving references to the agonism of the Greeks are made in this context. She contrasts the ancient concern to distinguish oneself in public before one's peers with the conformist behaviour of modern society and its equality based on sameness. In Athens, she writes, the public realm 'was permeated by a fiercely agonal spirit, where everybody had constantly to distinguish himself from all others, to show through unique deeds or achievements that he was the best'.[46] The public realm 'was the only place where men could show who they really and inexchangeably were'.[47] Arendt turns to the experience of the *polis* to articulate a conception of the political as a space of appearances, 'the organization of the people as it arises out of acting and speaking', an emergent space which 'can find its proper location almost anytime and anywhere'.[48]

Now it is of course true that scholars inspired by Arendt's agonistic conception of politics do acknowledge that her strict separation of the social and the political is untenable since it precludes matters of social justice from public debate and privatises social suffering. But what is untenable on the one hand must simultaneously be presupposed on the other. For the separation of the social and the political underlies Arendtian agonism in order to explain how *socially* determined identities can be transcended through *political* action in which new subject positions are enacted. Yet, as Jean-Philippe Deranty and Emmanuel Renault

[43] *Ibid* 36, 37.
[44] *Ibid* 212.
[45] *Ibid.*
[46] *Ibid* 41.
[47] *Ibid.*
[48] *Ibid* 198.

argue convincingly,[49] this account of the transcendence of oppressive identities is inadequate because it fails to account for how social experience can be constitutive for political action. Indeed, what is required is an account of the *modes of politicisation* through which the social comes to be viewed as political, how the suffering that Arendt associates with necessity is revealed as socially produced.[50] But, as we have already seen, it is precisely in response to such an understanding of exploitation that Arendt formulates her distinction between the social and the political.

Might it then be possible, nevertheless and despite Arendt's own intentions, to recast her *spatial* conception of the political (with its sharp distinction between the separate 'realms' of necessity and freedom) as a *process* of politicisation (that enables a mediation between necessity and freedom)? This is the suggestion argued by James Clarke,[51] who suggests that a revised Arendtian approach enables us to understand how human needs might be 'politicized' insofar as they can become the object of interpretation and discussion. If we acknowledge that the social is the terrain both of state intervention and wider political contestation, we can understand the relation between the social and the political in terms of the logics of depoliticisation and repoliticisation. On the one hand, the social can thus be understood as the realm of sedimented political practices in which needs become naturalised. When these needs are asserted in the public sphere as given, obdurate and incontestable, this can lead to an anti-political politics. On the other hand, when the interpretation of the origin, nature and appropriate form of satisfaction of needs is treated as an object of public debate, needs might be politicised.

On this account, relations of domination that have been naturalised through the private/public distinction are not *immediately* political. Rather, they *become* political when *meditated* through public action, when a 'we' emerges that recognises social relations as contingent and therefore potentially transformable. Although the effects of oppression are always personally experienced, oppression 'only becomes political when others recognize it as a shared reality and, further, when it can become the basis for solidarity and action'.[52] In other words, demands for the satisfaction of needs become political only when they carry with them the world-disclosing potential that for Arendt is the defining feature of action. On this

[49] J-P Deranty and E Renault, 'Democratic Agon: Striving for Distinction or Struggle against Domination and Injustice?' in A Schaap (ed), *Law and Agonistic Politics* (Farnam, Ashgate, 2009) 43.

[50] See H Pitkin, 'Justice: On Relating Private and Public' (1981) 9 *Political Theory* 327, and R Bernstein, 'Rethinking the Social and the Political' in R Bernstein, *Philosophical Profiles* (Philadelphia, University of Pennsylvania Press, 1986) 238, much-cited criticisms of the untenability of Arendt's attempt to distinguish between the 'social' and 'political' aspects of a single issue such as 'housing', and the way her thematisation of the distinction undercuts any attempt to relate private and public by publicising the social causes of personal suffering.

[51] J Clarke, 'Social Justice and Political Freedom: Revisiting Hannah Arendt's Conception of Need' (1993) 19 *Philosophy and Social Criticism* 333.

[52] *Ibid* 342.

account it is possible to imagine an agonistic politics of need that would involve the politicisation of social suffering.[53]

And yet even this careful Arendtian account of becoming-political stumbles on Arendt's very starting points. An Arendtian conception of the political is inadequate for thematising acts of politicisation because it only allows for the emergence of a 'we' in a situation where political actors are *neither for nor against but only 'with' others*. The agonistic striving for distinction can take place only within a community of equals. Consequently, the struggle to overcome social domination can be understood only as a pre-political act of liberation, following which a new political freedom might be inaugurated. And it is here, perhaps, above all that Arendt may have stood to learn something from Marx had she not been so quick with her wholesale dismissal.[54] As neo-Marxists (Negri, Badiou and Rancière amongst them) have variously argued, the productivity of political action, the constitution of new forms of commonality or subjectivity first emerge precisely in moments of political antagonism. Far from being a necessary precondition for politics, equality is more often than not the object of political dispute, in situations where equality (even visibility) must be claimed by actors from an opponent who denies it to them. By engaging in a struggle for recognition, parties to a conflict *demonstrate* their equality; and in doing so, disclose new subject positions and another possible world.

Citing John Adams in *On Revolution*, Arendt asserts that the fundamental deprivation suffered by the poor is that of appearance within a common world. She observes sympathetically that 'Marx's effort to rewrite history in terms of class struggle was partially at least inspired by the desire to rehabilitate posthumously those to whose injured lives history had added the insult of oblivion'.[55] Rancière agrees that the political wrong suffered by the poor consists in their invisibility. However, he rejects Arendt's suggestion that only someone such as Adams, who had experienced the joy of public life, could appreciate what it would mean to be deprived of the *bios politikos*. On the contrary, he points out that the politics of the poor have invariably concerned 'precisely their mode of visibility'.[56] If Arendt misses this, it is due to her stubborn insistence on the dichotomy between necessity and freedom. And where there are moments in Arendt's work where her *historical* observations seem to bring her close to the realisation of how freedom can be enacted through an antagonistic politics aimed at abolishing inequality, these moments are quickly passed over through the reassertion of a political ontology that constitutively undercuts that realisation before it can surface.

[53] See, eg, A Schaap, 'The Politics of Need' in A Schaap, D Celermajer and V Karalis (eds), *Power, Judgment and Political Evil: In Conversations with Hannah Arendt* (Farnam, Ashgate, 2010) 157.

[54] See B Parekh, 'Hannah Arendt's critique of Marx' in M Hill (ed), *Hannah Arendt: The Recovery of the Public World* (New York, St Martin's Press, 1979); C Holman, 'Dialectics and distinction: Reconsidering Hannah Arendt's critique of Marx' (2011) 10 (3) *Contemporary Political Theory* 332–53.

[55] Arendt, above n 2, 69.

[56] J Rancière, 'Ten Thesis on Politics' (2001) 5 *Theory & Event* 1, 26.

III. DEPLETING THE SPACE OF APPEARANCES

There is a less-discussed section in *The Human Condition* that bears out the contradictions in Arendt's thought in a revealing way. It is where Arendt interrupts her phenomenological analysis to remark on 'the extraordinarily productive role which the labour movements have played in modern politics'.[57] This political productivity came about when those involved in the labour movement took it upon themselves to self-organise, developing their own ideas and practices of self-government, exemplified in the brief flourishing of council democracy. She says:

> When the labour movement appeared on the political scene, it was the only organization in which men acted and spoke *qua* men—and not *qua* members of society. For this political and revolutionary role of the labour movement … it is decisive *that the economic activity of its members was incidental* and that its force of attraction was never restricted to the ranks of the working class. If for a time it almost looked as if the movement would succeed in founding, at least within its own ranks, a new public space with new political standards, *the spring of these attempts was not labour*—neither the labouring activity itself nor the always utopian rebellion against life's necessities—but those injustices and hypocrisies which have disappeared with the transformation of a class society into a mass society and with the substitution of a guaranteed annual wage for daily or weekly pay.[58]

The argument is riddled with circularity and contradiction.

Arendt begins by conceding the 'apparently flagrant discrepancy between *historical fact*—the political productivity of the working class—and the *phenomenal data* obtained from [her] analysis of the labouring activity'.[59] 'Apparently flagrant' is an odd formulation that captures something of her unease at the wedge she herself has driven between the history of constituent political power of the labour movement and her political ontology that denies them that their action is political, let alone constituent. To get herself out of this 'apparently flagrant discrepancy' she will claim that the labour movement was really only incidentally about labour. It was not the 'necessities' associated with a decent wage, decent working conditions, a degree of control over the productive process, the re-appropriation of the means of production, the scope of claims that one would assume make the labour movement a *labour* movement. Instead, for Arendt, it was about 'founding a new public space' where workers would act '*qua* men—and not *qua* members of society', 'at least', she concedes enigmatically, 'within its own ranks'. Are we to assume that the meaning of that confinement (its own ranks) is to some form of workplace democracy?

Obviously Arendt has nothing so confining in mind, and in order to rescue the political from the social, she will go on to insist that the contradiction into which she is led by her political ontology is only apparent. For, she argues, the world-disclosing (and therefore 'properly political') aspect of the labour movement

[57] Arendt, above n 35, 216.
[58] *Ibid* 219.
[59] *Ibid* 217.

'stemmed from its fight against society as a whole'. But with this desperate gesture to cleanse the movement from its origin in and connectedness to the social, in order to restore it untainted as properly political, Arendt tips the balance the other way. A 'fight against society as a whole' imports antagonism, a fight not on a political plane but against those who have appropriated that plane: against, thus, the bourgeois appropriation of the public sphere on the basis of the particular configuration of the public/private distinction.[60] Arendt is right to sense in the labour movement a challenge to precisely that configuration, one that relegates the demands of those at work to the private sphere and thus submits her valued principles of association—as non-political—to capitalist accumulation. A reaction of this kind and magnitude can only be antagonistic, not productive, to the public sphere as given. But now Arendt is caught. On the one hand her insistence on 'natality' draws her to world-disclosure of a different kind, that breaks into the given with the promise of the new. On the other hand her political ontology and the entrenchment of the social/political distinction prevents her from acknowledging what is distinctive about what the labour movement discloses to politics, because that would be founding the political in the social.

If antagonism was the condition of possibility for the dramatic appearance of the labour movement on the political scene, Arendt's conception of constituent power is emaciated precisely because she wants to isolate it from the social struggle—with *its* stakes, *its* subject-positions and *its* opportunities of disclosure—that gives rise to its appearance in the first place. She deprives it of any possible political purchase by abstracting world-disclosure from the material social context within which political actors come into conflict.

There is something both profound and disquieting in all this. Arendt's phenomenology is about what appears as political, with its attendant attributes and functions of disclosure. To distil this emergence of the political and identify the possibilities of action that pertain to it she will resist any form of 'instrumentalization of action and [with it] the degradation of politics into a means for something else', and she will cleanse it of its origin in social divides and hierarchies. To this, she will establish a principle of formal equality and plurality as proper to the political—proper in the fundamental sense of constitutive—where discrimination and sheer difference characterise the social. That is how the political is first enabled in the mapping out through the specific binarisms and the opportunities they sustain.

Arendt has been celebrated for her uncompromising defence of the political and her eloquent analysis of all that it sustains and makes possible: new beginnings,

[60] Negri makes the insightful point that in Arendt's thematisation of constituent power, the 'antagonistic event disappears' (Negri, above n 13, 18). For Negri, in contrast, the creative moment of politics emerges not in agonism but antagonism: 'there can be no creation without antagonism'. See A Negri and C Casarino, *In Praise of the Common: A Conversation on Philosophy and Politics* (Minneapolis, University of Minnesota Press, 2008) 129. Negativity is a productive principle: 'because negativity produces, it destroys the dialectic, that is, it produces an unassimilable surplus' (*ibid*).

solidarity, wordliness. And she has policed the boundaries of the political from all aspects of society's life that would impinge on it with claims that are properly those of administering and dealing with necessity. As in ideology's most pervasive move, the enabling move displaces alternatives that are simultaneously occluded and forgotten. Forgotten in the sense that their occlusion is what enables the appearance, furnishes the modality of appearance. If freedom cannot be tied dialectically to necessity it is because to retrieve necessity is to deny freedom, it is to fold or collapse the space for the appearance of freedom. There is no political space in Arendt in which the social question can find political expression, because political expression—the realm of the in-between, of freedom and the rest—is what necessity *is not*. The effacement is at the level of context, at the level of what opens up meaningfully to perception.

If the phenomenological moment is what is most valuable in Arendt—the process, that is, of the appearance of the political with all its world-disclosing brilliance—it is an emergence that Arendt can only *tentatively* sustain and sustain at a huge *cost*. The cost has to do, as we saw, with the bracketing from the sphere of properly political action and debate of all that which for her would contaminate it with society's concerns and the administration of life's necessities. 'Tentatively' because the political must be maintained as agonistic rather than antagonistic at all costs, maintained that is through the distribution of speaking positions that guarantees a certain confluence along given coordinates. Against this confluence, antagonism would import a constitutive negativity. And import it, for Arendt, in a way that would undercut the political. In the forms that Arendt was perhaps most eager to excise, it aimed to resist the move itself that discloses politics and sustains the plane of appearance as reductive, because depleted of what could in fact alone be constitutive of it as 'common': the equal share in the processes of social labour and the fruits of social production.

6

The Role of the Supreme Court in Arendt's Political Constitution

MARCO GOLDONI AND CHRIS MCCORKINDALE

IT IS SLIGHTLY curious that despite her clear interest in questions of law and legal process (see, for example, her analysis of Eichmann's trial in Jerusalem, her reflections on the Supreme Court's rulings on racial segregation, her analysis of the 'juridical person' in man, her formulation of the right *to have* rights), lawyers themselves have spent almost as little time on Arendt's work as Arendt scholars have on her legal thought. Then again, perhaps this should *not* be surprising. Arendt, after all, was noted for her neglect of 'normal' politics and a corresponding fascination with the 'extraordinary'.[1] And yet, given that her optimism for mankind in the *Origins of Totalitarianism* was based on the hope of founding new legal structures, given too that her pessimism in *On Revolution* was based on the failure of America's Founding Fathers to *institutionalise* the revolutionary spirit by which that republic was made, it would seem that a comprehensive account of Arendt's political thought is necessarily incomplete absent any dedicated analysis of those institutions within which she believed that the spirit of (political) action could endure.

For its constitutional implications, as well as for the way it captures the ambivalent treatment given by Arendt to law more generally, in this essay we focus on just one such institution—the US Supreme Court—and the ambiguous role attributed to it, and to the function of judicial review in particular, found scattered throughout her writing. We begin to explore this question from chapter five of *On Revolution*, where both the potential and the limits of the Supreme Court as a republican institution emerge. To date, and to our knowledge, only two papers seriously consider Arendt's views on the possibility of politics being played out in the court room; papers which offer polar opposite accounts of her faith in the judicial branch. The first is Jan Klabbers' 2007 piece, 'Possible Islands of

[1] See, eg, G Kateb, 'Political action: its nature and advantages' in D Villa (ed), *The Cambridge Companion to Hannah Arendt* (Cambridge, Cambridge University Press, 2000) 134–35; A Kalyvas, *Democracy and the Politics of the Extraordinary: Max Weber, Carl Schmitt and Hannah Arendt* (Cambridge, Cambridge University Press, 2008).

Predictability: The Legal Thought of Hannah Arendt'.[2] Here Klabbers says of Arendt:

> She would have been ... sympathetic to the idea of judicial review, provided that the idea remain limited to testing whether legislation and administrative action had ... come about in the right manner, and provided there were a clear constitutional mandate. She said kind words about the US Supreme Court, which while powerless, exercised great authority, and did so in a purely legal function.[3]

Klabbers, then, interprets from Arendt a somewhat narrow role for judicial review, something akin to John Hart Ely's procedural approach.[4] Taking from her work the warning that 'getting judges to solve political debates or fix political outcomes under the heading of judicial review would run into serious difficulties',[5] Klabbers proceeds from there to build his own argument against juridification on the international plane.

The second paper is Andrew Arato and Jean Cohen's 2009 article, 'Banishing the Sovereign? Internal and External Sovereignty in Arendt'.[6] In a marked contrast with Klabbers' interpretation, here the authors see in Arendt's work a far more expansive scope for judicial review. Indeed, they go as far to say that Arendt embraced 'a constitution of judges', putting 'a glowing senatorial aura on Wilson's rather negative depiction of the Court as "a constituent assembly in permanent session"'.[7] Thus Cohen and Arato find in *On Revolution* a Supreme Court 'capable of usurping sovereignty'.[8] This interpretation is not entirely implausible, and would place Arendt within a tradition of American legal scholars for whom a republican revival in American constitutional *thought* has meant, above all, placing the US Supreme Court to the front and centre of constitutional *design*.[9] Indeed, and as we shall see, in *On Revolution* Arendt certainly seemed to look upon the Supreme Court with something of the reverence depicted in Cohen and Arato's analysis. By looking beyond *On Revolution*, however, in particular to two essays, 'Reflections on Little Rock' and 'Civil Disobedience', this essay sets out to offer a more nuanced account of the authority and power of the Supreme

[2] J Klabbers, 'Possible Islands of Predictability: The Legal Thought of Hannah Arendt' (2007) 20 *Leiden Journal of International Law* 1, 1.

[3] *Ibid* 21–22.

[4] JH Ely, *Democracy and Distrust: A Theory of Judicial Review* (Cambridge, Mass, and London, Harvard University Press, 1980).

[5] Klabbers, above n 2, 22.

[6] J Cohen and A Arato, 'Banishing the Sovereign? Internal and External Sovereignty in Arendt' (2009) 16 *Constellations* 307.

[7] *Ibid.*

[8] *Ibid*, 317.

[9] The leading works are Cass Sunstein's 'Beyond the Republican Revival' (1988) 97 *Yale Law Journal* 1539, and Frank Michelman's 'Law's Republic' (1988) 97 *Yale Law Journal* 1493. For a strong counter-point, see K Abrams, 'Law's Republicanism' (1988) 97 *Yale Law Journal* 1591: 'The legal foray into republicanism,' says Abrams, of Sunstein's and Michelman's efforts, 'has been sidetracked by its intellectual premises. Straitened by the distinctive problems and perspectives of liberal legalism, it has produced a muted hybrid, oddly focussed on the role of the courts' (at 1591).

Court which is to be found in Arendt's work; a position which sits somewhere between that of Klabbers and that of Cohen and Arato. In the first place, we shall show that Arendt was much more ambivalent in bestowing authority upon the Supreme Court than the latter suggest, finding in that institution not the dynamism and vitality of the founding moment, but rather (and merely) the conservative interpretation of the written Constitution. *Contra* Arato and Cohen, secondly we trace the steps which led Arendt, finally and explicitly, to *reject* 'a constitution of judges'.

I. THE SUPREME COURT BETWEEN POWER AND AUTHORITY

In her (in)famous reconstruction of that which she believed to have been the most successful among modern revolutions, the American Revolution, Arendt traced the roots of its success to a distinction drawn by the Founding Fathers between the seat of *power* and the source of *law*. The Founding Fathers, she said, 'were never tempted to derive law and power from the same origin. The seat of power to them was the people, but the source of law was to become the Constitution, a written document, an endurable objective thing'.[10] It was 'in-between' these different sources that Arendt discovered the novelty of the Supreme Court, which stood to protect that object from the ebb and flow of power (always moving, always changing, always *subjective*) embodied in the legislative and executive branches. For she, the Court—together with the institution of judicial review—was directly linked to the *preservation* of that object, the Constitution,

> which, to be sure, one could approach from many different angles and upon which one could impose many different interpretations, which one could change and amend in accordance with circumstances, but which nevertheless was never a subjective state of mind, like the will.[11]

It is here, in Arendt's view of the Constitution as a *lasting* object, that one can begin to understand the role which she attributed to the Supreme Court. What she saw as characteristic of this institution was its being the seat of authority, and neither the *locus* of power (the people) nor the source of law (the written Constitution). In order to understand the nature and the scope of the Supreme Court (at least as Arendt saw it), allow us to consider this assumption a little more carefully.

For Arendt, the failure of the French Revolution (beyond the troublesome social question) could be traced precisely to the attempt to derive *both* law and power from the same source, through the deification of the people. There, the contradiction between the principle of political legitimacy (the national will) and the aim of institutions (to create the conditions for political stability) was brought into a sharp focus. Because the will is by definition the most transient among

[10] H Arendt, *On Revolution* (London, Penguin, 1963) 157 (hereafter 'OR').
[11] *Ibid.*

the human faculties, and therefore the least able to provide for a solid (and this is to say, permanent) institutional ground, Arendt saw that any conflation of power and law—of the subjective will and the objective constitution—was bound to fail.[12]

For Arendt, a stable and durable political community could only be secured through an institution capable of mediating between these two distinct concepts, the *power* of the new beginning (the founding moment) and the *stability* of the constitution (that which was founded). 'If,' she said, stating the paradox which faced the men of the revolution, 'foundation was the aim and the end of revolution, then the revolutionary spirit,' which was to say, the spirit of *action*, 'was not merely the spirit of beginning something new but of starting something permanent and enduring … From which it unfortunately seems to follow that nothing threatens the very achievements of revolution more dangerously and more acutely than the spirit which has brought them about'.[13] The Founding Fathers' 'novel and unique'[14] solution to this 'unsolvable'[15] problem was to recover for the modern age the Roman concept of authority.

It was characteristic of Arendt to give idiosyncratic (and at times hotly-contested) meaning to commonplace terms of political theory. In this instance, she distinguished 'authority' from 'violence' (defined by coercion *over* men) and 'power' (defined by persuasion *between* men). The 'hallmark [of authority],' as she saw it, 'is unquestioning recognition by those who are asked to obey; neither coercion nor persuasion is needed'.[16] To be sure, Arendt was never clear as to the nature of this act of faith: that is to say, just why it was that one institution could or should attract the *unquestioning* support of the people. She did begin to make a move in this direction, however, by exploring the etymology of the word, which she traced from *augere*, to augment. Here she left us the clue that the nature of authority derives from the continued augmentation of the republic's founding principles.[17]

In Rome, those who were recognised as having authority (*patres*) constituted the Senate. Their duty was to preserve the founding principles of the city by ensuring, through their deliberation and advice, that present and future laws remained faithful to them.[18] The past, in this sense, became a guide—a banister—to the coming generations; a legacy bestowed upon them by the Senators. Thus, no

[12] On Arendt's conception of the will, see 'Willing', in H Arendt, *The Life of the Mind* (New York, Harcourt & Brace, 1978) 93; on this see S Jacobitti, 'Hannah Arendt and the Will' (1988) 16 *Political Theory* 53; J Martel, 'Amo: Volo ut Sis. Love, Willing and Arendt's Reluctant Embrace of Sovereignty' (2008) 34 *Philosophy & Social Criticism* 287. See, also, V Liska, ch 4 of this volume.

[13] OR 232.

[14] *Ibid* 228.

[15] *Ibid* 232.

[16] H Arendt, *The Crises of the Republic* (New York, Harcourt & Brace, 1972) 144.

[17] OR 201.

[18] This is not the place to question why Arendt found the Roman conception of authority so persuasive. For some clue, however, see the pages on memory and heritage in H Arendt, *The Human Condition* (Chicago, Ill, The University of Chicago Press, 1958) 160–64 (hereafter 'HC').

generation was an island: each generation—past, present and future—was bound by a common world, both spatially and temporally:

> The common world is what we enter when we are born and what we leave behind when we die. It transcends our life-span into past and future alike; it was there before we came and will outlast our brief sojourn in it. It is what we have in common not only with those who live with us, but also with those who were here before and with those who will come after us.[19]

How Arendt conceived of this temporal dimension is both counter-intuitive and yet at the same time essential to understanding her conception of authority. It is natural to think of growth, and therefore of augmentation, as an activity which is exclusively orientated to the future, distancing us from the past. For Arendt however, the opposite was true. Thus, she said, for the Romans:

> Old age, as distinguished from mere adulthood ... contain[ed] the very climax of human life; not so much because of accumulated wisdom and experience as because the old man had grown closer to the ancestors and the past. Contrary to our concept of growth, where one grows into the future, the Romans felt that growth was directed toward the past.[20]

The Senate, then, derived its authority from the fiction that in it were permanently recreated the founding fathers of Rome themselves:

> Through the Roman Senators, the founders of the city of Rome were present, and with them the spirit of foundation was present, the beginning, the *principium* and principle, of those *res gestae* which from then on formed the history of the people of Rome.[21]

It was not the founding moment, but its (mythical) reincarnation in a political institution which tied the changes of the present to the vitality of beginning, to the vibrancy of the constitutive *act* of foundation; which tied, in other words, future generations to their constitutional origins.

In America, however, the seat of authority was *not* a political institution but a legal one. Judicial control of executive and legislative power drew *its* authority not from the political act of foundation, but rather from that which was founded: from the written document of the Constitution. As such, the role of the Court was neither to deliberate nor to advise, but rather to *interpret* that document.[22] If the Roman Senate sat as the (fictional) personification and institutionalisation of a *constituent* power, the very embodiment of action, the Court sat as the (fictional) personification of the Constitution itself. Accordingly, for the Romans, the

[19] *Ibid* 58.

[20] H Arendt, 'What is Authority?' in H Arendt, *Between Past and Future* (London, Penguin, 2006) 123 (hereafter 'WiA?').

[21] OR 201.

[22] Close to this reading of Arendt's approach to the role of the Supreme Court is Kalyvas, above n 1, 278–80.

> uninterrupted continuity of [constitutional] augmentation and its inherent authority could come about only through tradition, that is, through the handing down, through an unbroken line of successors, of the principle established in the beginning. *To stay in this unbroken line of successors meant in Rome to be in authority*...[23]

Corresponding to the meaning—if not the practice—of authority, in America to act *according to* the Constitution, to act *intra vires*, was to be in authority, the ongoing interpretation and *re*interpretation of legitimate *vires* being the role—the *only* role—reserved for the Supreme Court.[24] If this seems a rather banal position, we shall come to see its significance when, in sections III. and IV., we turn our attention to the criticisms which Arendt levelled at the Court in two specific instances. Before we do so, however, we must delve deeper into the nature of the Court and its authority.

II. POWERLESS BUT LASTING JUDGES

Taking Federalist number 78 as the basis for the claim that power and authority were kept separate by the Founding Fathers,[25] Arendt emphasised two features of the Supreme Court which bound it to the latter. 'Institutionally,' she said, 'it is [i] lack of power, combined with [ii] permanence of office, which signals that the true seat of authority in the American Republic is the Supreme Court'.[26] Allow us, then, to consider each of these features in turn.

The first—lack of power—speaks to the difficulty of producing in a constitutional court those matters which Arendt saw as being the two conditions of power: a space of appearance, and a common world.[27] To constitute a space of appearance, an institution should allow a plurality to appear, to speak, to act and to be preserved *qua* plurality. Typically, a court does not constitute such a space, and this for intrinsic reasons. First, in most actions before the court there stand only two actors, who face each other in an adversarial, zero-sum game with no (or limited) space for resolution *between* the parties. Secondly, in contemporary practice those two parties are, more often than not, constituted by the government on the one side and another (legal or physical) person on the other.[28] Thirdly, restrictive rules on standing mean that the latter must (generally) have suffered some harm in order to bring a claim against the former; third party and

[23] OR 201 (emphasis added).

[24] Woodrow Wilson, as quoted in OR 200.

[25] This is the passage quoted by Arendt: '[T]he majesty of national authority must be manifested through the medium of the courts of justice' because the judiciary branch, possessing 'neither Force or Will but merely judgment ... was beyond comparison the weakest of the three departments of power' (*ibid*).

[26] *Ibid*.

[27] HC 58. On the space of appearance, see J van der Walt, ch 3 of this volume.

[28] This theme resonates in J Waldron, *Law and Disagreement* (Oxford, Oxford University Press, 1999).

public interest standing, where the plaintiff represents a broader plurality, has actively been discouraged by the court: 'judicial power,' as the traditional reading has it, 'exists only to redress or otherwise to protect against injury to the complaining party'.[29] Thus, putting the three together, judicial review is often painted as a forum for the expression of what Berlin has famously called 'negative freedom'[30]: the protection of individual, private rights vis-à-vis the weight of the (presumably interfering) federal government.[31] For Arendt, freedom meant something more than this. Hers was an active and unashamedly demanding freedom: it meant, she said, 'the "right to be a participator in government", or it meant nothing'.[32]

Because of its powerlessness, political freedom—at least as Arendt saw it here—*could not* be exercised by a constitutional court. Thus, in a brief passage of *What is Authority?*, Arendt flirts with Montesquieu's definition of judicial power (a definition which clearly influenced the Founding Fathers themselves), approving his dictum that judicial power was 'somehow nil' and yet at the same time the highest authority.[33] Montesquieu's definition of the judiciary was, of course, tied to a specific institutional setting: his interpretation of the English Constitution, which—he said—guaranteed that judges were simply '*le bouche de la loi*'. Taking from this famous passage support for her belief that the authority of a constitutional court was to be measured in the respect and reverence held for the institution itself, and not from its ability to command, persuade or coerce, one of Arendt's key insights into the separation of constitutional powers lies in her distinction between constitutional judgments and their enforcement. Lacking the means to enforce its decisions—and in so doing to open up the possibility of a new beginning (and we shall return to this theme in section IV.)—the Court must restrict itself to decisions which authoritatively guide the other branches of government. In other words, when posed a constitutional question, the range of possible answers available to the Court were narrowed: the Court had a duty to interpret the Constitution, but could go no further.

The second feature of the Court, permanence of office, corresponds to the lifetime appointments of its judges; a feature which reveals the peculiar connection between the Court and 'constitutional time'. The Founding Fathers were particularly attentive to the importance of periodic constitutional renewal as a bulwark against political corruption; so it is that both the composition of Congress (the legislative branch) and the Presidency (the executive branch) are renewed and refreshed according to staggered political terms. However, this feature does not apply to the Supreme Court, whose judges are appointed for their lifetime. Even if justices are often appointed along political lines, and through a political process,

[29] *Warth v Seldin* 422 US 490 (1975) 499. For a recent reaffirmation of the restrictive test, see Justice Scalia's opinion in *Vermont Agency of Natural Resources v United States ex rel Stevens* 529 US 765 (2000).

[30] I Berlin, *Two Concepts of Liberty* (Oxford, Clarendon Press, 1958).

[31] OR 143.

[32] *Ibid* 218.

[33] WiA? 122.

lifetime appointments seem to achieve at least two things. First, they place the Court on a different temporal plane from the legislature and the executive. In that respect, and in keeping with Arendt's Roman understanding of authority, it seems that it was the task of the Supreme Court to solve the riddle of action and permanence, of foundation and preservation. Secondly, whilst a judge's appointment is the product of a political process, and therefore possibly exposed to the prevailing political winds at that time, her lifetime appointment transcends the moment of her appointment, elevating her (in theory, at least) to a degree of independence from the constant flux of political opinions. What, then, can we glean from these conceptual (the meaning and implications of the Court being the seat of authority) and institutional (lack of power, lifetime appointments) features, and—in particular—how do they help us explain the awe in which that institution is held?

Among American constitutional lawyers, Paul Kahn has proposed a political-theological explanation of just why it is that Supreme Court decisions are obeyed, both by the people and by the other political branches, even in controversial cases such as *Bush v Gore*.[34] Kahn's 'constitutional theology' transfers the body of the sovereign to the institutional body of the Supreme Court. This is plausible, he says, because the Supreme Court testifies with its activity to the sacredness of the act of foundation. In other words, the Supreme Court is the second of the 'two bodies of the king',[35] the other one being the mystic body of the revolutionary people. In this model, the Supreme Court gives voice to the sovereign people because the source of its *charisma* comes from the revolutionary past. Grounded in the idea of the citizen's revolutionary willingness to sacrifice herself for the polity, Kahn's explanation is one which justifies the authority of the Supreme Court in terms of the citizens' faith.[36] In other words, according to Kahn's theological reading, the authority of the Court does not rely on a rational conception of judgment and interpretation, but on the sacredness that surrounds the highest judicial body. In this sense, 'the voice of the Court is the voice of the People'.[37] Arendt's conception of authority is not an act of faith, however. She does not demand the sacrifice of the citizens' judgment even to perverse decisions from the Court. For Arendt—*contra* the implications of Cohen and Arato's interpretation that Arendt's is a 'constitution of judges'—the authority of the Court is not a given. Quite the opposite, it is an 'authority [that] implies an obedience in which men retain their freedom'.[38] Thus, in the next sections of this essay we shall see that for Arendt

[34] 531 US 98 (2000). On this contested decision see, among several publications, B Ackerman (ed), *Bush v Gore. The Question of Legitimacy* (New Haven, Yale University Press, 2002); R Dworkin (ed), *A Badly Flawed Election* (New York, New Press, 2002).

[35] The quotation is from E Kantorowicz, *The King's Two Bodies* (Princeton, NJ, Princeton University Press, 1957).

[36] P Kahn, *Putting Liberalism in Its Place* (Princeton, NJ, Princeton University Press, 2005).

[37] P Kahn, *Political Theology: Four New Chapters on the Concept of Sovereignty* (New York, Columbia University Press, 2011) 85.

[38] WiA? 93.

it has been possible for the Court to *lose* its authority, both by going beyond interpretation and attempting to engineer social change ('III. Reflections on Little Rock'), and, in another instance, by forgoing its duty of interpretation altogether ('IV. Towards Civil Disobedience').

III. REFLECTIONS ON LITTLE ROCK

For its rebuke of the Supreme Court's seemingly progressive judgments in the school desegregation cases *Brown v Board of Education*[39] and *Cooper v Aaron*,[40] 'Reflections on Little Rock' counts amongst Arendt's more controversial pieces. Indeed, so stinging was the criticism of the essay that she felt compelled to publish a defence of her position: a direct response to two critics in particular—David Spitz and Melvin Tummin—in which she claimed that her original article 'was not understood in the terms [that she] wrote it'.[41] The liberal line of attack was clear: here was Arendt—purveyor of the infamous 'social question'[42]—effectively denying the authority of federal intervention where it was aimed at enforcing racial integration. Yet, as we shall see, it was not—for Arendt—the Supreme Court's jurisdiction which was the problem here: she was clear that there *was* a constitutional question to be asked, and capable of being given a judicial answer. What Arendt found so troubling was, rather, the overreach of the Court in going *beyond* that question, '[f]or the crucial point to remember'—and this, she believed, the Supreme Court had not—'is that it is not the social custom of segregation that is unconstitutional, but its *legal enforcement*'.[43] In order to understand this, and in so doing to understand 'Reflections on Little Rock' in the terms that she wrote it, let us begin with an example used by Arendt herself.

For Arendt, 'the right to marry whoever one wishes is an elementary human right': more so, even, than the right to sit where one pleases on a bus, or—at issue in *Brown* and *Cooper*—to attend an integrated school. Had Southern anti-miscegenation laws, those most striking violations of the principles of equality and citizenship, been brought to the attention of the Supreme Court, Arendt felt sure of two things: first, that the Court would (and ought to) hold those laws to be unconstitutional; secondly, that the Court would not (and ought not to) *enforce* mixed marriages. To do so, she believed, would go far beyond the Court's authority to *interpret* the Constitution, and would in effect amount to an exercise in social engineering requiring persuasion or, more likely, coercion.[44] Allow us, then, to extend this to the issues at stake in *Brown* and *Cooper*.

39 347 US 483 (1954).

40 358 US 1 (1958).

41 H Arendt, 'Reflections on Little Rock' in P Baehr (ed), *The Portable Hannah Arendt* (London/New York, Penguin, 2000) 243 (hereafter 'RLR').

42 Cf E Christodoulidis and A Schaap, ch 5 of this volume.

43 RLR 236.

44 *Ibid.*

For Arendt, it would have been perfectly within the authority of the Court to determine that the laws which entrenched racial segregation within the public school system amounted to unlawful violations of the 14th Amendment. What she found so objectionable in these cases, however, was that by *enforcing* integration the Court had forgotten 'principle[s] … uppermost in the minds of the founders of the Republic'. First, she said, the decisions read too much into the principle of equality, taking it from its proper place, the political realm, and transposing it into the social realm, where discrimination was justifiable (if not always justified).[45] The dangers of doing so were clear to see in the iconic images of the time: black children being transported to newly-integrated schools amid 'jeering and grimacing' mobs.[46] It would seem that for Arendt (and perhaps in the reaction of the Southerners we can see some evidence of this), to remove the *legal enforcement* of segregation was to remove the barriers to a voluntary (and therefore deeper?) social integration; on the other hand, to *enforce desegregation* seemed to erect obstacles to that end by bringing to the surface the anger and frustrations of those touched by the decision. Secondly, Arendt was concerned by the underlying conflict between the Federal Government and the Southern states. Decisions such as *Brown* and *Cooper*, in her view, evidenced something of a bias in favour of the Federal Government which went beyond the text of the Constitution itself. Because, for Arendt, power generates more power when it is dispersed, it followed that the states' rights had to be at least preserved. Thus, by exercising a centripetal role, the Supreme Court, as she saw it at least, was no longer *interpreting* the Constitution but (in the sphere of education) *changing* the Constitution: appropriating for the Federal Government new powers over education, whilst with the same move disregarding the principle (captured by the first four articles of the Constitution) that the American political system is 'strengthened by the division of power'.[47]

The consequence of the Court's overreach—its going beyond the bounds of interpretation—was no less than the loss of its defining characteristic: authority. The authority of the Court, we recall, meant for Arendt an 'unquestioning respect' for its decisions. This she distinguished from power and action, which depended upon *persuasion*, and from violence, which depended upon *coercion*. That the authority of the Court had been lost could be seen, then, in two moments. First, Arendt herself pointed to the fact that the grounds for respecting the Court's decision clearly *were* questioned. Thus she took as support for her argument the results of public opinion polls which showed not only that 92 per cent of Virginians were opposed to integration, not only that 65 per cent were willing to forgo public education in light of integration, but, and this is the point, that 79 per cent denied *any obligation* to accept the Supreme Court decisions as

[45] M Canovan, *Hannah Arendt: A Reinterpretation of Her Political Thought* (Cambridge, Cambridge University Press, 1992) 243.
[46] RLR 236.
[47] *Ibid* 243.

binding.[48] Secondly, if Arendt's conception of authority was one distinguished from violence, then we must add that the *need* of the Federal Government to resort to coercion—by deploying the military to secure the ends of integration—was itself evidence of the Court's *loss* of authority. It was the very fact that respect for those decisions had been questioned—that integration would not happen *as result of the decision itself*—which required the Eisenhower Administration to act with such force.

IV. TOWARDS CIVIL DISOBEDIENCE

If Arendt found 'most startling'[49] the Court's over-reach in cases such as *Cooper* and *Brown*, it was (less paradoxically than it may seem) the *reluctance* of the judicial branch to exercise its authority which led Arendt, finally, to lose faith in the very institution of judicial review (and, therefore—if she ever had supported it-the constitution of judges). So, when she said that '[t]he establishment of civil disobedience among our political institutions might be the best possible remedy for [the] *ultimate failure* of judicial review,' she did so against the backdrop of the hugely controversial Vietnam war, and the many and varied attempts by citizens of the United States to challenge the legality of that war in the court room.[50] Judicial review, she believed, had 'failed' because, by the Court's response to these challenges, 'the sovereignty principle and the reason of state doctrine [had been] permitted to filter back, as it were, into a system of government which denies them'.[51] In other words, she believed that by its *refusal* to ask questions of the legality and constitutionality of the war, the judiciary—that separate and independent guardian of the Constitution—had failed to exercise its constitutional role, that is, authoritatively to interpret the Constitution.[52] Let us explain: at the heart of Arendt's criticism lies what she perceived to be the Court's use of 'the political question doctrine' to deny *certiorari* to the Vietnam cases. The very existence of the doctrine is itself contested,[53] whilst it has been argued that the trend in contemporary jurisprudence is a shift away from the doctrine[54] and

48 *Ibid* 235.

49 *Ibid.*

50 H Arendt, 'Civil Disobedience', in H Arendt, *Crises of the Republic* (New York, Harcourt Brace, 1972) 101 (hereafter CD).

51 *Ibid* 100.

52 *Ibid* 100–02. On the difference between civil disobedience and judicial review, see W Smith, ch 7 of this volume.

53 L Henkin, 'Is There a "Political Question" Doctrine?' (1976) 85 *The Yale Law Journal* 597.

54 See, eg, M Tushnet, 'Law and Prudence in the Law of Justiciability: The Transformation and Disappearance of the Political Question Doctrine' (2002) 80 *North Carolina Law Review* 1203. Most notably, in modern times, the doctrine has been challenged by the decision of the Supreme Court in the infamous case of *Bush v Gore*. See, eg, R Hirschl, 'Resituating the Judicialization of Politics: Bush v. Gore as a Global Trend' (2002) 15 *Canadian Journal of Law & Jurisprudence* 191.

towards what Ran Hirschl has called 'juristocracy'.[55] At the time of writing, however, Arendt was in no doubt that this doctrine, according to which certain acts of the two other branches of government, the legislative and the executive, 'are not reviewable by the courts',[56] was a corruption of the American Constitution and not, as it has otherwise been defended, a cornerstone of the separation of powers.

In a provocative and influential article which appeared in a 1976 edition of *The Yale Law Journal*, Louis Henkin suggested that the 'political question doctrine' could be thought of in two ways. 'That there are political questions—issues to be resolved and decisions to be made by the political branches of government and not by the courts—is,' he said, 'axiomatic in a system of constitutional government built on the separation of powers'.[57] In one respect, the 'political question doctrine' applied by the courts might take the shape of 'the ordinary respect of the courts for the political domain'.[58] In other words, if competence for a particular matter has been committed by the Constitution to the executive or legislative branch of government then, so long as the subsequent actions of that branch remain *intra vires*, the courts should recognise and respect that fact by refusing itself the jurisdiction to review those acts. Such questions, said Henkin, are the normal course of constitutional government, and so stand in no need of particular doctrinal protection. However, '[a] more meaningful political question doctrine,' in Henkin's view, 'implies something more and different: that some issues which prima facie and by usual criteria would seem to be for the courts, will not be decided by them but, extra-ordinarily, left for political decision.' It was *this* doctrine that was, by Henkin's own admission, invoked in his day 'to deny judicial review of constitutional issues raised by our national misfortunes associated with Vietnam'.[59] When it was argued before the courts that the President had acted *ultra vires* by engaging in a war not declared by Congress, several[60] held that questions of war and peace, fitting into the broad spectrum of international relations, were political questions best answered elsewhere. Thus, when Robert Luftig, a private in the US Army, sought to challenge his pending transfer to Vietnam on the basis of the war's illegality and unconstitutionality, an appellate court told him:

> It is difficult to think of an area less suited for judicial action than that into which the appellant would have us intrude. The fundamental division of authority and power established by the Constitution precludes judges from overseeing the conduct of foreign

[55] R Hirschl, *Towards Juristocracy: The Origins and Consequence of the New Constitutionalism* (Cambridge, Mass, and London, England, Harvard University Press, 2004).

[56] CD 100.

[57] Henkin, above n 53, 597.

[58] *Ibid* 598.

[59] *Ibid* 599.

[60] The constitutionality of the Vietnam War was challenged in over 70 cases.

> policy or the use of and disposition of military power; these matters are plainly the exclusive province of Congress and the Executive.[61]

On the face of it, the court's reasoning seems (at least) justifiable. As Lon Fuller has said, there are some disputes, some decisions, which by their very nature are not suited to adjudication in the court room.[62] By invoking the political question doctrine in the Vietnam cases, the courts seemed to be saying that both Congress and the Executive were better placed to determine questions of foreign policy. They had greater expertise, they were democratically accountable for those questions of high politics, and they had access to information, such as intelligence reports, which were not available to the judges. This is all well and good, but for the fact that Robert Luftig had not *asked* the courts to oversee the conduct of US foreign policy. Rather, the question which he had put to the courts was subtly different and, *prima facie*, certainly justiciable: '[H]as the Executive branch of government exceeded its constitutional powers by committing American troops to a war in Vietnam without the requisite declaration of war by Congress?'[63]

By invoking the 'political question doctrine' to escape even this question, a question of interpretation—that is to say, the interpretation of constitutional *vires*—the courts had not only left individual citizens without a judicial remedy against (the potential) abuse of power by the executive, but, as Michael Malakoff has said, they had also made 'a binding decision on justiciability which in effect holds that federal courts will *never* question the President's authority to wage war'.[64] It was then *this* evasion which Arendt found so damning when she penned her essay on civil disobedience. Judicial review had failed, in her mind, because the Court had consciously neglected to interpret the Constitution. The Court, she seemed to believe, feared the loss of authority—its defining characteristic—should it have declared the conflict unconstitutional, only for war be waged regardless:

> Whatever the theory, the facts of the matter suggest that precisely in crucial issues the Supreme Court has no more power than an international court: both are unable to enforce decisions that would hurt decisively the interests of sovereign states and both know that their authority depends on prudence, that is, in not raising issues or making decisions that cannot be enforced.[65]

Arendt's observation, however, was that the Court nevertheless suffered an even more striking loss of authority. If the authority of the Supreme Court lay in its duty of interpretation—if this was how the Court ensured that 'the beginning … is

[61] *Luftig v McNamara* 373 F 2d 664 (DC Cir 1967), 665–66. *Certiorari* was subsequently denied by the Supreme Court, 389 US 934 (1967).
[62] L Fuller, 'The Forms and Limits of Adjudication' (1978) 92 *Harvard Law Review* 353.
[63] M Malakoff, 'The Political Question and the Vietnam Conflict' (1969-70) 31 *University of Pittsburgh Law Review* 505.
[64] *Ibid* 513.
[65] CD 100–01.

remembered whenever constitutional questions come into play'[66]—then a loss of authority was the inevitable result where it elected to *forgo* that duty. Nowhere was this loss of authority more clear than in the eruption of civil disobedience which followed. Civil disobedience, Arendt believed, was a predictable result because the Constitution—as (not) interpreted by the Court—had left nowhere (no space of appearance) for those citizens to turn. Arendt, in other words, had faced in 'Civil Disobedience', and in her analysis of the 'political question doctrine', the problem of political exclusion—for this was precisely the effect of decisions such as *Luftig*—and discovered that by that exclusion, those same citizens had been *included* in the 'deliberative outcomes' of those (here the executive and judicial branches) who presumed to speak for the American people,[67] be that by the deployment in war of members of the armed services, or by the unquestioning obedience demanded of the citizens as a whole; by the engineering, it would seem, of their tacit consent and the rendering impotent of the power of dissent.

In our reading of Arendt's views on the role of the Supreme Court, there is then (despite, perhaps, first appearances) in fact a line of continuity which connects chapter five of *On Revolution*, through her 'Reflections on Little Rock' and finally to 'Civil Disobedience'. The normative aspect in each of these three works remains constant: that the role of the Court is a narrow, albeit important one, to interpret the Constitution; and that the discharge of this function was the very source of its authority. Thus, when the Court exceeded that role (Little Rock), or neglected it (*Luftig*), Arendt could not help but see in this a resulting *loss* of authority.

V. CONCLUDING REMARKS

In one sense, the aim of this essay has been limited in scope and ambition: to disprove the thesis put by Arato and Cohen that in chapter five of *On Revolution* Arendt subscribes to a 'constitution of judges'. By looking beyond that text to her particular reflections on the Court's over-reach in *Cooper*, as well as to its under-reach in those cases such as *Luftig*, we can see that for Arendt the proper place of the Supreme Court was a much more nuanced one: narrower in the sense that Court's role was restricted to one of constitutional interpretation, yet no less significant for that. As we see in 'Reflections on Little Rock', the Court could *only* interpret: it could not go further and engineer (even progressive) social change, lest it surrender its defining and legitimating characteristic—authority—in so doing. On the other hand, when we turn to 'Civil Disobedience', and the use of

[66] J Frank, *Constituent Moments: Enacting the People in Postrevolutionary America* (Durham, NC, Duke University Press, 2010) 56.

[67] On this theme, see J Bohman, 'The Moral Costs of Political Pluralism: The Dilemmas of Difference and Equality in Arendt's "Reflections on Little Rock"' in L May and J Kohn (eds), *Hannah Arendt: Twenty Years Later* (Cambridge, Mass, and London, England, The MIT Press, 1996) 53, 64.

the political question doctrine to *evade* its duty of interpretation, we see that whilst the Court may *only* interpret, it *must* interpret—even where interpretation brings before the judiciary questions of war and peace.

Thus, whereas *prima facie* there might appear to be something of a disconnect between the 'magisterial aura' bestowed upon the Supreme Court in *On Revolution* and the sharp criticisms which she reserved for that institution in 'Reflections on Little Rock' and 'Civil Disobedience', it is our view that reading Arendt's take on the Supreme Court in this way—to take from her the interconnectedness of the Court's authority with the *performance* of its duty of interpretation—one can see that, in fact, there is a consistent thread which runs through those three texts. What was considered 'magisterial' in *On Revolution* was not the institution of the Supreme Court itself, but the founding moment in which the American republic was given birth. The unquestioning recognition which was given to the Court (the very hallmark of Arendt's conception of authority) was unquestioned *only in so far as* that branch could be seen to interpret that moment anew. Indeed, the consistency with which she held that view shines through an oft-neglected passage of 'Civil Disobedience' which we shall quote at length, first, because it reinforces what has been the thrust of our argument, but, secondly, because it reveals, in our view, an insight of considerable relevance to contemporary constitutional discourse: the *limits* of juridification:

> Because of the unprecedented rate of change in our time and because of the challenge that change poses to the legal order—from the side of the government ... as well as from the side of disobedient citizens—it is now widely held that changes can be effected by law, as distinguished from the earlier notion that 'legal action [that is Supreme Court decisions] can influence ways of living'. Both opinions seem to me to be based on an error about what the law can achieve and what it cannot. The law can indeed stabilize and legalize change once it has occurred, but the change itself is always the result of extra-legal action.[68]

In the remainder of this Part of this volume, we shall leave it to William Smith and Kari Palonen to explore the possible sites in which such action might take place.

[68] CD 80.

7

A Constitutional Niche for Civil Disobedience? Reflections on Arendt*

WILLIAM SMITH

IN HIS INSIGHTFUL critique of Hannah Arendt's political philosophy, George Kateb expresses surprise at her inclination to affirm, even *celebrate*, the phenomenon of civil disobedience.[1] Arendt's inclination to commend this form of political protest can be explained only in part by her enthusiasm for its then most prominent practitioners, the civil rights and student movements. As Kateb reminds us, 'not all student activism was civilly disobedient; thus to take satisfaction in activism need not have extended to celebrating civil disobedience'.[2] Although her admiration for these movements doubtless influenced her judgement, Arendt appears to have discerned merit in the specific *modus operandi* of the civilly disobedient citizen. Hence her startling claim that 'it would be an event of great significance to find a constitutional niche for civil disobedience—of no less significance, perhaps, than the event of the founding of the *constitutio libertatis*, nearly two hundred years ago'.[3]

The fact that Arendt's enthusiasm for civil disobedience extends to a recommendation that it be accorded a 'constitutional niche' is indeed surprising. To be sure, several writers—notably John Rawls and Jürgen Habermas—have argued that civil disobedience is compatible with constitutional government. On the issue of how the State should respond to civilly disobedient minorities, however, these authors are content to advocate tolerant attitudes and a reduction or suspension of legal sanctions.[4] Arendt, by contrast, argues that civilly disobedient citizens should

* A first version of this essay was published as 'Reclaiming the Revolutionary Spirit: Arendt on Civil Disobedience' (2010) 9 *European Journal of Political Theory* 149.

[1] G Kateb, *Hannah Arendt: Politics, Conscience, Evil* (Oxford, Martin Robertson, 1984) 98. Civil disobedience is defined here as public, non-violent and illegal protest, carried out in support of political change.

[2] *Ibid* 98–99.

[3] H Arendt, 'Civil Disobedience', in *Crises of the Republic* (New York, Harcourt Brace Jovanovich, 1972) 49–102, 83–84. Citations to this essay will henceforth appear in the text with the abbreviation '*CD*'.

[4] J Rawls, *A Theory of Justice: Revised Edition* (Oxford, Oxford University Press, 1999) 339; J Habermas, 'Civil Disobedience: Litmus Test for the Democratic Constitutional State' (1985) 30 *Berkeley Journal of Sociology* 95, 106; see also D Lefkowitz, 'On a Moral Right to Civil Disobedience'

be given access to the very heart of law-making. In the context of the United States, she recommends that representatives of civilly disobedient minorities be invited to 'influence and assist Congress by means of persuasion, qualified opinion, and the numbers of their constituents' (*CD* 101). This proposal effectively to *institutionalise* civil disobedience—to take it off the streets and into government—is unprecedented within political theory. For this reason, it arguably deserves more attention than it has hitherto received in either the contemporary literature on civil disobedience or the extensive critical literature on Arendt's political philosophy.[5]

The aim of this essay is to explore and ultimately to defend Arendt's admittedly strange claim that the constitutional State should institutionalise civil disobedience. In the first section, I argue that the proposal to institutionalise civil disobedience follows from Arendt's peculiar interpretation of this mode of protest. She sees it as an unexpected yet welcome echo of the 'revolutionary spirit' that accompanied the foundation of the American republic. By embedding civil disobedience within the institutional fabric of the republic, Arendt hopes to remedy the historical tragedy of a revolution that, notwithstanding its other triumphs, failed to nourish and sustain the spirit that drove it. In the second section, I move from a reconstruction of Arendt's argument to a critical appraisal of the proposal itself. The principal value of the proposal, I suggest, is that it improves upon more familiar liberal and democratic arguments about how the constitutional State should respond to civilly disobedient citizens. At the same time, I argue that the proposal can be presented as compatible with liberal and democratic theories, provided that the grounds for it are detached from the more controversial aspects of Arendt's conception of political action. In the third section, I draw the discussion to a close by addressing several objections that might be raised against the claim that civil disobedience should be accorded a constitutional niche.

I. CIVIL DISOBEDIENCE AND THE REVOLUTIONARY SPIRIT

Given her diagnosis of civil disobedience as a resolutely political phenomenon, it is unsurprising that Arendt enjoins her readers to pursue a 'political approach to the problem' (*CD* 99). The fact that her preferred approach involves institutionalising civil disobedience, however, is more surprising. This section reconstructs

(2007) 117 *Ethics* 202, 218–23; K Brownlee, 'The Communicative Aspects of Civil Disobedience and Lawful Punishment' (2007) 1 *Criminal Law and Philosophy* 179, 189–91.

[5] Despite the huge critical literature on Arendt, her ideas on civil disobedience have seldom received in-depth analysis. Brief but helpful discussions may be found in D Villa, *Arendt and Heidegger: The Fate of the Political* (Princeton, NJ, Princeton University Press, 1996) 36–37; JC Isaac, 'Situating Hannah Arendt on Action and Politics' (1993) 21 *Political Theory* 534, 538; M Canovan, *Hannah Arendt: A Reinterpretation of Her Political Thought* (Cambridge, Cambridge University Press, 1992) 182–84 and 216–18; J Ring, 'The Pariah as Hero: Hannah Arendt's Political Actor' (1991) 19 *Political Theory* 433, 449. More detailed appraisals may be found in Kateb, *Hannah Arendt*, above n 1, and JL Cohen and A Arato, *Civil Society and Political Theory* (Cambridge, Mass, The MIT Press, 1992) 593–99.

the reasons behind her proposal by, first, showing how she understands civil disobedience as a political mode of action, secondly, examining how she associates civil disobedience with a particular interpretation of the spirit of American law and thirdly, placing her proposal within her broader reconstruction of the revolutionary tradition.

A. Civil Disobedience, Conscience and Law

A theme that runs throughout Arendt's essay on civil disobedience is that lawyers typically fail to grasp its true meaning: 'whenever the jurists attempt to justify the civil disobedient on moral and legal grounds, they construe his case in the image of either the conscientious objector or the man who tests the constitutionality of statute' (*CD* 55). She rejects these characterisations of civil disobedience as 'moral' (conscientious objection) or 'legal' (constitutional testing) in favour of a more political portrayal.

Conscientious objection is, for Arendt, an 'unpolitical' act, a potentially commendable but ultimately subjective and, in a sense, self-interested protest (*CD* 62).[6] This assessment stems from her analysis of conscience as an internal voice—a party to a 'soundless dialogue between me and myself'—whose counsels we must heed in order to achieve inner harmony (*CD* 63). She claims that our counsels of conscience 'are always expressed in purely subjective statements', which resist inclusion in the give and take of opinions in the public realm (*CD* 62). Our conscientious convictions 'cannot be generalized' because 'what I cannot live with may not bother another man's conscience' (*CD* 64). Conscience is more interested in the self than the world; it calls on us to disassociate ourselves from injustice, rather than to turn all our attention towards the removal of injustice from the world (*CD* 60–61).

Civil disobedience differs from conscientious objection because it is orientated towards the public realm. Its political character is illustrated by its mode of organisation. Civilly disobedient citizens are 'organized minorities, bound together by common opinion, rather than by common interest, and the decision to take a stand against the government's policies' (*CD* 56). As a member of a group, the dissenting citizen no longer relies on conscience but on a 'common opinion' forged through deliberation with her comrades: 'their concerted action springs from an agreement with each other, and it is this agreement that lends credence and conviction to their opinion' (*CD* 56). Such common opinions can be supported through beliefs that may, in principle, be debated, shared or criticised by others. Civil disobedience is also political in terms of its agenda. It is, in Arendt's account, a worldly mode of protest, driven by a heightened feeling or care for

[6] M Passerin D'Entrèves, *The Political Philosophy of Hannah Arendt* (London, Routledge, 1994) 148–51.

the world.[7] Its practitioners have an active interest in what goes on within the world and, crucially, a willingness to safeguard its durability and integrity. Civilly disobedient minorities aim to defend and develop the stable worldly structures that house political life. This ethos of worldliness resonates with Arendt's more general conception of political activity. As her many interpreters have pointed out, political activity is, for her, essentially 'self-contained', orientated towards the 'creation and preservation of the public sphere'.[8] In the civil disobedience carried out by civil rights and student activists, Arendt discerned an underlying commitment to 'protect' and 'perfect' the American republic.[9] Its associative nature, coupled with its ethos of worldliness, renders civil disobedience a political activity far removed from the individual acts of non-compliance carried out by conscientious objectors.

Constitutional testing, by contrast, is less self-interested than conscientious objection, but is still categorised by Arendt as unpolitical. The constitutional tester appeals to the legal system to rule on the validity of a particular law or policy. The legal system, according to Arendt, is part of the 'framework of stability' that allows mankind to survive 'the flux of change' (*CD* 79). The 'stabilizing' function of law means that it takes on a restraining and conservative character, particularly in times of turmoil and change. Although law can 'influence' ways of living, it cannot itself 'effect' or initiate change: 'the law can indeed stabilize and legalize change once it has occurred, but the change itself is always the result of extralegal action' (*CD* 80). Such 'extralegal action' takes place not in the judicial sphere, the site of constitutional testing, but in the political realm.

Civil disobedience can share a superficial similarity with constitutional testing, insofar as both may be employed as part of an orchestrated campaign against allegedly unconstitutional statutes (*CD* 74). Civil disobedience differs from constitutional testing, though, because it typically involves the violation of valid laws, such as 'traffic regulations', symbolically to contest other acts of government (*CD* 56). They also differ in their respective functions; while civil disobedience may be employed to uphold established constitutional norms, it can also adopt a more proactive complexion by initiating 'necessary and desirable change' (*CD* 75). This instigation of *change*, in the sense of promoting innovations in law and policy and, more importantly for Arendt, changing the nature and complexion of public opinion, reveals the political character of civil disobedience against the essentially juridical nature of constitutional testing. The intended audience of an act of civil disobedience is not primarily, or at least not solely, the legal system, but the political community as a whole. Through initiating changes in public opinion, civil disobedience creates the climate within which legal institutions decide whether to hear cases against the constitutionality of statute (*CD* 80). The initiatory function of civil

[7] On the idea of 'worldliness', see W Smith, 'Cosmopolitan Citizenship: Virtue, Irony and Worldliness' (2007) 10 *European Journal of Social Theory* 37.

[8] Villa, above n 5, 36–37.

[9] Kateb, above n 1, 21.

disobedience perhaps explains why Arendt is unwilling to follow the convention of assuming a hard-and-fast distinction between it and revolution: 'the civil disobedient shares with the revolutionary the wish "to change the world", and the changes he wishes to accomplish can be drastic indeed' (*CD* 77). Civilly disobedient citizens, with their capacity to instigate change, enjoy an affinity with the revolutionary spirit that undermines any attempt at neat conceptual separations.[10]

B. Civil Disobedience, Consent and the Republic

Although she does not wish to sever the tie between civil disobedience and the revolutionary spirit, Arendt clearly believes that the former can be compatible with established institutions of government. She pursues this insight in the context of the United States through arguing that civil disobedience, despite its illegality, is compatible with the 'spirit' of the laws (*CD* 83). And on the basis of this compatibility, she argues that the republic should find 'a recognized niche for civil disobedience in [its] institutions of government' (*CD* 99).

According to Arendt, 'consent, not in the very old sense of mere acquiescence, with its distinction between rule over willing subjects and rule over unwilling ones, but in the sense of active support and continuing participation in all matters of public interest, is the spirit of American law' (*CD* 85). Consent is identified as the outcome of a social contract; the contract is not 'vertical', as one between rulers and ruled, but 'horizontal', as one between 'all individual members' of society (*CD* 86). The 'moral content' of this contract is the 'promise' of all parties to abide by its terms; in so doing, each party gives a 'reliable assurance as to his future conduct' (*CD* 92).[11] Arendt concedes that the idea of consent may be dismissed as a 'fiction' both 'legally and historically', but not, she insists, 'existentially and theoretically' (*CD* 87). The familiar thought here is that 'tacit consent' is a presupposition of our survival in the world: 'a kind of consent is implied in every newborn's factual situation; namely, a kind of conformity to the rules under which the great game of the world is played in the particular group to which he belongs by birth' (*CD* 88). This consent can be voluntary only if *dissent* is a 'legal and *de facto* possibility'. As she puts it, 'dissent implies consent, and is the hallmark of free government; one who knows that he may dissent knows also that he somehow consents when he does not dissent' (*CD* 88).

[10] M Reinhardt, *The Art of Being Free: Taking Liberties with Tocqueville, Marx, and Arendt* (London, Cornell University Press, 1997) 163.

[11] On the centrality of promising to Arendt's view of politics, see A Keenan, 'Promises, Promises: The Abyss of Freedom and the Loss of the Political in the Work of Hannah Arendt' (1994) 22 *Political Theory* 297; and B Honig, 'Declarations of Independence: Arendt and Derrida on the Problem of Founding a Republic' (1991) 85 *American Political Science Review* 97, 103–04.

Civil disobedience is compatible with this interpretation of consent as 'active participation'. Although a general agreement to abide by the law is an outcome of the social contract, any 'promise' to do so is not immutable. According to Arendt, 'we are bound to keep our promises provided that no unexpected circumstances arise and provided that the mutuality inherent in all promises is not broken' (*CD* 93). This formulation suggests that any promise or obligation to obey may, at least in certain circumstances, cease to be binding. In fact, there appear to be two such circumstances. First, civil disobedience may be a legitimate response to illegal or unconstitutional acts of government; this 'failure of the established authorities to keep to the original conditions' violates the 'inherent mutuality of promises' and so releases citizens from their obligation to obey the law (*CD* 93). Secondly, civil disobedience may be a legitimate response to the gradual erosion of meaningful opportunities for citizens actively to participate in public affairs. Arendt tells us that civil disobedience occurs 'when a significant number of citizens have become convinced … that the normal channels of change no longer function and grievances will not be heard or acted upon' (*CD* 74). It is a response to a 'crisis' in a representative government that has 'lost, in the course of time, all institutions that permitted the citizens' actual participation' (*CD* 89). In such circumstances, civil disobedients appeal to the principles of 'consent and the right to dissent' that were the original inspiration behind the 'art of associating together' in America (*CD* 94).

Given this continuity between civil disobedience and the spirit of its laws, Arendt insists that the republic should make every effort to accommodate it. She quickly rejects the idea that civil disobedience could be legalised, arguing that the conceptual and practical difficulties involved in attempting to offer legal justifications for illegal acts are 'prohibitive'. Instead she articulates 'a political approach', by comparing the situation of civilly disobedient minorities with that of 'special interest' and 'pressure' groups. These groups are similar to civilly disobedient citizens in that they are organised minorities; they differ, though, in that special interest and pressure groups enjoy a more entrenched and vocal place in public life. Through their representatives, 'registered lobbyists', these groups 'are permitted to influence and "assist" Congress by means of persuasion, qualified opinion, and the numbers of their constituents' (*CD* 101). Arendt's proposal is that civilly disobedient minorities should be treated in the same way:

> These minorities of opinion would thus be able to establish themselves as a power that is not only 'seen from afar' during demonstrations and other dramatizations of their viewpoint, but is always present and to be reckoned with in the daily business of government. (*CD* 101)

The proposal depends entirely on her understanding of civil disobedience as a group activity. Her assumption is that citizens who engage in public protest will be affiliated to a larger group or organisation. The idea is that representatives of these groups be given access to decision makers and hence gain a foothold in the institutions of government.[12] Arendt also calls for a new constitutional amendment to take account of the fact that, in her view, the First Amendment 'neither in language nor in spirit covers the right of association as it is actually practiced in this country' (*CD* 101).

C. Reclaiming the Revolutionary Spirit

The conclusion of Arendt's analysis—that the republic should find a 'recognised niche' for civil disobedience in its institutions—is bold and provocative. At first glance it is difficult to see why she would recommend institutionalising an activity that appears to flourish outside of existing mechanisms of government. In order to understand the thinking behind Arendt's proposal, I suggest, it is necessary to situate her analysis of civil disobedience within her broader analysis of the revolutionary tradition and the decline of the American republic.

In *On Revolution*, Arendt sets out to reconstruct what she identifies as the 'lost treasure' of the revolutionary tradition.[13] This lost treasure is identified by Arendt as 'the revolutionary spirit … the principles which, on both sides of the Atlantic, originally inspired the men of revolutions … public freedom, public happiness, public spirit'.[14] Public freedom is identified with our 'participation in public affairs' and our 'faculty to begin something new'.[15] The essence of freedom involves a two-fold dynamic of entering the public world and, in so doing, adding something new to it. As James Miller puts it, freedom is 'the ability of a human being, through action, to reach out and attain, in deed, gesture, and word, realms, feelings, and thoughts heretofore unimagined'.[16] In Arendt's reconstruction, the aim of revolution is to create a permanent space within which public freedom can be enjoyed.[17] Public happiness is the peculiar sensation that accompanies active participation in public life; it reveals itself in 'the joys of discourse, of legislation, of transacting business, of persuading and being persuaded'.[18] The joy to be derived from public participation stems in part from the experience of acting in public; as

[12] The defence of political representation is ironic, given that Arendt is generally seen as a harsh critic of representative democracy (eg see Kateb, above n 1). A revealing analysis of Arendt's attitude towards representation, which suggests that she is more ambiguous on this issue than is often assumed, is presented in R Fine, *Political Investigations: Hegel, Marx, Arendt* (London, Routledge, 2001) 123–26.

[13] H Arendt, *On Revolution* (London, Penguin, 1990 [1965]).

[14] *Ibid* 221.

[15] *Ibid* 32, 34.

[16] J Miller, 'The Pathos of Novelty: Hannah Arendt's Image of Freedom in the Modern World' in MA Hill (ed), *Hannah Arendt: The Recovery of the Public World* (New York, St Martin's Press, 1979) 177–208, 178.

[17] A Wellmer, 'Arendt on Revolution' in D Villa (ed), *The Cambridge Companion to Hannah Arendt* (Cambridge, Cambridge University Press, 2000) 220, 222.

[18] Arendt, above n 13, 131.

has been noted by Dana Villa, Arendt often alludes to the 'theatricality' of public life and the virtues of 'playacting'.[19] Public spirit describes a heightened care or feeling for the public realm. It is displayed by those who 'have demonstrated that they care for more than their private happiness and are concerned about the state of the world'.[20] These citizens combine an appreciation for the delights of public happiness with an acute sense of responsibility for the maintenance of the polity.

Arendt's unwillingness to sever the tie between the revolutionary spirit and civil disobedience has been alluded to above. There are, in fact, striking affinities between her reconstruction of the revolutionary spirit and her interpretation of civil disobedience. Each of the three principles associated with the revolutionary spirit manifests itself in her analysis of the latter. Civil disobedience is described by Arendt as a means by which citizens assert their public freedom—their right to participate in public affairs—in the face of failings in established political institutions. Civil disobedience affords citizens the opportunity to add something new to the world. As we have seen, civil disobedience can preserve *or* innovate; it can be a vehicle for the protection of established constitutional norms or a means for promoting 'necessary and desirable change' (*CD* 75).[21] Civil disobedience can also be a vehicle for public happiness. In her reflections on the protest movements of the 1960s, she observes that 'what really distinguishes this generation in all countries from earlier generations is its determination to act, its joy in action'.[22] Civil disobedience is a means for organised minorities not merely to address the public but to act *in* public, discovering in the process the delights of public happiness.[23] The theatrical dimension of public happiness is relevant here; civil disobedience is, at least in part, a public performance, an attempt to capture the attention of the public through an extraordinary act.[24] And finally, civil disobedience is a means of displaying public spirit. Civilly disobedient citizens demonstrate a willingness to assume responsibility for the health and integrity of the public realm. These minorities display their public spirit through allowing their care for the world not only to inspire but also, if necessary, to *restrain* their actions. The civilly

[19] D Villa, *Politics, Philosophy, Terror: Essays on the Thought of Hannah Arendt* (Princeton, NJ, Princeton University Press, 1999) 138.

[20] Arendt, above n 13, 279.

[21] The initiatory dynamic of civil disobedience is perhaps most dramatically illustrated in 'pre-figurative' protest, when the organisation and presentation of protest is intended to embody an alternative vision of society. See B Epstein, 'The Politics of Prefigurative Community: The Non-Violent Direct Action Movement' in M Davis and M Sprinker (eds), *Reshaping the US Left: Popular Struggles in the 1980s* (London, Verso, 1988) 63–92.

[22] H Arendt, 'Thoughts on Politics and Revolution', in Arendt, *Crises of the Republic*, above n 3, 202.

[23] *Ibid* 203. This insight into the experience of protest is also discussed in the testimonies of contemporary political activists. See, eg, B Shepard, 'Joy, Justice, and Resistance to the New Global Apartheid' in B Shepard and R Hayduk (eds), *From ACT UP to the WTO: Urban Protest and Community Building in the Era of Globalization* (London, Verso, 2002) 389, 390.

[24] C Cartei, 'The Adelante Street Theatre Project: Theatricalizing Dissent in the Streets of New York City' in Shepard and Hayduk (eds), above n 23, 242.

disobedient citizen allows the urgency of conscience to be tempered by a sense of responsibility for the world.[25]

The fact that the three principles figure so prominently in her analysis suggests that Arendt regards civil disobedience as a manifestation of the revolutionary spirit. If so, then this casts a revealing light on her proposal to find a place for civil disobedience in government. In advancing this proposal, she aims to reclaim the revolutionary spirit by embedding it in the institutional fabric of the republic. This interpretation allows us to understand the proposal as a response to what Arendt diagnosed as the great *tragedy* of the American republic: its failure to nourish and sustain the revolutionary spirit that inspired its foundation.[26] This failure, or 'loss', derives in part from a post-revolutionary amnesia when it comes to the joys of public participation. The Constitution came to be seen as a way of guaranteeing only 'liberty' and the pursuit of 'private happiness', not also 'public freedom' and the pursuit of 'public happiness'.[27] The ebbing of the revolutionary spirit also derives from a growing tendency to view stability and change as opposing, rather than complementary, forces. The durability of the body politic is thus seen as threatened by the very spirit of freedom and initiation that accompanied its creation.[28] And finally, its decline stems from the failure of the revolutionary tradition to leave as part of its legacy an institution to house the revolutionary spirit. This failure inspires Arendt's lament for the councils, which had the untapped potential to preserve a space for continual public participation and the enjoyment of public happiness.[29] The urge to institutionalise civil disobedience—or at least to ensure that civilly disobedient citizens are brought into the ebb and flow of government—is surely born of a fear that this unexpected and spontaneous echo of the revolutionary spirit will, like the councils before it, disappear without concerted efforts to preserve it.

II. CIVIL DISOBEDIENCE AND THE CONSTITUTIONAL STATE

The preceding analysis helps us to understand why Arendt advocates institutionalising civil disobedience. It does not, though, amount to a vindication of her proposal. Indeed, the very idea of institutionalising civil disobedience in the name of a supposed 'revolutionary spirit' may strike some readers as too idiosyncratic to be taken seriously. Despite the difficult and incomplete nature of the proposal, however, I believe that it can be defended as a valuable contribution to debates

[25] On the issue of civil disobedience and responsibility, see L Thomassen, 'Within the Limits of Deliberative Reason Alone: Habermas, Civil Disobedience, and Constitutional Democracy' (2007) 6 *European Journal of Political Theory* 200, 215–16.

[26] Cohen and Arato, above n 5, 196–97.

[27] Arendt, above n 13, 132.

[28] *Ibid* 223–32.

[29] *Ibid* 264–65. Arendt's enthusiasm for the councils—and her lament for their decline—is neatly summarised by Canovan, above n 5, 232–38.

about how constitutional government should respond to civil disobedience. In this section, I make good this claim by, first, reformulating her proposal, secondly, offering some considerations that argue in its favour and, thirdly, showing that the proposal does not depend upon Arendt's controversial account of political action.

A. A Republican Forum for Civil Disobedience

The principal difficulty with Arendt's proposal is that, as it is not discussed by her at any length, she gives us little by way of detail about how it could be implemented. The little that she does say on this issue, such as her suggestion that the representatives of civilly disobedient minorities be treated like registered lobbyists, is not particularly helpful to addressing this concern. The influence of lobbyists is often a matter of informal networks, built up over many years by persons with extensive knowledge and experience of government.[30] It is not immediately clear how the representatives of civilly disobedient minorities could attain a similar influence, or be guaranteed the same kind of opportunities to advance their agendas.

The practical difficulties of seeking to address this concern may turn out to be insurmountable. At the same time, it is at least possible to furnish the proposal with rather more substance than Arendt provides. This can be achieved through appealing to recent developments in republican political theory. In particular, Arendt's proposal to bring civilly disobedient minorities into government bears a striking resemblance to Philip Pettit's recent defence of institutionalised consultative and appellate resources in a deliberative republic. Consultative resources, such as advisory bodies, public hearings and inquiries, are designed to facilitate citizen input to the formulation and design of policy. Pettit argues that these bodies are particularly important in allowing citizens to contest policy proposals on the grounds that they do not accurately track the public interest, or on the grounds that they treat minorities in a deleterious way.[31] Appellate resources, such as courts, tribunals and ombudsmen, must 'provide citizens with a capacity to challenge a government initiative on three more or less distinct counts: for its legality under public law; for its substantive merit; and for its general propriety'.[32] These bodies have the power to consider and, in some cases, adjudicate citizen complaints against government decisions.[33] They allow citizens to provoke deliberation throughout the polity and, in many cases, bring them into direct contact

[30] D Austen-Smith, 'Information and Influence: Lobbying for Agendas and Votes' (1993) 37 *American Journal of Political Science* 799.

[31] P Pettit, 'Democracy, Electoral and Contestatory' in I Shapiro and S Macedo (eds), *Designing Democratic Institutions* (New York, New York University Press, 2000) 105, 131.

[32] *Ibid* 132.

[33] N Lewis and P Birkinshaw, *When Citizens Complain: Reforming Administration and Justice* (Buckingham, Open University Press, 1993); P Cane, *Administrative Law*, 4th edn (Oxford, Oxford

with their political representatives.[34] Consultative and appellate mechanisms must be responsive to the concerns of citizens, in the sense that their reasoned complaints receive deliberative up-take in the law-making process.

There are several ways in which Arendt's proposal could be interpreted in light of these republican ideas. The complaints of civilly disobedient groups could be treated as inputs to either consultative or appellate mechanisms, depending on whether their protest is against a proposed or existing law or policy. A civilly disobedient group might be given the opportunity of delegating representatives to petition government at a specially convened public commission or inquiry. Alternatively, there may be existing institutional forums or committees, relevant to the contested policy area, to which civilly disobedient citizens could be given access. The most ambitious suggestion is that a *permanent body* could be set up for the purpose of hearing complaints of representatives from among the ranks of the groups whose members engage in civil disobedience. The permanent body would provide a stage for a confrontation between activists and government representatives. This confrontation would be deliberative insofar as it enabled civilly disobedient minorities to articulate their grievances, receive explanations from those in power and respond to counter-criticisms that are put to them by institutional actors. The dialogue between activist and government representatives in the permanent body could be moderated and adjudicated by a panel that is, as far as possible, impartial between the two sides. The panel might be selected from legislative assemblies, its members drawn from the ranks of major political parties with no particular party or grouping enjoying a majority. The culmination of the confrontation could be a summary document, which presents the collective judgement of the panel and its non-binding recommendations. In the event of disagreement among panel members, the body could follow the practice of law courts by drafting a 'majority' and 'minority' report. The government, and perhaps the civilly disobedient group, could 'complete' the deliberative process by drafting a response to the report and recommendations of the panel.

The idea behind this suggestion is to create a space for genuine dialogue between disobedient citizens and government representatives. The proposal to create a formal body where such confrontations might occur, to reiterate, is merely one way in which such confrontations could be structured. In any case, the arrangements that are finally chosen to accommodate civilly disobedient protest should be established, in line with the spirit of Arendt's proposal, as part of the public political rules of the republic. There is a certain irony in appealing to Pettit's republicanism in this context, given that he identifies consultative and appellate mechanisms as *alternatives* to popular protest as a means of petitioning

University Press, 2004) part IV; D Longley and R James, *Administrative Justice: Central Issues in UK and European Administrative Law* (London, Cavendish, 1999) 95–102.

[34] P Pettit, *Republicanism: A Theory of Freedom and Government* (Oxford, Oxford University Press, 1997) 239.

government.[35] An interesting connotation of Arendt's proposal, however, is that there is no need to draw such a sharp separation between institutional and non-institutional strategies of political contestation. It is not necessary to posit a continuum between institutional and non-institutional strategies, or to argue that there is no difference in kind between these two modes of political participation. One can instead regard the two strategies as different but *complementary* methods of political engagement. A civil disobedience campaign might aim in part at gaining access to institutional forums, which would give minorities a means of communicating their concerns directly to those in government. This may be particularly valuable for marginalised groups with little or no effective access to political elites. At the same time, attention-grabbing acts of civil disobedience can aim to activate public opinion and create a climate of public interest prior to the articulation of grievances in formal institutionalised settings. This may be particularly valuable insofar as groups want to combat deficiencies in the wider public sphere, such as insufficient or inadequate public discussion of a particular issue. In this way, a civilly disobedient minority can pursue institutional and non-institutional paths of exercising political influence and changing public opinion.

B. A Political Approach to Civil Disobedience

The preceding discussion suggests one way in which Arendt's proposal might be developed. The full value of the proposal, however, still remains to be ascertained. The reconstruction of the revolutionary spirit offered above suggests one line of argument: institutionalising civil disobedience can be defended on the grounds that it creates opportunities for dissenting citizens to participate directly in institutions of government. But there are also other considerations, less intimately tied to Arendt's controversial vision of political life, which may be invoked to support the proposal.

The first consideration is that providing an institutional forum for civilly disobedient groups would guarantee them an opportunity to articulate the reasons behind their grievances. It might be objected that this opportunity is redundant, in view of the fact that civil disobedience is already an effective means of creating publicity for oppositional views.[36] The shortcoming of this sort of publicity, however, is that it is often difficult for protesters to communicate their intended message and to ensure that media outlets report their protest in a fair and balanced way. An institutional forum of the sort envisaged by Arendt will enhance the opportunities for civilly disobedient minorities to receive a proper hearing for their concerns. It would also enable political representatives or other institutional actors to cross-examine these minorities to test the plausibility of their

[35] *Ibid* 195–96.

[36] J Habermas, *Between Facts and Norms: Contributions to a Discourse Theory of Law and Democracy* (trans W Rehg) (Cambridge, Polity, 1996) 382.

convictions. The institutionalisation of civil disobedience would, then, cohere with Habermas's conception of a 'two-tier' deliberative politics; the formal deliberation that would take place within newly-convened institutional forums would not replace but complement the informal debate and discussion in civil society provoked by campaigns of civil disobedience.[37]

The second consideration refers to the specifically political complexion of the forum that Arendt aims to establish. The forum would offer an alternative to pursuing complaints against government through legal-judicial bodies. This is important because courts—with their strict rules of evidence and narrow terms of reference—may not be the most conducive arenas for the advancement and assessment of the grievances that lead responsible citizens to engage in civil disobedience. Civilly disobedient citizens who rely on having a 'day in court' to publicise their cause are often unable to translate their concerns into plausible arguments that have legal standing. Arendt explores this difficultly in relation to the so-called 'political question doctrine' in the US, according to which the judiciary may refuse to hear a complaint against the other two branches of government (*CD* 99–101). She goes so far as to suggest that 'the establishment of civil disobedience among our political institutions of government might be the best possible remedy for this ultimate failure of judicial review' (*CD* 101). The creation of a political forum for civilly disobedient minorities would at least offer a means for citizens to contest law and policy in institutionalised settings that are not subject to the restrictive rules of argument that obtain in judicial bodies.

A third consideration appeals to a difficulty with more familiar liberal and democratic approaches to civil disobedience, which Arendt's proposal manages to avoid. As I mentioned in the introduction, liberals and democrats tend to argue that the constitutional State should respect civilly disobedient citizens and reduce, or even suspend, legal sanctions. This is the strategy of Jürgen Habermas, who argues that a constitutional democracy must avoid treating civil disobedience as a common crime and extend a 'tolerant spirit' to its dissenting citizens.[38] This is also the attitude of John Rawls, who argues that, when asked to rule on such cases, 'courts should take into account the civilly disobedient nature of the protester's act'.[39] It is notable that, as well-intentioned as these arguments may be, such proposals do not require any sort of *engagement* with dissident voices on the part of those in political authority. Still less do they require any kind of formal or informal response on the part of government to the concerns of protesters. The constitutional State can display a high-minded tolerant attitude, by electing not to subject civilly disobedient citizens to disproportionate sanctions, without

[37] *Ibid* 304–08.

[38] This toleration is conditional on civil disobedience satisfying certain conditions in its conduct and justification. See J Habermas, 'Religious Tolerance—The Pacemaker for Cultural Rights' (2004) 79 *Philosophy* 5, 9; W Smith, 'Civil Disobedience and Social Power: Reflections on Habermas' (2008) 7 *Contemporary Political Theory* 72.

[39] Rawls, above n 4, 339.

committing to listen to or take account of the complaints of dissenting minorities. The strength of Arendt's proposal is that it requires the constitutional State not merely to tolerate civil disobedience, but also to provide an institutional space where the arguments of dissenting citizens can be heard. It also requires that representatives of government be called upon to answer the complaints of citizens and—at the very least—provide a public justification for the contested law or policy. In this way, the proposal guards against the danger—implicit in orthodox liberal or democratic accounts—that the 'tolerant' constitutional State will simply ignore the grievances of civilly disobedient minorities. A positive by-product of this engagement might also be to restore, to some degree at least, the faith of alienated or disaffected citizens in the institutions of the republic.

C. The Broad Appeal of the Proposal

Despite the fact that Arendt's proposal contrasts with and improves on standard approaches, I do not believe that it is fundamentally incompatible with liberal and democratic accounts of civil disobedience. This is because the grounds for the proposal—particularly the three arguments considered above—do not presuppose Arendt's controversial conception of political action. In other words, liberals and democrats can accept, from within their own theoretical frameworks, the value of granting civilly disobedient citizens a political forum in which to express their grievances.

The proposal does require accepting at least one aspect of Arendt's broader approach to civil disobedience, namely, the distinction between it and conscientious objection. Her claim is that civilly disobedient minorities, bound together by common opinion rather than individual conscience, should be given institutional access to decision-makers. Given that Arendt bases the distinction between conscientious objection and civil disobedience on a controversial separation between morality, as concerned with the integrity of the self, and politics, as concerned with the integrity of the world, this might be thought drastically to limit the appeal of the proposal. In fact, although liberal and democratic theorists may not accept the way in which Arendt draws this distinction, it is now fairly commonplace to distinguish between conscientious objection and civil disobedience. Rawls, for example, notes that civil disobedience is a 'political act' in the sense that, unlike conscientious objection, it is not carried out solely for reasons of 'personal morality' or 'religious doctrine' but also on the basis of 'political principles'.[40] Habermas also endorses this view, arguing that civilly disobedient citizens do not act merely on the basis of 'private convictions' but primarily on the basis of 'valid constitutional principles'.[41] In fact, the widespread tendency to distinguish

[40] *Ibid* 321.

[41] Habermas, above n 4, 107.

between civil disobedience and conscientious objection may by due in no small part to the influence of Arendt's arguments on this point.

The grounds for the proposal can, and should, be detached from more problematic aspects of Arendt's conception of political action. One such aspect is her belief that a 'self-contained politics' must exclude from its agenda any concern with social justice. This is apparently because addressing questions of 'necessity' in the public realm will somehow compromise a genuinely political *praxis*, which, for Arendt, consists solely of the exercise of public freedom and the experience of public happiness.[42] This implausible exclusion of social justice from the realm of politics has been the subject of much warranted criticism.[43] In any case, one can endorse Arendt's proposal to institutionalise civil disobedience without excluding issues of social justice as appropriate grounds for political protest. This does not mean abandoning her view that civil disobedience should be motivated by care for the public realm, but entails a more inclusive view of what this 'public spirited' ethos entails.[44] On a less restrictive view, concern for the protection and perfection of the public realm might be compatible with, or perhaps even require, the promotion of social justice.[45] The point is not that none of Arendt's reasons for supporting the proposal can figure in a reasonable case for it; for example, she may be right to argue that institutionalising civil disobedience will increase opportunities for citizens to participate in the public realm and initiate 'necessary and desirable' change. The point, rather, is that a case for the proposal can be articulated that does not presuppose all aspects of her contentious conception of the 'political'.

III. OBJECTIONS TO INSTITUTIONALISING CIVIL DISOBEDIENCE

The preceding discussion has substantiated Arendt's proposal to institutionalise civil disobedience and offered arguments in its favour that do not presuppose all of her own reasons for endorsing the policy. The key point is that providing a political forum within which civilly disobedient citizens can lobby government will help to ensure that those in power must engage with dissident voices. Despite this attempt to strengthen and broaden the case for the proposal, however, it remains vulnerable to several powerful objections. The first objection raises the practical concern that, in institutionalising civil disobedience, there is a risk of creating incentives for groups to civilly disobey. If an organised minority wanted to advance its agenda, it might think it worthwhile to engage in civil disobedience if it could be reasonably sure of gaining for its representatives a hearing in government. This incentive to

42 Villa, above n 5, 29.

43 S Benhabib, 'Models of Public Space: Hannah Arendt, the Liberal Tradition, and Jürgen Habermas' in C Calhoun (ed), *Habermas and the Public Sphere* (Cambridge, Mass, The MIT Press, 1992) 3, 74–81.

44 W Smith, 'Democracy, Deliberation and Disobedience' (2004) 10 *Res Publica* 353.

45 RJ Bernstein, 'Rethinking the Social and the Political' in RJ Bernstein, *Philosophical Profiles: Essays in a Pragmatic Mode* (Cambridge, Polity Press, 1986) 238–59.

disobey may unduly threaten the stability of a republic based on respect for law and a general willingness to comply with democratic decisions.[46]

There are two ways of responding to this concern. First, it is important to remember that Arendt does not call for the legalisation of civil disobedience. This implies that groups who break the law may still have to face some kind of punishment or penalty, even at the same time as they receive the benefits of an institutional hearing.[47] It is true that Arendt appears to be rather ambivalent about the idea of punishing civilly disobedient citizens, reserving particular criticism for the view that disobedient citizens should welcome their punishment as a mark of their civic virtue (*CD* 66). In the context of institutionalising civil disobedience, however, the threat of punishment or penalties does perform a valuable function. It acts as a disincentive for groups to engage in civil disobedience unless they judge that their cause is especially grave; as Andrew Sabl points out, it serves to dissuade 'frivolous and insincere acts'.[48] Secondly, it is important to bear in mind the threat to stability that emerges when a democratic society does not take active steps to engage with dissenting citizens. The willingness of large numbers of citizens to risk the costs of transgressive protest is as likely to arise from genuine alienation from conventional politics as from a calculation of the relative costs and benefits of lawful and unlawful strategies. The danger of not responding to this alienation in an appropriate fashion is that disaffected citizens may be pushed further from the mainstream and thus countenance more aggressive forms of resistance. Arendt emphasises this point when she attributes the 'crisis' in America during the 1960s to a lack of responsiveness on the part of its political authorities to the reasonable dissent of vast numbers of citizens (*CD* 101–02). The proposal to channel civil disobedience into an institutional process of contestation is a means of managing the profound risks to stability that are posed when large numbers of citizens are tempted to turn their backs on democratic institutions.

A second objection is slightly different, in that it focuses on the type of minorities that might exploit opportunities to access institutions through disobedience. The idea of finding a constitutional niche for civil disobedience may be attractive if it will be thought to benefit public-spirited movements of the sort that inspired Arendt's reflections. It may, however, seem less attractive if it will benefit minorities engaging in civil disobedience to promote less commendable objectives, such as groups seeking to block certain policies on the basis of interest or prejudice. On occasion, Arendt appears to suggest that the associative nature of civil disobedience—the fact that it is carried out not by individuals but by groups—means that it will generally be supported through 'strong' opinions (*CD* 68). The limitations of such a view are suggested later in her essay, when she warns that protest movements can become 'infected' through 'ideologies' that may undermine

[46] Kateb, above n 1, 143.

[47] On the distinction between punishing and penalising civilly disobedient citizens, see Lefkowitz, above n 4, 218–23.

[48] A Sabl, 'Looking Forward to Justice: Rawlsian Civil Disobedience and its Non-Rawlsian Lessons' (2001) 9 *Journal of Political Philosophy* 307, 323.

the association and distort their grounds for dissent (*CD* 98). There is, then, no guarantee that civil disobedience will not be undertaken by groups for reasons that may be judged bad, mistaken or offensive.[49]

This is a challenging objection, but it is not compelling enough to undermine Arendt's proposal and may, in fact, even support it. In order to see why, it is helpful to look at how Pettit responds to similar concerns about his proposal for enhanced consultative and appellate mechanisms. He is well aware that not every appeal made through these avenues will be persuasive; in many instances, a minority view should not be allowed successfully to challenge the majority position. In order to minimise this possibility, consultative and appellate resources should be designed to maximise the scope for reason and argument to prevail. This is to be achieved through establishing deliberative processes within which the claims of citizens can be advanced and thoroughly examined.[50] The proposal to accommodate civilly disobedient groups is, as we have seen, styled in a similar fashion. As well as allowing activists to put forward their views, institutional actors should be given the opportunity to interrogate and assess their concerns. In fact, the case for the proposal is strengthened because it enhances the possibility that the reasons for a minority's opposition to policy will be subjected to public scrutiny. The requirement to provide a reasoned articulation of grievances within institutional forums might off-set the danger that protest movements will rely solely on inflammatory and obfuscating rhetoric to generate political influence.

A third objection focuses less on the stability and integrity of the republic and more on consequences of institutionalisation for civil disobedience itself. It might be argued that any move to institutionalise civil disobedience would amount to a strategy of co-optation by those in power. In other words, by granting a 'niche' for civilly disobedient citizens, the constitutional State would in fact be containing and, in a sense, 'disciplining' dissent. The force of this concern may be illustrated through the example, discussed by Iris Marion Young, of the recent attempt by the WTO to convene a public encounter with its critics prior to its annual meeting. Those civil society activists who attended the meeting were disappointed, though probably not surprised, to find that the agenda had been pre-set, and the majority of their time was spent listening to speeches by officials. Activists quickly concluded that this 'deliberative forum' had been organised simply to 'co-opt and dampen' opposition to WTO proceedings.[51] This objection might be sharpened further by arguing that any attempt to institutionalise civil disobedience as a 'public-spirited' mode of protest risks de-legitimising more radical acts of resistance that aim fundamentally to challenge prevailing self-understandings of the republic.[52]

49 *Ibid* 328–29.

50 Pettit, above n 34, 195–200.

51 I Marion Young, 'Activist Challenges to Deliberative Democracy' (2001) 29 *Political Theory* 670, 680–81.

52 A similar concern is articulated by Lasse Thomassen in his deconstructive critique of Habermas's approach to civil disobedience (Thomassen, above n 25, 209–12).

The concern that radical dissent may be co-opted is a powerful but, I think, not decisive complaint against a proposal to create an institutional forum for dialogue between activists and government. First, notwithstanding plausible scepticism about the limitations of institutionalised politics or the motivations of power-holders in democratic societies, it would surely be wrong to deny what may be a legitimate desire on the part of marginalised minorities directly to influence or participate in imperfect political institutions. A group which engages in civil disobedience might not aim to initiate a radical critique of institutional politics, but instead to raise the profile of a neglected or marginal issue. The opportunity to take up this issue in a highly-publicised dialogue with law-makers should not be taken away on the basis of speculative concerns about diminishing the nascent radicalism of civil disobedience. Secondly, and more importantly, the availability of this opportunity enables civilly disobedient groups to enhance the symbolic meaning of their protest. The thought here is not that groups could exploit an institutional forum to publicise their radical agenda, though this is certainly a possibility. The idea, rather, is that a civilly disobedient group may elect *not* to request an institutional hearing for its concerns, or may decide to decline an official invitation to participate in such a forum. The freedom to reject such an opportunity is important precisely because groups may not want to be incorporated into the political-institutional process. This may seem to be a trivial point, but the public refusal to take advantage of institutional resources can, in fact, add an important layer of meaning to a civil disobedience campaign. The decision to snub the government, in favour of concentrating on public appeals to the wider political community, is an important means of amplifying political opposition. The refusal by a civilly disobedient minority to participate in an institutional dialogue with the powerful signifies and underlines its thoroughgoing opposition to the existing administration or to prevailing ways of doing politics.

IV. CONCLUSION

Arendt's writings on civil disobedience contain much that is unorthodox and surprising. She explores the initiatory capacity of this mode of protest, reveals its link with the revolutionary spirit and calls for it to be given a permanent home in the institutional fabric of the republic. It is this final claim that most distinguishes Arendt's approach from that of liberals like Rawls and democrats like Habermas. It reflects her belief that the constitutional State must be compelled not only to tolerate but also to engage with civilly disobedient minorities. In and through this engagement, she hopes that the moribund institutions of representative democracy may once again recapture some of the political energy that is manifest in the annals of the revolutionary tradition. And—as I have argued throughout this essay—we have good reasons to take her provocative proposal seriously.

8

The Search for a New Beginning: Hannah Arendt and Karl Jaspers as Critics of West German Parliamentarism

KARI PALONEN

I. INTELLECTUALS AND PARLIAMENTARISM IN POST-WAR GERMANY

THE DISGUST FELT by intellectuals towards parliamentary regimes and parliamentarians is a commonplace. Parliaments come to decisions by counting votes, and participation in parliamentary debates requires getting elected. These are conditions that are, indeed, indispensable for parliamentary politics, which has been based since early modern Britain on principles, such as free elections, free mandate, free speech and freedom from arrest (parliamentary immunity), that also aim at guaranteeing fair play and mutual equality between parliamentarians.

In the wake of the celebrations of the sixtieth anniversary of the German *Grundgesetz* (Basic Law) from 1949, we have to remember that the criticism of the Bonn Republic and its parliamentary practices was widespread in the era of Adenauer and Erhard.[1] Intellectuals, in particular, were suspicious of parliamentary government: on the right, these included Carl Schmitt, Ernst Forsthoff and Hans Freyer; on the left, from Jürgen Habermas to Johannes Agnoli; and also many in the middle of the political spectrum. They all shared an extremely pessimistic view on the prospects of the Federal Republic, its parliamentary practices and the *Grundgesetz*.

Hannah Arendt was one of the most eloquent apologists of the activity of politics in the twentieth century, but she was never well acquainted with the political and rhetorical practices of the parliamentary regime. Even she failed fully to appreciate that parliamentarians, due to both their daily political experiences and the distinct parliamentary procedures of deliberation and debate, are frequently superior to scholars in political judgement.

[1] See, eg, S Ulrich, *Der Weimar-Complex* (Göttingen, Wallstein, 2009).

In a previous piece,[2] I have written a critical comparison between Arendt and Max Weber regarding their relationship to the acceptance of representative democracy, discussing mainly Arendt's *On Revolution* from 1963. In this essay, I continue this topic with Arendt's comments on the politics of the German Federal Republic. However, it turned out that she did not have so much to say on the subject.[3] Arendt long held the Federal Republic to have been a failure, and she expected it to run its course and expire.[4]

For this reason I decided to include in this discussion two pamphlets by Arendt's teacher and friend, the philosopher Karl Jaspers (1883–1969), *Wohin treibt die Bundesrepublik*[5] and his reply to critics of the first, *Antwort*.[6] Jaspers had been a professor in Basel since 1949, but he remained a German citizen. His books are strongly indebted to Arendt's early critique of West German politics and deal with a distinctly Arendtian problem, the planned statute of limitations (*Verjährung*) on the criminalisation of Nazi crimes. Jaspers analyses the parliamentary debate on this proposal, which ultimately failed in the *Bundestag*, and regards the entire debate as symptomatic of the state of the Federal Republic.

My aim in this essay is first to interpret Arendt's and Jaspers's political thought in its relation to parliamentarism, specifically as realised in the Federal Republic of Germany and the forms and practices of the West German polity. I consider Arendt and Jaspers as examples of anti-parliamentary tendencies among scholars who are otherwise sympathetic to democracy. My approach is that of a historically-oriented political theorist, rhetoric and Max Weber scholar.

II. PARLIAMENTARISM AS RHETORICAL POLITICS *PAR EXCELLENCE*

My analysis extends the concept of parliamentarism, viewing it not merely as a technique of government, but as an ideal type of distinctly rhetorical political culture. We can construct a typology of parliamentarism consisting of four dimensions: parliamentary government in the sense of the responsibility of government to parliament; parliamentary politics based on the rhetorical practices of 'government by speaking' (Macaulay); the procedural character of *pro et contra* parliamentary debate; and the indispensable role of professional politicians in parliamentary politics. Each dimension manifests a slightly different aspect

[2] K Palonen, 'Imagining Max Weber's Reply to Hannah Arendt: Remarks on the Arendtian Critique of Representative Democracy' (2008) 15 *Constellations* 56.

[3] See K Sontheimer, *Hannah Arendt* (München, Piper, 2005); H König, 'Kein Neubeginn. Hannah Arendt, die NS-Vergangenheit und die Bundesrepublik' in D Geppert and J Hacke (eds), *Streit um den Staat* (Göttingen, Vandenhock & Ruprecht, 2008) 113.

[4] Compare L Köhler and H Saner, 'Vorwort' in H Arendt and K Jaspers, *Briefwechsel 1926–1969* (München, Piper, 1985) 17–33.

[5] K Jaspers, *Wohin treibt die Bundesrepublik?* (München, Piper, 1966).

[6] K Jaspers, *Antwort zur Kritik meiner Schrift Wohin treibt die Bundesrepublik* (München, Piper, 1967).

of the deliberative genre of rhetoric. We can also detect a specific variant of anti-parliamentarism corresponding to each dimension: rejection of the parliamentary responsibility of government, of parliamentary 'bavardage', of the proceduralism of parliamentary politics and debate, and of the professionalisation of parliamentarians.

These aspects of parliamentarism and anti-parliamentarism may have differing emphases in different countries. We can imagine, for example, rhetorical excellence in the parliaments of presidential regimes, such as in the United States at certain stages of its history, or parliamentary governments that have been highly suspicious of rhetoric, as in the Scandinavian countries. For this reason, when discussing how a specific regime relates in the political thought of an individual thinker to an ideal type of parliamentarism, all four aspects and their respective differences deserve to be discussed.

Parliamentarism in West Germany after World War II had its special features. The parliamentarism of the Bonn Republic was not that of high eloquence, notwithstanding the brilliant rhetoricians, such as Herbert Wehner, in the *Bundestag*. The strong position of the parties in the electoral system, with half of *Bundestag* members chosen on the basis of party lists, and even directly-elected members dependent on the parties, has been a major reason for the generally low quality of rhetoric in the *Bundestag*.

Of equal importance is the ambiguous formulation in the *Grundgesetz* combining the free mandate of individual members with the party-based parliamentary practices.[7] The constitutional lawyer Gerhard Leibholz even declared the free mandate of the members practically outdated in a 'party state'.[8] This view tends to eliminate the procedural character of the parliament as a deliberative assembly and to make it, in Edmund Burke's terms, a 'congress of ambassadors',[9] with the parties as mandatants. Leibholz's thesis has been severely criticised by scholars[10] and parliamentarians.[11] The ambiguity of the *Grundgesetz* remains, and the 'party state' aspect indicates a limit to how far the Federal Republic can be called a fully parliamentary regime.

Hannah Arendt does not join anti-parliamentarians such as Thomas Carlyle and Carl Schmitt in anti-rhetorical denunciations of parliament as a talk shop (*Schwatzbude*). For her, speech is an inherent part of politics, and a silent politics is *contradictio in adjecto*.[12] Especially in her *Denktagebuch,* Arendt is a strong admirer of ancient rhetoric with its agonistic political culture of debating in the *Agora*.[13] Her

[7] C Möllers, *Das Grundgesetz* (München, Beck, 2009) 53–57.

[8] G Leibholz, *Strukturprobleme der modernen Demokratie* (Frankfurt, Fischer, 1974).

[9] E Burke, 'Speech to the Electors of Bristol' in *Selected Works of Edmund Burke*, retrieved at <http://oll.libertyfund.org/?option=com_staticxt&staticfile=show.php%3Ftitle=659&chapter=20392&layout=html&Itemid=27> (9 February 2008).

[10] W Hennis, *Auf dem Weg zum Parteienstaat* (Stuttgart, Reclam, 1998).

[11] H Hamm-Brücher, *Der Politiker und Sein Gewissen* (München, Piper, 1983).

[12] H Arendt, *Vita activa oder Vom tätigen Leben* (München, Piper, 1981).

[13] H Arendt, *Denktagebuch 1950–1973* (München, Piper, 2002).

admiration for the debates in the non-elected assemblies, from the wards of New England to the soviets of the 1956 Hungarian Revolution, is also well known.

Arendt and in particular Jaspers were critical of the strong parties of the Bonn regime. Nonetheless, the core of their critique seems to reach deeper, to the parliamentary form of representative democracy itself. The critique suggests a failure to recognise the importance of parliament as a representative and deliberative institution as well as the procedural character of parliamentary politics, based as it is on the principle of debating agenda items from opposed points of view.

III. ARENDT ON THE AFTERMATH OF NAZI RULE

In 1950 Hannah Arendt published in *Commentary* the article 'The Aftermath of Nazi Rule: Report from Germany', based on her three-month visit to the country just after the first *Bundestag* elections and the formation of the Adenauer Government. What was striking for Arendt was the lack of republican 'new beginning' after the Nazi regime, due to the failure of German citizens, politicians and academics to confront the Nazi past. Arendt was at that time completing *The Origins of Totalitarianism*, stressing the unique novelty of the Nazi regime in its militarily meaningless destruction of the Jews. She was struck by the experience of how this destruction was not seen in Germany as the main point of the Nazi rule: 'A lack of response is evident everywhere.'[14]

Arendt interprets her conversational informants in Germany as fleeing from the reality of the destruction, and who produced all kinds of excuses instead of manifesting guilt or remorse. Matters of fact are 'treated as if they were mere opinions',[15] and the totalitarianism seemed to have led to a deficient sense of judgement.[16] The bold currency reform of Ludwig Erhard was producing 'feverish busyness'[17] instead of efficient production. The arbitrary and half-heartedly implemented practices of the Allied denazification initiative, while holding the promise of a break with past, appeared to her to have been squandered, thus destroying the ability clearly to judge right and wrong and producing 'a moral confusion'.[18] In particular, the Americans' advertising campaign style against the Nazi horrors was experienced as counter-productive. She also parodied the State-centric thinking of the Germans, to which neither business nor the trade unions could form a counter-weight; she further parodied the trust in the universities as the arena that would lead the way out of the misery.

[14] H Arendt, 'The Aftermath of Nazi Rule: Report from Germany', in *Essays in Understanding 1930–1954* (New York, Schocken Books, 1994) 249.

[15] *Ibid* 251.

[16] *Ibid* 252.

[17] *Ibid* 254.

[18] *Ibid* 259.

An interesting point in Arendt's disappointment with Germany concerns her harsh political judgement of the federal character of the new Republic. She had expected that federalism would both prevent a concentration of power and provide grounds for citizens to express their immediate interests in the form of 'grass-root democracy in the field of communal and local affairs'.[19] However, she regarded the *Länder* governments as a complete failure due to the deficiencies in the denazification programme as well as to the social consequences of Erhard's economic policies. The West German local government appeared to Arendt to be a mere combination of folklore and corruption,[20] and she had the impression that the Federal Government in Bonn and the *Länder* governments did not exercise any control of each other, the apparatus of the parties forming their only connecting link.

For Arendt the main problem of German politics was the party system based on pre-Hitler era parties that had been easily destroyed by the Nazis.[21] In the German parties, tactics triumphed over the exhausted ideologies, and the party machines seemed geared mainly to providing jobs and perks for their members.[22] The parties thus provided an area for mere opportunists, who refused to draw lessons from history. All of this drove Arendt to the conclusion that the legacy of totalitarianism had not been overthrown. The only hope that remained for her was the vision of a federative Europe.[23]

These were the main points in Arendt's narrative on the intellectual and political situation in West Germany in the months following the foundation of the Federal Republic and the constitution of the first *Bundestag* and the Adenauer Government.[24] Her narrative was lucid, but in many respects dilettantish.

Take the case of parties. The party landscape of West Germany, though it may have replicated with only slight modifications the Weimar parties, did correspond to the broad pattern of post-war West European parties. The party constellations were based on the opposition between Social Democrats and Conservatives or—as in Italy, France and Belgium—Social Democrats and Christian Democrats (the latter were re-founded in West Germany on an inter-confessional basis). The Liberals, the Communists and others played a minor role in other West European multi-party regimes too. To imagine a spontaneous, bottom-up formation of parties on a local or regional basis without ideological or tactical considerations is not a realistic political judgment of the general party constellations in post-war Europe.

Arendt's Report is remarkable, above all, because she does not mention at all any of the new, unique features of West German constitutional politics. There is

[19] *Ibid* 267.
[20] *Ibid.*
[21] *Ibid* 262.
[22] *Ibid* 268.
[23] H Arendt, 'Approaches to the "German Problem"', in *Essays in Understanding*, above n 14.
[24] For Jaspers's praise of Arendt's 'Report from Germany', see Arendt and Jaspers, above n 4, 197.

no hint of the debates of the *Parlamentarischer Rat* consisting of the representatives of the *Länder* for the preparation of the interim constitution, the *Grundgesetz*.[25] The *Grundgesetz* itself contained decisive new elements, such as the constructive vote of no confidence and the individual right to asylum. She also does not comment upon the first *Bundestag* elections of the 1949, their consequent results and the election of Konrad Adenauer as Federal Chancellor by a one-vote majority.

Probably for Arendt, the lack of a new beginning in Germany after World War II was manifested primarily by the absence of a constituent assembly. Why does she not consider the deliberations of the *Parlamentarischer Rat* as an attempt to form new foundations for the Federal State? We can imagine that she, as did Jaspers later, held it to be too dependent on the decisions of the Allied powers and not formed on a spontaneous contract between local initiatives. But was such a contract even remotely thinkable in the post-war situation in which, by Arendt's own admission, the citizens were lacking in the capacity for sound political judgement?

Of course, Arendt was less interested in the political institutions themselves than in the political culture as their 'substrate'. She did not talk so much with the politicians acting in the parliaments, governments and parties, but rather with academics and literati. The cultural perspective was for her reason enough to doubt the legitimacy of the new institutions and practices, without considering them in detail. She blames also the Allied powers, which did not provide the conditions for a new beginning, either in radically breaking with the Nazi past or in leaving the Germans to form their own institutions spontaneously from the local level without the intervention of the parties.

With the formation of the Federal Republic and the preceding establishment of the *Länder* parliaments, procedures and institutions for the parliamentary process of debating and judging were established. To claim that the parties dominated this process is not inaccurate, but the factual domination of the parties should be distinguished from the institutionalisation of the parliaments. The parliaments' procedures refer to a condition for acting politically that is more dependent on parliamentary form than on historical and national tradition. The procedural mode of parliamentary politics conceptually precedes the formation of parties in terms of the importance of the former's deliberation of agenda items. The procedure also gives individual MPs the right to oppose their own parties, although ultimately at the cost of diminishing their own chances for re-election.

It seems that Arendt took the contractarian narrative of the constitution, which she later discussed in detail in *On Revolution*, as the only possible foundation of the modern State. She could not imagine alternatives to it. Her analysis of the new West German polity can be discussed in these terms.

An alternative apparently not considered by Arendt was provided by Max Weber, who in his essay on 'objectivity' proposes to replace psychologistic

[25] See M Feldkamp, *Der Parlamentarische Rat 1948–1949* (Göttingen, Vandenhoek & Ruprecht, 2008).

explanations in economics with institutional ones, insisting that institutions have the power to shape the personal qualifications.[26] In a similar manner, the parliamentary and democratic institutions can be considered as mighty forces to mould and alter the *Lebensführung*, that is, the experiences and qualities of the persons acting in and through them. Neither the pre-parliamentary personal qualities of the members nor the origins of the institutions are by themselves decisive for determining political practice; however, the members' involvement in parliamentary procedures and institutions can parliamentarise their style of politics independent of their personal histories and pre-parliamentary commitments. All of which, indeed, did take place in West Germany from the 1960s on, with the renaissance of a more debate-oriented political culture.[27]

IV. JASPERS ON THE CRISIS OF THE FEDERAL REPUBLIC

The lack of insight into the value of institutions and procedures was a major reason for Arendt's pessimistic judgement of post-war German politics. I now move to the question of how far these Arendtian reasons were used in Jaspers's critique of the regime from the mid-1960s.

Karl Jaspers was originally a medical doctor specialising in psychiatry, but turned to philosophy, becoming a professor in the 1920s. Arendt defended her thesis on Augustine to him at the University of Heidelberg in 1928. Jaspers's double training as a scientist and as a philosopher left its mark on his political thought, one of the effects being his conviction that philosophy is superior to rhetoric, which he more or less identified with demagoguery. From such a perspective he also had obvious difficulties in understanding the singularity of parliamentary politics, as he was looking for philosophical 'foundations' for politics in general.

Wohin treibt die Bundesrepublik? from 1966 starts with a debate between Jaspers and Rudolf Augstein, the editor of *Der Spiegel*, a liberal journal opposed to the restorative tendencies in West Germany.[28] Jaspers analyses the *Bundestag* debates on the proposal of *Verjährung*, the statute of limitations on Nazi crimes, which was finally rejected after the Christian Democrats switched sides, leading to resignation of Minister of Justice Ewald Bucher (FDP). In the bulk of the book Jaspers discusses the state of intellectual life, parliament and government before the 1965 *Bundestag* elections. A final chapter is written after the elections which confirmed the Erhard coalition of Christian and Free Democrats.

Jasper's reply to his critics, *Antwort*, was published in 1967, after the fall of Erhard and the formation of the grand coalition with Christian Democrat Kurt-Georg

[26] M Weber, '"Die Objektivität" sozialwissenschaftlicher und sozialpolitischer Erkenntnis' in *Gesammelte Aufsätze zur Wissenschaftslehre* (Tübingen, Mohr, 1973 [1904]) 188–89.

[27] T Mergel, *Propaganda nach Hitler. Eine Kulturgeschichte des Wahlkampfes in der Bundesrepublik 1949–1990* (Göttingen, Wallstein, 2010) 145–52.

[28] See Jaspers's position on the *Spiegel-Affäre* of 1962 in *Briefwechsel*, above n 4, 527.

Kiesinger as the Federal Chancellor and the Social Democrats as the junior partner, with Willy Brandt as Foreign Minister. The Government's proposal for emergency legislation (*Notstandsgesetze*) is a major concern in Jaspers's books. Although his critique sometimes resembles that of the rising left-wing extra-parliamentary opposition in Germany, his proposals and arguments are definitely different.

Arendtian *topoi* shape the entire argumentation of Jaspers. He insists on a radical break with the criminal Nazi regime and calls for the insight and will to re-found the State, '*der uneingeschränkte Wille zum Abbruch der Kontinuität zu dem Verbrecherstaat, die Erkenntnis und der Wille zur Neugründung*'.[29] The Federal Republic had made merely an external break, without reaching the hearts and minds as well as the political convictions of the people ('*ein äußerlich gefügtes Ordnungsgebilde ... ohne Ursprung in den Herzen und Köpfen des Volkes, ohne eine neue politische Gesinnung*').[30] In this sense the Republic remained an external institution, not an idea embraced by the citizens ('*eine äußere Institution, nicht eine innere des Denkens der Bürger*').[31]

Jaspers yearns for 'a jump to a new beginning' from the Federal Republic ('*der Sprung zum neuen Anfang*').[32] The longing for a political origin based on a constituting event, *Gründungsereignis*,[33] directly corresponds to the point of Arendt's critique from 1950 and her *On Revolution*. Such views give the impression that a moral conversion of every citizen would have been required as a condition for the new State. Jaspers's demand for a new conviction (*Gesinnung*) in the singular is a further example of a thinking that sets unity before plurality.

Nonetheless, Jaspers also parodies the search for consensus (*Einmütigkeit*) when looking at the spirit of solidarity between professional politicians in the *Bundestag* debate ('*Geist einer Solidarität der Berufspolitiker*').[34] At the same time the Federal Republic was still lacking a common ethico-political (*sittlich-politische*) foundation.[35] In other words, Jaspers rejects only 'false' forms of consensus. Despite his yearning for freedom, he remains much more a moralist and consensus-driven thinker than Arendt.

That a philosopher would analyse parliamentary debate is interesting, but unfortunately Jaspers reads the debate as though the facts would speak for themselves,[36] without properly considering either the political constellation or the genre of parliamentary debate. He accuses the Government of leaving decision-making to the parliament alone.[37] Chancellor Erhard kept his silence, though he sat the plenum.[38] Jaspers regards the speeches of Benda (CDU) and Jahn (SPD) as

29 Jaspers, above n 5, 22.
30 *Ibid* 67.
31 *Ibid* 128.
32 *Ibid*.
33 *Ibid* 68.
34 *Ibid* 97, 112.
35 *Ibid* 115.
36 On this method, see Jaspers, above n 6, 116–17.
37 Jaspers, above n 5, 58.
38 *Ibid* 56.

the highlights of the debate, but sees the result as a thin compromise that merely postponed the deadline for decriminalisation.[39] He charges that the debate was conducted merely inside the CDU parliamentary *Fraktion* which changed its position on the outdating of the Nazi crimes.[40] This change was, however, decisive for the result and also for the resignation of minister Bucher. In short, Jaspers judges the parliamentary debate by academic criteria and regards the compromise as a deplorable product of the kinds of tactics used by politicians to obtain majorities.

Jaspers is worried at the same time of too little as well as of too much debate. He is longing for a Nietzschean *große Politik*, and sees the West German parliamentarians as failing to meet the challenges of the great questions of the day. The parliamentarians were without deep personal convictions, and were not 'manly enough' (*'Man findet unter ihnen nicht viele eigentliche "Männer"'*).[41] This is a vulgar interpretation of Weber's concepts of *Leidenschaft* (passionate dedication to a cause), *Gesinnungsethik* (ethics of conviction) and *Verantwortungsethik* (ethics of responsibility) from *Politik als Beruf*,[42] while neglecting *Augenmaß* (approximate judgement, 'measurement by the eyes'). Jaspers idealises the committed politician, but not Weber's anti-dogmatic counter-type, who is capable of discussing consequences and political constellations and making approximate judgements.

Common to both Arendt and Jaspers is trust in the people (*das Volk*) as the last authority in politics. They remain suspicious of representation, parliament and the procedure of debating *pro et contra*. The founders of the *Grundgesetz* avoided the Weimar combination of presidential and plebiscitarian elements, and did not attribute the failure of the Republic to its parliamentarism. Jaspers reproaches them for minimising popular participation to voting in elections every fourth year on the basis of party lists.[43] He, furthermore, sees parties as having turned into appendages of the State due to their funding by the State. In addition, he rejects constitutional innovations such as the constructive vote of no confidence (*konstruktives Mißtrauensvotum*) to bring about the fall of the Government, the lack of referenda and the 5 per cent threshold clause for parties to enter the *Bundestag*.[44] As a counterweight to the party government he proposes an independent federal president and, with reference to Arendt, popular councils from below, *'politische Zusammenschlüße von unten aus dem Volk, … Räte'*.[45] With such measures he hopes to counter the over-emphasis on political stability and oppose the paralysis of political thought among the population and the Government: *'Das politische Denken im Leben der Bevölkerung wie der Regierenden ist gelähmt.'*[46]

39 *Ibid* 58.
40 *Ibid* 94.
41 *Ibid* 117.
42 M Weber, *Politik als Beruf. Max-Weber-Studienausgabe* I/17 (Tübingen, Mohr, 1994 [1919]) 35–88.
43 Jaspers, above n 5, 137.
44 *Ibid* 133–35.
45 *Ibid* 135–36.
46 *Ibid* 150.

Along with Max Weber and Theodor Eschenburg, a major figure in West German constitutional law and political science, Jaspers admires the independence of parliamentarians, comparing them in this respect to professors.[47] The *Bundestag*, however, is all too dependent on the parties and all too weak in parliamentary control of government. The Opposition was unable to control the Government, when the Social Democrats with their 1959 Bad Godesberg programme gave up the socialist economic policy and accepted the 'social market economy' of their adversaries in order to appear as plausible alternative for the voters. A parliamentary State that has not yet realised an alternation in government does not, for Jaspers, really deserve the name.[48]

This critique appears appropriate insofar as the dangers destructive to the Weimar Republic no longer existed. Nonetheless, the proposals miss the point. A few years after De Gaulle's rise to power and the de-parliamentarisation of the French Fifth Republic, the dangers of a Bonapartist-type alliance between the people and the president were by no means absent in Germany either. In that sense, both the constructive vote of no confidence and the five per cent clause strengthened the parliamentary powers against such dangers.

The *Parteienoligarchie*,[49] an old *topos* of intellectuals, forms the nucleus of Jaspers's critique of the West German politics. Leibholz's interpretation of the *Grundgesetz* and the party-list electoral system gave to it a certain credibility in post-war Germany. Jaspers denounces the quasi-monopoly and cartel of the parties, and the dangers of a grand coalition or all-party government.[50] He does not, however, even mention the role of interest groups and lobbies, which both inside and across party lines wielded oligarchic power beyond the control of the voters and the parliament.

The demand that the Chancellor should nominate 'independent' ministers[51] is a remnant of the Hegelian 'objective spirit' incarnated in the officials above the dirty game of politics. Jaspers seemingly supports Weber's proposal of parliamentary control commissions, but unlike Weber he does not aim at increasing the parliamentarians' control over the knowledge and power of the officialdom.[52] On the contrary, he wants to include in the commission non-partisan experts and ethically and politically reliable non-parliamentarians ('*parteilose Sachkündige, angesehene, ethisch-politisch zuverlässige Nichtparlamentarier zuzuziehen*').[53] His point is not to strengthen debate by introducing additional perspectives, but rather indirectly to rehabilitate old objections to parliamentary democracy. Even more naive is

47 *Ibid* 132.
48 *Ibid* 136–38.
49 *Ibid* 133.
50 *Ibid* 154.
51 *Ibid* 136, 194.
52 M Weber, *Parlament und Regierung im neugeordneten Deutschland. Max-Weber-Studienausgabe* I/15 (Tübingen, Mohr, 1988 [1918]) 235–48.
53 Jaspers, above n 5, 196.

his trust in the 'objectivity' of labour market policy experts.[54] This is strongly opposed to the Weberian perspectivistic and rhetorical concept of 'objectivity'[55] and Weber's calls for parliamentary control of the officialdom on both aspects.[56]

Jaspers does not advocate a new electoral system or strengthening parliamentarians in relation to their parties. His suggestions include plebiscitarian demands for petitions, restricting party-based appointments, directly electing an *ombudsman* according to the model of the Roman popular tribune, and instituting a presidential veto over the appointment of ministers and high officials. All this would have weakened the parliamentary powers of deliberation and decision in relation to the Government and the bureaucracy.

More radical are his Arendtian calls to the people spontaneously to organise and to participate in candidate nomination and local government.[57] He offers, however, no procedures for dealing with disputes between partisan and non-partisan powers. There is no guarantee whatsoever to prevent Jaspers's combination of presidential, expert and plebiscitarian reforms from increasing the power of non-elected officials, lobbies and pressure groups at the cost of parliamentary control of government. Furthermore, 'the people' of Jaspers appears, once more, as a monolithic figure, and he is not willing or able to analyse the divisions, conflicts and cleavages within 'the people', or to develop procedures for debate analogical to those in the parliament.

V. JASPERS'S REPLY TO CRITICS

In *Antwort zur Kritik meiner Schrift Wohin treibt die Bundesrepublik*, Jaspers takes up some of the polemics of his critics and reformulates his analysis and proposals to apply to the new grand coalition of Kiesinger–Brandt. He states that he does generally accept the parliamentary democracy of the Federal Republic and want his proposals to be understood as reforms or improvements.[58] He insists, however, on discussing politics from the 1,000-year perspective of a philosopher.[59] Whereas Arendt regards politics as a question of present appearances, Jaspers devaluates politics by setting it into a perspective of the perennial questions.[60]

In terms almost directly taken from Arendt's 1950 'Report from Germany', Jaspers's autobiographical narrative on the origins of the Federal Republic simply

[54] *Ibid* 276.

[55] M Weber, '"Die Objektivität" sozialwissenschaftlicher und sozialpolitischer Erkenntnis', above n 26.

[56] On both aspects, see K Palonen, 'Max Weber, Parliamentarism and the Rhetorical Culture of Politics' (2004) 4 *Max Weber Studies* 273; Palonen, above n 2; K Palonen, *'Objektivität' als faires Spiel. Wissenschaft als Politik bei Max Weber* (Baden-Baden, Nomos, 2010).

[57] Jaspers, above n 5, 198–200.

[58] Jaspers, above n 6, 11.

[59] *Ibid* 13.

[60] Compare the parody by Q Skinner, 'Meaning and Understanding in the History of Ideas' (1969) 8 *History and Theory* 3.

reiterates how the Republic was founded by the Allied powers and party leaders, not spontaneously from below. With the election of the first *Bundestag* in 1949 the possibilities for a new beginning were lost: '*Alle vorhandenden Möglichkeiten waren verschwunden.*'[61] The result was a parliamentary democracy of passive subjects who did not know the proper point of voting in elections ('*Ein Parlamentarismus von der Art, in dem die Untertanen, die noch gar nicht wissen, was das eigentlich ist, wählen*').[62] This is the classical academic argument against suffrage reforms, relying on educational[63] instead of political institutions to provide experiences for political judgement.

Unlike the student movement's idealisation of workers' councils, Jaspers recognises the indispensability of parties in a mass democracy.[64] Nonetheless, his party-bashing contains conspiratorial claims about parties as a small oligarchic minority that is alien to the people.[65] The epithet *volksfremd* indicates how Jaspers's idealisation of 'the people' could sound almost similar to the Nazis' jargon. Strangely, he also claims that the 'absolute Herrschaft' of the parties was unique to West Germany ('*gibt es nirgends außer bei uns*'),[66] whereas the practical identification of politics with party politics was the rule in all West European countries at that time.

To the critics Jaspers offers some clarifications of the concept of the people, *das Volk*. He sees both the people and the politicians as the target audience of his book, calling both to *Besinnung*, to reflect upon the state of affairs.[67] Characteristically, here is the very opposition of the people *versus* the politicians. Although Jaspers distances himself from the Rousseauvian idealisation of 'the good people', he sticks to the denunciation of 'bad politicians', considering them as separate and inherently opposed entities to the citizens, a concept that features prominently in his argumentation. Jaspers's dualism of good citizens *versus* bad politicians contains an implicit polemics against Weber's view of citizens as occasional politicians (*Gelegenheitspolitiker*).[68]

Das Volk is for Jaspers neither a mere quantitative entity (*die Menge*) nor a myth, but an *Idee*,[69] one which serves as a justificatory principle for democracy based on trust in the people ('*das Vertrauen des Volkes*').[70] This trust in the people legitimises distrust in the politicians, holding them responsible for accepting Nazi power in 1933: '*Das Mißtrauen nach 1933 ist in erster Linie gegen die Politiker zu richten.*'[71] Again, the polemics against 'the politicians' is an anti-parliamentary and

[61] Jaspers, above n 6, 67.
[62] *Ibid.*
[63] *Ibid* 98–105.
[64] *Ibid* 113.
[65] *Ibid* 86: '*Eine kleine innerlich volksfremde Parteienminorität und darin die Parteienoligarchie ist fast zur Herrschaft gelangt.*'
[66] *Ibid.*
[67] *Ibid* 125.
[68] Weber, above n 42, 41. Cf K Palonen, *Eine Lobrede für Politiker* (Opladen, Leske-Budrich, 2002).
[69] Jaspers, above n 6, 126.
[70] *Ibid* 127.
[71] *Ibid* 129.

anti-democratic *topos* of the nineteenth-century suffrage reforms.[72] Imputing the Nazi rise to power to 'the politicians' without further qualification manifests this anti-parliamentary tendency.

Jaspers admits the lack of institutional thinking as a weakness of *Wohin treibt die Bundesrepublik?* He regards institutions as possessing value only as instruments of control,[73] although, referring to Weber, he also emphasises that an interplay between persons and institutions might enable the rise of 'great statesmen'.[74] Weber, however, would not oppose persons to institutions, for the institutions contribute to the formation of certain types of persons, their experiences and competences. The Weberian *Chances* involved in institutions are not necessarily the ones aimed at, Weber contends, since unintended consequences are a regular part of political activities.[75]

Jaspers refers to the renowned German political science professor Wilhelm Hennis and his views on the reform of the *Bundestag*. Hennis puts his trust in reform from within, but Jaspers sticks to philosophical foundations, for otherwise political thought would remain bottomless ('*bodenlos*').[76] He reserves for philosophy a special role in making political judgements and in evaluating institutions.[77] Here we can note a Platonic tone in Jaspers's philosophy, whereas the political mode of institutional thinking about the actions taken remains for him an alien idea.[78] Arendt with her rhetorical insights is closer than Jaspers to understanding politics from within.

In reply to Kurt Sontheimer, another political science professor, Jaspers even regards the grand coalition to be close to irrevocably ruining democracy in West Germany ('*die Demokratie sich schneller abgeschafft hat als ich fürchtete*').[79] Such terms indicate a failure to maintain a clear distinction between democratic and non-democratic regimes in institutional and procedural terms. For Jaspers it was the Federal Republic alone—not Gaullist France or Austria (the latter had been ruled by a grand coalition for the entire post-war period)—that was abolishing parliamentary democracy.

The clarifications and concessions that Jaspers makes in the *Antwort* are not sufficient to make him a friend of parliamentary democracy. His alarmist situational analysis, his superficial concern for institutions, and his strange admiration of both the people and the experts rather accentuate his anti-parliamentary tendencies.

[72] See the classical studies of J Bryce, *The American Commonwealth* (Indianapolis, Ind, Liberty Fund, 1995) and M Ostrogorski, *La démocratie et les partis politiques* (Paris, Fayard 1993).
[73] Jaspers, above n 6, 145.
[74] *Ibid* 144.
[75] Weber, above n 42, 45–46.
[76] Jaspers, above n 6, 146.
[77] *Ibid* 147.
[78] *Ibid* 185–86.
[79] *Ibid* 184.

VI. ARENDT'S REVIEW OF JASPERS

Hannah Arendt was a successful propagandist of Jaspers's philosophy in the United States. *Wohin treibt die Bundesrepublik?* was translated in part and published with her foreward as *The Future of Germany* in 1967. She regarded it as the most important German political book of the post-war period.[80] This is a remarkable judgement when one considers the debt Jaspers owed to Arendt herself, whom Jaspers had always considered to be the better political thinker of the two.[81]

Arendt finds the core of the book to be the proposition that the Federal Republic is about to destroy its parliamentary democracy.[82] She accuses the American public of not being worried about the grand coalition led by a former member of the Nazi party, about the rise of the NPD in the local elections and about other signs of a revival of Nazism in Germany. Arendt welcomes the book as a wake-up call, and emphasises that certain unfortunate tendencies, such as the passage of emergency legislation, have become even stronger in Germany since the time when Jaspers's book was written. Quoting Jaspers from the *Antwort,* she warns of an ethico-political catastrophe facing the Germans.[83]

In their shared pessimistic analysis of the contemporary world situation,[84] Jaspers and Arendt tend to find alarming signs everywhere. Arendt compares the emergency legislation of the grand coalition with Brüning's emergency decree of 1931.[85] Such judgement was commonplace among the left-wing extraparliamentary opposition in Germany, but the comparison ignores crucial differences with respect to the powers of the parliament, which were suspended by Brüning's *Notverordnungen*. Equally misplaced is Jaspers's alarm about the danger of a military dictatorship similar to Schleicher's project of 1932.[86] Arendt repeats her old thesis about the lack of a new beginning after the war, and she agrees with Jaspers as to the ghost of a '*Politiker-Diktatur*.'[87]

Arendt's conclusions based on historical parallels led her to ask why Jaspers's book became a bestseller. His *Geistige Sitution der Zeit* also sold well in 1931. Of course, Arendt was not predicting an imminent military coup in Germany, but she did refer with Jaspers to warning signs in that direction. Her foreword illustrates that Arendt shared with him a pessimistic situational analysis, as well as a lacking of regard for the institutions, procedures and practices of parliamentary politics.

80 H Arendt, '"Wohin treibt die Bundesrepublik?"' in H Arendt, *In der Gegenwart* (München, Piper, 2000) 64.

81 For Arendt's praise of Jaspers's attitudes towards the Federal Republic, see Arendt and Jaspers, above n 4, 656.

82 Arendt, above n 80, 64: '*befindet sich auf dem besten Weg, die parlamentarische Demokratie abzuschaffen*'.

83 *Ibid* 66: '*Eine neue sittlich-politische Katastrophe steht bevor.*'

84 See also H Arendt, *Between Past and Future* (Harmondsworth, Penguin, 1962).

85 Arendt, above n 80, 66.

86 Jaspers, above n 5, 168–69; Arendt, above n 80, 67.

87 Arendt, above n 80, 67.

VII. KALYVAS ON SCHMITT AND ARENDT

Arendt's unwillingness to give the Federal Republic a chance may also have other conceptual grounds, which Jaspers also took up. In a remarkable recent study, Andreas Kalyvas suggests that there are interesting similarities between Arendt and Carl Schmitt as theorists of democracy.[88] Both, for example, give the figure of 'the people' precedence over procedures and institutions.

Of course, Schmitt's decisionism as a modern form of politics of the will instead of action was rejected by Arendt.[89] Nonetheless, the similarities that Kalyvas presents are striking, and deserve attention as a perspective on the question of why Arendt does not discuss the constitutional and procedural questions of the Federal Republic, and of why Jaspers much later retains a fundamental dislike of the practices of German parliamentary culture.

Kalyvas's point of departure is the opposition between ordinary and extraordinary politics. The key passage reads:

> During these extraordinary moments, the slumbering popular sovereign wakes up to reaffirm its supreme power of self-determination and self-government and to substantially rearrange or alter the fundamental norms, values and institutions that regulate ordinary legislation and institutionalized politics. In extraordinary moments, politics opens up to make room for conscious popular participation and extrainstitutional, spontaneous collective intervention. The means and scope of political action undergo considerable changes. For instance, formal, procedural rules that regulate normal, institutionalized politics are supplemented by or subordinated to informal, extraconstitutional forms of participation that strive to narrow the distance between rulers and ruled, active and passive citizens, representatives and represented.[90]

Some of the main points may be noted here. First, the assumption that there exists a figure called 'the popular sovereign' as something that is always present but 'wakes up' only in extraordinary situations, which are marked by the very end of this 'slumber'. The second point is the low regard for procedures and institutions as something secondary—needed in ordinary circumstances, but to be questioned when the 'popular sovereign wakes up'. A more implicit assumption is the unity of the 'popular sovereign'. It is this that renders the link between the extraordinary and the non-procedural intelligible. This assumption shows that the popular sovereign does not need any procedures or institutions to mediate conflicts and debates between actors. If we explicate this point made by Kalyvas, we find that the 'means and scope of political action' are also reduced in importance during the extraordinary moment.

[88] A Kalyvas, *Democracy and the Politics of the Extraordinary* (Cambridge, Cambridge University Press, 2008).

[89] See the discussion of her critique of Schmitt's conception of sovereignty, *ibid* 210–12.

[90] *Ibid* 7.

Kalyvas claims that Carl Schmitt is an author who has well understood, especially in his *Constitutional Theory*,[91] this constituting, pre-institutional moment of democracy. A key thesis in his defence of Schmitt is the claim that 'the belief that democracy requires popular unity and collective solidarity is one of the oldest maxims in political thought, as well as of the democratic, republican and socialist traditions'.[92] This thesis may be disputed in historical terms. In any case, such an assumption of unity is not shared by the parliamentary style of political thought, from Renaissance rhetoric to Max Weber and beyond. The parliamentary tradition, on the contrary, relies on a rhetorical epistemology in which debating *pro et contra* is the basic *modus operandi* of the parliamentary institutions. The Canadian rhetoric scholar James De Mille puts the point as follows: 'The aim of parliamentary debate is to investigate the subject from many points of view which are presented from two contrary sides. In no other way can a subject be so exhaustively considered.'[93]

Kalyvas objects, however, to Schmitt's elimination of the moment of discussion: 'He did incorrectly assume that voice, discussion, judgment and deliberation were inherent, constitutive attributes of classical bourgeois parliamentarism,' whereas for Kalyvas 'the origins of those practices were located … at the very origins of the democratic experience, the ancient Greek *polis*'.[94] Such a view is common in the contemporary literature of rhetoric and of deliberative democracy. Unlike Schmitt and many other antiparliamentarians who turned against parliamentary proceduralism, this view tends to miss the significance of parliamentary procedure and its innovations in the institutionalisation of debate. To locate the origins of the political culture of debate in the Greek *polis* fails to appreciate the crucial dissentious character of parliamentary procedure and politics.

This disinterest in procedure also holds for Kalyvas's defence of Arendt's apology of deliberation in the popular councils as 'a public, diffused process of deliberation, debate, argumentation, and opinion formation'.[95] In contrast to Schmitt, Arendt is also a thinker of radical plurality. In the very first sentence of *Was ist Politik?*, from the 1950s, she declares that politics is based on the fact of plurality: '*Politik beruht auf die Tatsache der Pluralität der Menschen.*'[96] Consistent with this emphasis is Arendt's sympathy for the Sophist-style rhetorical theory of knowledge, which is based on the possibility of defending opposite *logoi*.[97] How is one to deal with such a radical plurality and its corresponding demands to debate issues *pro et contra* in political institutions?

[91] C Schmitt, *Constitutional Theory* (Durham, NC, Duke University Press, 2008).
[92] Kalyvas, above n 88, 122.
[93] J De Mille, *Elements of Rethoric* (1878) 473, retrieved at <http://www.archive.org/stream/elementsrhetori01millgoog> (accessed on 15 July 2009).
[94] Kalyvas, above n 88, 125.
[95] *Ibid* 276.
[96] H Arendt, *Was ist Politik?* (München, Piper, 1993) 9.
[97] See Arendt, above n 13, 390–92, 408–10.

The ancient debate paradigm defended by both Arendt and Kalyvas is in many respects more moderate than its parliamentary institutionalisation. In the *polis*' debates the moment of dissensus was to be overcome by the catharsis of unity, whereas in parliamentary politics the dissensus is the procedural principle of its intelligibility, the political basis of a rhetorical epistemology. A thorough understanding of a question presupposes both the presentation of opposed perspectives and a debate between them, the choice between them being decided by vote counting, not disputing the legitimacy of the minority perspectives.

The spontaneous character of debates in the popular councils that Arendt admires allows merely the cathartic type of debate on issues in which the opinions and perspectives of the participants do not radically oppose each other. This might also be the reason why she supports the power of constitutional courts over parliamentary institutions.[98] The advantage of the parliamentary style of politics is that it allows a more radical dissensus and the distinct parliamentary form of deliberating in a peaceful manner on the items, whether they concern the polity, the procedures or the agenda questions.

VIII. TOWARDS A PARLIAMENTARY INTERPRETATION OF 'THE PEOPLE'

It is an old problem: Are insiders or outsiders better political analysts? The dangers of parochialism[99] among the insiders and of dilettantism among the outsiders must be carefully weighed one against the other. Arendt's and Jaspers's views remain curiosities of the time, relevant only to understanding post-war West German parliamentary politics, whereas West German political theorists such as Wilhelm Hennis and Theodor Eschenburg are still a part of the political and constitutional debate. Arendt's distance from German politics was, of course, much greater than that of Jaspers, who tried to turn accusations of dilettantism into marks of honour.[100]

Their lack of insider access to parliamentary practices imposed limits on Arendt's and Jaspers's ability to analyse West German parliamentarism. Arendt's memory of the Weimar Republic and the US style of presidential government may have prevented her from interesting herself in the parliamentary politics of Germany. For Jaspers the question was approached from the habitus of a philosophy professor, and he was not without contempt for the 'mere politics' of politicians.

Jaspers applied Arendt's political and constitutional ideas to the West German politics of the 1960s. Their common points concern the need for a radical break

[98] See the discussion in Kalyvas, above n 88, 272, 278–79. Cf M Goldoni and C McCorkindale, ch 6 of this volume; W Smith, ch 7 of this volume.

[99] See Skinner, above n 60.

[100] Jaspers, above n 6, 184–85.

with the Nazi past and for a real 'new beginning' from below, according to, as suggested in Arendt's 'Report from Germany' of 1950, the US model of founding a republic. Jaspers explicitly refers to Arendt in his emphasis on trusting 'the people' as the basis of democracy and on the need for spontaneous popular organisations. His Platonic-Hegelian trust in the independent experts is, however, completely alien to Arendt, although her contractarianism also presupposes the unity of 'the people'. Jaspers does recognise parliamentarism and political representation as practical necessities, as for the moment the only possible way to freedom,[101] but he does not link this liberty to the deliberating character and rhetorical style of politics as institutionalised in parliament. He accepts instead a minimalist interpretation of parliamentary government, ie one without a political culture of parliamentary rhetoric.

Neither Arendt nor Jaspers was familiar with the rhetorical background of parliamentarism. Their German academic *Bildung* did not include, for example, William Gerard Hamilton's *Parliamentary Logick*, the rhetorical advice-book for parliamentarians based on maxims collected from the second half of the eighteenth century,[102] although it was available in German. The same is the case with the rhetorical literature of the nineteenth century, which regarded parliamentary oratory as an independent rhetorical genre.

The personal link between Max Weber and Karl Jaspers is well known, but Jaspers used Weber's concepts for his own purposes without connecting them to Weber's political context or style of thinking. In his early writings Jaspers attempted to make Weber a philosopher.[103] He hardly understood that, for Weber, politics was superior to philosophy and required a more rhetorical mode of thinking than Jaspers was prepared to accept, for example, regarding the concept of objectivity and parliamentary control of the knowledge of the officials.

In his brochure *Wahlrecht und Demokratie*, published at the end of 1917, Weber defends the view that a non-parliamentary form of democracy might, in practice, support uncontrolled rule by the officialdom.[104] In his *Parlament und Regierung im neugeordneten Deutschland* from spring 1918, he then drafts a programme for parliamentary control over officials and their allegedly superior knowledge. This explicitly shows that Weber was indebted to rhetorical tradition and to the procedures and practices of Westminster.[105] Neither publication by Weber is mentioned in Arendt's or Jaspers's comments on the parliamentary regime of Germany.

Another difference may be found in their views on 'the people'. In a letter to Robert Michels from 4 August 1908, Weber declares that he holds figures such as

[101] *Ibid* 11: '*die zur Zeit für die Bundesrepublik einzig reale Weg zur Freiheit*'.

[102] W Hamilton, *Parliamentary Logic*, with an introduction and notes by CS Kenny (Cambridge, Heffer, 1927).

[103] K Jaspers, *Max Weber. Gesammelte Abhandlungen* (München, Piper, 1988) 52–114.

[104] M Weber, *Wahlrecht und Demokratie in Deutschland. Max-Weber-Studienausgabe* I/15 (Tübingen, Mohr, 1988 [1917]) 187.

[105] M Weber, above n 52, 235–48; see Palonen, '*Objektivität*', above n 56.

'the will of the people' to be mere fictions.[106] This has been widely regarded as an expression of a scepticism towards democracy on Weber's part. I would suggest another interpretation: it is against the concept of a united people that Weber's statement is directed.

Both Weber's defence of parliamentarism and his rhetorical epistemology, ie his view of knowledge based on *pro et contra* disputes, emphasise division and dissensus. Weber's strong emphasis of these aspects prompts me to radicalise this thesis. Instead of viewing in the parliament a miniature model of 'the people', we should, on the contrary, view the dissensus among the citizens, or 'the people' in a constitutional sense, as serving to amplify the parliamentary mode of debating *pro et contra*.

Hannah Arendt's vision of a radical plurality of human beings also hints in the same direction, though she had reservations about Weber's uncompromising *Meisterstück der Nüchternheit*.[107] Inexperienced in parliamentary politics, Arendt lacked the tools to transfer this radical plurality to the procedural and institutional level, and she never considered parliament from the rhetorical perspective of being the institution of debate *par excellence*. Arendt with her non-voluntaristic contractarianism, according to the paradigm of the Mayflower compact[108] presupposes a consensus superior to the dissentious aspects and regards the principle of representation itself as something to be questioned.

Rousseau's dictum that the English are free only on election day does not preclude the possibility of defending a parliamentary and representative style of politics. From the Weberian perspective, we might say that on the election day, membership of the parliament expands to include the entire electorate. Since their votes determine the composition of the parliament, they are already participants in the debates of the next parliament.[109]

[106] M Weber, *Max-Weber-Briefe 1906–1908* (Tübingen, Mohr, 1990) 615.
[107] Arendt and Jaspers, above n 4, 186.
[108] Kalyvas, above n 88, 233–40.
[109] K Palonen, 'The Parliamentarisation of Elections' (2010) 14 *Redescriptions* 133.

Part III

Beyond the Nation State: Hannah Arendt and International Law

A. Public International Law

9

Facing the Abyss: International Law Before the Political

FLORIAN HOFFMANN

There is an art … or rather, a knack to flying. The knack lies in learning how to throw yourself at the ground and miss. (Douglas Adams, *Hitch Hiker's Guide to the Galaxy*[1])

I. A DISCIPLINE OF CRISIS

IN MANY WAYS, Hannah Arendt may be called a philosopher of crisis. It is a recurrent theme in Arendt's thought, notably the crisis of republicanism, the crisis of education; indeed, the crisis of modernity itself.[2] It is as much a heritage of her philosophical upbringing as of her witnessing of the quintessential crisis of the project of modernity.[3] And it is, not least, a product of her classicism, that is, her seeing through the defining terms of modernity to their Greek-Roman origins which, to her, revealed the fundamental issues of human existence in a clearer way than modern civilisation has been able to. It is, arguably, primarily in the latter sense that Arendt can be said to have been a philosopher of crisis, as she did not see crisis only as the breakdown of normality, but as an instance that calls for a response to a question and, thus, as a moment of decision, which, in turn, requires judgement.[4] In this classical sense, crisis is, for Arendt, the opposite of an undesirable state; it is, in fact, a crucial element for a modernity that does not fail itself by falling to hyperbole. For Arendt, it becomes a crisis in the modern sense only when the question to which a response is sought is either forgotten or no longer heard. And that question is, arguably, the question of political authority which, to her, is constitutive of the world itself.[5] That world is, of course,

[1] D Adams, *The Hitch Hiker's Guide to the Galaxy* (London, Del Ray, 1995).

[2] See, in particular, her collection of essays in *Between Past and Future* (Chicago, Ill, University of Chicago Press, 1961) as well as *Crises of the Republic* (New York, Harcourt, 1972); see also M Antaki, 'The Critical Modernism of Hannah Arendt' (2007) 8 *Theoretical Inquiries in Law* 253.

[3] See E Young-Bruehl, *Hannah Arendt: For Love of the World* (New Haven, Conn, Yale University Press, 2004).

[4] Antaki, above n 2, 252.

[5] Arendt, *Between Past and Future*, above n 2; see also S Humphreys, 'Nomarchy: On the Rule of Law and Authority in Giorgio Agamben and Aristotle' (2006) 19 *Cambridge Review of International Affairs* 331.

the 'now', ie that which bridges the 'gap between past and future' and which thereby provides a firm footing over the abyss that looms below.[6] Until the dawn of modern thought, that bridge consisted of authority in what Arendt defines as its Roman mode, notably authority as an act of foundation reiterated across time. Vested in those who represent past foundation, the elders, it was expressed through tradition and as such literally made (up) the world of the ancients.[7] That world, however, is gone, and modernity is, to Arendt, not just its replacement but the ongoing lamentation of its demise, not just a new thinking triggered by crisis but crisis itself. For modernity represents the breakdown of authority, and the essential modern condition is to face that predicament. It is, for Arendt, a specifically *political* predicament, that is, one in which the bridging activity has become individualised and bestows upon each and every one the need to act for oneself, to make world, to think critically.[8] The *political* is, hence, woven into the fabric of modernity; yet it has all too often been obscured. Recovering the political under conditions of modernity was, in any case, one of Arendt's primary quests and the task she placed on those passing through her thought.

Arendt's diagnosis of the inherently critical condition of the modern world is echoed in historiographical reflection on the dawn of the enlightenment.[9] Reinhard Koselleck, for one, notoriously argued that it was the 'discovery' of historical contingency that led to the critique of traditional authority, and its eventual replacement with an unholy melange of authoritarianism and utopianism.[10] He located this crisis in the eighteenth century, which, following Otto Brunner, he called the 'saddle period' (*Sattelzeit*).[11] Like Arendt, Koselleck's reflection on the modern condition took place against the backdrop of what would have seemed to both of them modernity's catharsis, the catastrophes of the first half of the twentieth century, and both would retain a degree of ambivalence about the modern project because it stemmed from, and indeed represented, crisis. Somewhat earlier, Paul Hazard had argued that it was the emergence of the modern State system after the Peace of Westphalia in the seventeenth century that represented a 'crisis of European conscience'.[12] Hazard argued, not unlike Arendt, that it

[6] Arendt, *Between Past and Future*, above n 2, 'Preface: The Gap Between Past and Future' 3; see also A Herzog, 'Political itineraries and anarchic cosmopolitanism in the thought of Hannah Arendt' (2004) 47 *Inquiry* 20, 26.

[7] H Arendt, *The Human Condition* (Chicago, Ill, Chicago University Press 1958) 90; see also B Constant, *The Liberty of the Ancients Compared to that of the Moderns* (New York, Peerless Press, 2010).

[8] Arendt, *Between Past and Future*, above n 2; see also T Bonacker, 'Die Politische Theorie des freiheitlichen Republikanismus: Hannah Arendt' in A Brodocz and G Schaal (eds), *Politische Theorien der Gegenwart* (Stuttgart, UTB, 2009).

[9] On the historiography of 'crisis', see R Starn, 'Historians and "Crisis"' (1971) 52 *Past and Present* 3.

[10] R Kosellek, *Critique and Crisis: Enlightenment and the Pathogenesis of Modern Society* (Cambridge, Mass, MIT Press, 1998); see also AJ LaVopa, 'Conceiving a Public: Ideas and Society in Eighteenth Century Europe' (1992) 64 *The Journal of Modern History* 79.

[11] R Koselleck, 'Einleitung' in O Brunner, W Conze, R Koselleck (eds), *Geschichtliche Grundbegriffe* (Stuttgart, Klett Cotta, 1979).

[12] P Hazard, *La Crise de la Conscience Européenne* (Paris, Le livre de Poche, 1994).

was the loss of religious authority which vouched for the reality of transcendent meaning that brought about a critical juncture and the eventual emergence of rational absolutism as the *materia prima* of the modern concept of sovereignty and the modern State system. Unlike Arendt, Hazard did not see all that followed as crisis but focused on the transitory moment of crisis which he evocatively called '*une zone uncertain … malaise*',[13] that is, a time in between, a moment to be seized, a *kairos*. Crisis as decision, as Arendt well perceived, links the concept not only to its etymological roots but also to the sphere into which it emerged in its native Greece, namely the public sphere of assemblies and courts, later of medicine and, of course, (military) history.[14] To these ancients, the idea of crisis introduced an element of disruption and contingency into more archaic concepts of repetition, 'eternal return' or the 'Golden Age', thus creating a sense of time at once organic and fragmented, and bringing about an incipient sense of historical contingency and relativity.[15] Much later, this critical contingency of the flux of history would, in turn, be re-framed so as to express the deeper logic of history itself. Augured in by the likes of Jean-Jacques Rousseau or Thomas Paine at the dawn of the 'age of revolutions', it was Marx who, by historicising the altogether uncritical Hegel, came to be the arch-thinker of the modern philosophy of crisis.[16]

Here crisis is the necessary consequence of the deeper logic of economic production; indeed, it arises from overproduction, and it necessarily forces the system of production to reconfigure itself in a historically more advanced form.[17] Thus crisis drives historical evolution through revolution, the ingenious formula on which Marxist philosophy of history is premised. Yet this deterministic view of history came to be opposed by a different strand of late nineteenth-century historiography, notably that inaugurated by Jacob Burckhardt, which gave crisis near equal prominence in its historical narrative, if from a very different perspective. For in the incipient historicist tradition, crises as events mark the narrative stepping-stones of history. It is, hence, through breaks with the regular flow of history, through upheaval and disruption that historical flux may be discerned and described, though without there being an overarching meta-narrative and clear-cut teleological direction of history.[18] Arendt, in turn, may be said to have attempted to budge this choice between crisis as structure or as event. Her critique of Marx centered, amongst others, on historical materialism's elimination of the historical significance of the event, and the resulting reduction of freedom

[13] *Ibid*, 'Preface' 4.

[14] Crisis derives from the ancient Greek *krisis* meaning 'judgement'; it, in turn, derives from the verbs (*krinein*) 'to separate, to decide, to judge' and 'to dispute, to contend, to explain', which has the (hypothetical) proto-Indo-European root *kri-*, 'to sieve, to discriminate, to distinguish'; the '*krites*' is, then, the judge; see Online Etymology Dictionary at <http://www.etymonline.com/index.php?search=krinesthai&searchmode=none>.

[15] Starn, above n 9, 5.

[16] See E Hobsbawm, *The Age of Revolution: 1789–1848* (New York, Vintage, 1996).

[17] Starn, above n 9, 7.

[18] *Ibid* 8.

to the recognition of objective necessity.[19] Yet her 'libertarian existentialism' placed her at an equal distance from mainstream historicism with its interest in observing the event as an external occurrence. For her, the event is not accidental but the result of pure, non-utilitarian action which interrupts the normal flow of historical time. It is, at least according to the exceptionalist interpretation of Arendt's thought, crisis action;[20] it implies a moment of choice, a bifurcation in the course of history which forces one to decide and move on, lest one ventures to abandoned history itself.

Is international law, then, in crisis? Has it, as a discourse and discipline, reached a dead end, and do global actors need to chart new territory to conceive of their relations? Or is there no crisis? The relation between international law and crisis is complex and multi-faceted. First, there is what might be termed international law *and* crisis. This is, arguably, the most common and, to many international lawyers, intuitive association with crisis, and it refers to those numerous yet discrete 'international incidents' which represent a breakdown of 'normal' inter-State relations and which raise the spectre of violence or humanitarian catastrophe.[21] This is the sort of crisis that international lawyers thrive on, for, as Hilary Charlesworth has critically remarked, 'it provides a focus for the development of the discipline and it also allows international lawyers the sense that their work is of immediate, intense relevance'.[22] Charlesworth's point here is that international lawyers tend to focus on one particular type of incident, notably individual instances of crisis, to the exclusion of the deep structures that produce what she terms 'everyday life' and which account for far greater human suffering than the aggregate of isolated incidents.[23] This is, of course, an elaboration of the general contention that international law's blind spot with regard to the deep structure of the international is no coincidence but a consequence of the project it articulates, notably the reconstruction of global politics as a liberal polity governed by a neutral rule of law.[24] Yet, perhaps ironically, while this project sees international legality as the norm and its violation as the exception, it is largely through these exceptional 'incidents' that international law is reaffirmed and reproduced.[25] It is during times of crisis that international law, by demarcating international 'normality', becomes a privileged episteme through which to frame the exception as exception and through which to articulate restorative action.

[19] E Müller, 'Hannah Arendt's Marxkritik' (2003) 14 *Berliner Debatte INITIAL* 104; see also WA Suchting, 'Marx and Hannah Arendt's The Human Condition' (1962) 73 *Ethics* 47, and J Ring, 'On Needing Both Marx and Arendt: Alienation and the Flight from Inwardness' (1989) 17 *Political Theory* 432.

[20] Müller, above n 19; see also PF d'Arcais, *Libertärer Existenzialismus: Zur Aktualität der Theorie von Hannah Arendt* (Frankfurt am Main, Neue Kritik, 1993).

[21] See most notably M Reisman and A Willard, *International Incidents: The Law that Counts in World Politics* (Princeton, NJ, Princeton University Press, 1988).

[22] H Charlesworth, 'International Law: A Discipline of Crisis' (2002) 65 *MLR* 377.

[23] *Ibid* 388.

[24] See S Marks, 'The End of History? Reflections on Some International Legal Theses' (1997) 3 *European Journal of International Law* 449.

[25] See G Agamben, *State of Exception* (Chicago, Ill, University of Chicago Press, 2005).

It is also these moments which, as Charlesworth observes, bestow a critical role onto international lawyers, namely as the scribes whose privileged knowledge of the grammar of international affairs opens to them the prince's ear.[26] Hence, in a world in which 'normal' law, Charlesworth's 'law of everyday life', is largely hidden within the private life of States, 'incidents' represent instances when international law becomes public and is affirmed as the *telos* of global political action. As such and paradoxically, the crises that dominate the international political agenda and that, to many external observers, reveal a failure of the international rule of law, are not, by and large, seen or felt as crises *of* international law by its practitioners.[27] Indeed, for many an international lawyer, non-compliance does not challenge the reified view of international law as a factual system of rules governing inter-State conduct. Neither does it weaken the underlying conviction that this system enshrines progressive values which make it the most desirable *modus operandi* for inter-State relations.[28]

There is, however, a second sense in which international law is associated with crisis, and in this one, crisis does seem to affect the discipline and discourse itself, namely in the form of the phenomenon commonly referred to as 'fragmentation'. The latter challenges, on empirical grounds, the idea that one unified body of rules governs all international conduct, and it implies three threats to the traditional conception of international law: the segmentation of rule applicability; the pluralisation of interpretative authority; and the colonisation of some legal regimes by others. All three may be viewed as dangerous cracks in the edifice of 'normal' international law which, if taken to their logical conclusion, would imply a dissolution of international law 'as we know it'.[29] However, while some scholars have expressed concern over the potential loss of coherence, and with it of legal certainty, predictability and equal treatment that fragmentation may represent, this has hardly been viewed as life-threatening for international law.[30] Hence, in its *Report on the Fragmentation of International Law* the International Law Commission concluded that the available body of rules and accumulated precedent already contained all the tools necessary either to overcome or to manage regime pluralism and potential regime clash. Indeed, it stressed that

[26] See M Koskenniemi, 'Epilogue' in *From Apology to Utopia: The Structure of International Legal Argument* (Cambridge, Cambridge University Press, 2005); see also F Hoffmann, 'An Epilogue on an Epilogue' (2007) 7 *German Law Journal* 1095.

[27] For a forceful if polemical defence of international law, see P Sands, *Lawless World: America and the Making and Breaking of Global Rules* (London, Penguin, 2005).

[28] See M Koskenniemi, *The Gentle Civilizer of Nations: The Rise and Fall of International Law 1870–1960* (Cambridge, Cambridge University Press, 2001) 494ff.

[29] What a global legal pluralism might look like has been conceived, inter alia, by A Fischer-Lescano and G Teubner, 'Regime-Collisions: The Vain Search for Legal Unity in the Fragmentation of Global Law' (2004) 25 *Michigan Journal of International Law* 999.

[30] For concern about fragmentation, see PM Dupuy, 'The Danger of Fragmentation or Unification of the International Legal System and the International Court of Justice' (1999) 31 *New York University Journal of International Law and Politics* 791.

> the very effort to canvass a coherent legal-professional technique on a fragmented world expresses the conviction that conflicts between specialized regimes may be overcome by law, even as the law may not go much further than require a willingness to listen to others, take their points of view into account and to find a reasoned resolution at the end. Yet this may simply express the very point for which international law has always exited [*sic*].[31]

Here, international law is advertised not just as a necessary moderating device in international relations, but as being its own meta-law. It is taken to contain not only its own rules of recognition, but also its own rules of integration through which the different legal regimes are made to cohere.

Is international law, thus, resistant to crisis? If political crises are but international law's basic nutrient, and if international legal pluralism is but its natural evolution, then its critique would be besides the point, that is, analytically misconceived and politically naive or even dangerous. Yet there is, arguably, a third way in which international law may be associated with crisis, notably as itself denoting crisis, or rather, as a symptom of the structural crisis that pervades global politics. That crisis is rooted in a lack of political authority in the international sphere and the replacement of political action by strategic politics. The latter is built on the Vatellian model of atomistic statehood and antagonistic national interest which is premised on the idea of (State) sovereignty. A product of the absolutist era, such sovereignty, in Arendt's view, confounds freedom with free will, and therefore defines politics as the antagonistic encounter of sovereign wills.[32] Anthony Carty has called this a 'false ontology' which provides the intellectual ground for what to him is a Hobbesian (mis-)conception of order in the international sphere. The latter is based on the

> apparent construction of order based upon the opposition of the domestic and the foreign, and the paradox of a state system which rests upon the mutually exclusive suppositions that each is a self for itself and an other for all the others.[33]

Thus, (State) action is conceived of as inherently strategic and utility-oriented, driven, as it were in Arendt's terms, by capitalism and nationalism, and international affairs become a network of private economic and military engagements, with the State being, in essence, an *animal laborans* writ large.[34] The private pursuit of survival comes to constitute the public sphere of States, while the public pursuit of freedom is relegated to the private sphere of civil society. The crisis that modernity represents for Arendt is, hence, also one of the modern State system

[31] International Law Commission, *Fragmentation of International Law: Difficulties Arising from the Diversitification and Expansion of International Law—Report of the Study Group of the International Law Commission* (A/CN.4/L.682 of 13 April 2006) at 246.

[32] Arendt, *Between Past and Future*, above n 2; see also J Keedus, '"Human and nothing but human": How Schmittian is Hannah Arendt's critique of human rights and international law?' (2011) 37 *History of European Ideas* 190, 193f.

[33] T Carty, *The Philosophy of International Law* (Edinburgh, Edinburgh University Press, 2007) 161.

[34] Arendt, above n 7.

and of international relations. As such it is one, too, of the modern international legal project; for the latter is, as Martti Koskenniemi has shown, inherently paradoxical in its 'structural coupling' of utopian legalism and the apology of sovereignty.[35] On the one hand, international law's near exclusive focus on the State enshrines the idea of antagonistic sovereignty and creates a false *nomos* of politics; on the other hand, its articulation of universal features of humanity abstracts from concrete human beings and inverts cause and effect of (their) political action.[36] Both result in a reduction of the space for politics and, thus, of freedom. For Arendt, the law of the modern nation State is unable to maintain, by itself, the balance between *demos* and *ethnos*, the rule of law and popular sovereignty.[37] It may well, on the contrary, serve to cover up any imbalance in the name of an abstract humanity and to substitute technical solutions for political ones, a phenomenon now frequently referred to as managerialism.[38]

It is, hence, international law itself that demarcates the crisis of international politics. It embodies the fundamental tension between the universal and the particular which modernity, Sisyphus-like, continuously strives but fails to overcome. By enshrining the identity-creating particularism of the State system, international law produces the conditions of its own demise. To balance this sliding scale, it covers its particularist traces in an air of universalism which, however, abstracts from its concrete foundation in modern statehood and surrenders government through law to governance under law. Hence, the more the law is put in question in *international* relations, the more it is reasserted in *trans-national* ones; the less States seem to govern (through law), the more governance there is (by law). It is modernity's mode of functioning, namely, to cover up the loss of foundation through a simulacrum of foundation. If political authority is the foundation, law mimics it in form but not substance. To conceal that lack of substance, its formal authority must continuously expand and reaffirm itself on new sites. Indeed, it must inherently strive to cover all the discursive space of, in this case, international relations in order to protect its authority and eliminate the possibility of uncovering its lack of (political) substance. As such, (international) law strives to rule, and the ideal of the (international) rule of law is a reflection of modernity's imperialist discursivity. Its concrete shape is that of international legalism, that is, of the continuous expansion of the rule of law in international affairs. As a phenomenon, this has for long been known in (domestic) legal sociology as 'juridification', that is, as the gradual infiltration of the functional logic, or code, of law into other codes, most notably that of

[35] Koskenniemi, above n 26.

[36] Keedus, above n 32.

[37] Bonacker, above n 8.

[38] See here, in particular, Koskenniemi's recurrent critique, developed, inter alia, in 'Constitutionalism, Managerialism and the Ethos of Legal Education' (2007) 1 *European Journal of Legal Studies* 1; 'The Politics of International Law' (1990) 1 *European Journal of International Law* 4; 'The Politics of International Law—20 Years Later' (2009) 20 *European Journal of International Law* 7; 'Miserable Comforters: International Relations as New Natural Law' (2009) 15 *European Journal of International Relations* 395.

politics. The early Habermas described this, of course, as a process of colonisation which, at the time, he critically thought shifted legitimacy away from the political and onto the legal sphere.[39] In fact, insofar as international legalism is, necessarily, articulated against international politics, it is itself a political project, namely, one that champions international law as the better international politics.

As with modernity in general, international law is paradoxically instrumental both in bringing about the loss of political authority and in trying to cover it up. It can obscure its failure to fill out entirely the hole left by political action only by hypertrophying, yet it provides, thereby, a sense of foundation and reassurance. It does so, of course, by laying claim to two legitimating discourses outside of its own remit, notably justice and peace. It is in the name of these two that international lawyers justify their 'intervention' in international politics, notably as a morally, sociologically and perhaps even politically necessary shifting of language games, out of politics and into law. Yet while expansive legalism is driven by the deep logic of the modern project of international law, international lawyers have scarcely been awake to its inherent contradictions or to the (ethical) need to take position on account of them. Instead, the abyss between real and ideal, power and norm, apology and utopia has largely been ignored in theory and plastered over by compromise formula in practice. Indeed, many international lawyers have felt emboldened by the legalisation of ever more subjects of international politics, be it international trade, environmental degradation and climate change, or mass atrocity in conflict situations.[40] The seeming centre-stage place taken by legal—as opposed to political—discourse when it comes to dealing with situations such as those in Sudan, Kosovo or Iraq, is often enough to distract the discipline from its actual state. A culture of muddling through has taken hold, whereby international law's relevance and legitimacy is taken at face value, and where international lawyers mechanically apply their expert idiom to whatever (political) reality presents itself to them. As a result, those insisting on taking the project's critical condition seriously have been pushed to the margins of the discipline, while, at the same time, the language itself has become, by grammatical standards, impure and inconsistent, as well as inflated with the neologisms of governance and management. As with modernity, international law seems to run its own end-game.[41]

II. OUT OF THE MUD? (NEO)FORMALISM V (NEO)NATURALISM

Awareness of this end-game usually surfaces only during critical periods when the contingency of the concepts and institutions that make up 'the world' becomes

[39] J Habermas, *The Theory of Communicative Action*, vol 2 (Boston, Mass, Beacon Press, 1987) 355.

[40] See T Skouteris, *The Notion of Progress in International Law Discourse* (The Hague, Asser, 2010).

[41] A Wellmer, *Endgames: The Irreconcilable Nature of Modernity* (trans D Midgley) (Cambridge, Mass, MIT Press, 1998).

undeniable.[42] In Euro-American history, it is times such as the *fin-de-siècle* of the nineteenth century, the inter-War years or, indeed, the contemporary post-Cold War, post-9/11 period which are marked by soul-searching and an uneasy recognition of the need to reconsider and reconstruct. In contemporary international law, the post-Cold War period has seen a prolonged soul-searching both for the role of law in international affairs and for the state of the international legal project and the discipline of international law. The picture that has emerged here is more complex than would appear at first sight, most notably because of a cross-cutting of theoretical concerns and (perceived) geo-political position. Broadly put, one axis of the matrix that represents contemporary international legal theorising shows the divide between what has been described above as the 'muddling through' position, notably the non self-reflexive formalist 'practitioner's approach',[43] on one hand, and those approaches self-consciously critical of it and commonly grouped under the label of 'critical legal studies', on the other hand. This divide is both about the status of theory in the discipline and about the appropriate theoretical perspective on it, namely, either the internal perspective of legal positivism or the external perspective of auxiliary disciplines such as philosophy or sociology.

The formalist 'mainstream' forms, as Stanley Fish might have put it, an interpretive community in which a received canon of primary and secondary rules is applied to concrete cases rather than theoretically reconstructed with reference to anything beyond that canon.[44] There is, hence, in this position an inherent critique of theory as necessarily critical, that is, as being essentially about reconstructing law through terms outside of it. The underlying epistemology is, of course, that of legal positivism, which has combined an analytical critique of the 'impurities' of legal analysis with a political critique of the alleged primacy of certain theoretical meta-narratives over others.[45] Instead, law is seen as an autonomous field of norms and normative relations, a specific code that can be properly understood only from the vantage point of its own syntax and grammar. This turn to a positivistic mindset in international law as of the nineteenth century has also meant a shift away from scholarly argument to judge-made law, with the emphasis on formal legal process reducing the reflective space for theorising. If theory is accorded any relevance at all in this 'practitioner approach', it is as doctrine or, as Anthony Carty would have it, as dogmatics, that is, as the interpretation of

[42] For a popular if enlightening argument to that end, see P Blom, *The Vertigo Years: Europe 1900–1914* (New York, Basic Books, 2010).

[43] Carty, above n 33; see also BS Chimni, 'An Outline of a Marxist Course of International Law' in S Marks (ed), *International Law on the Left: Re-Examining Marxist Legacies* (Cambridge, Cambridge University Press, 2006).

[44] See S Fish, *Is There A Text in This Class* (Cambridge, Mass, Harvard University Press, 1980) 147ff.

[45] For good overviews of the tenets of legal positivism in international law, see J Von Bernstorff, *The Public International Law Theory of Hans Kelsen: Believing in International Law* (Cambridge, Cambridge University Press, 2010); and J Kammerhofer, *Uncertainty in International Law: A Kelsenian Perspective* (London, Routledge, 2010).

legislation and jurisprudence understood as a logically coherent system of rules and not concerned with the values informing legal precepts, nor with their meaning in relation to history, society or politics.[46] Such a legal dogmatic approach corresponds, of course, to a hermetic shielding-off of the legal from the political language game and to a (political) denial of the need to provide (theoretical) justification. This is the impulse behind the prevalent muddling through.

Yet with this being so, alternatives have, by and large, been articulated in and through opposition to the 'mainstream' position, notably as critical theories (about international law) and critical meta-theories (about international lawyers). They broadly fall into three methodological streams, notably *postmodern* perspectives inspired, inter alia, by French post-structuralism, linguistics and psychoanalysis, and they are interested mainly in the indeterminacy of legal language and the (micro-) politics behind the law;[47] *Marxist* perspectives drawing on an historical-materialist framework of analysis and mainly interested in international law's implication in imperialism, colonialism and global capitalism;[48] and *pragmatic/legal Realist* perspectives focusing on the techniques and strategies of international legal governance.[49] However, in line with the broader project of critical theorising, these 'critiques' of international law operate on the level of critical hermeneutics that aim to reconstruct an existing social reality in different terms. They thereby essentially seek to produce emancipation through enlightenment, notably by theoretically recharging practice. The international legal project as such is, however, not questioned as such; indeed, it is the building block for critical theorising, and the majority of self-conscious 'crits' continue to see themselves as international lawyers. Much critical legal theorising has, in effect, engaged in driving the 'mainstream' deeper into its mud, rather than in systematically articulating alternatives.

In the shadow of the ongoing engagement between the formalist 'mainstream' and the 'crits', two other positions have established their theoretical niches, namely, sociological approaches and law and economics. The former purport to be strictly analytical and reconstruct international law in legal sociological terms, drawing on international relations theory, administrative law and comparative political science. From the international perspective of formalism, these approaches, too, are external to the law, though the main difference from critical approaches is their primary goal of developing a systematic approach to all forms of international normativity. Their premise is that canonical doctrine no longer captures the reality of that normativity, with phenomena such as fragmentation or the non-State actor predicament calling for new vocabularies and new systematic

[46] AJ Arnaud, *Dictionnaire encyclopédique de théorie et de sociologie du droit* (Paris, Librarie générale de droit et de jurisprudence,1993); Carty, above n 33.

[47] See A Rasulov, 'International Law and the Poststructuralist Challenge' (2006) 19 *Leiden Journal of International Law* 799.

[48] See Marks (ed), above n 43.

[49] See D Kennedy, 'Spring Break' (1985) 63 *Texas Law Review* 1377.

for international law.[50] 'Law and economics' or rational choice, or simply realist approaches to international, have emerged relatively recently as a reflection of the predominant position this 'school' has reached in American domestic jurisprudence. Besides drawing on the rational choice perspective developed in neo-classical economics, it builds on the realist scepticism of the relevance of norms in international relations, and consequently represents a strong critique of the international legal project as such. Indeed, authors such as Jack Goldsmith or Eric Posner go one step further and, unlike their realist colleagues in international relations, not only downplay the role international law may possibly occupy, but hold out as positively perilous the international legalism that follows from the formalist project.[51]

While the international legal theory matrix has produced a wealth of critical reconstructions of international law, few have ventured to point to a way out of the mud to either a critically recharged or an entirely alternative practice. From an Arendtian perspective, this undermines the very political, and politically progressive, character that critical theory claims for itself;[52] and it leaves politically relevant action to a 'profession' which, as such, is inherently averse to recognising that it is engaging in such practice. However, two recent theoretical projects stand out in this respect: one for attempting to provide 'mainstream' practice with a critical underpinning and explicitly to reframe it as progressive political practice; the other as an experimental revisiting of humanist natural law as an alternative to the State-centric Vattellian-Hobbesian scheme that underlies today's notion of international law. Both are, thus, attempts at redefinition, albeit from opposite angles, and both share a commitment to international law as law and to the empirical relevance and theoretical importance of the international legal project.

The first, conceived by Koskenniemi, goes down the path of formalism. As has been seen, he began his phenomenology of international legal discourse with the identification of the latter's paradoxical structural coupling of power and norm. He then went on to trace the historical actualisation of this discursive configuration and found that, as a self-consciously modern conceptual framework, international law had left its utopian origins as a politically progressive intervention into power politics and steadily developed into an apologetic provider of debating chips for the (State) powers that be. On the basis of this, Koskenniemi has, arguably, gone one step further and ahead of most other critical projects and offered a new and future-oriented perspective for the discipline in the form of the 'culture of formalism'. In (simplified) essence, the 'culture of formalism' seeks to reframe international legal discourse from within, notably by showing it to contain all the elements necessary to move it back from the current apologism to the political progressive

[50] See N Krisch, B Kingsbury and RB Stewart, 'The Emergence of Global Administrative Law' (2005) 68 *Law and Contemporary Problems* 15.

[51] See E Posner, *The Perils of Global Legalism* (Chicago, Ill, Chicago University Press, 2009).

[52] Arendt, *Between Past and Future*, above n 2.

utopias of global peace and social justice. Koskenniemi affirms that the vocabulary of formal (legal) norms and the judicial and quasi-judicial institutions within which it is performed provide the most hopeful platform for transformative politics under current global conditions—provided such strategic legal interventionism is aware of its own contingency and refrains from essentialising its lacking centre through reified concepts such as governance, human rights, constitutionalisation, etc. Indeed, the emphasis is all on strategic processes that avoid crystallisation into firm institutions or structures and thereby stay clear of the legal managerialism which, being devoid of political commitment, has, in Koskenniemi's mind, taken over the profession. Even though the theoretical underpinnings of the 'culture of formalism' clearly betray its critical pedigree, it has nonetheless left a big door open for well-intentioned practitioner-positivists, since 'canonical' professional practice would appear to be quite compatible with 'strategic formalism', if only the latter's professed political intentions were deemed progressive, as would arguably be the case with many practitioners of 'lawfare', especially in such legal fields as human rights, humanitarian law, environmental law or labour law. It is, perhaps, for this reason that the 'culture of formalism' has seemed to win the day over other critical projects. Indeed, it has asked the question of international legal theory about what else there is or ought to be apart from traditional international legal language and the interpretative community of international lawyers.

One international lawyer who has taken up this challenge is Anthony Carty, whose humanist neo-naturalism represents the other grand attempt at a way out of the mud.[53] As already hinted, it is diametrically opposed to neo-formalism, in that it fundamentally challenges the very notion of international law that informs the formalist canon. The latter is, to Carty, a Hobbesian/Vattellian plot that reduces the international to the 'deuteronomic' antagonism of sovereign States.[54] Carty's 'original sin' lies in this paradigm shift in the seventeenth century, with the turn to positivism in the nineteenth century only denoting the formalisation and canonisation of this scheme. His remedy against this plot consists, in essence, of (re-)philosophising international affairs through the 'development of a method for valid, legitimate, or otherwise convincing argument'. This is both a critical method aimed at exposing the unreality of the concepts of modern international law, and a way of exploring the 'real' being of society and political community, and the law at its basis. Unlike Koskenniemi, Carty believes that a 'real' international law is 'out there', waiting to be found, if only (methodological) 'right reason' were properly applied. While he shares with Koskenniemi the historical critique of the Vatellian conception and the role it has given to international lawyers, he radically differs in his vision of an alternative. For Koskenniemi, arguably the only cure must be the disease itself, which is why the agency of international lawyers is necessarily reduced to strategic intervention rather than containing a capability

[53] Carty, above n 33.
[54] *Ibid* 143.

to originate an entirely alternative praxis. The viability of such an alternative praxis is produced through the dual nature of the international: it is, at once, an episteme mediated by language *and* a set of material circumstances. As language, it is amenable to interpretation, and thus to a plurality of meanings; as a set of material circumstances, it is rooted in the social and political 'reality' of the people inhabiting the world.

For Carty, the 'mainstream' conception represents a distorted account of this 'reality' produced by international lawyers. It is hence up to them to pierce the veil of traditional statehood and its law, and to chart what they find behind it. The method Carty proposes to achieve this is what he calls 'an ethnographic phenomenology of human conduct, whereby the place of language as an all-determining structure is accepted up to the point that our minute instances of surface consciousness, general social perspectives can be read'.[55] Basing himself, amongst others, on the thought of Paul Ricoeur, Carty seeks to re-conceive the international as a space inhabited by 'cultural (and) historical communities' for whom the figure of the 'state is the institutional or procedural framework they give themselves for the conduct of their public affairs'.[56] These communities are culturally incommensurate, and are themselves made up of distinct individuals in a continuous search for identity. They are engaged in continuous conflict and struggle, though this engagement does not, as in Hobbes, take the necessary form of enmity, but on the contrary of mutuality. This is so because there are shared moral motivations among all participants, motivations which inhere in the human person. At the bottom lies the fundamental solicitude of human beings, their opaqueness and the need to work with rather than against this basic 'human condition'. Law, in this scenario, is the medium through which mutuality through (diplomatic) tact is expressed in the form of reasoned (public) opinion by international lawyers, subject to mistakes and misjudgement or, rather, to the intransparency of the effects of agency. In this way, the Hobbesian order of fear may be replaced by an order of respect in which 'tact in the face of perplexity has to take the place of fear in the face of the unknown and apparently threatening'.[57] This, then, is a sophisticated revisiting of natural law, or, rather, (legal) humanism as it developed within the historical natural law tradition. It aims to reconstruct a naturalistic world view in which law primarily denotes a complex morality that inheres in human community and is subject to rational exploration. It denotes only secondarily 'positive' precepts meant to regulate human conduct according to that overarching morality. And it reserves for the lawyer the role of the public intellectual engaged in a continuous debate about the content of the good (not of the right).

Are, then, either neo-formalism or neo-naturalism viable ways out of the mud? Can they address the Arendtian challenge of restoring the political to international

[55] *Ibid* 17.
[56] *Ibid* 18.
[57] *Ibid* 245.

relations? Do they conceive of a law that guards against, rather than articulates, either totalitarian or technocratic impositions? And are they apt for practice? It would go beyond the scope of this discussion to redescribe either conception in Arendtian terms. Yet, in a nutshell, one might argue that Koskenniemi's neo-formalism has a problem with politics, whereas Carty's neo-naturalism has one with the law. The 'culture of formalism', for one, is all about how to orient the particular language game that States play when dealing with each other towards certain political objectives. Yet there is no concept of the political and of the substantive objectives that flow from it in the 'culture of formalism'. On the contrary, it must preserve the autonomy of the law and legal institutions if it is to succeed in making law the better politics. Indeed, all legal formalism must be anti-political, and neo-formalism as politics can thus not itself be political. Nor does international law in Koskenniemi's conception play the role either of the *nomos* in the Greek *polis*, notably by providing the 'architectural' conditions of possibility for political action, or of the Roman *lex* that creates linkages between interlocutors. For formal law is, to Koskenniemi, a language game that derives its progressive potential precisely from its indeterminacy that permits its speakers to interpret and negotiate over meaning. That meaning, in turn, is stabilised through formalised grammatical rules which theoretically bind all speakers. Law thereby becomes, for Koskenniemi, the privileged discourse of (international) politics, a position curiously similar to Carty's notion of diplomatic tact at the basis of his new naturalism. Ultimately, both envisage (international) law as a sort of hypothetical ideal speech situation in which, in Koskenniemi's case, formalised language, in Carty's case a formalised morality, provides the barrier to (undue) power asymmetries. Yet as far as the 'culture of formalism' is concerned, it is not only power that is (theoretically) kept outside, but also politics itself, or rather the sort of political action of which Arendt speaks. As was seen, formal law abstracts and diverts from 'pure' non-instrumental political speech, and it imposes its own rules of causality and accountability. The politics which the 'culture of formalism' is meant to foster lies outside of the law, in a space which Koskenniemi leaves largely unexplained and unaccounted for. It might well be a private space, or a network of private spaces, yet, at any rate, not the public space which, for Arendt, is an essential feature of genuine political action.

By contrast, Carty's humanistic neo-naturalism appears to have much in common with Arendt's conception of politics and law. The stylised conversation among diplomats, the disinterested opinion (formation) of well-educated, generalist counsellors seem not too distant from the debate of (male) Athenians in their *agora* or Arendt's own experience of jury duty.[58] Even the central role of legislation in political action is compatible with Carty's idea of humanistic international relations. Yet Carty's naturalism is ultimately bound to define the law substantively, a 'rightly-reasoned' public

[58] H Arendt and K Jaspers, *Correspondence 1926–1969* (L Kohler and H Saner eds) (Boston, Mass, Houghton Mifflin Harcourt, 1992) 666.

morality that conceptually conflicts with Arendt's idea of the inherently unpredictable nature of the political. Law, to Arendt, may be instrumental to political action but it is not identical to it; politics must remain an autonomous field, a 'pure politics' accompanied by a fairly pure law, as Jan Klabbers has insightfully observed.[59] Yet, as the space of freedom, it cannot be filled out either by formal law, nor by substantive morality, but must remain open and unpredictable.

III. FACING THE ABYSS: RE-POLITICISING THE INTERNATIONAL

Yet can there be an Arendtian alternative to Koskenniemi's enlightened legalism and Carty's legalised enlightenment? The core challenge any response to this question faces is that that which lies beyond formalism and naturalism is not a promised conceptual land out there to be occupied but, as it were, a territory contested by two opposing meta-narratives, notably (Schmittian) realism and (Marxian) materialism. Neither can (yet) be said to have been articulated in the same systematic and explicit way in relation to international law as have neo-formalism and neo-naturalism, though in combination they set the threshold over which any alternative conception of the international must pass. It is a threshold which Arendt also perceived and over which she recurrently laboured.[60] Its Schmittian component consists, in essence, of the claim that politics is fundamentally about determining and maintaining identity through power which is articulated as sovereign will. It is a line of thought that stretches from Hobbes to Schmitt, from Morgenthau's realism to, arguably, the contemporary 'law and economics' approach.[61] It postulates that political action is necessarily antagonistic and decisionist, based on an irreducible *pouvoir constituant*. Law, including international law, is, if anything, a function of that *pouvoir*, and politics is the continuous affirmation of the latter among distinct polities in the international sphere.[62] It is what is colloquially referred to as 'power politics' and what gives politics the bad name it has among many critical thinkers. For Arendt, as has been seen, it is really a conception of an anti-politics that usurps the name of the political and eliminates the space for political action.[63] The other component of the threshold is, of course, (Marxian) historical materialism, that is, the affirmation that both (international) law and political action are but epiphenomena of a deeper structure, namely that of capital reproduction. Arendt's reading of Marx was, of course, critical but complex, with both sharing the analytical entanglement

[59] See J Klabbers, 'Possible Islands of Predictability: The Legal Thought of Hannah Arendt' (2007) 20 *Leiden Journal of International Law* 1.

[60] H Arendt, *Denktagebuch: 1950 bis 1973* (Munich, Nordmann, 2002).

[61] See A Vermeule and E Posner, 'Demystifying Schmitt' in A Vermeule and E Posner (eds), *The Cambridge Companion to Carl Schmitt* (Cambridge, Cambridge University Press, forthcoming)—manuscript available as University of Chicago Public Law Working Paper No 333.

[62] Keedus, above n 32, 195.

[63] Arendt, above n 7.

of the theory of action with the theory of society.[64] In relation to politics, her main critique of Marx was the determinism that resulted from his elevation of a materialist theory of labour to the main driving force of history. This, to her, leaves no space for genuine (political) freedom, as politics is, for Marx, not an autonomous concept but premised on social relations. This makes Marx, to Arendt, as anti-political as Schmitt, if on entirely different grounds; it reduces freedom to the insight into objective necessity, and politics to the enactment of that insight.

Schmittian realism has, of course, found expression in and through part of international relations discourse, whereas Marxist materialist readings of international law have occupied one of the niches of critical legal thought; sometimes both have entered into what some would describe as an unholy alliance.[65] What is common to both, and definitive of the threshold for any alternative conception, is that political action in Arendt's sense, as non-utilitarian inter-subjective speech focused on 'promising, combining, and covenanting',[66] is considered as essentially inexistent and derided as at best naive and at worst dangerous. Neither is (international) law accorded any emancipatory role, too deeply is it thought to be contingent on the power either of historical agents such as States, or of history itself. Arendtian international thought must, hence, make its way in-between the imperialist legalism of the 'mainstream' and the totalitarian realism of the sceptics. However, both are incomplete accounts of contemporary international affairs, they leave questions open, or rather they cease to ask certain questions, which is precisely a symptom of the crisis of authority that modernity represents. It is that crisis which, if recognised as such, opens up a horizon for the genuinely political.

Yet of what would such international political action consist, and what, if any, would be the role of international law in relation to it? These are, of course, the hard questions all those interested in Arendtian thought have been asking themselves all along, and Arendt's refusal to present her thought as a system has left ample room for a plurality of interpretations. The, perhaps, dominant line today might be described as the 'normalist' reading of Arendt,[67] in which her conception of politics is made to resemble the Habermasian reconstruction of modern constitutional (and liberal) democracy with a special emphasis on the role of civil society and public opinion.[68] However, Arendt herself undermines the 'normalisation' of her political thought through her own complex fascination with revolution and moments of revolutionary re-foundation. Indeed, an 'exceptionalist'

[64] *Ibid*; and H Arendt, *On Revolution* (New York, Viking Press, 1963).

[65] C Mieville, *Between Equal Rights: A Marxist Theory of International Law* (Chicago, Ill, Haymarket, 2006); for an appreciative if not uncritical review, see A Carty, 'Marxist International Law Theory as Hegelianism' (2008) 10 *International Studies Review* 122.

[66] Arendt, *On Revolution*, above n 64, 212.

[67] Müller, above n 19.

[68] See, for instance, S Benhabib, *The Reluctant Modernism of Hannah Arendt* (London, Sage Publications, 1996).

reading of Arendt has her espouse the interruption of the 'normal' flow of history, the 'human condition' of unpredictability, the recurrent 'out-of-jointness' of time as the conditions of possibility for political action, moments when human action is freed from the automatisms of institutions and procedures—indeed of law (!)—and thrown into a condition of radical responsibility. To be sure, Arendt seems herself to have been ambivalent about the implications of the exceptionalist side of her thought, as she was well aware that a theory build on the permanent exception would be a contradiction in terms.[69]

Yet her libertarian exceptionalist existentialism has to be seen in the context of her reading of modernity as crisis. For it is not self-conscious agency that produces revolutionary moments, but the fundamental contradictions of modern life that are kept at a constant simmer by the lack of any overarching and integrative authority. This continuously generates exceptional moments, moments of crisis, though, as has been seen, it also plasters these over with simulacra of normality. One of these simulacra is, of course, law, namely, when it functions to substitute political authority and becomes an instrument of the bureaucratic usurpation of the space of politics. It goes along with a de facto political disenfranchisement through massified democratic process. It is only when this plaster is forced open by the magnitude of crisis that sensitivity for a genuine constitutional moment returns, a moment which, for Arendt, is one of egalitarian, if also aristocratic republicanism. She derives it from real-life experiences of exception, such as the American Revolution, the Paris Commune, the early Soviet and other syndicalist experiences, even the Hungarian uprising of 1956[70]—and one might add any subsequent spontaneous moments of intense political action from the fall of the Berlin Wall to the uprisings in Burma, Iran, or the Arab world. It is moments that are not made but offer themselves up as a stage for communal political performance. The, perhaps, central element of that performance is, of course, responsibility, which, like political action, can be experienced only in those (exceptional) moments when all mechanisms by which responsibility is delegated and represented are suspended. It is only then that exposure is unmediated and that the audience can judge properly. Again it the law of the modern State that absorbs a good part of that responsibility and thereby creates a veneer of de-politicised normality over modernity's semi-liquid surface.

Law plays an ambivalent role in this. Although it is clearly marked out as an element of the crisis of modernity, Arendt also recognised its indispensability. The necessary antinomianism of constitutive moments is coupled with an elective espousal of law as both a precondition (as *nomos*) and a consequence (as *lex*) of political action. Some have contended that Arendt saw law as 'islands of predictability' necessary to navigate the sea of unpredictability that is the human

[69] Müller, above n 19.

[70] Arendt, *Between Past and Future*, above n 2; see also S Auer, 'The Lost Treasure of the Revolution: Hannah Arendt, Totalitarianism and the Revolutions in Central Europe: 1956, 1968, 1989' (2006) *Eurozine* 10 (available at <http://www.eurozine.com/articles/2006-10-25-auer-en.html>).

condition;[71] others have argued that she deconstructs the dichotomy between law and politics all together.[72] What is clear is that she resisted any and all 'imperative' conceptions of law as threatening the autonomy of the political, and that she did not agree with strategic uses of the law in lieu of political debate, to which her controversial stand on legal desegregation in the United States bears witness.[73] Perhaps law was, to Arendt, a particular form of political action, not qualitatively distinct from it and without a logic of its own. As such it would represent both the self-reflexive awareness by all (political) actors of their own 'actorness', as well as the heightened sense of responsibility that the promise, once made, implies. Its essence would be the process of legislation, that is, the continuous making, unmaking and re-making of laws by a body politic acting out of mutual responsibility and not obligation. Recovering the political in 'world affairs', cannot, hence, mean merely to squeeze a complex set of issues—Afghanistan, Iraq, North Korea, Palestine, Darfur, Geneva—into a legal iron cage in order to advance particular solutions. Neither can it mean to treat the values and aims behind these solutions as pre-political and situate them, as Koskenniemi (perhaps inadvertently) does, in the private choices of individual strategists. What it can mean, however, is to espouse political agency and responsibility; to name things; to insist on argument; to attempt to grasp people and things, as best as possible, in their infinite complexity; to resist conclusion; to face up to contingency; to make promises as a marker of seriousness and commitment to an ongoing conversation; and to dare to throw oneself into the abyss of politics!

[71] Klabbers, above n 59, 9.

[72] C Volk, 'From Nomos to Lex: Hannah Arendt on Law, Politics, and Order' (2010) 23 *Leiden Journal of International Law* 759.

[73] H Arendt, 'Reflections on Little Rock' (Winter 1959) *Dissent Magazine* 47; see also D Allen, 'Law's Necessary Forcefulness: Ralph Ellison vs. Hannah Arendt on the Battle of Little Rock' in AS Laden and D Owen (eds), *Multiculturalism and Political Theory* (Cambridge, Cambridge University Press, 2007).

10

*International Law and Human Plurality in the Shadow of Totalitarianism: Hannah Arendt and Raphael Lemkin**

SEYLA BENHABIB

I. INTRODUCTION

HANNAH ARENDT AND Raphael Lemkin were witnesses to the twentieth century. They both experienced the dislocating transformations on the European continent as a consequence of two World Wars, lost their States as well as their homes in this process, narrowly escaped the clutches of the Nazi extermination machine, and made it to the New World through sheer luck and fortuitous circumstance. Their thought is marked by the cataclysms of the last century, and they have in turn emerged as indispensable interlocutors for all of us in understanding this past.

Arendt and Lemkin were contemporaries, and there are astonishing parallels in their early biographies. She was born in Hannover in 1906 (d 1975) and grew up in Koenigsberg in East Prussia. After the First World War, the Polish Corridor was created and cut East Prussia and Koenigsberg off from the rest of Weimar. In 1945, Koenigsberg was occupied by the Soviets and renamed Kaliningrad. Lemkin was born in Bezwodene in 1900, then part of Tsarist Russia. Between the two World Wars (1918–39) Bezwodene became part of Poland, and today is Bezvodna in Belarus.

When Arendt was arrested by the Gestapo in the Spring of 1933 and was forced to flee to Paris via Prague with her mother, she had been carrying out research in the Prussian State Library at the request of Kurt Blumenfeld on anti-Semitic measures undertaken by Nazi non-governmental organisations, business associations

* This chapter is reprinted from S Benhabib, 'International Law and Human Plurality in the Shadow of Totalitarianism: Hannah Arendt and Raphael Lemkin' (2009) 16 *Constellations* 331; reprinted with revisions in S Benhabib, *Politics in Dark Times. Encounters with Hannah Arendt* (Cambridge, Cambridge University Press, 2010), 219–47. An abridged version has also appeared in S Benhabib, *Dignity in Adversity. Human Rights in Troubled Times* (Cambridge, UK and Malden, MA: 2011) 41–57.

and professional clubs to exclude Jewish members. Her Zionist friend, Kurt Blumenfeld, in turn, was preparing to present this material at the 18th Zionist Congress. During those very same years, Ralph Lemkin was a young clerk in the Polish State Prosecutor's office who had been collecting documents on Nazi war legislation, particularly those affecting cultural, linguistic, religious activities and artifacts of cultural and religious groups. In 1933, he had sent a paper to a League of Nations conference in Madrid, in which he proposed that 'the crimes of barbarity and vandalism be considered as new offences against the law of nations'.[1] In 1939, he fled from Poland and reached Stockholm, where he continued to do extensive research on Nazi occupation laws throughout Europe. On 18 April 1941, he arrived in the United States via Japan. That very same year, Arendt and her second husband, Heinrich Bluecher, arrived in New York via Portugal.

Yet in contrast to Arendt, who acquired world-wide fame after her arrival in the USA with her many works and university appointments, Lemkin, after the general acclaim he received with the passage of the Genocide Convention by the United Nations in 1948, fell into obscurity and died a lonely death, destitute and neglected in New York in 1959.

It is certainly fascinating to speculate whether these Jewish refugees, who were caught up in the great dislocations of their time, ever met one another in some location or association in the United States. We simply do not know. What is even more astonishing is the lack of any discussion in Hannah Arendt's work of Lemkin's great book on the concept of genocide,[2] or any evidence that Lemkin knew Arendt's work on totalitarianism, which certainly was the most powerful historical documentation and philosophical analysis in the early 1950s of the unprecedentedly murderous character of the Nazi regime. Arendt and Lemkin appear to have existed in the same time and space coordinates without ever encountering one another. It is thus incumbent upon retrospective readers of their work to put together the pieces of the puzzle in this missed encounter.

This missed encounter may itself be viewed as a metaphor for the ways in which not only their lives but also their thought ran so close to each other and

[1] This, and other biographical information on Ralph Lemkin, is drawn from S Power, *'A Problem from Hell': America and the Age of Genocide* (New York, Basic Books, 2002) 17–87; A Curthoys and J Docker, 'Defining Genocide' in D Stone (ed), *The Historiography of Genocide* (New York, Palgrave Macmillan, 2008) 9 ff. See also DJ Schaller and J Zimmerer, 'From the Guest Editors: Raphael Lemkin: the "founder of the United Nation's Genocide Convention" as a historian of mass violence' (2005) 7(4) *Journal of Genocide Research* 447.

[2] Cf R Lemkin, *Axis Rule in Occupied Europe. Laws of Occupation, Analysis of Government, Proposals for Redress* (Washington, DC, Carnegie Endowment for International Peace, 1944). In 1945, upon the publication of *Axis Rule in Occupied Europe*, the *New York Times Book Review* devoted its cover to this work. It is hard to believe that Arendt, who resided in New York City at that time, and in view of her general interests in and knowledge of these questions, would not have been familiar with Lemkin's book. See OD Tolischus, 'Twentieth Century Moloch: The Nazi Inspired Totalitarian State, Devourer of Progress—and of Itself', *New York Times Book Review*, 21 January 1945: 1, 24, as cited in Power, above n 1, 525, fn 35.

yet remained so distant.[3] In 1944, Ralph Lemkin published *Axis Rule in Occupied Europe*, in which he demanded that a new category in the law of nations be formulated in order to reckon with and bring to justice war crimes committed by Nazis and their Allies against the many peoples of Europe. He was concerned that international law ought to recognise the unprecedented nature of the genocide of Jews and other peoples. In 1951 Hannah Arendt published *The Origins of Totalitarianism* which also exposed the unprecedented political nature of totalitarianism as a novel form of political rule in history—in fact, as a transformation of the sphere of the political as such. Yet, unlike Lemkin, Arendt was quite sceptical that declarations of human rights, international conventions and the like could help restore the destroyed political fabric of the world after the Second World War. In a passage which almost seems to take aim at Lemkin's efforts to pass the Genocide Convention, Arendt wrote:

> Even worse was that all societies formed for the protection of the Rights of man, all attempts to arrive at a new bill of human rights were sponsored by marginal figures—by a few international jurists without political experience or professional philanthropists supported by the uncertain sentiments of professional idealists. The groups they formed, the declarations they issued show an uncanny similarity in language and composition to that of societies for the prevention of cruelty to animals. No statesman, no political figure of any importance could possibly take them seriously and none of the liberal or radical parties in Europe thought it necessary to incorporate into their program a new declaration of human rights.[4]

Did Arendt possibly have Lemkin in mind when she referred in dismissive terms to those 'international jurists without political experience'? And could she have been referring to Eleanor Roosevelt, the tireless force behind the passage of the Universal Declaration of Human Rights in 1948, when she takes a swipe at 'professional philanthropists supported by the uncertain sentiments of professional idealists'? There are no references in Arendt's work, as far as I can tell,[5] to Raphael Lemkin.

[3] A subtle analysis of the sensibility of Arendt, Lemkin and others in terms of the category of 'citizen of the world' is given by Ned Curthoys, who writes: 'As emigre scholars and public intellectuals, Arendt, Jaspers, Spitzer, Auerbach and Lemkin were dedicated to illuminating generous and unorthodox methodological approaches imbued with the restless exigencies of personal experience and hermeneutic inituition.' See N Curthoys, 'The Emigre Sensibility of "World Literature": Historicizing Hannah Arendt and Karl Jaspers' Cosmopolitan Intent' *Theory and Event* 8, no 3, accessed online at <http://muse.jhu.edu/journals/theory_and_event/v008/8.3curthoys.html>.

[4] H Arendt, *The Origins of Totalitarianism* (New York, Harcourt, Brace and Jovanovich, 1979) 292 (hereafter 'OT'). Originally published in Britain as *The Burden of Our Time* (London, Secker and Warburg, 1951).

[5] There is still no serious cataloguing of the contents of the 80-odd boxes deposited in the Library of Congress in Washington, DC, although microfilm collections exist in several universities. The same is true of the extensive Hannah Arendt and Heinrich Bluecher Library which is located in Bard College. Attempts are underway to catalogue its holdings. The electronic catalogue contains no references to Lemkin.

Ironically, though, by 1963, when she writes *Eichmann in Jerusalem*, Arendt has not only accepted the categories of the Genocide Convention, she goes even beyond Lemkin to provide a philosophical condemnation of the crime of genocide in the light of her concept of human plurality. Genocide, in Arendt's view, destroys plurality and is a crime against the human condition as such. In the dramatic Epilogue to *Eichmann in Jerusalem* she states that the 'justice of what was done in Jerusalem would have emerged to be seen by all if the judges had dared to address their defendant in something like the following terms'.[6] In astonishingly pointed language, she then delivers her own verdict against Adolph Eichmann:

> You admitted that the crime committed against the Jewish people during the war was the greatest crime in recorded history, and you admitted your role in it … Let us assume, for the sake of argument, that it was nothing more than misfortune that made you a willing instrument in the organization of *mass murder*; there still remains the fact that you have carried out, and therefore actively supported, a policy of *mass murder* … And just as you supported and carried out a policy of not wanting to share the earth with the Jewish people and the people of a number of other nations—*as though you and your superiors had any right to determine who should and who should not inhabit the world*—we find that no one, that is, no member of the human race, can be expected to share the earth with you. This is the reason, and the only reason, you must hang.[7]

I want to suggest that these two quotations—from *The Origins of Totalitarianism* and from *Eichmann in Jerusalem*—are like book-ends marking the evolution of Arendt's thought from scepticism towards international law and human rights[8] in the 1950s toward a cautious confirmation of their role in shaping politics among nations in the 1960s. And this change of heart on Arendt's part was, whether or not she personally was acquainted with or knew Ralph Lemkin's work, indebted to his achievement. He remained one of those 'obscure international jurists', in her words, who single-handedly and tirelessly worked to craft the Convention on Genocide and saw it adopted by the United Nations on 9 December 1948. I shall argue in this essay that with her claim that Eichmann must die because he 'carried out a policy of not wanting to share the earth with the Jewish people and the people of a number of other nations', Arendt not only confirmed Raphael

[6] H Arendt, *Eichmann in Jerusalem: A Report on the Banality of Evil* (New York, Penguin Books, 1965) 277 (hereafter 'EIJ').

[7] *Ibid* 211–79.

[8] There continue to be contentious exchanges around Hannah Arendt's concept and justification of human rights. See J Isaac, 'Hannah Arendt on Human Rights and the Limits of Exposure, or Why Noam Chomsky is Wrong About the Meaning of Kosovo' (2002) 69(2) *Social Research* 263; S Benhabib, *The Rights of Others. Aliens, Citizens and Residents* (Cambridge, Cambridge University Press, 2004) 49–61; C Menke, 'The "Aporias of Human Rights" and the "One Human Right": Regarding the Coherence of Hannah Arendt's Argument' (2007) 74(3) *Social Research. Hannah Arendt's Centenary* 739; P Birmingham, *Hannah Arendt and Human Rights: The Predicament of Common Responsibility* (Bloomington, Indiana University Press, 2006); and S Benhabib, 'Another Universalism: On the Unity and Diversity of Human Rights' (2007) 81(2) *Proceedings and Addresses of the American Philosophical Association* 7.

Lemkin's understanding of the crime of genocide as the 'intent to destroy, in whole or in part, a national, ethnical, racial or religious group, as such',[9] she gave it a firm ontological grounding in the human condition.

In tracing this transformation in Arendt's thought, the first step will be to delve into her analysis of the dilemmas of the modern European nation state and the role of this institution in the rise of European anti-Semitism; the second step is to consider her discussion of the problem of minorities and of statelessness in the inter-war period. For Arendt, anti-Semitism is not an eternal aspect of the human condition or of human history. It originates with the interlacing of historical, socio-economic, political and cultural circumstances around the rise of the modern nation state and the emancipation of European Jewry. These two political developments in turn fuel her profound pessimism about the role of modern political and legal institutions in the European continent, and encourage her scepticism that they are unable to resolve the paradoxes that they themselves create.[10]

Raphael Lemkin, by contrast, is a jurist trained in the law of nations, and for him the rise of European anti-Semitism and the eventual destruction of European Jewry need not be explained in terms of the fate of the Jews alone. He considers genocidal anti-Semitism to be *one* episode *among others* in the long history of the cultural extermination of human groups; the Holocaust is to be singled out for its intensity and extent rather than its logic. Lemkin retains his faith in the relative autonomy of legal institutions *vis-à-vis* the political process, but instead of documenting the folly of the League of Nations and of Minority Treaties, as Arendt does, he strives to put into legal coda the unfulfilled promises of this institution, in particular with respect to minority rights and vulnerable peoples. In the 1950s both agree, however, that the 'rule of law' in the American republic has reached the right balance between politics and the law.[11] Above all, they believe

[9] United Nations Convention on the Prevention and Punishment of the Crime of Genocide. Adopted by Resolution 260 (III) A of the UN General Assembly on 9 December 1948 (Chapter II). See the rather dramatic description of the events surrounding and leading up to the adoption of this Convention in Power, above n 1, 54–60.

[10] I have discussed these paradoxes extensively in *The Rights of Others*, above n 8, ch 2, 'The Right to Have Rights: Hannah Arendt on the Contradictions of the Nation-State', 49–71. See also C Volk, 'The Decline of Order. Hannah Arendt and the Paradoxes of the Nation-State' in S Benhabib (ed), *Politics in Dark Times: Encounters with Hannah Arendt* (Cambridge, Cambridge University Press, 2010) 172.

[11] Ann Curthoys and John Docker report that only 11 months after the Genocide Convention went into effect, in December 1951, 'a petition entitled *We Charge Genocide* was presented by Paul Robeson and others to the UN Secretariat in New York' on behalf of African-Americans, charging that slavery was a form of genocide. See Curthoys and Docker, above n 1, 15 ff. The General Assembly did not adopt the petition and furthermore, '[w]ithout exception, law academics were adamantly opposed because any attempt to apply the Genocide Convention to the US situation would affect the integrity of "our nation".' Lemkin was among these academics and, within the context of the Cold War, he saw these accusations as Soviet attempts to 'divert attention from the crimes of genocide committed against Estonians, Latvians, Lithuanians, Poles and other Soviet-subjugated peoples' (from a *New York Times* interview of 18 December 1951). On this, see Curthoys and Docker, above n 1, 19. See also for further discussion, A Rabinbach, 'The Challenge of the Unprecedented—Raphael Lemkin and the Concept of Genocide' (2005) 4 *Simon Dubnow Institute Yearbook* 397. In Lemkin's

that political traditions in the United States have helped ameliorate the fatal confusions which recurred on the Continent as between the supremacy of the will of the nation, understood as a homogeneous ethno-cultural entity, and the constitution of a State, which ought to guarantee equality in the eyes of the law and equal rights to all its citizens regardless of their ethnic origin.[12]

I begin with a brief consideration of Arendt's analysis of the origins of European anti-Semitism and the failure of the Minority Treaties in the inter-war period. I turn then to Lemkin's crucial innovations in international law with the introduction of the concept of 'genocide'. I argue that underlying this legal concept is an 'ontology of the group'. While little noted in the literature on Lemkin, this concept has two origins: one is the legal category of 'minorities' as defined by President Wilson's 14 Points; and the other is a Herderian belief in the group as the *conditio sina qua non* of all human artistic and cultural achievement.[13] Arendt, by contrast, only harbours scepticism towards such group concepts. Yet, like Lemkin, she believes in the ontological value and irreducibility of *human plurality*. It is because we inhabit the world with others who are *like* us and yet always different *from* us that the world is perspectival and can manifest itself to us only from a particular vantage point. Nevertheless, plurality need not be constituted through the 'ascribed' groups of ethnicity, nationhood, race or religion alone. Quite to the contrary. It is only when ascription is transcended through association and human beings come together for a joint purpose in the public sphere that plurality, which is the human condition, is most strikingly revealed. I shall argue that Arendt's philosophical grounding of the concept of plurality provides the concept of genocide with one of its strongest moral and existential underpinnings.[14]

case as well, we encounter a certain 'colour blindness', an insensitivity to the problem of race as colour, as opposed to race defined through ethnicity, language and religion. Hannah Arendt has often been criticised on this account, and in particular for her controversial essay on desegregation in southern schools, published as H Arendt, 'Reflections on Little Rock' (1959) 6(1) *Dissent* 45. See my analysis of Arendt on black–white relations in the US and on race in Africa in S Benhabib, *The Reluctant Modernism of Hannah Arendt* (New York and Toronto, Rowman and Littlefield Publishers, 2003) 146–55, and Richard King's essay on the invisibility of race among emigré intellectuals: R King, 'On Race and Culture: Hannah Arendt and Her Contemporaries' in Benhabib (ed), above n 10, 113.

[12] For a more sceptical consideration of these claims with regards to sovereign power and executive privilege in the US experience, see A Arato and J Cohen, 'Banishing the Sovereign: Internal and External Sovereignty in Arendt' in Benhabib (ed), above n 10, 219.

[13] DM Segesser and M Gessler, 'Raphael Lemkin and the International Debate on the Punishment of War Crimes (1919–1948)' (2005) 7(4) *Journal of Genocide Research* 453.

[14] For further considerations on the concept of groups, see AD Moses, 'Moving the Genocide Debate Beyond the History Wars' (2008) 54(2) *Australian Journal of Politics and History* 248, 267. On the place of *existential* as distinct from *moral* values in Arendt's work, see the illuminating essay by George Kateb, 'Existential Values in Arendt's Treatment of Evil and Morality' in Benhabib (ed), above n 10, 342.

II. ANTI-SEMITISM AND THE NATION STATE IN ARENDT'S THOUGHT

In her reflections on anti-Semitism in the aftermath of the Holocaust and after the fate of German-Jewry had become sealed, Arendt put forth a radical contention: anti-Semitism, she argued, far from being an 'eternal' dimension of the relationship between Jews and gentiles, represented, rather, a thoroughly modern phenomenon.[15] As such, it reflected the disintegration of traditional political structures in Europe, and, in particular, the decline of the nation state in the aftermath of European imperialism in the second half of the nineteenth century. According to Arendt, anti-Semitism had to be understood not in isolation, but in the context of a crisis of Western civilization that far exceeded the importance of the 'Jewish Question'.

In thus framing the 'Jewish Question' against a much broader political background, Arendt challenged a number of traditional views on anti-Semitism. Foremost among them was the idea that modern anti-Semitism simply represented a new form of religiously-motivated 'Jew hatred'. Against this view, Arendt argued that, in effect, 'even the extent to which the former derives its arguments and emotional appeal from the latter is open to question'. As she wrote in a crucial and characteristically controversial passage from the *Origins of Totalitarianism*:

> The notion of an unbroken continuity of persecutions, expulsions and massacres from the end of the Roman Empire to the Middle Ages, the modern era, and down to our own time, frequently embellished by the idea that modern antisemitism is no more than a secularized version of popular medieval superstitions, is no less fallacious (though of course less mischievous) than the corresponding antisemitic notion of a Jewish secret society that has ruled, or aspired to rule, the world since antiquity.[16]

Arendt's strong language in this passage is meant to drive home her point unambiguously: to understand the new in light of the old was, she suggests, fundamentally to misunderstand it. No amount of historical detail about the persecution of Jews could explain what she considered an unprecedented phenomenon. An adequate understanding of modern anti-Semitism therefore required new categories of thought.[17] Underpinning all these contentions, and thus Arendt's

[15] Parts of this section have previously appeared in S Benhabib and R Eddon, 'From Anti-Semitism to the "Right to Have Rights: The Jewish Roots of Hannah Arendt's Cosmopolitanism' in *Babylon: Beitraege zur juedischen Gegenwart*, no 22 (Frankfurt, Verlag Neue Kritik, 2007) 44. For general discussions on the significance of Jewish politics for Arendt's conception of politics and philosophy, see R Bernstein, *Hannah Arendt and the Jewish Question* (Cambridge, Mass, MIT Press, 1996); Benhabib, above n 11. Cf also J Kohn, 'Preface: A Jewish Life: 1906–1975' in J Kohn and RH Feldman (eds), *Hannah Arendt: The Jewish Writings* (New York, Schocken Books, 2007) ix–xxxiii.

[16] OT xi.

[17] Arendt's insistence on the centrality of Jews to the larger story of the moral and political collapse of Europe reveals a complex and ambivalent philosemitism that underpins her theory of anti-Semitism. While she famously declared that 'I have never in my life "loved" any people or collective,' and, indeed, that the '"love of the Jews" would appear to me, since I am myself Jewish,

theory of anti-Semitism as a whole, was a fundamental paradox: modern anti-Semitism rose as the modern nation state declined; therefore, the suggestion that anti-Semitism was a by-product of extreme nationalism was simply mistaken. As she explained, '[u]nfortunately, the fact is that modern anti-Semitism grew in proportion as traditional nationalism declined, and reached its climax at the exact moment when the European system of nation-states and its precarious balance of power crashed'.[18] It was only in light of these events, unfolding on a European and indeed a global scale, that it was possible to understand what would have been an otherwise deeply perplexing development: the enormous significance that the 'Jewish problem' acquired for the Nazis.

The group of Jews who had inherited their wealth from the Court Jews of the absolutist State seemed ideally suited to serve the purposes of the modern nation state, since they were the only group in society that 'did not form a class of [its] own and … did not belong to any of the classes in their countries'.[19] As a result, they could offer the emergent State both the financial backing and the political loyalty it so desperately needed. The distance from Court Jew to European banker seemed but a short step away. And indeed, the European banker continued to be of use to the State even as it subsequently achieved a higher degree of consolidation. Even as their political role diminished as the result of subsequent political developments, Jewish bankers nevertheless remained useful as international mediators *among* nation states.

The peculiar economic position occupied by the Jews as lenders and bankers, bailing out and supporting first the absolutist regimes of Europe and subsequently national governments, gave them a unique and problematical profile. They were 'within the nation' but never really 'of the nation'. They enjoyed a 'supra-national' and almost 'proto-cosmopolitan' existence, which at one and the same time called forth and belied the universal belief in 'the rights of man'. The Jews seemed to represent 'human rights as such'. Yet at the same time, their problematic position within the nation also evidenced their vulnerability in virtue of not clearly belonging to a collectivity that would stand up for them. This is why for Arendt, as well as for Theodor Herzl, the Dreyfus case was so significant. Even after the legacy of the French Revolution, and within the 'civic nation' of France, the Jews remained outsiders. After the Franco-Prussian War

as something rather suspect', she nevertheless attributed to Jews a privileged cultural as well as political role in European history. [See H Arendt, *The Jew as Pariah* (RH Feldman (ed)) (New York, Grove Press, 1978) 247. Cf the expanded and revised edition of the essays from *The Jew as Pariah*, supplemented by other materials in *Hannah Arendt*, *The Jewish Writings*, above n 15.] In one sense, for example, in the figure of the *schlemiel* as embodied by Heinrich Heine and in Bernard Lazare's *pariah*, Arendt discerned a unique model of humanity, which, 'excluded from the world of political realities', could at one time 'preserve the illusion of liberty'. While Nazi totalitarianism erased this illusion, Arendt regarded the pariah's humanity and independence of mind as eminently political qualities in her own time—indeed, as the conditions *sine qua non* of human freedom.

[18] OT 3.

[19] *Ibid* 13.

(1870–71), Dreyfus, an Alsatian Jew and an officer in the French army, was accused of being a spy for the Germans. Jewish existence thus revealed the fragile balance between the universalistic aspirations of the modern nation state and the principle of 'national sovereignty'. Such sovereignty would repeatedly be defined not in terms of a community of citizens and equals, but in terms of an *ethnos* of blood and belonging.[20] Particularly after the collapse of the nation state system in Western Europe in the wake of overseas imperialism, and the destruction of the Kaiserreich, the Russian, the Austro-Hungarian and Ottoman Empires in central and eastern European territories, a political and legal chaos exploded to which the nation state system as a model of 'inter-State order' was unable to provide answers.[21]

It is also at this point that the threads connecting the experiences of the failed liberal emancipation of the German Jews to whom Arendt belonged with the collective experiences of the majority of Eastern European Jews, as articulated for us most poignantly through Lemkin's category of 'genocide', become visible.

In *Axis Rule in Occupied Europe*, Lemkin also considers the legal status of the Jews in chapter VIII.[22] He observes matter-of-factly that the definition of a Jew was based by Axis powers (among which are included not only Germany, but Italy, Hungary, Bulgaria and Rumania too) upon the Nuremberg laws: 'A Jew is any person who is, or has been, a member of the Jewish faith or who has more than two Jewish grandparents.'[23] The latter are considered Jewish if they are, or have been, members of the Jewish faith. Lemkin is particularly attentive to differences in the treatment of Jews from France, Norway, Belgium and The Netherlands in the hands of the Nazis, in contrast with those hailing from the eastern European territories; but after the deportation *en masse* to Poland of western European Jews, he claims, these differences among different Jewish nationalities evaporated.

In contrast to Arendt's reflections, there is no social, economic, psychological or cultural analysis of European anti-Semitism in this work, but rather a very detailed account of the race-policies of the Nazis and their attempts at the Germanisation of the European continent. Whereas Arendt attempts to understand the *causes* of anti-Semitism, Lemkin focuses on the *consequences* of racialist Nazi ideology. Prejudice and genocide, among human groups—which in his unpublished Notes is extended as far as the colonisation of the Aztecs and the Incas, the destruction of early Christians by the Romans, and less controversially, to the genocide of Ottoman Armenians—appear rooted for him in a deep-seated anthropological

[20] These philosophical theses on the contradictions between 'human rights' and 'national sovereignty' are more clearly analyzed in H Arendt, *On Revolution* (New York, Penguin Books, 1963). For a more detailed discussion of these themes, see Benhabib, above n 11, ch 2.

[21] Cf C Volk, in Benhabib (ed), above n 10, 172.

[22] Lemkin, above n 2, 75–78.

[23] *Ibid.*

predilection of the human species.[24] It is the law and human institutions which can counter this. 'Only man has law,' he is reported to have said.[25]

Arendt's and Lemkin's analyses of anti-Semitism thus show little affinity: for her the emergence of the Jewish Question in the heart of nineteenth- and early twentieth-century Europe requires a full-scale analysis of the paradoxes of the modern nation state system, whereas he sees deep-seated tendencies throughout human history towards the persecution of vulnerable groups, and among them the Jews. It is the goal of law to protect the vulnerable against the predator and the exploiter, but the law cannot eradicate evil from human heart.

It is in their reflections on the question of minorities in Europe between the two World Wars that Arendt and Lemkin tread some common ground.

III. ARENDT ON STATELESSNESS, THE MINORITY TREATIES AND 'THE RIGHT TO HAVE RIGHTS'

The dissolution of the multinational and multiethnic Russian, Ottoman and Austro-Hungarian empires, and the defeat of the Kaiserreich in 1918, led to the emergence of nation states, particularly in eastern-central European countries that enjoyed little religious, linguistic or cultural homogeneity. These successor States—Poland, Austria, Hungary, Czechoslovakia, Yugoslavia, Bulgaria, Lithuania, Latvia, Estonia, the Greek and the Turkish republics—controlled territories in which large numbers of so-called 'national minorities' resided. On 28 June 1919, the Polish Minority Treaty was concluded between President Woodrow Wilson and the Allied and Associated Powers, to protect the rights of minorities who made up nearly 40 per cent of the total population of Poland and consisted at that time of Jews, Russians, Germans, Lithuanians and Ukrainians. Thirteen similar agreements were then drawn up with various successor governments, 'in which they pledged to their minorities civil and political equality, cultural and economic freedom, and religious toleration'.[26] Not only was there a fatal lack of clarity as to how a 'national minority' was to be defined, but the fact that the protection of minority rights applied only to the successor

[24] 'In my early boyhood, I read *Quo Vadis* by Henry Sienkiewicz—this story full of fascination about the sufferings of the early Christians and the Romans' attempt to destroy them solely because they believed in Christ … It was more than curiosity that led me to search in history for similar examples, such as the case of the Huguenots, the Moors of Spain, the Aztecs of Mexico, the Catholics in Japan, and so many races and nations under Genghis Khan … I was appalled by the frequency of evil, by great losses in life and culture, by the despairing impossibility of reviving the dead or consoling the orphans, and above all, by the impunity coldly relied upon the guilty.' R Lemkin, 'Totally unofficial', manuscript, undated, New York Public Library, Manuscripts and Archives Division, The Raphael Lemkin Papers, Box 2.

[25] The full quote is: 'Only man has law … You must build the law!' Quoted in Power, above n 1, 47, 55.

[26] C Fink, 'Defender of Minorities: Germany in the League of Nations, 1926–1933' (1972) 4 *Central European History* 330. Also, C Fink, *Defending the Rights of Others. The Great Powers, the Jews and International Minority Protection* (Cambridge, Cambridge University Press, 2004).

States of the defeated powers, and not to the victors—Great Britain, France and Italy—who refused to consider the extension of the Minority Treaties to their own territories, created cynicism about the motivations of the Allied Powers in supporting minority rights. This situation led to anomalies whereby, for example, the German minority in Czechoslovakia could petition the League of Nations for the protection of its rights, but the large German minority in Italy could not. The position of Jews in all successor States was also unsettled: if they were a 'national minority', was it by virtue of their race, their religion or their language that they were to be considered as such, and exactly which rights would this minority status entail? For Arendt, the growing discord within and the political ineptitude of the League of Nations, the emerging conflicts among so-called national minorities themselves, as well as the hypocrisy in the application of the Minority Treaties, were all harbingers of developments in the 1930s. The modern nation state was being transformed from an organ which would execute the rule of law for all its citizens and residents, into an instrument of the nation as a narrowly 'imagined' ethnonational community: 'The nation has conquered the state, national interest had priority over law long before Hitler could pronounce "right is what is good for the German people."'[27] This statement from Hans Frank, the former German Minister of Justice and Governor General of occupied Poland, is also cited by Lemkin, who renders it as '[l]aw is that which is useful and necessary for the German nation'.[28]

The perversion of the modern State from an instrument of law into one of lawless discretion in the service of the ethnic nation was evident when States began to practice massive denaturalisations against unwanted minorities, creating millions of refugees, deported aliens and stateless peoples across borders—special categories of humans created through the actions of nation states. In a territorially bounded nation state system, or in a 'State-centric' international order, one's legal status is dependent upon protection by the highest authority which controls the territory upon which one resides and issues the papers to which one is entitled. One becomes a *refugee* if one is persecuted, expelled and driven away from one's homeland; one becomes a *minority* if the political majority in the polity declares that certain groups do not belong to the supposedly 'homogeneous' people; one is a *stateless* person if the State whose protection one has hitherto enjoyed withdraws such protection, nullifying the papers it has granted; one is a *displaced* person if, having been rendered a refugee, a minority or a stateless person, one cannot find another polity to recognise one as its member and remains in a state of limbo, caught between territories, none of which desire one to be its resident. It is here that Arendt concludes:

> We become aware of the existence of a right to have rights (and that means to live in a framework where one is judged by one's actions and opinions) and a right to belong

[27] OT 275.
[28] Lemkin, above n 2, 31.

> to some kind of organized community, only when millions of people emerge who had lost and could not regain these rights because of the new global political situation … The right that corresponds to this loss and that was never even mentioned among the human rights cannot be expressed in the categories of the eighteenth-century because they presume that rights spring immediately from the 'nature' of man … the right to have rights, or the right of every individual to belong to humanity, should be guaranteed by humanity itself. *It is by no means certain whether this is possible.*[29] (emphasis added)

Written in 1951, three years after the adoption of the Genocide Convention by the UN General Assembly, this quotation betrays Arendt's profound ambivalence towards the nation state system. It remains one of the most puzzling aspects of her political thought that, although she criticised the weaknesses of this system, she was equally sceptical toward all ideals of a World State and in fact, at this stage in the early 1950s, towards all instruments of international law to resolve these problems.

Arendt's philosophical and political ambivalence towards the nation state has complex dimensions. The nation state system, established in the wake of the American and French Revolutions, and bringing to culmination processes of development at work since European absolutism in the sixteenth century, is based upon the tension, and at times outright contradiction, between human rights and the principle of national sovereignty. The modern State has always been a specific nation state.[30] This is the case even when this nationalism is civic in form, as is usually associated with the American, French, British and Latin American models, or ethnic, as is usually associated with the German and east-central European models. The citizens of the modern State are always also members of a nation, of a particular human group who share a history, language, culture, religion and tradition, however conflictually this identity may be constituted, and however 'imagined' the identity of the nation may be (Benedict Anderson). Between the principles of national self-determination and universal human rights there are always potential, and often actual, conflicts. The ethno-cultural nation can trample upon the rights of vulnerable minorities.

Ironically, although she never accepted Zionism as the dominant cultural and political project of the Jewish people, and chose to live her life in a multi-national and multicultural liberal democratic State, the catastrophes of the Second World War made Arendt more appreciative of the moment of new beginning inherent in all State formations. 'The restoration of human rights,' she observed, 'as the recent

[29] OT 296–97.

[30] Scheuerman makes an excellent case about the dominance of the French Revolution as a negative model and counter-example which is often juxtaposed to America in Arendt's work. He argues that Abbé Sieyès' influential conception of the nation 'is remarkably free of the ethnicist qualities'. See WE Scheuerman, 'Revolutions and Constitutions: Hannah Arendt's Challenge to Carl Schmitt' in D Dyzenhaus (ed), *Law as Politics: Carl Schmitt's Critique of Liberalism* (Durham, NC, Duke University Press, 1998) 252, 259. Scheuerman concludes that '[f]or her as for [Carl] Schmitt, the intellectual legacy of the French Revolution merely reproduces the most heinous features of Absolutism, particularly its vision of an indivisible, omnipotent, and legally unlimited sovereign' (*ibid* at 261). Of course, the critique that concepts such as the sovereignty of the nation reproduce absolutist tendencies was first voiced by Alexis de Tocqueville in his *The Ancien Regime and the French Revolution.*

example of the State of Israel proves, has been achieved so far only through the restoration or establishment of national rights.'[31] Arendt was too knowledgeable and shrewd an observer of politics not also to have noted that the cost of the establishment of the State of Israel was the disenfranchisement of the Arab residents of Palestine and hostility in the Middle East until the present. She hoped throughout the 1950s that a binational Jewish and Palestinian State would become a reality.[32]

What can we conclude from the historical and institutional contradictions of the idea of the nation state? Is Arendt's begrudging acceptance of this political formation a concession to political realism and historical inevitabilities?[33] Could Arendt be saying that no matter how contradiction-fraught the nation state may be as an institutional structure, it is still the only one which defends the rights of all who are its citizens—at least in principle, even if not in practice?

The answer to this question in part depends on Arendt's own evolving appreciation of international law and international institutions. Between the 1951 publication of *The Origins of Totalitarianism* and the 1963 appearance of *Eichmann in Jerusalem*, post-Second World War politics were transformed with the creation of the United Nations in 1946, the Universal Declaration of Human Rights in 1948 and the adoption of the Genocide Convention by the General Assembly that same year. Although Arendt never abandoned her belief in the priority of self-determination of peoples for guaranteeing human as well as citizens' rights, her faith in international law and institutions grew. The complex relationship between republican self-government and new developments in the international sphere, including international law, are part of the subtext of Arendt's reflections on the trial of Adolph Eichmann in Jerusalem.[34] And this new world constellation comes about, in no small measure, through Lemkin's tireless efforts in drafting and advocating the acceptance of the Genocide Convention.

IV. FROM THE ORIGINS OF TOTALITARIANISM TO THE GENOCIDE CONVENTION

Transforming the memory of the persecution not only of Jews, but of other peoples such as the Gypsies, the Poles, the Slovenes and the Russians, into a

[31] OT 179.

[32] For an extensive discussion of this issue as it relates to Arendt's reflections on Palestine, see Benhabib, above n 11.

[33] There is renewed interest in Arendt's views of world politics and international relations. For an original reading, see P Owens, *Between War and Politics. International Relations in the Thought of Hannah Arendt* (Oxford, Oxford University Press, 2007); D Klusmeyer, 'Hannah Arendt's Critical Realism: Power, Justice, and Responsibility' in AF Lang Jr and J Williams (eds), *Hannah Arendt and International Relations: Readings Across the Lines* (London, Palgrave, 2005) 113.

[34] See L Bilsky, 'The Eichmann Trial and the Legacy of Jurisdiction' in Benhabib (ed), above n 10, 198. See also, for an in-depth discussion of the jurisprudential issues behind the Eichmann trial, S Benhabib, *Another Cosmopolitanism: The Berkeley Tanner Lectures* (Oxford, Oxford University Press, 2006) ch 1.

universal legacy for mankind, actionable under the law of nations, was Lemkin's desideratum. In the Preface to *Axis Rule in Occupied Europe*, he writes:

> The practice of extermination of nations and ethnic groups as carried out by the invaders is called by the author 'genocide,' a term deriving from the Greek word *genos* (tribe, race) and the Latin *cide* (by way of analogy, see homicide, fratricide).[35]

These few famous lines offered a term for what Churchill, referring not only to the extermination of European Jewry but to German war conduct in eastern Europe generally, called 'a crime without a name'.[36]

Lemkin himself, it has been pointed out, did not insist on the uniqueness of the Holocaust but attempted to formulate 'a broad theory and definition of genocide, in which the Holocaust served as prime example, not as an exception'.[37] This broad conception of genocide in the meantime has spawned a new field of 'comparative genocide studies'.[38]

Lemkin's picture of Nazi ambitions and of the Holocaust was based on an immensely detailed knowledge of the legal framework of the occupation regimes. From a historian's point of view, Dan Stone writes that

> perhaps Lemkin's most original contribution … is his inclusion of the murder of the Jews in a wider policy for the demographic reshaping of Europe. Historians … have shown the extent to which the genocide of the Jews was part of a broader plan for the 'resettlement' of ethnic Germans and the expulsion of millions of Slavs, as encapsulated in the *Generalplan Ost* (General Plan East). Where Lemkin does not adumbrate contemporary concerns is in his failure to see that attack on the Jews as driven by a radical ideology … Today historians accept that the murder of the Jews was not the full extent of the Nazis' ambitions, but … there are good reasons why the Jews were targeted first and most tenaciously, and equally that the Jews had a special place in the Nazi *Weltanschauung*.[39]

[35] Lemkin, above n 2, xi.

[36] WS Churchill, *The Churchill War Papers: The Ever Widening War*, vol 3: 1941 (M Gilbert (ed)) (New York, WW Norton, 2000) 1099–1106; as cited by Power, above n1, 29, fn 32.

[37] D Stone, 'Raphael Lemkin on the Holocaust' (2005) 7(4) *Journal of Genocide Research* 539, 546.

[38] See the special issue of the *Journal of Genocide Research*, 7, no 4 (December 2005), devoted to the work of Raphael Lemkin; MA McDonnell and AD Moses, 'Raphael Lemkin as historian of genocide in the Americas', *ibid*, 501–29; and A.D Moses, 'The Holocaust and Genocide' in D Stone (ed), *The Historiography of the Holocaust* (Houndsmills, Palgrave Macmillan, 2004) 535.

[39] D Stone, above n 37, 545. Arendt was well aware of this 'imperialist' aspect of Nazi ideology, and therefore distinguished between 'overseas' and 'continental imperialism' in OT, 222–67. But see the following distinction made by Lemkin between the Nazi persecution of Slavs (pragmatic colonisation reasons) *versus* the Jews and Gypsies (purely racial reasons): '[T]he Nazi plan of Genocide was related to many peoples, races, and religions, and it is only, because Hitler succeeded in wiping out 6 million Jews, that it became known predominantly as a Jewish case … [As] a matter of fact, Hitler wanted to commit G against the Slavic peoples, in order to colonize the East, and to extend the German Empire up to the Ural Mts. Thereupon after the completion of the successful war he would have turned to the West and to subtract from the French people the 20 million Frenchmen he promised in his conversation with Rauschning. Thus the German Empire would have reached from the Ural Mts. to the Atlantic Ocean. Nazi Germany embarked upon a gigantic plan to colonize Europe, and since there are no free spaces local populations had to be removed in order to make room for Germans. Nazi Germany did not have a fleet to protect overseas possessions. Moreover Germany had never good experiences in the past with overseas colonization. It was thus much simpler to colonize the European

Not only in terms of historical research, but also in terms of more technical legal considerations, Lemkin's various definitions of genocide are elastic, and exhibit an '"instability" between the historical and the legal, between the cultural and the "ethnical," between intent and consequence'.[40] According to the Genocide Convention, adopted on 9 December 1948,

> genocide means any of the following acts with intent to destroy, in whole or in part, a national, ethnical, racial or religious group, as such: (a) Killing members of the group; (b) Causing serious bodily or mental harm to members of the group; (c) Deliberately inflicting on the group conditions of life calculated to bring about its physical destruction in whole or in part; (d) Imposing measures to prevent births within the group; (e) Forcibly transferring children of the group to another group.[41]

Debates as to the degree of 'intent' which must accompany these acts, the definition of 'the group', whether social classes should or should not be considered as groups, what degree of destruction of the cultural legacy of the group constitutes genocidal intent as distinct from forced assimilation, ethnic cleansing or displacement, have accompanied these words from their inception and will continue to do so. But Lemkin not only brought legal imagination and perspective to the understanding of anti-Semitism and the extermination of the Jews, he also introduced the category of 'the group' and insisted that a genocidal plan would be characterised by the following:

> The objectives of such a plan would be the disintegration of the political and social institutions, of culture, language, national feelings, religion, the economic existence of *national groups*, and the destruction of the personal security, liberty, health, dignity, and even the lives of individuals belonging to *such groups*. Genocide is directed against *the national group as an entity*, and the actions involved are directed against individuals, not in their individual capacity, but as members of *the national group*.[42] (emphasis added)

continent … [H]itler's plan covered the Poles, the Serbs, the Russians, the Frenchmen … [T]he main purpose of the Nazis was a commission of a G against nations in order to get hold of their territory for colonisation purposes. This was the case of the Poles, and the Russians and the Ukrainians. The case against the Jews and the Gypsies was not based upon colonisatery [*sic*] but upon racial considerations … The case against the Jews and Gypsies was of a purely racial rather than emotional political nature. The race theory served the purpose of consolidating internally the German people. The Germans had to be shown that they are racially valuable Nordics. Their favorable racial classifications could be understood better by comparing them with those who were called and classified as vermin of the earth—the Jews and the Gypsies.' As cited by A.D Moses, 'Intellectual History and Conceptual Questions' in AD Moses (ed), *Empire, Colony, Genocide: Conquest, Occupation and Subaltern Resistance in World History* (New York, Berghahn Books, 2008) 20–1. Moses is quoting from Raphael Lemkin, 'Hitler's Case-Outline', Jacob Radar Marcus Center of the American Jewish Archives, Collection 60, Box 7, Folders 12 and 13. The spelling has been corrected in part by Moses.

[40] A Rabinbach, 'The Challenge of the Unprecedented—Raphael Lemkin and the Concept of Genocide' (2005) 4 *Simon Dubnow Institute Yearbook* 397, 401.

[41] United Nations Convention on the Prevention and Punishment of the Crime of Genocide. Adopted by Resolution 260 (III) A of the UN General Assembly on 9 December 1948 (Chapter II).

[42] Lemkin, above n 2, 79.

The famous chapter IX of *Axis Rule in Occupied Europe* is dedicated to showing why Nazi and Axis actions in occupied Europe constitute a crime that requires a *new* conception. Admittedly, given his insistence that genocide against groups has been a constant feature of human history, it is at times unclear whether Lemkin thinks that this is an *old* crime which requires a *new* name, or a *new* crime which differs from historical precedents so radically that it must be called by a *new* name. He thinks it is the latter.[43] Lemkin is concerned to prove that the Nazis are waging an unprecedented 'total war' since they make no distinction between the nation and the State: '[T]he nation provides the biological elements for the state.'[44] Such total war is the antithesis of the Rousseau-Portalis Treaty[45] that ought to have governed war among sovereign States and which was, he believes, implicit in the Hague Regulations of 1907: 'This doctrine holds that war is directed against sovereigns and armies, not against subjects and civilians.'[46] The Nazis violated this principle not only by waging total war, but even prior to war, through their policies of Aryanisation of the German race (by forbidding mixed marriages with Jews and others; employing euthanasia on the feeble-minded and the retarded, etc); through the Germanisation of peoples such as Dutchmen, Norwegians and Luxembourgers, and the Germanisation of the soil alone of people *not related* to Germans by blood such as Poles, Slovenes and Serbs; and finally, when it came to the Jews, through their total extermination.[47]

Lemkin is first and foremost concerned to establish that there are no existing instruments of international law to deal with such crimes. The Hague Convention on 'Respecting the Laws and Customs of War on Land' (signed on 18 October 1907) has rules addressing 'some (but by no means all) of the essential rights of individuals; and these rules do not take into consideration the interrelationship of such rights with the whole problem of nations subjected to virtual imprisonment'.[48] The Hague rules deal with 'the sovereignty of a state', but not with preserving 'the integrity of a people'.[49] In a subsequent essay, Lemkin names genocide a 'composite crime'.[50] By his own account, as far back as 1933, he formulated two new international law crimes—the crime of *barbarity*, 'conceived as oppressive and destructive actions directed against individuals as members of

[43] *Ibid.*

[44] *Ibid.*

[45] The Rousseau-Portalis doctrine provides basis for the combatant-non-combatant distinction. In the 1801 opening of the French Prize Court, borrowing heavily from Jean-Jacques Rousseau (*The Social Contract*, Book 1, ch 4), Portalis said: 'War is a relation of state to state and not of individual to individual. Between two or more belligerent nations, the private persons of whom these nations are composed are only enemies by accident; they are not so as men, they are not so even as citizens, they are so only as soldiers.' Cited in MS McDougal and FP Felicioano, *Law and Minimum World Public Order* (New Haven, Conn, Yale University Press, 1994) 543.

[46] Lemkin, above n 2, 80.

[47] *Ibid* 80–81.

[48] *Ibid* 90.

[49] *Ibid.*

[50] R Lemkin, 'Genocide as a Crime Under International law' (1947) 41(1) *American Journal of International* 145, 147.

a national, religious, or racial group',[51] and the crime of *vandalism*, 'conceived as malicious destruction of works of art and culture because they *represent the specific creations of the genius of such groups*'.[52] In 1944 he is convinced that neither these terms nor the Hague Conventions are adequate to deal with the crime being perpetrated by Axis powers.

Yet why is the destruction of the life, works, culture and life-form of a national group more heinous than the destruction of the individuals belonging to this group? According to Lemkin, insofar as 'the actions involved are directed against individuals, not in their individual capacity, but as members of *the national group*',[53] they violate the *moral* principle that innocents shall not be harmed; the *legal* principle that the law punishes individuals for what they do, not for what or who they are; as well as *the laws of war and peace* that innocent civilians must be spared and must not be treated as collateral damage. There is an added dimension of legal criminality and moral culpability when destruction is aimed at the *national group as such*. To make this point Lemkin returns here to the Minority Treaties of the inter-war period, much as Arendt did, and observes that

> National and religious groups were put under a special protection by the Treaty of Versailles and by specific minority treaties, when it became obvious that national minorities were compelled to live within the boundaries of states ruled by governments representing the majority of the population.[54]

Not only the life and well-being, but also the 'honor and reputation' of such groups were to be protected by the legal codes at that time.[55] Already then, legal developments in the inter-war years anticipated the need for special protection of the life and well-being as well as the 'honor and reputation' of such groups.

But why privilege the national/ethnic/religious group in this fashion? In a passage that remains frequently uncommented upon, Lemkin lays bare what I shall call his 'ontology of groups':

> The world represents only so much culture and intellectual vigor as are created by its component national groups. Essentially the idea of a nation signifies constructive cooperation and original contributions, based upon genuine traditions, genuine culture, and a well-developed national psychology. The destruction of a nation, therefore, results in the loss of its future contributions to the world. Moreover, such destruction offends our feelings of morality and justice in much the same way as does the criminal killing of a human being: the crimes in one case as in the other is murder, though on a vastly greater scale.[56]

[51] Lemkin, above n 2, 90.
[52] *Ibid.* (emphasis added)
[53] *Ibid* 79. (emphasis added)
[54] *Ibid* 90–91.
[55] *Ibid* 91.
[56] *Ibid.*

This passage is noteworthy for a number of reasons: Lemkin is quite unconcerned about the definition of a 'national group,' considering it almost self-evident and using it interchangeably with 'ethnos';[57] he often includes race and religion, as well as social groupings in need of protection.[58] The Genocide Convention speaks of a 'national, ethnical, racial or religious group', without much specification as such. Whether one considers Lemkin's own formulations or refers to the text of the Genocide Convention, it is the 'ascriptive' group, the group into which one is *born* or into which one is *thrown* (to speak with Martin Heidegger), that constitutes his reference point. Such groups are not created, they are found; they are not invented but discovered.

Most significantly, Lemkin's understanding of the group is culturalist, defined in terms of the 'genuine traditions, genuine culture, and well-developed national psychology'.[59] Culture, in turn, is viewed fairly conventionally as 'high culture', as 'original contributions' to the world. In a popular piece addressed to a large audience in the *American Scholar*, Lemkin writes:

> We can best understand this when we realize how impoverished our culture would be if the peoples doomed by Germany, such as the Jews, had not been permitted to create the Bible, or to give birth to an Einstein, a Spinoza; if the Poles had not had the opportunity to give to the world a Copernicus, a Chopin, a Curie; the Czechs, a Huss, a Dvořák; the Greeks, a Plato and a Socrates; the Russians, a Tolstoy and a Shostakovich.[60]

Is there a distinction to be made, then, between cultures which contribute to world civilization and others which have not or cannot? Is there a lurking distinction between 'genuine traditions' and 'genuine culture' and 'non-genuine', inauthentic traditions and cultures? And would such distinctions affect the claim of some cultures to be preserved and protected more than others? Is Lemkin's ontology of the group based upon an implicit hierarchy of cultures and their contributions?

My goal here is not to engage in postmodernist scepticism about holistic concepts of groups and culture against Lemkin. Even beyond postmodern scepticism, however, the definition of the 'group' that is deemed worthy of legal recognition remains a contentious matter in all debates on group rights, and has consequences as to *which* collective rights groups are deemed to be entitled as opposed to the individuals who are members of such groups.[61] Lemkin's own understanding of the national group has two sources: from a legal point of view, he reverts to the

[57] *Ibid* 79.

[58] *Ibid* 93. It is all the more puzzling, therefore, that Lemkin would be so resistant to extending the Genocide Convention to cover conditions of slavery in the Americas.

[59] *Ibid* 91.

[60] R Lemkin, 'Genocide' (1946) 15(2) *American Scholar* 228, quoted in Power, above n 1, 53.

[61] See W Kymlicka, *Multicultural Citizenship. A liberal Theory of Minority Rights* (Oxford, Oxford University Press, 1995); W Kymlicka, *Citizenship in Diverse Societies* (Oxford, Oxford University Press, 2000); for a general discussion of these issues in contemporary debates, cf S Benhabib, *The Claims of Culture. Equality and Diversity in the Global Era* (Princeton, NJ, Princeton University Press, 2002); within the American context of dilemmas raised by group-based classifications, see R Post and

instruments of the Minority Treaties of the inter-war period, which as we saw above, through Arendt's analysis as well, were themselves hardly unproblematic. Philosophically, Lemkin is heir to a romantic and nationalist Herderian tradition which sees national groups, broadly conceived, as sources of a unique perspective on the world, as originators of a mode of disclosing the world.[62]

This privileging of national groups leads Lemkin to conclude that:

> genocide is a problem not only of war but also of peace. It is an especially important problem for Europe, where differentiation into nationhood is so marked that despite the principle of political and territorial self-determination, certain national groups may be obliged to live as minorities within the boundaries of other states. If these groups should not be adequately protected, such lack of protection would result in international disturbances, especially in the form of the disorganized emigration of the persecuted, who would look for refuge elsewhere.[63]

M Rogin (eds), *Race and Representation: Affirmative Action* (New York, Zone Books, 1998); J Sleeper, *Liberal Racism* (New York, Viking, 1997).

[62] There has been ongoing debate about Johann Von Gottfried Herder's legacy. Some classify him as a 'German nationalist'. Karl Popper, for example, in *The Open Society and its Enemies* (London, 1945), 'includes Herder in a sort of Hall of Shame recapitulating the rise of German nationalism', as noted by MN Forster (ed and trans), 'Introduction' in JG Von Herder, *Philosophical Writings: Cambridge Texts in the History of Philosophy* (Cambridge, Cambridge University Press, 2002) xxxi, fn 33. Others, such as Isaiah Berlin and Charles Taylor, view Herder as a precursor of a kind of cultural and value pluralism which is distinct from relativism. See, eg, C Taylor, 'The Importance of Herder' in EA Margalit (ed), *Isaiah Berlin: A Celebration* (Chicago, Ill, University of Chicago Press, 1992). By pointing to this Herderian connection, my point is not to charge Lemkin with a kind of 'relativist nationalism of vulnerable peoples'! Rather, I wish to draw attention to the concept of the group in his writings which is philosophically under-explored, in as much as language, race, ethnicity and religion are often used, either together or individually, as markers of group identities. Lemkin does not explore either the conflicts or the ambiguities to which the use of these markers can give rise in the law or society. We know, by contrast, that for Herder the nation is a linguistic and cultural and not a racial group. See, eg, JG Herder, 'Treatise on the Origin of Language' [1772], in *Philosophical Writings* (above), 65. See also Letter 114 in 'Letters for the Advancement of Humanity: Tenth Collection' and the Fragment on 'Purified Patriotism' for Herder's condemnation of wars among nations and of imperialism (in *Philosophical Writings*, 380 ff, 406). Lemkin undoubtedly would have shared Herder's sentiments in full, as expressed by the following: 'What, generally, is a foisted, foreign culture, a formation [*Bildung*] that does not develop out of [a people's] own dispositions and needs? It oppresses and deforms, or else it plunges straight into the abyss. You poor sacrificial victims who were brought from the south sea islands to England in order to receive culture … It was therefore not otherwise than justly and wisely that the good *Ch'ien-lung* acted when he had the foreign vice-king rapidly and politely shown the way out of his realm with a thousand fires of celebration. If only every nation had been clever and strong enough to show the Europeans this way' (*Philosophical Writings* at 382). Cf Arendt's very interesting reflections on Herder's significance for the Jews after the Enlightenment. She credits Herder with rendering Jewish history visible in Germany, 'as history defined essentially by their possession of the Old Testament': H Arendt, 'The Enlightenment and the Jewish Question' in Kohn and Feldmen (eds), above n 15, 12. At the same time, insofar as this history is theological history and not history connected to that of the world at large, for Herder 'the Jews have become a people without history within history. Herder's understanding of history deprives them of their past' (*ibid* at 16). Philosophically, as well as historiographically, the question is one of balancing the universal and the particular, the general history of humanity and the specific memories, trajectories and suffering of specific peoples. I cannot pursue this matter further here, but have attempted to do so in Benhabib, above n 8.

[63] Lemkin, above n 2, 93.

Lemkin's thought here slides from the crime of genocide to the peacetime protection of 'minority rights', which, as he admits, is a matter of civil and constitutional and not criminal law.[64] Whereas for Hannah Arendt the division of people within a nation state into minorities amid a majority is the source of the problem itself, Lemkin sees strengthening protection for minority rights to be necessary in peacetime as well. He thereby tries to use legal means to address political questions which are properly matters of State organisation and which concern the design of political constitutions and institutions—whether these be federalist or unitary.

Arendt presents a rather different understanding of the value of the group.[65] For her, the group is not ascribed but formed; it is not discovered but constituted and reconstituted through creative acts of human association. The value of the group does not lie first and foremost in its 'original contributions' to world culture and 'genuine traditions', but rather in its manifestation of human diversity; in its disclosing a new perspectival outlook on the world.[66] The world is disclosed for us through diversity and plurality.

V. PLURALITY AS A FUNDAMENTAL CATEGORY IN ARENDT'S WORK

No passage better expresses the concept of plurality in Arendt's work than the following:

> If it is true that a thing *is* real ... only if it can show itself and be perceived from all sides, then there must always be a plurality of individuals or peoples ... to make reality even

[64] *Ibid.*

[65] I conjecture that Arendt, emerging as she did out of the more liberal and individualistic tradition of German Jewish emancipation, would not be as accepting as Lemkin was—an eastern European and Polish Jew—of the concept of the group, or of the moral and political imperative to preserve groups. Arendt was quite sensitive to the differences among the experiences of German *versus* east European Jewish communities. See her critical remarks about the 'collective' *versus* 'individualistic' orientation of the *Ostjuden* as opposed to German Jews in the letter to her husband Heinrich Bluecher. For further discussion, see S Benhabib, 'Arendt's Eichmann in Jerusalem' in D Villa (ed), *The Cambridge Companion to Hannah Arendt* (Cambridge, Cambridge University Press, 2000) 65. For a philosophical analysis of anti-Semitism in the works of Arendt and the Frankfurt School, as refracted through the German Jewish experience, see S Benhabib, 'From "The Dialectic of Enlightenment" to "The Origins of Totalitarianism" and "The Genocide Convention". Adorno and Horkheimer in the Company of Arendt and Lemkin" in W Breckman, PE Gordon, AD Moses, S Moyn and E Neaman (eds), *The Modernist Imagination: Essays in Intellectual History and Cultural Critique. For Martin Jay on his 65th Birthday* (New York, Berghan Books, 2009) 299; reprinted in: Seyla Benhabib, *Dignity in Adversity. Human Rights in Troubled Times* (Cambridge, UK and Malden, MA, Polity Press, 2011) 20–41.

[66] Does not this voluntarist concept of the group contradict Hannah Arendt's own assertive defence of her own Jewish identity? I would argue that it does not, in that Arendt insists on defining the conditions and the meaning of her own belonging to the Jewish people. For her it is not the Halachachic definition of the Jew, as one born to a Jewish mother, that is paramount, but rather one's conscious and self-chosen identification with the fate of a collectivity and a people. This individualist, perhaps existentialist, dimension of Arendt's Judaism is at the root of her conflict with Gerschom Scholem, and it is what distinguished her from other thinkers such as Leo Strauss who argued that one could not separate out the cultural and theological meanings of Judaism as sharply as Arendt herself wished to. I have explored these questions further in S Benhabib, (2009) above n 65, 316–17.

> possible and to guarantee its continuation. In other words, the world comes into being only if there are perspectives … If a people or a nation, or even just some specific human group, which offers a unique view of the world arising from its particular vision of the world … is annihilated, it is not merely that a people or a nation or a given number of individuals perishes, but rather that a portion of our common world is destroyed, an aspect of the world that has revealed itself to us until now but can never reveal itself again. Annihilation is therefore not just tantamount to the end of the world; it also takes its annihilator with it.[67]

As Patricia Owens observes,

> wars of annihilation that aim to wipe out a particular group attack the basic fact of human plurality and violate the 'limits inherent in violent action.' With genocide we are not 'just' talking about large numbers of dead but something that is potentially immortal. The public, political world, the political constitution of a people, the outcome of people's living together, and debating their common affairs is also destroyed with genocide.[68]

Genocide violates 'an altogether different order', writes Arendt in *Eichmann in Jerusalem*.[69]

The category of plurality is no less ontological in Arendt's thought than that of the group is in Lemkin's. That is to say, for both authors these categories represent some element and principle which is part of the order of being human in the universe. Arendt names this 'the human condition', that is, 'the basic conditions under which life on earth has been given to man'.[70] Plurality is the fact that corresponds to our irreducible sameness as members of the same species, and yet at the same time expresses our irreducible difference from one another. 'Plurality is the condition of human action because we are all the same, that is, human, in such a way that nobody is ever the same as anyone else who ever lived, lives, or will live.'[71] This plurality is the precondition of the possibility of all political life: because we are members of the same species who have speech and reasoning, or who are capable of *legein* (reasoned speech), we can communicate with one another, build a world together as well as destroy one another. And since we are all subject to similar bodily needs and face likewise the struggle with nature, we face the 'circumstances of justice', ie of how to establish just institutions under conditions of vulnerability and scarcity.

Plurality is also what enables diversity and perspectivality:

> In acting and speaking, men show who they are, reveal actively their unique personal identities and thus make their appearance in the human world, while their physical

[67] H Arendt, 'The Promise of Politics' in J Kohn (ed and intro) *The Promise of Politics* (New York, Schocken Books, 2005) 175.

[68] Owens, above n 33, 110.

[69] EIJ 272.

[70] H Arendt, *The Human Condition*, 2nd edn (Chicago, Ill, The University of Chicago Press, 1998) 7 (hereafter 'HC').

[71] HC 8.

> identities appear without any activity of their own in the unique shape of the body and sound of the voice. The disclosure of 'who' in contradistinction to 'what' somebody is—his qualities, gifts, talents and shortcomings, which he may display or hide—is implicit in everything somebody says and does.[72]

We live in a world constituted by narratives about the 'who' as well as the 'what' of action; this web of narratives is the medium through which the multiplicity and diversity of perspectives on human affairs converge and conflict, are woven together and torn apart.

These ontological theses of Hannah Arendt are well known. Her concept of plurality enables Arendt to escape both the ascriptivism and the culturalism of Lemkin's concept of the group. Groups for Arendt are enduring associations, rooted in the human capacity to create a world in common that is shareable yet diverse, that is communicable yet open to misunderstanding, and that appears as one yet is refracted through many different narratives and perspectives. While from a philosophical point of view there can be little question about the brilliant acuity of Arendt's analyses, from a legal point of view, from the standpoint of the jurist, the protean aspect of Arendt's concept of plurality may be too volatile. The juridification of the category of the group brings with it inevitable ontological as well as sociological problems.

Ironically, her scepticism toward group concepts and her dynamic concept of plurality enable Arendt to deliver a trenchant account of the crime of genocide as constituting a 'crime against the human condition' as such. This, I believe, is the meaning of the passage from *Eichmann in Jerusalem*, already quoted above:

> And just as you supported and carried out a policy of not wanting to share the earth with the Jewish people and the people of a number of other nations—*as though you and your superiors had any right to determine who should and who should not inhabit the world*—we find that no one, that is, no member of the human race, can be expected to share the earth with you. This is the reason, and the only reason, you must hang.

Genocide is 'an attack upon human diversity as such, that is, upon a characteristic of the "human status" without which the words "mankind" or "humanity" would be devoid of meaning'.[73]

It is hard not to see in these passages of searing eloquence a belated vindication of those such as Lemkin whom Arendt seemed to dismiss little more than a decade previously as 'those few international jurists without political experience or professional philanthropists supported by the uncertain sentiments of professional idealists' but who, through their tireless efforts, transformed the meaning of the 'human status'. Abandoning her bitter irony of *The Origins of Totalitarianism* (1951), Arendt in *Eichmann in Jerusalem* in 1963, embraces and honours Lemkin's legacy, although it remains a mystery why she does not credit Lemkin by name.

[72] *Ibid* 179.
[73] EIJ 268–69.

VI. BRIEF EPILOGUE: ARENDT AND LEMKIN ON *UNIVERSAL JURISDICTION*

For Lemkin, no less than for Arendt, embracing the concept of 'genocide' raised the question of jurisdiction. In *Axis Rule in Occupied Europe*, Lemkin is ready to include the crime of genocide as amended under the Hague Regulations.[74] He later insists, however, that this crime must be independent of any prior Treaty or set of regulations. Furthermore, he notes that

> the adoption of the principle of *universal repression* as adapted to genocide by countries which belong now to the group of non-belligerents or neutrals, respectively, would likewise bind these latter countries to punish the war criminals engaged in genocide or to extradite them to countries in which these crimes were committed.[75] (emphasis added)

Universal repression makes the culprit liable not only in the country in which he committed the crime, but also 'in any other country in which he might have taken refuge'.[76] Astonishingly, Lemkin shows himself to be little concerned with the difficulties which might arise with the application of the principle of universal repression, such as the capacity of prosecutors in other countries to be able to collect evidence, provide for the adequate defence of the defendants, escape the semblance of 'victor's justice', and a myriad other procedural and substantive details which may go wrong in a criminal trial. By contrast, these and other details haunted Hannah Arendt with regards to the trial of Adolph Eichmann, and cast doubts for her on its full legality.

For Lemkin, 'genocide offenders should be subject to the principle of universal repression as should other offenders guilty of the so-called *delicta juris gentium* (such as, for example, white slavery and trade in children, piracy, trade in narcotics and in obscene publications, and counterfeiting of money)'.[77] There is something deeply unsatisfactory about singling out the radicalness of the crime of genocide, on the one hand, and comparing it to piracy, trade in narcotics and in obscene publications, etc, on the other. The only crime to which genocide can be compared, insofar as it too is a crime against the human status and the human condition, is slavery, and this is what Lemkin was not willing to do.

In *Eichmann in Jerusalem*, Arendt notes that the analogy between genocide and piracy is not new, and that the Genocide Convention expressly rejected the claim to universal jurisdiction and provided instead that

> persons charged with genocide … shall be tried by a competent tribunal of the States in the territory of which the act was committed or by such international penal tribunal as may have jurisdiction.[78]

74 Lemkin, above n 2, 93.
75 *Ibid* 92.
76 *Ibid* 94.
77 *Ibid.*
78 EIJ 262.

With the recognition of the crime of genocide as a 'crime against humanity', Arendt believes that the path has been cleared to entertain the likelihood that 'international penal law' will develop. Quoting Chief Justice Robert Jackson in the Nuremberg Trials, Arendt points out that international law is viewed as an 'outgrowth of treaties and agreements between nations and of accepted customs', and as long as that is the case she believes that 'in consequence of this yet unfinished nature of international law', it is ordinary trial judges who have to render justice by facing the unprecedented with the 'help of, or beyond the limitation set upon them through, positive, posited laws'.[79] She does not consider the negative consequences of 'judges making law', though on the whole she is very sensitive that law, whether domestic or international, be seen by a self-governing people to be 'its' law, and not imposed upon it by other instances.

Lemkin, on the other hand, in 1948 was fearful that an international criminal court would mean 'too great an affront to state sovereignty'.[80] Ironically, Arendt was willing to go beyond him in the principle as well as the practice of the persecution of the crime of genocide. Undoubtedly, though, both would have greeted enthusiastically the establishment of an International Criminal Court with the jurisdiction to try those accused of crimes against humanity and of genocide through the Treaty of Rome. They would also have been dismayed that their adoptive country, for whose constitutional traditions they had such reverence—the United States—first signed and then withdrew from the Treaty of the International Criminal Court. The weakening of the status of international law and the contempt toward international institutions is part of the 'crises of our republic' in the contemporary period, very much as the violation of the laws of war and peace, the collapse of the League of Nations, of the nation state system and the Holocaust were those of Arendt and Lemkin.

[79] *Ibid* 274.
[80] Power, above n 1, 56.

11

Power and the Rule of Law in Arendt's Thought

HAUKE BRUNKHORST

SINCE THE REVOLUTIONARY changes to the global order at the threshold of the 1990s, we have been able to observe a growing academic and political discussion on global constitutionalism, global fundamental laws, global statehood and global democracy. The public discourse on the constitution of the international community reaches back to the *constitutional moment* when the United Nations (UN) Charter was signed in San Francisco on 26 June 1945 by the representatives of the first 50 Member States.[1] The first three words of the Charter underline the revolutionary claim of that document: 'We the Peoples of the United Nations …' The text of the Charter describes itself as a Constitution of the international community that establishes a new global order of *power* and *law*. The Charter is designed as a *revolutionary* or *power-founding Constitution* which stipulates a global legal order that is no longer international but for the first time in history *supranational* (Articles 1, 2, 39 and especially 103 UN).

The idea of a *revolutionary Constitution* that establishes a *new political and legal order of powers* guided the authors of the UN Charter, and it is that idea that stands at the centre of Hannah Arendt's political theory. Arendt's theory is on power. What distinguishes all kinds of *power* (as *potentia*) from *violence* is—as it is written in the *Declaration of Independence* from 1776—the 'consent of the governed'. The *consent of the governed* is the basis for Arendt's main thesis on the *binding force* of power, and the fundamental relation between power and all political institutions: 'All political institutions are manifestations and materializations of power; they petrify and decay as soon as the living power of the people ceases to uphold them.'[2] The *living power of the people* is not organised coercive power but emerges spontaneously through conflicting public opinions. Therefore it needs deviant behaviour, negations, confrontations, disagreement—in short, the force of new ideas which Arendt calls *natality*. This is the Hegelian *power of the negative*. Even if Arendt loves

[1] B Fassbender, 'The United Nations Charter as Constitution of the International Community' (1998) 36 *Columbia Journal of Transnational Law* 529.
[2] H Arendt, *Macht und Gewalt* (München, Beck, 1970) 42.

to quote Burke's formulation of *acting in concert*—what she means is *acting in concert and conflict.*

I. POWER

Theories of power may be differentiated within two dimensions: first, *repressive* versus *constitutive* power; and, secondly, *action* versus *system* points of view.[3] If we combine these two pairs of distinctions within a simple cross-table then all major theories of societal power fit into one of its four boxes:

- *Actor-oriented repressive power* is the Hobbesian or Weberian power to impose *binding decisions* on others (box 1).
- *Actor-oriented constitutive power* is the Arendtian-Habermasian *power of public communication* that constitutes *in its performance* a group of people *as* a political actor (box 2).
- *Structurally repressive power* is *bureaucratically-organised power* of public or private organisations. Structurally repressive power is also effective in *ideologies* (Marx) or *systematically disturbed communications* (Habermas). Structurally repressive power is used to *impose binding decisions without the immediate threat of violence of physical coercion* (box 3).
- *Structurally constitutive power* is the institutions' founding power that is then embodied in these institutions as their productive power (Sieyès, Madison, Jefferson, Foucault). In its pure form it is binding because it is *backed by the consent of the governed only* (box 4).

The normative core of Arendt's theory of power is the idea of *empowerment of the people* by acting in concert and conflict (Table 2: box 2); but as we shall see, her concept of power is much richer and also implies an important notion of *structurally repressive power* as well as of *founding power that is productive.* Her paradigmatic case of structural repression is the social or *anti-political organisational* or *administrative powers* of *imperialism* and *totalitarianism* (Table 2: box 3), and her paradigm of a founding power that is productive is the *institutionalisation of a permanent revolution* by a *revolutionary constitution* (Table 2: box 4).

Table 1: Dimen sions of societal power[4]

Reference Concept	**Actor**	**System**
Repressive	1 Instrumental power	3 Administrative power
Constitutive	2 Communicative power	4 Institutionally-embodied founding power

[3] D Strecker, *Logik der Macht*, unpublished post-doctorate second thesis, called *Habilitationsschrift* in German (Berlin, FU, 2006) 60, 129.

[4] I follow with these distinctions Strecker, *ibid*, 60, 129.

Table 2: Arendt's theory of political power

Reference Concept	**Actor**	**System**
Repressive	1 Violence (*On Violence*)	3 Imperial/totalitarian power (*Origins of Totalitarianism*)
Constitutive	2 Communicative power (*Human Condition*)	4 Constitutional power (*On Revolution*)

The notion of 'violence' and the differentiation between power and violence is categorically infelicitous, and even mistaken. There is *no power* without the *backing of violence* that remains latent during powerful actions. Otherwise the talk about power does not make any sense. In the same way as tanks and police forces are the 'symbiotic' (Luhmann) backing of administrative power, the potential of the 'barricade' or the 'violence of revenge' (*rächende Gewalt*) is the backing of communicative power.[5] Implicitly Arendt knew that very well, because she again and again insists that 'action' and 'power' are the most dangerous ways man relates to himself (see below section V.).

II. STRUCTURALLY REPRESSIVE POWER

Arendt describes the *modern society* in sociological categories as a rational capitalist market society which is *structurally differentiated* from the public sphere (*res publica*).[6]

[5] On symbiotic mechanisms see: N Luhmann, ‚Symbiotische Mechanismen' in K Horn, N Luhmann, W-D Narr, o Rammstedt, K Röttgers, *Gewaltverhältnisse und die Ohnmacht der Kritik* (Frankfurt, Suhrkamp, 1974) 107–31.

[6] I take the phrase 'structural differentiation' from J Habermas, *Theorie des kommunikativen Handelns*, Vol 2 (Frankfurt, Suhrkamp, 1981) 229. Habermas distinguishes the *structural* differentiation between life-world and system as the fundamental differentiation of the modern society, and the basic structure on which *functional differentiation* is built. The modern society is a *structurally* and *functionally* differentiated society. Together with the *internal* differentiation of the life-world in different value-spheres, expert cultures and professions, an *external* sphere of functionally specialised social systems is *structurally differentiated* from the social life-world. Both internal and external processes of differentiation enforce each other. One could call the internal differentiation *discursive differentiation*, and the external one *functional differentiation*. All human societies are, according to Habermas, *socially integrated groups that are stabilised by systemic mechanisms and media* ('systemisch stabilisierte Handlungszusammenhänge sozial integrierter Gruppen' (*ibid* 228). On the central role of this definition, see A Nassehi, *Der soziologische Diskurs der Moderne* (Frankfurt, Suhrkamp, 2006). Hence, the decoupling of system and life-world that is specific for modern societies, means that (1) *social integration* becomes dependent more and more on discursive knowledge, and (2) *systemic stabilisation* no longer is feasible by segmentation (eg tribal units), differentiation of centre and periphery (eg cities and citizenship), class rule or stratification (eg aristocracy), the *only way left for stabilization* now being *functional differentiation*. The first author to have discovered this dependency was Karl Marx, in his famous analysis of the economic or capitalist system: K Marx, *Das Kapital*, Book 1 (Berlin, Dietz, 1969).

The most powerful driving forces of the modern society are *economic capital* and *social power*. If the powers which are emerging from social systems appear in the public sphere, they will become *negative* political or *anti*-political powers (Table 2, box 3). On Arendt's account, *capital accumulation* and *power accumulation* are both structural social processes that reinforce each other: '[A] society which had entered the path of never-ending acquisition'—in the German edition Arendt uses the Marxian term, *Kapitalakumulation*—'had to engineer a dynamic political organization capable of a corresponding and never-ending process of power generation (in German: *Machtakkumulation*).'[7] Both are based on a highly abstract, *reflexive mechanism* that she calls 'expansion for expansion's sake' or 'power for power's sake'.[8]

Together with the *differentiation* (Weber) and *des-embedment* (Polany) of the modern society from the political consent of citizens, capital and power became mere social forces which find and have to find all their ends in themselves. At first imperialism and later totalitarianism made obvious the developmental logic of the reflexive social power of modern organisations. 'Power,' Arendt writes at a key point in her book on totalitarianism, 'appears as a dematerialized mechanism which with its every move produces more power' and this mechanism causes an 'automatic accumulation' of 'total organizational power'.[9]

For Arendt the 'dematerialized mechanism' of reflexive *power accumulation* is a *structural* or *systemic* mechanism. It is one of the very origins of totalitarianism which, for the first time in history, was invented during the imperial rule of Europe over most of the rest of the world. Whereas only a systemic mechanism that works *without* or *independent* from the consent of the governed can explain the tremendous growth and technical improvement of power within the modern society, only a specific *ideological consent* that is reinforced by organised *administrative terrorism* can explain the—up to then—inconceivable repression, destruction and extermination, and in particular the *self-radicalisation*[10] and unprecedented *self-destruction*[11] conducted by totalitarian regimes. This is where Arendt draws

[7] H Arendt, *The Origins of Totalitarianism* (New York, Schocken Books, 2004) 146 (hereafter 'OT').

[8] *Ibid* 215, 217, 351. On reflexive mechanisms, see also N Luhmann, 'Reflexive Mechanismen' in *Soziologische Aufklärung* (Opladen, Westdeutscher Verlag, 1971).

[9] H Arendt, *Elemente und Ursprünge totaler Herrschaft* (München, Beck, 1991) 646. In the earlier American edition she writes that power has turned 'into a kind of dematerialized mechanism whose every move generates power as friction or galvanic currents generate electricity' (OT 418).

[10] H Mommsen, 'Der Nationalsozialismus. Kummulative Selbstradikalisierung und Selbstzerstörung des Regimes' in J Meyers, *Enzyklopädisches Wörterbuch* (Stuttgart, Klett, 1976) 785–90; U Herbert, *Biographische Studien über Radikalismus, Weltanschauung und Vernunft. 1903–1989* (Bonn, Dietz, 1996).

[11] OT 417. In the later German version of her book she writes in particular with respect to Stalin, 'dass die Fremdherrschaft, welche totalitäre Regierungen in jedem, auch dem eigenen Land errichten, nirgends schließlich furchtbarer und blutiger wütet als in dem eigenen' (*Elemente und Ursprübge*, 644). But this seems also true about the last year of the Nazi regime: 'The Nazis behaved like foreign conquerors in Germany when, against all national interests, they tried and half succeeded in converting their defeat into a final catastrophe for the whole German people' (OT 416). The self-destructive tendency of the fascist regime in Germany was analysed first by F Neumann, *Behemoth* (New York, Oxford University Press, 1942).

the distinction between *imperial* and *totalitarian* power. Imperialism presupposes the preservation of a stable difference between rule of law in the homelands and 'un-rule of law'[12] abroad—in the 'heart of darkness'.[13] What imperialism erected during the nineteenth century was a *global double state*: normative state (*Normstaat*) at home, 'prerogative' state (*Massnahmestaat*) abroad.[14]

III. IMPERIAL POWER

Arendt's concept of structurally repressive power, and in particular her distinction between imperial and totalitarian rule, fits nicely to the development of modern international law during the long period that lasted from the Treaty of Tordesillas 1494 until the unconditional surrender of the Nazi Regime and Japan in 1945. The Treaty that Spain and Portugal signed on 7 June 1494 divided the non-European world, and in particular the Americas, into two enormous spheres of occupation, expropriation and expansion; both legally excluded from the protection of the *public* European law of nations. The *Jus Publicum Europaeum* was valid for all the European Nation States, and based on the equal rights of these States to wage war (*ius ad bellum*), conduct treaties and coalitions, and declare neutrality, and it obliged all European States or kingdoms to obey the basic rules of the *ius in bellum*.[15] This was in some respect progress, because not only was war now legalised (as it had been much earlier in canon law of the twelfth and thirteenth centuries) but it was based on a clear distinction between law and morality. The legalisation and (not at all non-ambivalent) de-moralisation of international relations went hand in hand with European State-building.

Yet the 'darker side' of the new State-centered *Jus Publicum Europaeum* that accompanied its history, like a shadow,[16] was the transformation of the rest of the world into the potential and actual private property of European princes, and later European and American constitutional or democratic regimes, and even private or private–public companies (like the East India Companies in The Netherlands and England). During the whole period between 1494 and 1945, the basic discrimination that constituted international law never altered, and that was the discrimination between *European State equality* (later including America and Japan) and the *global imperialism* that was aimed at those from 'the other

[12] I take this terminological invention from G O'Donnell, 'Polyarchies and the (Un)Rule of law in Latin America: A Partial Conclusion' in H Brunkhorst and S Costa (eds), *Jenseits von Zentrum und Peripherie. Zur Verfassung der fragmentierten Weltgesellschaft* (München, Hamp, 2005) 53–80.

[13] J Conrad, *Heart of Darkness* (New York, WW Norton & Company, 2006).

[14] E Fraenkel 'Der Doppelstaat' (1941) in E Fraenkel, *Gesammelte Schriften* (Vol 2) (Baden-Baden, Nomos, 1999).

[15] C Schmitt, *Nomos der Erde im Völkerrecht des Jus Publicum Europaeum* (Berlin, Duncker und Humblot, 1988) 55, 57.

[16] C Joerges and N Singh Ghaleigh (eds), *Darker Legacies of Law in Europe. The Shadow of National Socialism and Fascism over Europe and its Legal Traditions* (Oxford and Portland, Ore, Hart Publishing, 2003).

heading'.[17] International lawyers functioned as 'sorry comforters'—Kant's *leidige Tröster*—who were most creative in justifying the ideological discrimination that constituted international law, and who fuelled it again and again with new legal concepts.[18] In Europe, for example, King Leopold is bound to *public international law*, but the 'heart of darkness' is declared to be his *private property*, and the Berlin conference about the future of Africa (1884–85) offered colonised peoples *authority* instead of *jurisdiction*, *private* prerogative law instead of *public* law equity, *prerogative measures* instead of *law*.[19]

From its very beginning, the progress of European public law was at the price of the anarchic spread and enlargement of structural repressive power in America, Asia, India, Africa and the Near East. But imperial and totalitarian power was excluded from the European borders until the twentieth century. The Nation State realised to *some* degree the *exclusion of inequalities*, and via crisis, social fights and radical reform transformed the ideology of equality into real-life effects. The horror of totalitarian rule was externalised to the 'heart of darkness', and this was one of the great and deeply ambivalent advances of the modern European Nation State which more or less quickly became a democratic *Rechtsstaat*.

Arendt has emphasised this advance strongly, in articles from the 1940s and in the first parts of *Origins*:

> Until now the greatest bulwark against the unlimited domination of bourgeois society, against the conquest of power through the mob and the introduction of imperialistic politics in the structure of Western states has been the nation-state. Its sovereignty, which once was supposed to express the sovereignty of the people, is now threatened from all sides.[20]

What happened during the first half of the twentieth century in Europe was, just as Arendt has analysed it in her book, the internalisation of imperialism to the world of the European States. Externalised imperialism became internalised totalitarianism—with the immediate consequence of a total destruction of the *Jus Publicum Europaeum*, the decay of the legal principle of equal sovereignty in the middle of Europe, and its replacement by imperial rule and imperial theories of the *Großraum*.[21] Whereas imperialism combines the European

[17] J Derrida, *The Other Heading: Reflections on Today's Europe*, trans Pascale-Anne Brault and Michael B Naas (Bloomington, Indiana University Press, 1992).

[18] A Anghie, *Imperialism, Sovereignty and the Making of International Law* (Cambridge, Cambridge University Press, 2004).

[19] M Koskenniemi, *The Gentle Civilizer of Nations. The Rise and Fall of International Law 1870–1960*, (Cambridge, Cambridge University Press, 2001) 126.

[20] H Arendt, *Die verborgene Tradition* (trans M Vatter and V Lemm) (Frankfurt, Suhrkamp, 1976) 29. German original: 'Das bisher stärkste Bollwerk gegen die schrankenlose Herrschaft der bürgerlichen Gesellschaft, gegen die Ergreifung der Macht durch den Mob und die Einführung imperialistischer Politik in die Struktur der abendländischen Staaten ist der Nationalstaat gewesen. Seine Souveränität, die einst die Souveränität des Volkes selbst ausdrücken sollte, ist heute von allen Seiten bedroht.'

[21] Carl Schmitt, ‚Großraum gegen Universalismus' in C Schmitt, *Positionen und Begriffe im Kampf mit Weimar—Genf—Versailles* (Duncker & Humblot, 1988) 295–302.

Normstaat (state of law) with the non-European *Maßnahmestaat* ('prerogative' state), totalitarianism brings the anti-state back to the European homelands. The externalised difference of *Norm-* and *Maßnahmestaat* is re-internalised during the 1920s, 1930s and 1940s.[22]

IV. CONSTITUTIONALISM

Yet the picture Arendt draws of the sovereign European State is a little too rosy. Arendt here follows far too narrow an idea of structural power, more or less reduced to imperialism/totalitarianism (Table 2: box 3). The modern State, which Arendt impressively describes as a 'bulwark' against the 'unlimited domination' of economic powers and political imperialism, could be such a bulwark only because it was the most important and mightiest producer and carrier of just *the same reflexive power* which appears in imperialism and totalitarianism 'as an immaterial mechanism which with its every move produces more power'.[23] Without the power of the modern Nation State, neither the transformation of aggressive religious pluralism into freedom of speech nor the constitutionalisation of despotic public power, nor the social re-embedment of modern capitalism, nor the establishment of modern democracy would have been possible. But without the same power of the State, the so-called 'mob', even if it performed the most terrible ideologies of the twentieth century—anti-Semitism, racism and populist nationalism—never could cause totalitarian rule, industrialised genocide or global war.[24]

It is not only imperialism and totalitarianism but the modern State as such that engenders and must preserve itself by the 'automatic accumulation' of 'total organizational power'.[25] Moreover, the powerful Nation State is not only a bulwark *against* internal imperialism, but at the same time the only organisation of power that could *enable and conduct* external imperialism. Arendt here misses the point that it is the *same* legally-bound State power that defends *us* (Europeans) and oppresses *them* or *the others* (non-Europeans). The totalitarian anti-State is not the self-destructive power station that hits the State from *outside*, but it is executive State power itself that becomes 'anti political', and hence destroys the State from *within*.[26]

Arendt misses this abysmally negative dialectic of executive State power, because her whole theory relies on a *dualistic distinction between inside and outside*, 'civilization' and 'barbarianism', that goes back to the dualism of the (human/

[22] Fraenkel (1941), above n 13.
[23] Arendt (1991), above n 8, 646.
[24] W Reinhard, *Geschichte der Staatsgewalt* (München, Beck, 1999).
[25] See already K Marx, *Der achtzehnte Brumaire des Louis Bonaparte*, Kommentar von Hauke Brunkhorst, (Frankfurt, Suhrkamp, 2007).
[26] Reinhard, above n 21.

civilised) *political* and the (non-human/barbarian) *social sphere of action*.[27] This dualism does not so much reproduce, as she herself represented it, the old Aristotelian difference between *polis* and *oikos*, civic and despotic rule, but is much more dependent on the right-wing Hegelian and German *Staatsrecht* tradition of *constitutionalism*. Constitutionalism means limiting an already existing power by a Constitution—or in the words of Georg Jellinek, the self-binding of the State by law. Constitutionalism relies on at least three basic distinctions:

(a) The *State* is split off from the *society* (or, in the more dynamic versions of Carl Schmitt and the later Arendt, the *political* is split off from the *social*). This dualism protects the bourgeois society *a priori* from democratisation, and protects private property from the regulatory access of public interest.[28]

(b) The constitutional regulations of organised State power, or the *constitutional law of check and balances*[29] (in German: *Staatsorganisationsrecht*) are detached from the *individual rights* of citizens. This has the twofold consequence that rights are kept away from egalitarian concretisation, and that the constitutional law of check and balances, and in particular the executive power, is protected from any shaping impact of basic rights.[30]

(c) The *State* as sovereign power finally is separated from rule of *law* (and the *pouvoir constituent* from the *pouvoir constitué*). This dualism between State and law allows the State (or those who are in power) to maintain a prerogative position beyond, behind or above the law, and in self-defined cases of emergency this position can be used to get rid of rule of law and the *Rechtsstaat*.[31] Therefore the so-called neutrality of the *Rechtsstaat* which Arendt (in the third part of *On Totalitarianism*) supposes to be a bulwark against nationalism, populism and the so-called 'mob', is nothing but ideology.

Switching from her early apologia of the French revolutionary idea of a republican Nation State to a Burkean or English constitutionalism, especially in

[27] Arendt explains the imperialistic outbreak of violence by appealing to the 'horror' and 'shock' that 'overcame Europeans when they got to meet the Negroes (Neger), not as individuals, exported exemplars, but as the population of an entire continent … The horror before the fact that even people like these were human beings, and the immediately following decision that such "human beings" could under no circumstances be their equal. … What distinguished them from other peoples was not the color of their skin; what also made them physically frightening and repulsive was their catastrophic … belonging to nature, against which they could not hold up a man-made world. Their unreality and ghostly wandering is due to this lack of worldliness … Their unreality lies in the fact that they are human beings and, nevertheless, completely lack a specifically human reality. It is this given unreality of the aboriginal tribes together with their lack of worldliness that seduced Europeans into murderous destruction and utter lawlessness they displayed in Africa.' (Arendt, *Elemente und Ursprünge*, above n 8, trans Vatter and Lemm, 646).

[28] H Kelsen, *Demokratie und Sozialismus* (Darmstadt, Wiss Buchges, 1967).

[29] LH Tribe, *American Constitutional Law* (New York, Foundation Press, 2000).

[30] On the latter, see F Müller and R Christensen, *Juristische Methodik II: Europarecht* (Berlin, Duncker & Humblot, 2003).

[31] P Römer, 'Die reine Rechtslehre Hans Kelsons als Ideologie und Ideologiekritik' (1971) 12 *Politische Vierteljahresschrift* 579.

the last part of her book *On Totalitarianism*, Arendt falls back to the German ideology of the neutral *Rechtsstaat*. Yet in her later book *On Revolution* she turns towards the American revolutionary idea of a federal republicanism that is not constitutionalist and neutral but power-founding and democratic from the very beginning (and in this respect the American constitutional revolution is not different from the French one as Arendt wrongly had assumed). Arendt now, and rightly so, criticises constitutionalism because of its political neutrality, or, as she says, because it is 'independent from the form of the state',[32] hence, compatible with nearly every regime; and even the Nazi regime of the 1930s could work only because it was—as Fraenkel has shown—half a *Normstaat* (which means that in this respect it kept being a *Rechtsstaat*).

V. A CONSTITUTION PRESERVING THE CONSTITUENT POWER

In *On Revolution* from 1963, Arendt introduced a concept of power that is internally related to, but different from, the *communicative power* of acting in concert and conflict (Table 2: box 2) which she had invented a couple of years before in *The Human Condition*. Yet the power that is at the focus of *On Revolution* is the specific power of *Constitutio Libertatis*. This is *higher level communicative power* that is stabilised by a revolutionary constitution (Table 2: box 4). How can a revolutionary constitution at once engender and stabilise the communicative power of the people?

The starting point in *On Revolution* is the observation from *The Human Condition* that communicative power cannot stabilise itself. The power of communicative action stems from the 'opinion upon which many have agreed in public'.[33] It 'springs up between men when they act together';[34] it is 'innovative' and 'experimental'[35]; it is nobody's private property;[36] it is socially inclusive and therefore 'from the start open to all'.[37] In performing communicative power an 'unlimited power' emerges that, without the use of violence, 'may engender an almost irresistible power' that can overcome even 'materially vastly superior forces'.[38] This 'tremendous potential of power' is as productive as it is destructive.[39] One 'cannot rely' on power, and *action* is 'the most dangerous of all human capacities and possibilities'.[40] Therefore, the 'men of the Revolution' always stare into an 'abyss'.[41]

[32] H Arendt, *Über die Revolution* (München, Beck, 1974) 186.
[33] H Arendt, *Macht und Gewalt* (München, Beck, 1970) 45.
[34] H Arendt, *The Human Condition* (Chicago, Ill, Chicago University Press, 1958) 200 (hereafter 'HC').
[35] Arendt, above n 29, 222f.
[36] H Arendt, *Vita activa oder vom tätigen Leben* (München, Beck, 1981) 194.
[37] H Arendt, *On Revolution* (New York, Vicking, 1963) 178 (hereafter 'OR').
[38] HC 201.
[39] OR 178.
[40] Arendt, above n 29, 228, in German 'ungeheures Machtpotential'; H Arendt, *Zwischen Vergangenheit und Zukunft. Übungen im politischen Denken 1* (München, Beck, 1994) 363.
[41] H Arendt, *Vom Leben des Geistes, Bd. 2: Das Wollen* (München, Beck, 1979) 30, 185 ff.

However, the communicative power of the people lasts only for the 'fleeting instant of acting in common' and 'vanishes the moment they (the people) disperse'.[42] Therefore the riddle posed by all revolutionary constitutions which *establish* power of the people is how to stabilise their communicative power to act in concert and conflict *without* repressing it; and if that means stabilising a power that in fact results in *engendering* a power that is *unlimited* and *almost irresistible*, can such power thus change, abolish and create any political institution?

Coming to this point of her argument, Arendt draws a sharp distinction between *constitutionalism* and a *revolutionary constitution* (or power-limiting and politically pseudo-neutral constitutions, and power-founding and democratic constitutions).[43] Whereas a constitutional regime (like the Prussian-German or British regimes of the nineteenth century) *limits*, as we have seen, the power of the ruler through *rule of law*, individual *rights* and a power-restricting *fragmentation* of powers, a power-founding constitution (like the US Constitution or the French JacobinConstitution of 1793) is designed not to limit but to *establish, enlarge and improve the power of the people*.[44] Arendt now describes *constitutionalism* as a 'counter-revolutionary' turn of a revolution, the purpose of which is to 'break' the 'revolutionary power of the people' and to institutionalise 'distrust against the people'.[45] Contrarily, the only purpose of a *revolutionary constitution* is to establish a government '*for* the people', '*by* the people' and '*of* the people'.[46] The revolution 'submits the constituent power to the people' and the only function of the *system of check and balances* here is to constitute, organise and stabilise that *constituent power*.[47]

Hence, the system of check and balances must be designed to coordinate all the constituted powers of a political community—legislative, judicial and executive bodies, as well as (and even more importantly) federal and State powers—for two purposes:

(a) to *prevent* the constituted powers, reciprocally, from 'destroying' the 'original' communicative power of the people;
(b) to *preserve* the 'growth' and capacity of the *constituent power* to 'engender new power', and to engender 'new centers of power'.[48]

Therefore the American constitutional system of check and balances applies power to power, 'confronts power with power' (John Adams), in a *reflexive* manner, not to weaken the internally differentiated political power but 'to make' it

[42] HC 200.
[43] Arendt, above n 29, 183ff.
[44] For a similar distinction between the 'dualistic' constitutionalism of the German *Kaiserreich* and the Weimar republican democracy with its *unification* of different powers, see R Thoma, 'Das Reich als Demokratie' in G Anschütz and R Thoma (eds), *Handbuch des Deutschen Staatsrechts, Bd 1* (Tübingen, Mohr, 1930) 119.
[45] Arendt, above n 29, 379, fn 7. Arendt here refers to Karl Löwenstein's *Staatssoziologie*.
[46] Abraham Lincoln, *Gettysburg Adress*, (19 Nov 1863), available at: http://de.wikisource.org/wiki/Gettysburg_Address.
[47] Arendt, above n 37, 193.
[48] *Ibid* 196f, 200.

'mightier' and to 'make the political community mightier than any centralized power' ever could be.[49] The revolutionary constitutional 'division of powers' is not so much a division but a *unification* of different powers: '*e pluritate unum*—but *without depriving*' the single elements—the federal states, different peoples and individual citizens—'*of their power*'.[50]

VI. A PERMANENT LEGAL REVOLUTION

In Arendt's final theory of power, the alternative to 'counterrevolutionary' constitutionalism consists in the idea of a *permanent revolution* that is *constitutional*. The idea of a revolution that is permanent is the right idea, Arendt argues in accordance with Jefferson and Trotzki, but the problem is that one can avoid the tendency of totalitarian self-destruction of the revolution then and only then, if it is possible to constitutionalise the permanence of the revolution (and to include the reflexive operation of a permanent revolution of the constitution itself).[51] This idea carries, and I quote from Susan Marks's brilliant book on *The Riddle of all Constitutions*, a 'meaning' of 'democratic self-rule and equity' that never can be 'reduced to any particular set of institutions and practices'.[52] The 'normative surplus'[53] of *democratic meaning* or the *meaning of democracy* depends on different and changing contexts and circumstances, and it always already transcends any concrete set of *legal procedures of democratic legitimisation*.[54] There is always a meaning of democracy that cannot be 'exhausted' by 'representative government' and 'national government' alone.[55] It is here where Arendt's idea of a power-founding, power-establishing and power-enlarging constitution coincides with Justus Fröbels' idea of a 'permanent legal revolution' and John Dewey's democratic experimentalism.[56]

Democracy is not, as the young Karl Marx once wrote, the 'solved riddle of all constitutions'[57] but *more radical*, as Susan Marks now writes, the 'unsolved riddle of all constitutions';[58] and revolutionary constitutions that are democratic have to keep the riddle open, simply because it is up to the individual and collective *self-determination* of the people to determine, interpret and reinterpret the altering

[49] *Ibid* 198f (Adams quoted from *Ibid*).

[50] Arendt, *Über die Revolution*, n 29 above, 198 (emphasis added). On the unification or coordination of powers in a law of check and balances that is democratic, see Thoma, above n 49, 119; and now extensively C Möllers, *Gewaltengliederung* (Tübingen, Mohr, 2005).

[51] Arendt, above n 29, 187. For normative *versus* nominalistic *versus* instrumental constitutions, see M Neves, *Symbolische Konstitutionalisierung* (Berlin, Dunker & Humblot, 1998).

[52] S Marks, *The Riddle of all Constitutions* (Oxford, Oxford University Press, 2000) 103, 149ff.

[53] T McCarthy, 'Philosophy and Critical Theory' in DC Hoy and T McCarthy (eds), *Critical Theory* (Oxford, Blackwell, 1994) 21.

[54] Arendt, above n 29, 188.

[55] Marks, above n 48, 2.

[56] H Brunkhorst (ed), *Demokratischer Experimentalismus* (Frankfurt, Suhrkamp, 1998).

[57] K Marx, 'Kritik des Hegelschen Staatsrechts' in K Marx and F Engels, *Werke 1* (Berlin, Dietz, 1976) 231.

[58] Marks, above n 48, 103.

meanings of democratic self-determination, self-rule and equity, again and again in ever-new terms of institutional design, be it representative or not, be it national, sub-national, transnational or supranational.

VII. TRAPPED IN CONSTITUTIONALISM

Unfortunately Hannah Arendt herself shrank back from the radical *democratic* consequences of her own argument, and that is because she never completely got rid of the fundamental dualistic distinctions of German *constitutionalism*. When it came to concretising her theory of check and balances, she suddenly tried to combine what is incompatible: the idea of a *revolutionary constitution* together with *constitutionalism*. Hence, she reconstructed the American constitutional institutions (not very plausible) as being designed for keeping the constituent power only for an *elite of politically active citizens*, on the one hand, and for taming, binding and reducing the assumed *anti-political* or *social* power of consumerist mass democracy, on the other hand. She then split (in a similar way to Carl Schmitt in *Legalität und Legitimität*)[59] the *higher legitimacy* of the original and substantial *founding consent* of the governed from the daily and formal procedures of *democratic legitimisation*—the first interpreted politically by the active elite (eg the Supreme Court), the second performed for the technical purposes of social welfare.

The inconsistent mix of constitutionalism and revolutionary constitution leads Arendt to an affirmation of the presidential prerogative in international affairs. This prerogative power in 1788 was designed as a copy of the constitutional monarchy of the British Commonwealth: an absolute kingdom for *them* (the alien nations) and democratic self-rule for *us* (the Americans). Here the combination of a *revolutionary democratic constitution* with *authoritarian constitutionalism* meets the political reality and the Morgenthauian *Realpolitik* of the United States.

VIII. DEMOCRATIC INCLUSION

Yet if we take Arendt's idea of a revolutionary constitution from its egalitarian side (*isonomia*), and drop elitist confusions which are related to the dualisms of constitutionalism, then we can use the idea of a revolutionary constitution as a critical measure for the present constitutionalism of inter-, trans- and supranational law and politics. Hence, we can take Arendt's outline of a power-establishing, constitutional law of check and balances as a blueprint for designing global democracy.

The Arendtian idea of a revolutionary constitution should not be abandoned if we turn our awareness to postnational levels if we understand it as a guiding principle for a Kantian *Reform nach Prinzipien*. The fundamental constitutional

[59] C Schmitt, *Legalität und Legitimität* (Berlin, Duncker & Humblot, 1993 (1932)).

and legal principle of a revolutionary constitution is the *principle of democratic inclusion*.[60] This principle now can be used to make explicit the democratic meaning of Arendt's famous but legally opaque and homeless idea of a *right to have rights*.

In the light of the principle of democratic inclusion, the *right to have rights* must be interpreted as the *emerging right* of any human being to have national *and* transnational civic and democratic rights. The declaration of 'We the peoples ...' in the Preamble to the UN Charter, with which I started my essay, already lays claim to a *second civic track of legitimisation* 'by' and 'through' the peoples. If the Preamble is more than the Preamble to a mere 'symbolic,' or 'instrumental' constitution, then the civic track of legitimisation should supplement the first track of *intergovernmental legitimisation* of international law.

Yet as a legal principle, the claim for democracy does not reappear in Chapter I of the Charter where it belongs. The right to democratic inclusion should be located internationally at the same legal level as today's most fundamental norm of international law, the principle of *sovereign equality of States*. This principle originally stems from the *Jus Publicum Europaeum*, but since the UN Charter was ratified in 1945, it has changed its meaning into a principle of *global constitutionalism*, ie: all States are equal *under* the law.[61] Democratic inclusion today is already a right in the making.[62] If democratic inclusion were to become one of two fundamental legal principles of international law, then *global constitutionalism* would begin to change into a *global revolutionary constitution*, and Chapter I, Article 2, paragraph 1 of the UN Charter would read as follows: 'The Organization is based on the sovereign equality of all its Member States, and on the democratic inclusion of all world citizens.'

Even if this suggestion sounds very abstract and idealistic, it is not that far-fetched. Although it is true that a new legal principle, and even a new legal textbook, will not change the world, legal principles and textbooks are not simply philosophical deliberations but have always had at least a latent impact on the real world, because they *can* be used *directly* in making and concretising legal norms with binding effects—for the good as well as for the bad, and (to be sure) usually in the interest (or not against the interest) of keeping in power the ruling classes. Therefore they usually are in favour of law and order. Once a court interprets the constitutionally guaranteed equality of *all* men before the law as the equality of *all* slave-holders (as they did in the US during the first half of the nineteenth century), human rights can work as an ideological structural power to stabilise a slaveholder regime. But the same legal principles and textbooks, even

[60] *Ibid*, 103, 109ff.

[61] Fassbender, above n 1.

[62] F Müller, *Demokratie zwischen Staatsrecht und Weltrecht* (Berlin, Duncker & Humblot, 2003) 52; T Franck, 'The Emerging Right to Democratic Governance' (1992) 86 *American Journal of International Law* 46; C Cerna, 'Universal Democracy' (1995) 86 *New York University Journal of International Law and Politics* 289; Marks, above n 48.

if they were designed as *Klassenjustiz* (legal system with a class bias) in the interest of the ruling classes (as was and partly is the case with communist constitutions, and as was the case with the property-centered early constitutions in France and America[63]), they can be used (and were and are used) by the oppressed classes. Therefore misused legal textbooks 'can strike back'.[64]

[63] The text (except the amendments) has been the same for nearly 250 years, but the constitution changed deeply, and even in a revolutionary sense, such as in the case of the sovereignty of the states.

[64] F Müller, *Wer ist das Volk? Eine Grundfrage der Demokratie, Elemente einer Verfassungstheorie VI* (Berlin, Duncker & Humblot, 1997) 56.

12

Hannah Arendt and the Languages of Global Governance

JAN KLABBERS

IT HAS BECOME rather fashionable to explore contemporary political issues by invoking the works of Hannah Arendt, and often this takes the form of starting with Arendt's thoughts on some topic or other, finding that her thoughts leave a few gaps, filling in those blanks, and then somehow hoping that the speculating is enough in line with what Arendt said and wrote to make it plausible. There is, obviously, a huge temptation to do the same with the broad topic of global governance—something that was not around when Arendt wrote, and most assuredly not under that name. In fact, it would even be arguable to say that even the discipline of international relations was still in its infant shoes when Arendt devoted attention to world politics, and that her most well-known comment (to the effect that the relations between States were not traceable to economic interests) would be considered outdated by most specialists these days.[1]

Given the methodological problems involved in what Besson, in chapter eighteen of this volume, refers to as 'Arendtology', I shall fiercely try to resist the temptation to read things into Arendt that may not be there—without fully succeeding, no doubt. Indeed, elsewhere I have suggested that Arendt is best seen not so much as a fount of wisdom, but rather as a source of inspiration: the unexpected connections she made, and the unorthodox ways in which she defined concepts and looked at what went on around her, shed unfamiliar light on familiar issues—even if it sometimes ended up generating more heat than light.[2] What I shall aim to do instead is try to sketch some connections between what Arendt wrote and what could be called 'global governance'.

[1] See H Arendt, *Between Past and Future* (London, Penguin, 1977) 155: 'Only foreign affairs, because the relationships between nations still harbour hostilities and sympathies which cannot be reduced to economic factors, seem to be left as a purely political domain.' Among the first explorations of the relevance of Arendt for the discipline of international relations is AF Lang, Jr, and J Williams (eds), *Hannah Arendt and International Relations: Readings Across the Lines* (New York, Palgrave Macmillan, 2005).

[2] See J Klabbers, 'Possible Islands of Predictability: The Legal Thought of Hannah Arendt' (2007) 20 *Leiden Journal of International Law* 1.

Arendt's biographer and former student, Elisabeth Young-Bruehl, recently remarked that 'Arendt's greatest gift as a political thinker was to identify novelties, to explore them, and when the exploration led to a generality, to state that generality clearly'.[3] One of Arendt's preferred methods of identifying these novelties was by zooming in on the language used, on the unspoken assumption that language is rarely neutral but often already steers discussion and debate into a certain direction, or, more importantly still, comes to function as a blanket, warming its users but obscuring relevant issues and opinions from view.

The aim of the present contribution is to tease out some of this, with special reference to global governance. It would seem that Arendt can offer useful insights about the language and concepts used in discussing, analysing and celebrating global governance, even if she did not say anything out loud. In what follows, I address first what global governance stands for: disputed as it is, it is not impossible to find something of a working concept. Secondly, I highlight some of the pitfalls of global governance: some issues keep puzzling analysts. Subsequently, I explore how an Arendtian frame of mind could be useful to analyse some of those topics. In doing so, I first address human rights, followed by a discussion on the use of language and concepts in global governance more generally. The reason for this distinction is that human rights law is one of the few manifestations of global governance about which Arendt did actively write, even if her writings on human rights are somewhat dispersed throughout her work. Hence, here her writings can offer some direct guidance. Inevitably, I shall be painting with a rather broad brush; the format of an essay does not allow for a more detailed exploration.

I. (SOME OF THE) HALLMARKS OF GLOBAL GOVERNANCE

What seems reasonably clear these days is that there is no single institution running the world. Power and authority are divided and, what is more, dispersed. Authority is exercised by States (some more than others), but not by States alone. Authority is exercised by intergovernmental organisations (think of the UN, the WTO, the World Bank), but again to varying degrees. Authority can also be found in the work of non-governmental organisations: entities such as Amnesty International or Greenpeace may have an influence on global affairs beyond what could reasonably be expected given their formal status.

In addition, companies and industries exercise authority. On the prosaic level, anyone who used WordPerfect as their preferred word-processing device will have realised that in the days of Microsoft, there is not much chance left to continue working with WordPerfect: Microsoft's systems are not highly compatible. The dominance of Microsoft makes free choice in the field of word-processing

[3] See E Young-Bruehl, *Why Arendt Matters* (New Haven, Conn, Yale University Press, 2006) 175.

well-nigh impossible. The picture is similar in other industries, as the 2009 global financial crisis made clear: some actors can set the tone, but the downfall of one can cause an economic avalanche beyond anyone's control. As a result, it is possible to argue that the problem resides not so much with companies, but with the markets on which these operate: authority, on this view, is located somewhere in these markets—and that makes things all the more difficult to control, or even to identify who exactly is influencing whom.[4]

What is also unclear is how global governance is exercised. Anne-Marie Slaughter has made a plausible case that much governance these days is being exercised through informal networks of civil servants, making deals and arrangements far from the spotlight and far from any democratic or judicial control.[5] Many of the results of such concord are, furthermore, laid down in instruments of uncertain legal status, ranging from summit statements and guidelines to codes of conduct, action programs and the like.[6] As a result, it is not just difficult to find out how global governance is exercised, but also, most disturbingly perhaps, what it consists of. Much the same applies to the guidelines and codes developed by industry representatives in such vital sectors as insurance and banking: their legal status is opaque, resulting in great uncertainty for audiences worldwide and well-nigh unlimited room for manoeuvre for the powers that be.[7]

James Rosenau, arguably among the first to identify governance in the absence of government, more or less accidentally defined governance as related to the exercise of governmental functions in the absence of 'organizations and institutions explicitly charged with performing them'.[8] Indeed, pivotal to global governance are 'the informal, non-authoritative dimensions that are so essential to the functioning of international orders and regimes'.[9]

The elusive nature of global governance has several consequences for research. One of these consequences is that global governance cannot be captured fully within the confines of a single academic discipline. While possibly most work to date has been done by those with a background in international politics, much of this work misses the legal dimension. International lawyers, in turn, have difficulties studying informal exercises of authority, precisely because these are informal and not institutionalised. Both lawyers and political scientists, moreover, might lack the sensibilities that come with training in the humanities. Theologians and moral theorists may offer valuable insights on the ethics of global governance (or the

[4] For a brief argument along these lines, see J Gray, *False Dawn: The Delusions of Global Capitalism* (London, Granta, 1998) 63.

[5] See A Slaughter, *A New World Order* (Princeton, NJ, Princeton University Press, 2004).

[6] See J Klabbers, 'Reflections on Soft Law in a Privatized World' (2005) 16 *Finnish Yearbook of International Law* 313.

[7] See Slaughter, above n 5. See also H Davies and D Green, *Global Financial Regulation: The Essential Guide* (Cambridge, Polity, 2008).

[8] See JN Rosenau, 'Governance, Order, and Change in World Politics' in JN Rosenau and E Czempiel (eds), *Governance without Government: Order and Change in World Politics* (Cambridge, Cambridge University Press, 1992) 1, 3.

[9] *Ibid* 9.

absence thereof), while sociologists and anthropologists may be better equipped to tease out presumptions on how people behave and, in particular, on how informal mechanisms relate to formal ones. It is perhaps no accident that trans-disciplinary approaches (think of legal anthropology, for example) are undergoing something of a renaissance in the context of global governance.

Global governance also stimulates a different research agenda. As Avant *et al* make clear, the study of global governance is not so much interested in the types of actors operating as in the character of relationships in the global sphere. They outline how authority, instead of flowing top-down through institutions and, it is hoped, bottom-up through democratic legitimation procedures, comes in different forms: authority can be institution-based, it can be delegated, it can be based on expertise, on principle, and it can be based on capacity. This checklist alone would suggest that a single disciplinary perspective no longer suffices.[10]

There is the additional circumstance that existing disciplinary paradigms may well no longer be suitable to address even aspects of global governance that could otherwise be said to fall within the province of that discipline, and perhaps the main example resides in the fragmentation of international law. It is not just the case that international law has great difficulties in classifying and analysing documents other than treaties (or other recognised manifestations of international law): the suggestive term 'soft law' already hints at these problems, carrying the connotation that such instruments are not hard law, and thus either not law at all or, at best, straddling the boundary between law and non-law. This alone would be tricky enough, but the greater difficulty resides in the circumstance that it is often not even clear where, in the great taxonomy of international law, a given issue properly belongs.

Fischer-Lescano and Teubner provide a telling example when they observe that the discussion concerning the spread of HIV-Aids and the availability of patented medication may be viewed in a variety of ways. Thus, so they suggest, the AIDS medication issue may be seen as a conflict between rights: pitting the right to life, and the right to a decent health care system, against the rights of patent-holders protected under the WTO Agreement on the Trade-Related Aspects of Intellectual Property (TRIPs Agreement). Alternatively, it may be seen as an issue between competing institutions, triggering a conflict between the WTO and the WHO. Or it may be seen as a conflict between different rationalities: the rationality of healthcare versus the rationality of trade.[11] The questions this provokes relate not just to what the TRIPs Agreement says, or whether a right to medication is reconcilable with intellectual property rights, but go deeper, and relate to how to decide between those different interpretations of the same issue: how can we even tell where we should begin to look for applicable law?

[10] See DA Avant, M Finnemore and SK Sell, 'Who Governs the Globe?' in DA Avant, M Finnemore and SK Sell (eds), *Who Governs the Globe?* (Cambridge, Cambridge University Press, 2010) 1.

[11] See A Fischer-Lescano and G Teubner, *Regime-kollisionen: Zur Fragmentierung des globalen Rechts* (Frankfurt am Main, Suhrkamp, 2006) 75–81.

While Arendt never wrote on global governance specifically, her work can be an inspiration to the study of global governance. This finds its cause, it would seem, in two related factors. First, Arendt's work has always been seen as a bit erratic and not terribly systematic,[12] and thus, it could be claimed, transgressing traditional academic divides almost inadvertently—although one suspects that much of it was intentional, given her oft-stated preference for 'thinking without banisters';[13] surely, such a stand is eminently compatible with an approach which leaves academic disciplines for what they are. Secondly, Arendt was erudite by any standard—well-read in politics, history and the social sciences, with formal training in philosophy and a more than passing acquaintance with religious studies. She even managed to write sensibly about law, something that is more exceptional than one might hope.[14] In short, as her critics often highlighted with some exasperation, her work was difficult to categorise and classify, and a bit elusive, which suggests that her work may be highly suitable for the purposes of approaching global governance—elusive phenomenon par *excellence.* In much the same way as Thomas Kuhn once observed that scientific breakthroughs are often achieved by relative newcomers to a field who have not yet been blinded by a field's paradigms,[15] so Arendt's reluctance to be pigeonholed may well result in her being able to offer useful insights into a phenomenon that refuses to be pigeonholed.

Global governance and globalisation would seem to go hand in hand: the rise of globalisation, however precisely defined, has been accompanied by the rise of global governance. In other words: global governance, it could be claimed, sets the parameters in which globalisation can develop and blossom. Not surprisingly, then, much of global governance is motivated by a desire to make the global economy function smoothly, in much the same way as modern legal systems took their shape in the late nineteenth century so as to facilitate the modern capitalist economy.[16] In this light, the current popularity of such topics as international trade law or international investment law is hardly a coincidence: these bodies of law are considered necessary to make the economy run smoothly, and are often portrayed as neutral arbitrators which help to 'level the playing field', as the popular phrase among WTO protagonists has it.

[12] A hint to this effect may be seen in Isaiah Berlin's acidic dismissal of everything coming out of *Mitteleuropa*, which had produced the likes of Arendt and (the direct target of the claim) Herbert Marcuse: '[T]he terrible twisted *Mitteleuropa* in which nothing is straight, simple, truthful, all human relations and all political attitudes are twisted into ghastly shapes by these awful casualties who, because *they* are crippled, recognise nothing pure and firm in the world!' Quoted in M Ignatieff, *Isaiah Berlin: A Life* (London, Vintage, 1998), 253.

[13] See, eg, the brief discussion in M Canovan, *Hannah Arendt: A Reinterpretation of her Political Thought* (Cambridge, Cambridge University Press, 1992) 278.

[14] For an exploration, see Klabbers, above n 2.

[15] See TS Kuhn, *The Structure of Scientific Revolutions*, 2nd edn (Chicago, Ill, University of Chicago Press, 1970) 90.

[16] See, eg, D Kennedy, 'Legal Education and the Reproduction of Hierarchy' (1982) 32 *Journal of Legal Education* 591, 597.

Accompanying this drive towards economic liberalisation and globalisation has been an erosion of traditional values. The neo-liberal economic philosophy upon which the globalising economy rests cannot be reconciled with any set of distinct values other than the value of *laissez-faire* which, in different settings, appears as toleration.[17] Religions are unsuitable chaperones to globalisation because of their truth claims—and as Arendt held in the 1950s, truth claims are naturally absolutist.[18] Likewise, grand ideologies are ill-suited companions, as these too tend to make the sort of truth claims that will not allow for liberal trade and investment flows. Yet some normative floors and ceilings are required; people need some guidance concerning what to do and what not to do in matters that do not directly impact their roles as producers and consumers—roles that may be shrinking, incidentally.[19]

In the globalised world, this guidance comes in (at least) two recognised manifestations: the rise of a set of predominantly liberal human rights since the 1970s, and the completion of a system of international criminal law, visible in the creation of the Yugoslavia and Rwanda tribunals of the 1990s and culminating in the creation of the International Criminal Court in 2002. Indeed, the last-mentioned is a most wonderful simulacrum of global governance: a well-developed institution, based on a set of detailed rules and even more detailed elaborations thereof, with nothing to do: it has yet to decide a substantive case, despite having been in existence for almost a decade.

II. (SOME OF THE) PITFALLS OF GLOBAL GOVERNANCE

Global governance comes in various shapes and guises—that much is clear. Some of its manifestations turn out to be highly problematic, and so are some of the manifestations of non-governance: it would seem, for example, that climate change could well benefit from some form of governance; some form of governance might be better than none at all. Or perhaps it is more accurate to say that governance is taking place in the form of a hyper-liberal approach: industrialised States take no measures whatsoever, neither do the large industrialising ones, and any attempts at reaching some form of international agreement fail miserably.

Likewise, issues of migration are still largely left to regulation by national governments: sovereign States have been highly reluctant to liberalise the movement of persons through global regulation, despite the circumstance that goods and services can nowadays move rather freely from one side of the globe to another. While products move freely and have been subjected to some kind of

[17] See generally M Walzer, *On Toleration* (New Haven, Conn, Yale University Press, 1997).

[18] See her essay on 'Truth and Politics', reproduced in *Between Past and Future*, above n 1, 227.

[19] See, eg BR Barber, *Consumed: How Markets Corrupt Children, Infantilize Adults, and Swallow Citizens Whole* (New York, Norton, 2007); R Urueña, *No Citizens Here: Global Subjects and Participation in International Law* (doctoral thesis, University of Helsinki, 2010—on file with the author).

global governance, most notably within the WTO, what economists refer to as production factors are less regulated. The movement of persons is deemed problematic; and if anything, national controls have strengthened, not just over the last decade (since 9/11), but already before: passports and visas are inventions of fairly recent origin.[20]

Financial regulation, including the movement of capital, would seem to be subject to some form of global governance, but without there being much regulation, so to speak. There are no formal intergovernmental institutions in existence to supervise the work of banks, central banks and the financial sector at large, and no rules exist to combat such things as currency speculation. Still, below the surface (on the 'legally subliminal level',[21] so to speak) it would seem that things do not happen randomly. There are networks of regulators in the financial sector, ranging from the Basel Committee to the International Organisation of Securities Commissioners or the International Accounting Standards Board, whereas heads of State meet (or used to meet) regularly in loose frameworks such as the G7, G8 or G20, debt issues may be discussed in the nebulous Paris Club, and security in the more visible but not less nebulous Organisation for Security and Cooperation in Europe. Companies and their accountants may be asked to (or stronger: expected to) follow International Financing Reporting Standards, so by any measure it would seem that some form of governance is going on. And yet the financial crisis of 2009 managed to take many by surprise, and accounting standards did little to prevent Enron from making a mess a decade ago—whatever governing takes place in the banking sector or concerning the behaviour of companies would seem to be insufficient. Moreover, scandals such as that involving Enron paved the way for aggressive unilateral legislation (think of the US Sarbanes-Oxley Act—itself a form of global governance).

By contrast, there are other sectors in which global governance can be seen to be present in abundance; perhaps too much so. One sector is the 'war on terror' (which will be further discussed below) which helps to legitimate the imposition of economic sanctions on individuals suspected of cooperating with terrorists or suspected of financing them. The problem here is not the absence of governance: the UN Security Council has adopted many resolutions, some even of a legislative nature, and those resolutions are implemented with enthusiasm by governments and the European Union.[22] The problem is rather that those resolutions, which may freeze an individual's property and therewith come close to criminal punishment, are not based on anything even remotely resembling a fair trial. There is no clear indication of how individuals come to be suspected of aiding terrorists; the procedure by which individuals become blacklisted is nebulous; there is no

[20] See generally C Dauvergne, *Making People Illegal* (Cambridge, Cambridge University Press, 2008).

[21] The term is gratefully borrowed from SC Neff, *Friends but No Allies: Economic Liberalism and the Law of Nations* (New York, Columbia University Press, 1990).

[22] Although the famous *Kadi* case suggests that there may be limits to the EU's enthusiasm. See Joined Cases C-402/05 P and 415/05 P, *Kadi and Al Barakaat* v *Council and Commission* [2008] ECR I-6351.

legal procedure for becoming de-listed, and at no point is a trial based on the rule of law envisaged. It is, moreover, difficult to challenge sanctions once they have been imposed, and there is not even a plausible indication, in any particular case, that the regime is effective. It may be that the regime as a whole is reasonably effective (in that it may help to prevent further terrorist attacks—then again, as a counterfactual this is impossible to prove or disprove), but it is by no means certain that sanctions on individuals X, Y or Z contribute anything to this, other perhaps than as serving as a deterrent. But such considerations are difficult to reconcile with any conception of the rule of law, liberal or otherwise: people should not be punished for what they have not done, and should not be punished, without established ground, just to set an example.[23]

Ironically perhaps, with the International Criminal Court in The Hague, an institution would be available to guarantee suspects a fair trial, but this institution, while it addresses political violence, has no jurisdiction to address the political violence of terrorism, let alone over acts of the Security Council. If anything, the Court works the other way around: it can be activated at the instigation of the Security Council, but cannot address acts of the Council itself. This provides a curious picture: one of the institutions of global governance—the Security Council—has carved out a special niche for itself, insulating itself from any form of legal control. The International Criminal Court is now a court with jurisdiction over crimes that happen only rarely; and typically, when they happen, they happen within a particular political context, which suggests that some of the effects normally associated with criminal courts (deterrence, for example) are bound to remain out of reach: the political criminal is not easily deterred by the prospect of having to spend time in jail, because he or she is unlikely to work on the basis of a regular criminal's cost–benefit analysis.[24] While Arendt pleaded passionately in favour of an international criminal tribunal, it is difficult to imagine that she would be very impressed by the International Criminal Court as it now exists.[25]

In yet other fields governance seems to exist, but does so in a highly dispersed way, and perhaps the best example resides in the regime relating to foreign direct investment. Over the last two decades or so, a veritable network of bilateral investment treaties has been concluded, protecting foreign direct investment against expropriation (or matters of equivalent or more or less similar effect) by the host States of these investments. The key to understanding the regime resides in its bilateral nature: the regime is the product of a network of bilateral

[23] See generally HLA Hart, *Punishment and Responsibility: Essays in the Philosophy of Law* (Oxford, Clarendon Press, 1968).

[24] See J Klabbers, 'Just Revenge? The Deterrence Argument in International Criminal Law' (2001) 12 *Finnish Yearbook of International Law* 249.

[25] Also because the International Criminal Court separates the individual suspect from his or her national context. See H Arendt, *Eichmann in Jerusalem: A Report on the Banality of Evil* (London, Penguin, 1977) 298: 'It is quite conceivable that certain political responsibilities among nations might some day be adjudicated in an international court; what is inconceivable is that such a court would be a criminal tribunal which pronounces on the guilt or innocence of individuals.'

engagements rather than any multilateral convention. An attempt to establish a multilateral agreement on investment, negotiated under auspices of the OECD, did not survive the opposition from civil society in the late 1990s, and civil society had possibly been alarmed by the earlier (and still fairly innocuous) creation of a limited set of multilateral rules in the framework of the WTO: the Agreement on Trade-Related Investment Measures (TRIMs Agreement).

Those bilateral investment treaties, on their face, tend to look politically neutral, but given the circumstance that developing countries are dependent on foreign investment while most of the companies doing the investing are from industrialised countries, a certain tilting of the scales seems inevitable. What is more conspicuous, however, is that these treaties come with firm arbitration provisions: as soon as a host State does something that diminishes the value of the investment, mandatory arbitration can set in, and often results in the finding that, indeed, the host State has done something unacceptable and should pay compensation. Problematically, this implies that changes in environmental legislation or labour legislation may be seen as equivalent to the taking of property, thus limiting the legitimate policy options for local governments in order to protect against environmental degradation, for example, or to improve labour conditions or minimum wages. Thus, the political space for local governments is limited by the existence of international procedures; these help shape the public law of States hosting investments.[26]

The popularity of investment law seems intimately connected to what is arguably the most remarkable human rights development of the last half century: the emergence of the right to private property. It is not, of course, the case that private property was never recognised: political theorists have long heralded its blessings, and the 1948 Universal Declaration of Human Rights protected the right to property in its Article 17. Yet thereafter it was to vanish for a while. The original European Convention on Human Rights did not address the right to property, and in the same spirit, the 1966 International Covenant on Civil and Political Rights does not mention the right to property either.[27]

In the European system, the right to property would come to be included two years after the conclusion of the original Convention, when the first Protocol was concluded, and even then in less than absolute terms: the very phrase 'protecting the right to property' immediately goes on to state that deprivation of possessions is allowed in the public interest. The format chosen comes close to having the exception overshadow the general rule, and the same applies to most other regional human rights conventions: the African Charter, the Inter-American Convention, the Commonwealth of Independent States Convention—they all protect the right to property, but all subject to the 'general interest or the 'public interest'.

[26] See generally G van Harten, *Investment Treaty Arbitration and Public Law* (Oxford, Oxford University Press, 2007).

[27] The documents mentioned here and below are conveniently collected in PR Gandhi (ed), *Blackstone's International Human Rights Documents*, 4th edn (Oxford, Oxford University Press, 2004).

In terms of legal phrasing, the hardest guarantee can probably be found in the Arab Charter, Article 25 of which specifies that

> Each citizen has a guaranteed right to own private property. No citizen shall under any circumstances be divested of all or any part of his property in an arbitrary or unlawful manner.

Compared to the other regional conventions, this is hard language, further borne out by the bilateral investment treaties. Intriguingly, what was quite difficult to conceive as a human right (the right to property) has proved immensely successful upon being rebranded in terms of a right of investors or, better still, as protecting investors against the risks inherent in a long-term business relationship.[28]

In conjunction with the liberalisation of world trade since the Second World War—with first, hesitantly, the conclusion of the General Agreement on Tariffs and Trade and a multitude of regional free trade arrangements (including the highly ambitious European Union with its free movement of goods, services, capital and, subject to migration control, workers), later followed by the creation of the WTO with its strongly legalised dispute settlement mechanism—the emergence of a strong (if dispersed) investment regime and the increased protection of private property sketch a picture of the overwhelming dominance of neo-liberalism on the global scene: this will be further discussed below.

III. (SOME OF THE) CONCEPTS OF GLOBAL GOVERNANCE

When the US Government labelled the attack of 9/11 an 'attack on America', it brought to mind the earlier attack, in 1941, on Pearl Harbor; and this, in turn, triggered all sorts of associations and analogies.[29] The immediate association was to be engaged in a war, and since no single State could be classified as 'the enemy', the concept of war was broadened to include a war on a method: the war on terror, in harmony with earlier rhetoric about a war on drugs. And in the absence of a concrete and identifiable enemy, the war can only be limitless: everyone can be a suspect, everyone can be an enemy. Not surprisingly, then, 9/11 triggered the reification of national security: the attack was not considered to be a matter for the New York police but involved the entire country, and through air traffic controls and limitations would come to involve the rest of the world as well. The US authorities could trample on the rights of suspects, subject people to lengthy security checks, create a new Department of Homeland Security, and even re-introduce the visa (for States whose citizens would not need one) under the different heading of ESTA (Electronic System for Travel Authorization). It is at least arguable that little of this would have happened had the attack been labelled differently: the label 'attack on

[28] This is how investment law is conceptualised in one of the leading textbooks: see R Dolzer and C Schreuer, *Principles of International Investment Law* (Oxford, Oxford University Press, 2008).

[29] Young-Bruehl, above n 3, 12, 61–66.

America' gave rise to a national siege mentality which is difficult to imagine had 9/11 been characterised as, say, an 'attack on New York' or as large-scale murder. In that sense, the terrorism stigma may be as convenient to governments as it is (one imagines) to terrorists: without this, numerous governmental measures would be difficult to justify or legitimate.[30]

If the above is a particularly poignant example of how the terminology employed can steer the subsequent debates and decision-making processes, much the same transpires from other terms that make up the 'global governance' vocabulary. One of these is the *fons et origo* itself: the very term 'globalisation' invokes all sorts of images about a shrinking planet, people travelling to pleasant destinations and being able to procure exotic products close to home. Indeed, some have claimed that 'globalisation' is more ideology than anything else, and that what looks pleasant and attractive from afar is in fact a ruthless process of producing winners and losers, and much more of the latter than of the former.[31]

'Global governance' too is a highly ambivalent term, suggesting, as it does, that some form of authority is being exercised on the global level. While it is clear that governance and government are different phenomena, nonetheless the term 'governance' suggests that someone is in charge, which gives the further impression that since there is someone at the helm, there is no need for the rest of us to bother: the proverbial ship of State, in the form of the 'ship of globe', is in safe hands, even if admittedly it is not very clear whose hands these are, or where the ship is being steered. Contrast the term with a possible competing description (say, 'global anarchy') and the difference becomes clear: elusive as global governance may be, it is decidedly not anarchy.

This is, quite obviously, an issue with two sides to it. The term 'global governance' is descriptively arguably more accurate than 'global anarchy'; indeed, the argument is that it has come to succeed the idea of anarchy, popular among international theorists, precisely because there seem to be some patterns of authority discernible in ways that do not apply in the earlier 'anarchical society'. Still, speaking of governance may also have the effect of lulling people to sleep or, more likely perhaps, making it seem that nothing much is to be gained by engaging in global politics. Put differently, the elusive nature of global governance (with its uncertain foci and methods of authority) may induce a sense of despair: whatever we do, it is impossible to influence the course of events, and things are too complex and difficult to handle at any rate. Hence, the global public realm is thought to be either absent or irrelevant, with the result that politics is being replaced by

[30] I explore the mutual dependence of States and terrorists in greater depth in J Klabbers, 'Rebel with a Cause? Terrorists and Humanitarian Law' (2003) 14 *European Journal of International Law* 299.

[31] See J Friedman, 'Globalization' in D Nugent and J Vincent (eds), *A Companion to the Anthropology of Politics* (London, Blackwell, 2004) 179.

managerialism, bureaucracy and technocracy, and without the types of control that one would expect (be it democratic control or judicial control).[32]

One of the buzzwords in global governance, especially perhaps among international lawyers, is 'constitutionalisation'. The argument is, with greater or lesser plausibility, that international law is going through a phase of constitutionalisation.[33] There might be several reasons for this. One is, no doubt, to counter the perceived problem of the fragmentation of international law: in a fragmented world, constitutionalisation offers the promise of some degree of unity. What might also be a relevant factor is a kind of *ennui* with the vocabulary of international law on the part of international lawyers: international law has been unable to tame the beast of politics, despite all its good intentions and despite the launching of concepts such as *erga omnes* obligations and *jus cogens* rules; perhaps, then, it is time to try a different vocabulary—the language of constitutionalism.

This might apply all the more so given the circumstance that constitutionalisation and like terms (constitution, constitutionalism) come with a set of associations that help explain its attraction. In the setting of global governance, where political legitimacy is at a premium, constitutionalisation offers such legitimacy: a constitutional order is almost (if not quite) by definition a legitimate order. It carries overtones about the exercise of authority in accordance with the Rule of Law; it carries an implicit promise that basic human rights shall be respected, and that a constitutional order is an order worth inhabiting and, what is more, worth supporting. The very inclusion of the term 'constitutionalisation' in the vocabulary of global governance therewith suggests that global governance too can be seen as legitimate. It may be the case that we cannot quite figure out who is governing, and how governance is exercised, but at least in a constitutional system there will be limits.

The association between global governance and constitutionalisation carries two faces. The suggestion that global governance is legitimate because it is somehow constitutional is risky in the same way the use of the term 'governance' is risky: it might induce a sense of complacency. On the other hand, the very use of the term and its obvious discrepancy with any version of reality (as discussed above) also suggests that much work remains to be done, and that it is not for nothing that constitutionalisation denotes a process rather than a finalised state of affairs.

Last but not least, global governance is strongly coloured by the ideology of neo-liberalism. While it might not be very helpful to sketch neo-liberalism as a form of political evil, as some commentators do,[34] nonetheless the influence of the neo-liberal discourse is so overwhelming that alternatives seem hardly feasible.

[32] See M Koskenniemi, 'The Fate of Public International Law: Between Technique and Politics' (2007) 70 *MLR* 1.

[33] See generally J Klabbers, A Peters and G Ulfstein, *The Constitutionalization of International Law* (Oxford, Oxford University Press, 2009).

[34] See P Hayden, *Political Evil in a Global Age: Hannah Arendt and International Theory* (London, Routledge, 2009).

Many of the institutions of global governance adhere to neo-liberalism, from the International Monetary Fund and the World Bank to the WTO, and the sheer numbers impede political discussion. This carries the substantial risk that political discussion is *a priori* excluded unless it fits within the dominant discourse, that is, with a view to markets and the marketability of human activity. Thus, institutions of learning (ranging from elementary schools to universities) are subjected to market demands and accompanying (or derived) ideas about cost-efficiency, measurement by output and demand, and the like, and the same applies to other issues such as healthcare and even policing. All this is then accompanied, logically, by a controlling urge: the achievements of students, police officers, health care professionals, etc are to be measured, and those measurements themselves are typically in the form of quantitative indicators—and how could it be otherwise? The result is what a leading accountancy scholar (and this is hardly a coincidence) has labeled 'the audit society',[35] denoting a society where each and every one is subject to scrutiny and control; where performances are deemed useful only if they are measurable and, within that frame, deemed to be quantitatively gratifying.

IV. (SOME OF THE) HUMAN RIGHTS IN GLOBAL GOVERNANCE

Human rights are often thought to function in global governance as something of a base level of ethics, as 'values for a Godless age'.[36] In a globalised world economy, where nothing is certain except job insecurity and where crises are the order of the day, human rights are thought to provide a normative safety-net. That sounds highly commendable, and human rights discourse has met, understandably, with many adherents and advocates. Law schools have offered human rights programs since the 1970s; there are courts in existence to deal with complaints from citizens; specialised journals exists, and there are even specialised training institutions for aspiring human rights workers, such as the Venice-based European Master's Program in Human Rights and Democratisation, the more or less official aim of which is to help train young professionals, by offering an 'action and policy-oriented approach' to human rights.[37]

And yet the human rights regime does little to come to the rescue of the ones left behind in the wake of globalisation; indeed, it is arguable that human rights law facilitates globalisation. The most potent rights, backed by the most potent judicial institutions, tend to be civil and political rights: the right to be free from torture, the traditional freedoms of expression and assembly, respect for private life and for family life. At the very least, the list is compatible with neo-liberal economics,

[35] See M Power, *The Audit Society: Rituals of Verification* (Oxford, Oxford University Press, 1997).

[36] See F Klug, *Values for a Godless Age: The Story of the United Kingdom's New Bill of Rights* (London, Penguin, 2000).

[37] See its website at <http://www.emahumanrights.org/about-us.html> (visited 16 November 2010).

something made abundantly clear perhaps by the addition, mentioned earlier, of the right to respect for one's property.

To put it more poignantly perhaps, the catalogue of human rights as usually conceived does not protect against the drawbacks of globalisation: it does not provide for job security, or stipulate a right to a minimum wage or a general basic income. While it does protect the freedom to form trade unions, it does not necessarily support a right to strike, or a governmental obligation to accept collective bargaining agreements or to force employers to accept these.[38] The same catalogue does not provide a safety-net against poverty and malnutrition, or emergency rights in times of food crises, and the right to education that is recognised in some documents detailing civil and political rights focuses on non-discrimination in education rather than anything else. Moreover, as Arendt anticipated in *The Origins of Totalitarianism*, those human rights catalogues do little to protect the stateless, or to protect the vulnerable group of migrants and their families. The one Convention specifically dealing with migrants' rights, moreover, is among the least accepted treaties: the Convention has 44 parties, but they are drawn exclusively from countries whose citizens tend to emigrate; it counts not a single western State among its signatories.[39]

Neither is human rights law usually seen to extend to refugees. Indeed, the notion of 'refugee' is defined as a person who flees from political persecution, and who flees across State boundaries: the Refugee Convention (including the 1967 Protocol[40]) does not protect those who seek to escape from poverty and a poor quality of life, and does not apply to those who move within a State, the so-called 'internally displaced persons'.

To some extent, this is offset by the conclusion of specific conventions addressing economic, social and cultural rights, but these suffer from a number of enforcement problems. Their language is often less than precise; few courts or other tribunals exist to give effect to them, and to the extent that these do exist, their findings are not considered binding. This lack of enforceability is sometimes explained by the circumstance that such things as poverty are not caused by the acts of individual agents (as, typically, 'regular' human rights violations are) but are, instead, caused by the structures of the global economy: capitalism comes inevitably with winners and losers, and protecting the losers can only be accomplished by changing the structures rather than blaming individual actors or even companies: the 'legal model' underlying human rights law is simply ill-equipped to deal with structures.[41]

[38] The leading textbook on the European Convention on Human Rights deals with trade union rights in a single page (out of close to 500), simply because there is not all that much to say. See C Ovey and RCA White, *Jacobs and White, European Convention on Human Rights*, 3rd edn (Oxford, Oxford University Press, 2002) 294–95.

[39] This concerns the 1990 International Convention on the Protection of the Rights of All Migrant Workers and Members of Their Families, reproduced in Gandhi, above n 27, 154.

[40] Reproduced in Gandhi, *ibid*, 31 and 41, respectively.

[41] The argument is made by J Galtung, *Human Rights in Another Key* (Cambridge, Polity, 1994).

Arendt had already warned, writing in the early 1950s, that not too much could be expected of human rights law. Her position, as is well known, was that people need a polity in which to thrive and, moreover, in which their rights can be guaranteed: the 'right to have rights' would be the ultimate right. This now is negated in the case of refugees, migrants and the stateless, who, even if they are, in some systems, protected against torture or slavery, often are not allowed to benefit from the two rights which are foundational of polities and make politics ultimately possible: the right to vote, and the right to run for political office. These rights are pivotal for participation in politics; and politics, to Arendt, was the lifeblood of humanity. Typically, the international law of human rights still does very little to guarantee precisely these two rights. Neither the International Covenant on Civil and Political Rights nor the European Convention on Human Rights guarantees these participatory rights; the European Convention comes closest perhaps in guaranteeing free elections in Article 3 of the First Protocol to the Convention, but without giving any indication as to whom the right applies. The American Convention on Human Rights, in Article 23, does guarantee rights to vote and be elected, but seems to be a lonely exception. While Article 23 appears to have inspired the drafters of the African Charter on Human Peoples' Rights, this particular provision has been omitted in the corresponding article (Article 13), and the Arab Charter of Human Rights too remains silent.

Of the 'single topic' conventions, it would seem that the 1952 Convention on the Political Rights of Women[42] and the later Convention on Elimination of All Forms of Discrimination against Women[43] both respect the rights to vote and to run for office (Articles I and II of the 1952 Convention; Article 7, paragraph a, of the 1979 Convention), but only to the same extent that these rights are enjoyed by men: these Conventions aim to achieve equality, even if it is merely equality in bad treatment. Much the same applies to the 1966 International Convention on the Elimination of Racial Discrimination (Article 5, paragraph c).[44]

Some human rights conventions go even further, and explicitly restrict the political rights of foreigners and stateless individuals. A clear example is the (relatively recent) Commonwealth of Independent States Convention on Human Rights and Fundamental Freedoms, concluded in 1995[45], which in the curiously drafted Article 30 holds that

> Nothing in Articles 11, 21 and 20 shall be regarded as preventing the Contracting Parties from imposing restrictions on the political activity of alien citizens and stateless persons.

What makes this extra poignant is that the articles in question address issues such as freedom of expression and equality before the law.

[42] Reproduced in Gandhi, above n 27, 43.
[43] *Ibid* 95.
[44] *Ibid* 55.
[45] *Ibid* 454.

Specific conventions dealing with those lacking the right to have general rights do little to remedy the situation. Neither the 1951 Refugee Convention nor the 1967 Protocol thereto provide anything by way of political rights. The 1990 Migrant Workers Convention (above) does provide for the right to vote and be elected, but only in migrant workers' State of origin (Article 41), not in the State where they reside. In the State of residence (the State of employment), migrant workers may have political rights only if that State grants them 'in the exercise of its sovereignty' (Article 42, paragraph 3). It would seem, moreover, that this is limited to the migrant workers themselves, and does not cover members of their families.[46]

The remedy for all this is not to claim that human rights are useless and admit defeat, and indeed this is not what Arendt proposed. Despite her critique, Arendt was a fierce proponent of human rights, but not in the naive or laudatory manner which has come to carry the day. What today's high priests of human rights often miss is the circumstance that far from being a critical vocabulary or providing a safety-net to the poor and dispossessed, human rights have become part of the establishment of which they are supposed to be critical—at least in the Western world. For all the nice rhetoric embodied in human rights documents, dispersed through human rights classes and specialised journals, endorsed by specialist non-governmental organisations and implemented through human rights 'mainstreaming' of policies, governments retain quite a bit of latitude in determining how to treat people, by having been granted a considerable 'margin of appreciation' and being able to build in limitations if these are considered 'necessary in a democratic society'.

In *The Origins of Totalitarianism*, Arendt points out with uncanny precision that the paradox at the heart of human rights is that these rights are supposed to be derived from human dignity but, in fact, depend on governments to make them work: it is precisely this paradox that was unmasked by her focus on the plight of the stateless and refugees: if you are not part of a polity, you have no human rights. The obvious response of human rights advocacy has been to diminish this reliance on governments and proclaim that sovereignty is a 'bad word', in Louis Henkin's evocative phrase, but doing so has succeeded only in shifting the reliance: instead of being asked to trust States and their highest courts to guarantee human rights, we are now asked to trust supranational institutions to guarantee human rights. Yet each of these has a limited jurisdiction (it could hardly be otherwise), and is not afraid to invoke this limitation whenever it is convenient to do so-witness the ease with which the European Court of Human Rights accepted the limits to its jurisdiction in relatively recent cases such as *Bosphorus*,[47] *Bankovic*,[48] or

[46] The Convention in most provisions spells out that rights apply to migrant workers and members of their families; in Art 42, para 3, though, the family members are not explicitly mentioned.

[47] These cases are most conveniently available at the HUDOC database of the ECtHR, http://www.echr.coe.int/echr/en/hudoc/. See *Bosphorus Hava Yollari Turizm ve Ticaret anonym Sirketi v Ireland*, app no 45036/98.

[48] See *Bankovic v Belgium and Sixteen Other States*, app no 52207/99.

Behrami and Saramati.[49] Still, then, human rights are dependent on polities, except that the polities have become bigger and are not really polities: the Council of Europe, home to the European Convention on Human Rights, can hardly be called a polity in any substantive sense, but is instead a gathering of States, some democratic, some a bit less so, where decision-making takes place on an intergovernmental basis through the concord of the governments making up the system, and without any plausible role for individuals other than through their national governments. Hence, the very attempt to undermine sovereignty may well have served to strengthen sovereignty: it is governments that decide what human rights we have; and it is governments that appoint the guardians of the regimes thus established—the judges. All this may be inevitable, and all this may even be commendable, but it is a far cry from anything having to do with human dignity: when Russia, France, Britain, Germany and the other States involved negotiate over how to treat their citizens and which categories of people are worthy of some kind of protection, human dignity will hardly enter the picture.

Hence, Arendt had already suggested that the problem resides not so much in sovereignty, but rather in the suggestion that human rights emanated from human dignity and were supposed to be inalienable. In fact, overcoming sovereignty could be counter-productive unless it were to be done radically: part of the problem, so she wrote, is that the world had become one. In a globalised world (she did not use the term, but the concept was clear enough), with a network of international legal documents in place, there is no escape left except through the cracks in the interstices—and then people are lost altogether: 'Only with a completely organized humanity could the loss of home and political status become identical with expulsion from humanity altogether.'[50]

Instead of relying on human dignity as given effect by sovereign States through reciprocal agreements (and coming with a baggage of idolatry, as Ignatieff would later point out),[51] the right to have rights could only be guaranteed by humanity itself. Reciprocal agreements would not be able to accomplish this, and not much could be expected from a world government or some such body either.[52] So how should humanity do this? Here, as so often, Arendt turned elusive, but the famous chapter in *The Origins of Totalitarianism* does contain a few hints. Thus, it would seem that human rights have to be built from the ground up. Mankind can build a common world, and can do so, in the public realm, with and between equals.[53] This equality should not be limited to people of a certain ethnicity only: precisely because foreigners (aliens) remind us of our private selves, they should

[49] See joined cases *Behrami & Behrami v France* (app no 71412/01), and *Saramati v France and Others*, app no 78166/01.

[50] See H Arendt, *The Origins of Totalitarianism* (New York, Harcourt, Brace & Company, 1966) 297.

[51] See M Ignatieff, *Human Rights as Politics and Idolatry* (Princeton, NJ, Princeton University Press, 2001).

[52] See Arendt, above n 50 , 298–99.

[53] Equality to Arendt was typically a public phenomenon, completely alien to the private realm: '[T]he public sphere is as consistently based on the law of equality as the private sphere is based on the law of universal difference and differentiation.' (*ibid* 301)

be treated publicly on equal footing. What this would seem to boil down to is, if not global democracy, then a seamless web of commitments by polities, so seamless as not to allow for any cracks—or even interstices. This may well be difficult to accomplish in its own right, but idle talk about human dignity or inalienable rights will not be very helpful; instead, the realisation that human rights must result from political action rather than adhere in humanity might just spur people into political action.

Generally a key theme for Arendt was that being human implies accepting a common responsibility for the public world, and she would no doubt agree, at least up to a point, with the idea that one should not treat others less favourably than one would treat oneself. This is not to insist on Kant's categorical imperative, but rather is a re-working of it, following which people aim to be true to themselves and not engage in activities they cannot live with and cannot bear to remember: human rights therewith presuppose, in an Arendtian conception, measurement by the 'standard of the self'.[54] As a result, it would seem that humans, when creating a normative safety-net in the form of human rights, would and should take care not to exclude anyone simply by reason of their being refugees, migrants or stateless. It is not so much that refugees, or migrants or the stateless would need special regimes; for Arendt, their situation functioned as the prism through which she could formulate her critique of human rights and hint at a different conception.

What this presupposes, though, is a realisation on everyone's part that human rights are politically produced. They are the common responsibility of all, for the greater benefit of all, and it is precisely this underlying concept that is hidden from plain view by insisting on human dignity as the basis for universal human rights, and by insisting on their, by definition unrealisable, inalienability. As it turns out, the choice for a certain terminology works in a manner so as to preclude proper understanding: it steers the debate into troubled waters, so redemption can only start by giving up the unhelpful terminology.

V. (SOME OF THE) POSSIBLE CONCLUSIONS

If Arendt were still alive, it would stand to reason that she would be writing critical tracts about global governance. She would most likely agree with Onora O'Neill's observation that the coming of age of the 'audit society' has led, and will further lead, to the erosion of trust; and without trust, no meaningful politics is possible.[55] She would be concerned about the managerial turn in global governance, with politics being replaced by governance in the form of technocracy, exercised by faceless bureaucrats; she would no doubt still insist that human rights should be severed from their rhetorical connection to human dignity, and she would

[54] This owes quite a bit to Young-Bruehl, above n 3, esp at 200.
[55] See O O'Neill, *A Question of Trust* (Cambridge, Cambridge University Press, 2002).

no doubt point to the dangers of the wholesale adoption of neo-liberal ideology: humans are no longer seen as citizens, but as market actors; Aristotle's *zoon politikon* has become *zoon ekonomikon*; *homo politicus* has become *homo economicus*.

The very first thing to do, then, perhaps, for any scholar of global governance, is to focus attention on the assumptions underlying much global governance, and on the role of neo-liberal thought. Even those who by and large embrace neo-liberalism cannot afford to buy its ideology wholesale, as the ideology is inextricably tied to global governance itself, including all its legitimation strategies. Perhaps the main lesson to be learned from Arendt with respect to global governance is that words matter, and that failing to grasp the influence of neo-liberalism on the way issues are framed and solutions are proposed will result in failing to understand global governance.

B. International Criminal Law

13

'How Dangerous it Can Be to Be Innocent': War and the Law in the Thought of Hannah Arendt

PATRICIA OWENS[1]

You know of course that all our war criminals are 'not guilty'. (Hannah Arendt to Mary McCarthy[2])

I. INTRODUCTION

MANY OPPONENTS—AND supporters—of recent US-led wars have suggested they were not only (or even) based on so-called 'humanitarian' or 'antiterrorist' grounds. They were quests by the United States for strategic influence; and in light of the current balance of power, that could only translate into a form of imperialism, whether judged pernicious or benign. Debates about the effectiveness of international law in recent wars have therefore coincided with a trend in both media and academia to describe the emergence of a new form of imperialism. It has also been suggested by those writing on contemporary imperialism that recent breaches of international law by the United States are not in keeping with some of the oldest democratic traditions of the country. Hannah Arendt's work suggests that the opposite may more accurately be the case. There is a close relationship between imperial foreign policy and the foundations of the law. It is a relationship, Arendt wrote, that emerged at the very 'beginning of the Western world … as a *world*', that is, as the in-between space for politics.[3]

Central to Arendt's explanation of the decline of the ancient Greek system of city-states was its inability to build a real empire. She located part of this failure in the Greek understanding of politics and law. Law established the boundary between political communities, and political relations were deemed to end at

[1] This chapter is reprinted from P Owens, *Between War and Politics: International Relations and the thought of Hannah Arendt* (Oxford, Oxford University Press, 2007), Chapter 5.

[2] H Arendt and M McCarthy, *Between Friends: The Correspondence of Hannah Arendt and Mary McCarthy, 1949–1975* (Carol Brightman ed and intro) (London, Secker & Warburg, 1995) 278.

[3] H Arendt, *The Promise of Politics* (New York, Schocken, 2005) 189 (hereafter 'PP' in the text).

the border. The law was both this wall-like structure and a system of 'precepts and prohibitions whose sole purpose is to demand obedience' (PP 189). Greek conduct in war was often brutal, including the annihilation of the enemy, because no political relations and alliances with former enemies were deemed possible. In contrast, the Romans were more successful in building an empire because they understood law as relational, not just a boundary or a system of rules to obey. Treaties and laws instituted a relationship *between* peoples, including enemies that were first encountered in battle. The expansive alliance system of the *societas Romana* captured the new arrangement, Arendt noted, 'in which peoples and lands were not only bound to Rome by temporary and renewable treaties, but also became Rome's eternal allies' (PP 186).

Law was an important part of the expansion of the Roman Republic and its transformation into the Roman Empire. As Mills describes,

> For the Romans there was no 'conflict' of laws—Roman universalism demanded the integration of other territory as part of the empire, not mutual respect of different people and their legal systems. Given the Roman conception of justice as unitary, absolute, universal ... international order was simply the universalization of the Roman order—a homogenization of law.[4]

But the Romans also suffered as a result of their conception of law. While they were able to establish a system of alliances and ties, the system itself was also without limits. As Arendt described, it 'forced them against their own will—indeed absent any will to power or lust for domination—to rule [what they believed to be] the entire globe, a dominion that once achieved could only collapse' (PP 187). Arendt's history of the constitutive relationships between power, law and war placed imperial expansion at the centre of the analysis. Unfortunately, the centrality of power and the constitutive relationship between law and war and expansion has been neglected in much international thought. In this field, such questions are usually framed in terms of the extent to which law articulates principles, norms and procedures as a check on brute force. Law is either considered irrelevant by some schools of thought, and therefore unworthy of much consideration, or it is considered a constraint, and research accordingly centres on questions of compliance with the law. Consider the legal injunction that States must distinguish between combatants and civilians, and take all reasonable precautions to avoid targeting non-combatants. High levels of US compliance with this norm—even when dysfunctional in purely strategic terms—reveal the power of law in shaping war. We are frequently told of occasions where US commanders called off attacks on strategically important targets when the risk of civilian casualties was deemed too high. In such circumstances, the United States is considered to be complying with the laws of war that protect civilians. In each school of international thought,

[4] A Mills, 'The Private History of International Law' (2006) 55(1) *International & Comparative Law Quarterly* 5.

the question of the relationship between power, law and war has overwhelmingly been addressed as one of various degrees of compliance.

But what if we understood law as more than simply regulative or completely extraneous? Is it possible to consider law—and assumptions about compliance with the law—as productive of the social and political context that makes possible certain forms of war and certain relations of hierarchy?[5] Law is not simply irrelevant. Neither it is simply a limitation with which, for example, US wartime actions must comply to remain legitimate. The point is not to spend time arguing that the Founding Fathers were explicit that when America reached its full potential it would walk the world stage undaunted, though indeed they did. Moreover, as Arendt wrote, European and later American imperialism was and is as 'different from national conquests in border-wars as it was from true empire building Roman style'.[6] Indeed, the word 'imperialism', she argued, 'does not mean a thing if it is used indiscriminately for Assyrian and Roman and British and Bolshevik history', and American history we might add.[7] The imperial histories of the Roman and the American republics are different. Nonetheless, Arendt's account of the relationship between law, war and imperial expansion suggests that perceived compliance with the law itself is partly productive of the global order in which contemporary war occurs.

Approaches to the relationship between law and power in international theory have been useful in capturing some important developments in the evolving system of the laws of war. Realist theory rightly argues that law alone can never be a match for political and military power; international society approaches and constructivism suggest why States often comply with various legal norms governing war that may not be in their narrow strategic interests; normative theory has suggested why the laws of war ought to be respected, and has raised the practical question of how to strengthen the law to provide a check to political and military power; post-Marxist scholars suggest that the law, when narrowly conceived, may be increasingly irrelevant given the resurgence of US imperial power. However, while capturing some central features of the current system of military power in relation to law, most international theory is limited in its capacity to capture this relationship, in particular the *productive* effect of law—what law can do. In pursuing this path with Arendt,

[5] HM Kinsella, 'Securing the Civilian: Sex and Gender and Laws of War' in M Barnett and R Duvall (eds), *Power in Global Governance* (Cambridge, Cambridge University Press, 2005) 249–72.

[6] H Arendt, *The Origins of Totalitarianism* (New York, Harcourt Brace Jovanovich, 1966) xvii (hereafter 'OT' in the text).

[7] H Arendt, *Essays in Understanding, 1930–1954* (New York, Harcourt Brace, 1994) 407 (hereafter 'EU' in the text). Arendt's broader point was that '[t]erms like nationalism, imperialism, totalitarianism, etc, are used indiscriminately for all kinds of political phenomena (usually just as highbrow words for "aggression"), and none of them is any longer understood with its particular historical background. The result is generalization in which words themselves lose all meaning' (EU 407). Elsewhere, she also noted the difficulty in comparing the British and the Roman empires, 'because, though Roman rule was presumably much crueler and intemperate, it was still a genuine empire and not merely imperialism, because the Roman conquerors forced Roman law on foreign peoples and by doing so avoided the disastrous bastardized governments of modern times': H Arendt and K Jaspers, *Correspondence, 1926–1969* (L Kohler and H Saner eds) (R and R Kimber trans) (New York, Harcourt Brace Jovanovich, 1992) 167l (hereafter 'AJ' in the text).

this essay moves away from an understanding in which law is merely a constraint on pre-existing power. Instead, we address how law plays a role in producing not only imperial power relations, but also the subjects of the law, in particular the civilian casualties of Western military campaigns.

II. POLITICS, LAW AND EXPANSION

The status of law in any political order is always fragile. But law is necessary to provide an element of stability and regulation to the always unpredictable character of political action. Since the Greeks, Arendt argued, the tradition of political thought has 'understood that laws are the stabilizing forces', the only check on the inherent unpredictability and instability of all political affairs (PP 186; OT 467). There was nothing intrinsic to political action that was stabilising and limiting. When left unchecked, it was the nature of political action—which after all emerges *in-between* people acting and speaking together and is not mediated by material things—to be boundless, to overrun existing rules, to bring about the new and unexpected. 'The stability of the laws,' she wrote, 'corresponds to the constant motion of all human affairs, a motion which can never end as long as men are born and die. The laws hedge in each new beginning and at the same time assure its freedom of movement, the potentiality of something entirely new and unpredictable' (OT 465).

The purpose of law was to offer some stability and form to what could otherwise seem so fleeting and transient, political words and actions. This was part of the greatness of political action, and why boundaries and laws were so important.[8] Arendt analogised the law with territorial boundaries, which 'protect and make possible the physical identity of a people'. Laws similarly 'protect and make possible its political existence'.[9] Law itself does not bring about change. It can 'stabilize and legalize change once it has occurred, but the change itself is always the result of extra-legal action', the result of politics.[10] Law and territorial boundaries provided the main limits to political action but, again, their capacity is limited; the 'limitations of law are never entirely reliable safeguards against action from within the body politic, just as the boundaries of the territory are never entirely reliable safeguards against action from without' (HC 191). The concept of territory is itself a legal and political as well as geographical term.

[8] The power that emerged out of people acting together in the political realm, Arendt wrote, could not 'be checked, at least not reliably, by laws … [They] are always in danger of being abolished by the power of the many, and in a conflict between law and power it is seldom the law which will emerge as victor'. H Arendt, *On Revolution* (New York, Viking, 1970) 150 (hereafter 'OR' in the text).

[9] H Arendt, *The Human Condition* (Chicago, Ill, University of Chicago Press, 1958) 191 (hereafter 'HC' in the text).

[10] H Arendt, *Crises of the Republic* (New York, Harcourt Brace Jovanovich, 1972) 80 (hereafter 'CR' in the text).

International law is similarly a product of customs, treaties and agreements between States.[11] To be enduring, any political space has to be 'hedged in by laws'. Without such conventions the world would truly be little more than a Hobbesian state of nature, or more accurately, in Arendt's words, a desert, a 'lawless, fenceless wilderness of fear and suspicion' (OT 466). In the absence of such laws the space in-between that emerges through political interaction would seem so ephemeral. Arendt believed the territorial principle established by the European comity of nations was praiseworthy to the extent that it reflected that 'the earth is inhabited by many peoples and that these peoples are ruled by many different laws' (EJ 264). These laws and boundaries served a limiting function to the extent that each member of the comity respected the principle of sovereignty. However, as Arendt's history of imperialism reminds us, this European comity and respect of plurality did not extend to the rest of the world, and indeed made possible the expansion of overseas empires. Indeed, crucially for our later discussion, Arendt never identified the law of this comity of nations as embodying potentially universal and abstract norms that could be divorced from force and imperial power.

Arendt did not focus in detail on the role of law in her study of the history of European imperialism at the end of the nineteenth century. She presented this new form of expansionist power politics as law*less*, and spent little time addressing the extent to which European lawyers had sought to make the power grab as orderly as possible. In her accounts of the ancient political systems of Greece and Rome, however, she did draw explicit links between politics and law, war and imperial expansion. In the Greek model of politics and war, politics was understood as the realm of non-violent speech and persuasion among equals that reached its limit at the boundary of the *polis* and the doorstep of the home. This system emerged as their self-conscience solution to the problem of violence in human affairs. As Arendt put it, they sought to turn 'struggle into an integrating component of the polis and the political' (PP 171) and simultaneously to exclude war and brute violence from conduct between citizens. The limited space of the Greek *polis* was protected, indeed constituted, through the exclusion of non-citizens, slaves and women, who therefore had no formal protection from violence. Ideals of citizenship were modelled on the practice of hoplite battle by farmer-warriors who would return to the city after a short, sharp battle. All this, Arendt reminds

[11] In this sense, territory does not first and foremost refer to territorial space on the earth, Arendt observed, but 'to the space between individuals in a group whose members are bound to, and at the same time separated and protected from, each other' by their traditions and laws. See H Arendt, *Eichmann in Jerusalem: a Report on the Banality of Evil* (New York, Viking Press, 1963) 262–63 (hereafter 'EJ' in the text). The organisation of politics, the human-made laws and conventions, is historically contingent as well as spatially (territorially) bound. 'Treaties and international guarantees provide an extension of this territorially bound freedom for citizens outside of their own country, but … the elementary coincidence of freedom and a limited space remains manifest.' (OR 279; HC 191)

us, was the peculiarly Greek response to the 'annihilating element of brute force, which destroys both the world and the political sphere' (PP 171).[12]

Legislative activities involved in building a system of laws were considered to be pre-political. Law-making was necessary to secure the structure of the public realm within which political action could then occur.[13] But this law, as Arendt wrote,

> was neither the content of political action … nor was it a catalogue of prohibitions … It was quite literally a wall … This wall-like law was sacred, but only the inclosure was political. Without it a public realm could no more exist than a piece of property without a fence to hedge it in. (HC 63–64)

Law, the Greek word *nomos*, was understood as constitutive of all subsequent political speech and inter-action, a necessary precursor for the properly political to begin. But the building of the protective walls around the *polis* contained an essence different from that of speech and persuasion among free and equal citizens. There was 'something violent about it in terms of both its origins and its nature. It comes into being by means of production, not action' (PP 181). The law is *made*, and as such 'contains in itself the violent force inherent in all production' (PP 181). This is captured in the notion that citizens are subject to the *force* of the law.

The means used to form the institutional, legal element of the Greek *polis* was not considered political, and neither was anything that went on outside the walls of the city. Law ceased to apply in interactions with other city-states. We have described the constitutive 'negative exclusion' of women, slaves and non-Greeks. This exclusion was so radical that anything outside the *polis* was deemed non-political. This is clear from the brutality of Greek conduct in war, especially against barbarians. Thucydides' description of the brutal lessons the Athenians sought to impose on the islanders of Melos has always been cited by the realist tradition as evidence of the timeless and often brutal power struggle between groups. Clearly the Greeks waged war according to the principle that it is 'might that makes right'. Foreign relations were necessarily violent. Moreover, in Arendt's words, 'negotiation and the conclusion of treaties [were] understood merely as the continuation of war by other means, the means of cunning and deception' (PP 165). Such talk was not deemed to be political speech, and no real 'ties and linkages' were believed to emerge out of them (PP 181). The most important thing was the border, which was not a bridge that connected but a barrier that separated. Once the Greeks had annihilated their

[12] '"Wherever you go, you will be a *polis*": these famous words became not merely the watchword of Greek colonization,' wrote Arendt, 'they expressed the conviction that action and speech create a space between the participants which can find its proper location almost anytime and anywhere' (HC 198). They expressed the creative and boundary-transgressing ethos of the political action of free and equal citizens.

[13] Another indication that laws and legislating were considered by the Greeks as pre-political, Arendt suggests, is that the 'lawgiver did not even have to be a citizen of the city but could be engaged from outside to perform his task' (PP 179).

enemies, they would retreat 'inside their walls, to be with themselves and their glory' (PP 178).

The bulk of Arendt scholarship is now clear that the Greek model of politics (and war) was not Arendt's, though elements of political agonism were attractive to her. Instead we find traces of a qualified endorsement of an alternative, though no less imperial, solution to the problem of war in politics and which emerged out of meeting in battle. The Greek solution to the problem was to define separate spheres and treat the legal boundary of the *polis* as the limit to authentic politics. But law can do more than secure boundaries and provide a structure of commandments that must be obeyed. Law can also institutionalise a relationship *between* people, that is, be constitutive of interaction in a newly public, political space. Arendt's alternative example is that of the rise of the Roman Republic, which from around 200 BC emerged as the most powerful political entity after the decline of the Greek city-states and which eventually evolved into the Roman Empire. The Roman word for law, *lex*, Arendt wrote, 'has an entirely different meaning; it indicates a formal relationship between people rather than the wall that separates them' (HC 63). The spatial significance of law in relating what would otherwise be separate had enormous implications for the conduct of war and the earliest meanings of foreign policy in the West. Indeed, Arendt argued that this alternative understanding was the beginning of what we now think of as foreign policy.

The Roman army as an instrument of the republic was very different from the Greek hoplite force, and more adaptable to the needs of imperial expansion. The Roman legion-based system, in common with all military systems, reflected the society from which it emerged. Roman society was less insular and more diverse than that of the Greek city-states. Expansion into new territories provided economic resources and land to divert social conflict, and some power was shared between the aristocracy and lower classes. With a larger population, a professional army was established and higher casualty figures could be absorbed. During the course of a campaign, one single battle did not necessarily bring a decision, as it had done with the Greeks. 'The real strength of the Roman Republic,' as Antonio Santosuosso writes, 'was the ability to remain at war until the enemy was exhausted, asked for a humiliating peace, or was utterly destroyed'.[14] Vast expansion into new colonies ensued. The native aristocracy did not face inevitable annihilation. Rather, they were often placed in positions of power. It may have been humiliating, but it was a peace nonetheless, a peace with a treaty.

Greek and Roman foreign policy—which was imperial foreign policy—diverged in terms of their respective thinking about politics, law and war. War was the beginning of Greek political existence; but this was only to the extent that they understood themselves as institutionalising agonistic struggle in the

[14] A Santosuosso, *Soldiers, Citizens and the Symbols of War: From Classical Greece to Republican Rome, 500–167 BC* (Boulder, CO, Westview Press, 1997) 205.

polis—'they became themselves,' in Arendt's words, 'through conflict and then came together to preserve their own nature' (PP 178). For the Romans, struggle with outsiders was not only an opportunity to discover the identity of the self; there was *recognition*, self-interested, imperial recognition, of the other. Indeed, Arendt ultimately explained the demise of the system of Greek city-states in these terms. The Greek understanding of law and war as pre-political came at a high cost, for they were unable to build an empire. They were unable to unite and join their colonies 'in a permanent alliance' (PP 187). It was simply beyond the Greek conception of what they were doing when they fought. The failure to 'transform wars of annihilation into political wars,' wrote Arendt, '... led to the ruin of the Greek city-states' (PP 164).

What does Arendt mean by political wars? Anything political involves speech. She thus pointed to the Roman beginnings of the tradition of the 'just war' as the origins of Western wars accompanied by verbal rationalisations. Arendt is not writing in support of this tradition. The Romans, she wrote, 'drew no line between aggressive and defensive warfare. "The war that is necessary is just", said Livy, "and hallowed are the arms where no hope exists but in them"' (OR 3). But the Greeks' sharp, definitionally and spatially enforced distinction between political and non-political life meant that violence needed no justification and few normative limitations. War was far less likely to be accompanied by the language of justice; violence was understood as purely instrumental, not the beginning of a new relationship. But the Roman concept of warfare, as Arendt described, was 'that unique and great notion of a war whose peace is predetermined not by victory or defeat but by an alliance of the warring parties, who now become partners, *socii* or allies, by virtue of the new relationship established in the fight itself and confirmed through the instrument of *lex*, the Roman law' (OR 211). The end of the war and conquest of new territory resulted in the signing of a binding peace treaty, a lasting tie. Fighting a political war instead of a war of annihilation enabled the literal creation of a new political order, indeed a new world, a space in-between the former enemies. This political outcome was possible only because violent hostilities were ended before the complete destruction of the life and world of the vanquished.

Rather than annihilating the enemy, the Romans acknowledged them, Arendt argued, 'precisely when that adversary revealed itself as such in war'. This was not out of compassion but 'for the sake of expanding Rome' (PP 185). This relationship between alien peoples was not a relationship of equality. The choice was between submission and destruction. The defeated could retain their life, and the Romans, in Arendt's words, 'gained ... a new political arena, secured in a peace treaty according to which yesterday's enemies became tomorrow's allies' (PP 178). As such, to meet in battle remained an encounter between people, and a new political realm emerged, expanded and endured from a meeting which originally occurred 'as war' (PP 183). Out of battle the creation of new lasting ties was possible. Law and legislative activity were the very things that secured these new relationships. Law itself indicated a 'lasting tie' and later 'contract'.

If for the Greeks to meet in battle meant the end of politics, then we might say that for the Romans it was the beginning; 'politics began as foreign policy' (PP 183). This was the beginning of the Western concept of foreign policy, that is, 'of *politics* in foreign relations' (PP 189). Law would assume different meanings throughout the centuries. But from the very beginning there emerged an association between politics, law and war that still resonates. Law can be understood as a necessary check on the inherently unpredictable nature and boundlessness of political action. In the tradition of international thought this relationship is considered in the terminology of compliance. How effective is law in restraining political action, especially the action of the most powerful State in the system? In contrast, Arendt pointed to an understanding of law that brings into being and justifies new power relations that did not previously exist. The tradition of international thought has been less good at asking questions about the productive or constitutive character of the law. To understand why this is the case we briefly review the dominant liberal assumptions concerning law that have shaped most international thought.

III. SOME PROBLEMS WITH INTERNATIONAL THEORY

The relationship between law and power in most international theory is fundamentally liberal. It mirrors the way in which John Locke and the liberal tradition position law in domestic society as a 'constant and lasting force', derived from the command of society and not the Leviathan.[15] Thomas Hobbes had asserted that Truth (State power) makes Law. With Locke and the emergence of liberal society, the origin of legal codes became deinstitutionalised and set apart as the emblem of society and social interaction, not the State. The public sphere, the privileged realm of the law in liberal theory, is imagined as cohering around and deriving force from more general social norms. Norms of economy and politics come together within the public sphere as codified law, and this process in turn instantiates a vast array of assumptions concerning public and private. 'In the "law", the quintessence of general, abstract, and permanent norms,' interpreted Jurgen Habermas, 'inheres a rationality in which what is right converges with what is just; the exercise of power is to be demoted to a mere executor of such norms'[16]

Locke's influential model of power and law is based, in part, on claims about the emergence of liberal society in the United States. Locke had gone as far as citing America as the exemplification of the original state of nature. 'Thus in the beginning,' he wrote, 'all the World was America'.[17] His conception of democracy

[15] J Locke, *Two Treaties of Government* (with Introduction and notes by Peter Laslett) (Cambridge, Cambridge University Press, 1963) 343.

[16] J Habermas, *The Structural Transformation of the Public Sphere: an Inquiry into a Category of Bourgeois Society* (translated by Thomas Burger) (Cambridge, MA, MIT Press, 1991 [1962]) 53.

[17] Locke, above n 15, 343, II §49.

derived from social contract theory and as the process of manoeuvring government in the interests of society. But political order could exist only when the many 'freely' submitted to be 'ruled'. Locke reversed Hobbes's image of the Leviathan as the supreme lawgiver securing the necessary conditions for civil society to emerge. This alternative narrative—followed closely by the American Founders (and later international theorists)—begins with the people (or States) assembling first and then agreeing to representative government through the social contract (or norms of international society). In the international domain, the counterpart to this conception of the role of law is the founding moment of 1648 and the Treaty of Westphalia, after which a system of international law developed in a new non-hierarchical society of independent sovereign States.

To be sure, the establishment of the legal apparatus in the United States was a major contributor to the democratisation of sovereignty. Similarly, the collective association of common interests, values, norms and legal institutions that developed in Europe served to limit some of the excesses of inter-State competition among Europeans. (This limitation on conflict facilitated imperial expansion into the rest of the world.) However, in both models the Lockean-liberal account of the origins of legal codes 'was less the law in any institutional form as it had in fact developed historically … and more the law now defined as general and abstract norms'.[18] Liberal theorists could accomplish this feat of sociological revisionism because, as an historical point, constitutionalism in the United States was asserted in the course of rebellion against an executive foreign power. Yet law at once provided a positive rationale for political rebellion against the Old World and the perfect instrument of empire, patriarchy and slavery in the 'New', the legal institutionalisations of which still resonate.

The American Revolution seemed to Arendt to offer at least a partial answer to *the* question of modern politics: How, in the absence of a king or god to impose authoritative principles on the public realm, could political freedom thrive and be stable? The most important act of the Revolution, Arendt believed, was in the 'necessarily relative' agreement of the Founders; 'those who get together to constitute a new government are themselves unconstitutional, that is, they have no authority to do what they have set out to achieve' (OR 184). The trick rested in the act of instituting law without reference to any pre-existing authority. Accordingly, in Thomas Jefferson's famous words, 'We hold these truths to be self-evident', Arendt emphasised the authority of the agreement 'We hold' rather than the 'self-evident' nature of the truth (OR 92–94). With this conception, we see the productive force contained in the act of speech. The Declaration of Independence was 'the perfect way for an action to appear in words' (OR 127). That its authority was contained within itself, that it derived its own legitimacy, meant that it met the dual yardstick of neither being autocratically enforced nor

[18] MR Somers, 'The Privatization of Citizenship: How to Unthink a Knowledge Culture' in VE Bonnell and L Hunt (eds), *Beyond the Cultural Turn: New Directions in the Study of Society and Culture* (Berkeley, University of California Press, 1999) 153.

needing to appeal to grounds outside the political sphere. At the moment of instituting a new legal system the law itself took on a powerful legitimating force. The liberal tradition, following Locke, was able to reinterpret the law as a 'constant and lasting force' originating from society as a whole, and not a reflection of existing social and economic power, as Arendt always understood it. In the moment of founding this law, the institution of new socio-economic power relations appeared simultaneously. The new system of law and justice, therefore, did not appear as merely the product of pre-existing forms of domination, relations of force that could manipulate law to its own end and produce the subjects of law. Law itself took on the appearance of being the 'Immortal Legislator' (OR 185) exterior to the prevailing distribution of power and control over the 'legitimate' means of violence. It accordingly became harder to criticise this and other forms of legally-sanctioned 'violence since one cannot summon it to appear before the institution of any preexisting law: it does not recognize existing law in the moment that it founds another'.[19]

The liberal conception of this political history meant that the rule of law appeared at least in principle independent of political domination. Yet we know that in both domestic and international society, liberal norms of what it has meant to be a good citizen or a sovereign State did not simply arise out of a natural democratic disposition or the fiction of sovereign equality. Liberal norms had to be produced. In 'international society', a process of forcible socialisation occurred before some societies—those outside Europe—were deemed fit to enter the society of States as equal sovereign actors. In other words, law does not only regulate the behaviour of already existing individuals and States. It often violently constitutes individuals and States as legal subjects and makes some forms of violence appear legitimate. The liberal vision obscures much of this sociological development of legal systems in both domestic and international society. But it has nonetheless been central to much recent legal theory. Indeed, such a vision enables the distinction between law and power necessary to pose the questions central to much international thought: How and in what way does law provide a check on political power and military force?

As indicated earlier, in international theory most legal thought focuses on measuring degrees of State compliance with existing legal norms, or how State and non-State actors may break old norms and create new ones. Different sovereign States, distinguished by their relative material and/or ideational power, are generally understood to shape legal norms through their interactions in the society of States or international public sphere. Power in most international theory is understood as 'the ability, either directly or indirectly, to control or significantly influence how actors … behave'.[20] Whether military, economic or moral power is conceived as a

[19] J Derrida, 'Force of Law: The "Mystical Foundations of Authority"' in D Cornell, M Rosenfeld and DG Carlson (eds), *Deconstruction and the Possibility of Justice* (London, Routledge, 1992) 40.

[20] M Byers, *Custom, Power and the Power of Rules: International Relations and Customary International Law* (Cambridge, Cambridge University Press, 1999) 4, 5, 35–50.

possession, and depending on the particular school of thought, is held by both State and non-State actors. This power is then used to 'construct' the evolving standards and 'norms' of the international legal order. The State with the most power in the system, the United States, is widely reckoned to be in the best position to break and create new norms with greatest ease. But this power is not unlimited even in the hard test case of war. Apparently strong US compliance with legal norms of non-combatant immunity, for example, has widely been attributed to the integration of 'humanitarian' norms into the law governing war.

Since the end of the Cold War, students of international relations have become more interested in law. The 'world', according to the editors of one text, 'is witnessing a move to law'.[21] There has been much talk about international punishment for war crimes. During the Bosnian conflict (1991–95), the International Criminal Court for the Former Yugoslavia was established at a relatively stunning speed, creating a supranational institution with independent decision-making powers to override Balkan State sovereignty. The permanent International Criminal Court (ICC) was established on 1 June 2002 at The Hague. The public event of a war crimes trial, even if the United States is immune, and the establishment or re-establishment of the rule of law can facilitate conflict resolution, and for many bring about a sense of justice and finally peace. Although the sheer scope of atrocities can sometimes make trials seem irrelevant, this has perhaps not been the case with a small number of recent conflicts. After the Holocaust, Arendt suggested that some 'are unable to forgive what [they] cannot punish and … are unable to punish what has turned out to be unforgivable' (HC 241). Several have analogised events in Bosnia, Rwanda, Kosovo and Iraq with elements of the Second World War. One difference, of course, is that punishment has factored greatly in the international response.

Arendt was an early advocate for the establishment of a permanent international criminal court, even though she believed Nazi crimes were so great that no legal system could ever mete out appropriate justice. The Nuremberg Trials after the Second World War were inadequate because Nazi crimes were not simply crimes of aggression and ruthless conduct—the expulsion, and murder of large numbers of people. None of these were unique to the Germans. Rather, Arendt argued that the Nazis had broken with 'that *consensus iuris* … the foundation-stone of international relations even under the conditions of war' (OT 462). The supreme crime had been the effort to remove an entire people, not only from German territory, but from the face of the Earth. The Nazis rejected the territorial principle that different political and legal systems can exist.[22] 'Both moral

[21] J Goldstein, M Kahler, RO Keohane and AM Slaughter (eds), *Legalization and World Politics* (Cambridge, Mass, MIT Press, 2001) 1.

[22] In a letter to Jaspers, Arendt intriguingly wrote, that her support for the right of Israel to try Eichmann might appear like she was 'attempting to circumscribe the political with legal concepts. And I even admit that as far as the role of the law is concerned, I have been infected by the Anglo-Saxon influence. But quite apart from that, it seems to me to be in the nature of this case that we have no tools to hand except legal ones with which we have to judge and pass sentence on something that cannot even be adequately represented either in legal terms or political terms' (AJ 417).

judgement and legal punishment presuppose this basic consent; the criminal can be judged justly only because he takes part in the *consensus iuris*' (OT 462).

The establishment of the ICC is clearly important. But Arendt's ideas suggest that some of its most fervent advocates set their sights too high. Lawyers have argued that the recent move to prosecute war crimes helps make possible 'the primacy of law over considerations of policy', thus constituting 'radical changes in the international constitutional order'.[23] Habermas is even more ambitious, suggesting that such developments indicate move away from the classical Westphalian system towards a 'cosmopolitan law of a society of world-citizens'.[24] Arendt would have been wholly suspicious of such claims.[25] She believed that the purpose of a trial could only be 'to render justice, and nothing else; even the noblest of ulterior purposes … can only detract from the law's main business: to weigh the charges brought against the accused, to render judgement, and to mete out due punishment' (EJ 253). Arendt's cosmopolitanism is far more modest than Habermas's. Here it is sufficient to note that ICC jurisdiction is not recognised by the United States, and 'Laws that are not equal for all,' as Arendt wrote, 'revert to rights and privileges' (OT 290).

In such circumstances, accusations of victors' justice are easy to make. As Arendt pointed out after the Second World War, Allied violations of The Hague Convention were never examined or prosecuted. But she also recognised the 'understandable feeling on the part of the Allies that they "who had risked everything could not admit neutrals"' (EJ 274). In the context of total war, little else but victors' justice could be expected. Deliberate and inhumane purpose was indeed found on the Allied side. The use of atomic weapons twice against Japan, Arendt believed, was a clear war crime. While saturation bombings of German cities may have been provoked by the Nazis' aerial bombing of London, Coventry and Rotterdam, this was not an argument that could be made to defend the nuclear destruction of Hiroshima and Nagasaki. The very 'existence' of these weapons, Arendt argued, 'could have been announced and demonstrated in many other ways' (EJ 256). The issue of victors' justice is obvious and clear, but is not the most 'potent' explanation Arendt offered for the one-sided nature of the trials. 'For the truth of the matter,' she wrote, 'was that … everybody knew that technical developments in the instruments of violence had made the adoption of "criminal" warfare inevitable … Hence, it was felt that … war crimes were only those outside all military necessities, where a deliberate inhuman purpose could be demonstrated' (EJ 256). The very foundations of the laws of war and the definitions necessary

[23] M Weller, 'The Kosovo Indictment of the International Criminal Tribunal for Yugoslavia' in K Booth (ed), *The Kosovo Tragedy: The Human Rights Dimensions* (London, Frank Cass, 2000) 207, 208.

[24] J Habermas, 'Bestiality and Humanity: A War on the Border between Law and Morality' in WJ Buckley (ed), *Kosovo: Contending Voices on Balkan Interventions* (Michigan, Eerdmans Publishing, 2000) 308.

[25] For a discussion see P Owens, 'Walking Corpses: Arendt on the Limits and the Possibilities of Cosmopolitan Politics' in C Moore and C Farrands (eds), *International Relations Theory and Philosophy: Interpretive Dialogues* (London, Routledge, 2010) 72–82.

to determine war crimes had become obsolete—'the distinction between soldier and civilian, between army and home population, between military targets and open cities' (EJ 256).

The distinctions between these categories, like all legal distinctions, are political. This has led to controversy over the extent to which Western States in more recent wars have properly adhered to them, as well as debates about the meaning of any such adherence.[26] Again, the question is usually framed in the language of compliance. For followers of realpolitik and post-Marxism, not much has changed.[27] International law is either instrumentally used by the United States when it suits its strategic ends, or it is abandoned as outmoded when it does not. 'The law …' in the words of EH Carr, 'cannot be understood independently of the political foundation on which it rests and of the political interests which it serves'.[28] From this perspective, the language of 'humanitarianism' that invariably accompanies Western wars is mere rhetoric. The causes of war remain the pursuit of power in the national interest and/or imperial foreign policy.[29] The recently trumpeted idea that humanitarian intervention is a breach of sovereignty to protect human rights is nothing new. Throughout history, powerful States have frequently and hypocritically superseded the 'right' to sovereignty of weaker States. 'Modern power conditions,' as Arendt wrote, 'make national sovereignty a mockery except for giant states' (OT 269).

The highly-disputed legal justification for the invasion and occupation of Iraq appears to confirm some of the worst suspicions about the philosophy of the administration of George W Bush in relation to international law. In 2003, war was deemed necessary by the United States to uphold existing Security Council resolutions that mandated Iraq cease its development of weapons of mass destruction. Certainly, the function of the UN system in restraining the use of force has been dramatically weakened if unilateral action 'in support' of past resolutions is now deemed an acceptable *ex post facto* legitimation. Remnants of legalist rhetoric endure, of course, as one among many vehicles to legitimise grand strategy. But from a realist perspective, recent US wars—and any attendant rhetoric of humanitarianism—have been ruled more by geopolitics than any background rules of international (or even increasingly domestic) law. The long-term political goal of the United States appears to be the diminution of the UN's legal authority to one of a number of policy instruments. While it is not in the US interest to

[26] HM Kinsella, 'Discourses of Difference: Civilians, Combatants, and Compliance with the Laws of War' (2005) 31 *Review of International Studies* 163.

[27] T Barkawi and M Laffey, 'Retrieving the Imperial: *Empire* and International Relations' (2002) 31(1) *Millennium: Journal of International Studies* 109.

[28] EH Carr, *The Twenty Years' Crisis, 1919–1939: An Introduction to the Study of International Relations* (London, Macmillan, 1939) 179.

[29] Arendt believed that the international affairs of her day were 'still based upon national sovereignty' and did not make sense or 'function without force or the threat of force as the *ultima ratio* of all foreign policy'. War remained the 'last resort' and she was not confident of any progress in this area. H Arendt, 'The Cold War and the West' (1962) 29(1) *Partisan Review* 11.

undermine the fragile international legal framework governing war for all States, the United States may be seeking to have its desire for exceptional status codified in international law. The legal claim of a right to pre-emptive war is the clearest indication of the imperial challenge to sovereign State equality.

Not all schools of international thought share the realist diagnosis of US compliance with the laws of war. Constructivists and international society scholars suggest that there is evidence that the existing fragile system may be robust enough to resist merely being used as a tool of the United States, and might even constrain imperial urges. The system of international law, including the law governing the use of force, exists as a legitimating normative structure that can be augmented in its own right. In principle, Arendt also held this view and quoted Justice Jackson from the Nuremberg Trials to this effect. 'Our own day,' he said, 'has the right to institute customs and to conclude agreements that will themselves become sources of a newer and strengthened international law' (quoted in EJ 273–74). Hence while the United States has taken great pains to avoid the appearance of needing to rely on international law to justify the right to fight, or *jus ad bellum*, it has also sought to avoid the admission that any of its wars are illegal. Law clearly remains central to the efforts to legitimate and de-legitimate apparent breaches of the laws of war.

In the two most important recent test cases, the Kosovo and Iraq campaigns, the language of law enforcement was central to arguments for military action. NATO claimed that it acted in Kosovo to avert a humanitarian catastrophe, and that this action was consistent with Resolutions 1160, 1199 and 1203 adopted under Chapter VII of the UN Charter. Others have argued that even if such US-led actions were illegal, they were still just.[30] We cannot know what Arendt's position would have been on these specific cases. However, writing on the trial of Nazi war criminal Adolf Eichmann, she noted that his initial abduction from Argentina was 'a clear violation of international law ... to bring him to justice' (EJ 263).[31] Israel 'violated the territorial principle' that recognises that different peoples are governed by different laws. However, Arendt also argued that 'he who takes the law into his own hands will render a service to justice only if he is willing to transform the situation in such a way that the law can again operate and his act can, at least posthumously, be validated' (EJ 265). She cited the example of two inter-war assassins who separately killed perpetrators of pogroms against the

[30] NJ Wheeler, 'Reflections on the Legality and Legitimacy of NATO's Intervention in Kosovo' in Booth (ed), above n 23, 145.

[31] In a letter to Jaspers, Arendt expressed sympathy for Israel's abduction of Eichmann in contrast to Jaspers's belief there was no justification and that he ought to be tried in an international court. Arendt argued that it was possible for Israel to claim that they captured a man who had already been indicted in Nuremberg for crimes against humanity but due to his escape he was now 'a *hostis humani generis*, the way pirates used to be'. They could also argue that he was kidnapped from Argentina because that country had 'the worst possible record for the extradition of war criminals' (AJ 414). Later she realised that the pirate theory was inadequate because pirates act for private (financial) and not public political motives (AJ 423).

Jews and massacres against Armenians. Each assassin immediately turned himself into the authorities and insisted on being tried in a public court. The purpose was 'to show the world through court procedure what crimes against his people had been committed and gone unpunished' (EJ 265; AJ 415). Both assassins were found not guilty.

It is difficult to imagine the United States insisting on being tried in an international court to establish justice after admitting an illegal act of war. After all, it is the position of the United States, and the influential school of neoconservative thought, that wars in defence of peace, in the name of freedom and the spread of democracy need no further justification. On this view, wars waged by the United States are justified because they rid the world of demonstrably evil regimes. Even from the perspective of conventional international theory, it appears that the United States is on strong ground. From the realist perspective, might makes right. There is no need for further debate. Liberal, constructivist and international society scholarship can either concede to realism that power trumps law, or agree with the United States that the cause was just even if technically illegal. They can also point to the US effort to abide by the norm of non-combatant immunity. Realists are sceptical of the power of *jus in bello* norms to rein in fighting in the heat of battle. But these other schools point to strong US compliance with international laws governing conduct *in* war, especially high standards of compliance with the founding principle of international humanitarian law, the distinction between combatant and civilian.

IV. ACCIDENTS AND CIVILIAN DEATH

During recent military campaigns, US commanders and politicians have made frequent pledges to spare innocent lives; 'due care', '*great* care' is always taken to prevent civilian death. American soldiers are trained in the laws of war, which in any case do not impose obligations to absolute civilian protection. The law only requires commanders to take reasonable precautions and to discriminate between civilian and military targets. Lawyers are consulted. Strict 'collateral damage' avoidance rules produce frequent occasions when targets are avoided, reviewed again and again, or even cancelled at the last moment. This apparent compliance with non-combatant immunity is a product of both technological advances in precision weapons and the evolving normative framework. But what is this normative framework, and what is its relation to imperial power and the law? Are Western wars simply becoming more humane? Can we question the too easy association between ethical practice and apparent compliance with non-combatant immunity? What forms of identity construction are maintained by the current application of military power and assumptions about its legality?

The United States must be able to present its wars as more humanitarian, more clinical and more civilised than the violence of its enemies. The deaths caused by the US military are seen as *fundamentally* different from the deaths caused by terrorists and rogue regimes. An important distinction has been constructed as almost beyond question or doubt—between the deaths inflicted accidentally by the United States which are aberrations in contrast to those that its enemies inflict deliberately.[32] The comparison between the 'due care' taken by civilised States and the indiscriminate killing by others has been constructed as so obviously valid as to be almost beyond question or doubt. Speaking of the war to topple the Taliban from 2001, then Secretary of Defence Donald Rumsfeld claimed he could not 'imagine there's been a conflict in history where there has been less collateral damage, less unintended consequences'.[33] Only military assets (at worst 'dual-use' sites) are targeted, and if on occasion they kill civilians in error, the United States surely cannot be blamed.

Rumsfeld has rightly echoed William Sherman in saying that 'war is hell', that civilians always die in war. It is both an admission and a justification of wars' detrimental effects. But it also serves as an authorisation. It plays on the narrow sense of liability disconnected from common notions of moral responsibility—the idea that we are responsible for the reasonably predictable consequences of our actions. With the removal of accountability from the equation, the risks of warfare are justified because no one in power saw or wanted their consequences. It is as if, to borrow Arendt's words, 'blessings and doom are meted out … according to accident and without any relation whatsoever to' anyone's actions (OT 296). Holding the United States responsible for its deeds during wartime seems less important than the charitable handling of victims through generous promises of reconstruction aid. It appears less expensive to be lavishly generous to the target society, or appear to be generous, than to tolerate open international adjudication of the actions of the US military.

Rather than frame questions about law and war in the language of compliance, we can ask how civilian deaths are legitimated and under what guises does this legitimation occur. How does it become possible that the humanity of Western-style war, rather than the savagery of all war, is reinforced by this construction of accidents? Widespread judgements about compliance with noncombatant immunity, made possible by advances in war-fighting technology, construct the deaths that do occur as 'accidents'. They appear like some ideal of an accident, where neither the victim nor the agent could possibly have been aware of the pending calamity. The issue at stake is not about compliance with law, or increasing or decreasing civilian casualty rates. The laws of war admit the possibility of collateral or unintentional damage, as they have since St Thomas Aquinas first wrote of an

[32] For a discussion see P Owens, 'Accidents Don't Just Happen: The Liberal Politics of High-Tech Humanitarian War' (2003) 32(3) *Millennium: Journal of International Studies* 595–616.

[33] Donald Rumsfeld, NewsHour, PBS, 3 January 2002. Available at <http://www.pbs.org/newshour/bb/terrorism/jan-june02/search_1-3.html>.

act 'beside one's intention'.[34] Rather, the intention is to raise questions about the very idea that some acts are 'beside intention' and what this idea allows.

Martin Shaw has convincingly written of the 'militarism of small massacres', military actions leading to the death of thousands of civilians but in discrete pockets of tens, twenties and even hundreds.[35] Accidental small massacres of civilians are legitimated through assumptions about compliance with international law and advances in weapons technology. Civilian casualties are made *more*, not less, permissible when constructed as 'accidents' and shown to be in accord with the law. Admission of responsibility for civilian deaths can perhaps never be fully declared. To accept liability would be injurious to the pre-emptive wartime spirit that sustains the current war on terror without end. The number of 'accidents' involving civilian death may increasingly be known. The potential of high-tech warfare to produce disaster may also be recognised. But 'accidental' small massacres of civilian populations have nonetheless—and perhaps necessarily—become normalised as part of the post-9/11 discourse of pre-emptive war.

V. CONCLUSION

Max Weber is widely considered to be the exemplary theorist of bureaucracy or 'rule by rules'. The rise of modern bureaucracy led to increasing efficiency, but it was soulless and inhumane, producing 'specialists without spirit'.[36] Yet it was Hannah Arendt, more influenced by Franz Kafka, who identified bureaucracy with something potentially more frightening than rule by rules. Bureaucracy was 'rule by nobody'. In *The Human Condition*, she argued that this was 'not necessarily no-rule; it may indeed, under certain circumstances, even turn out to be one of its cruelest and most tyrannical versions' (HC 40). In its extreme form, individuals are dehumanised, becoming mere 'functionaries of men, mere cogs in the administrative machinery' and the 'intricate system of bureaus' (RJ 58; CR 137). Donald Rumsfeld's powerful claim that the United States and its allies are not responsible for the predictable deaths of thousands of civilians—in wars of choice not necessity—is underpinned by what Arendt described as the imperial 'philosophy of the bureaucrat' (OT 213).

Bureaucracy, Arendt argued, is 'characteristic of all imperialist enterprise' (OT 213). It was central to European imperialism in the late nineteenth century as a 'principle of foreign domination … [and a] substitute for government' in the colonies (OT 185). The British administered their outposts with brutal and racist violence, but also with bureaucratic administration, a form of rule that 'grew out

[34] Saint Thomas Aquinas, *On Law, Morality, and Politics* (WP Baumgarth and RJ Regan (eds)) (Indianapolis, Hackett Publishing, 1988) 228.

[35] M Shaw, 'Risk-Transfer Militarism, Small Massacres, and the Historic Legitimacy of War' (2002) 16(3) *International Relations* 343–60.

[36] M Weber, *The Protestant Ethic and the Spirit of Capitalism* (new introduction by A Giddens, Talcott Parsons trans) (New York, Charles Sribner's Sons, 1976) 182.

of a tradition of military discipline' (OT 186). With the rule of bureaucracy in far and distant lands there was at once the appearance of order and also 'an atmosphere of anarchy and hazard … the daily accidents of incompetence and inconsistency' (OT 246). It would indeed appear as though 'the Accident', as Arendt put it, was 'the true Lord of Life' (OT 246). There are many differences between the means and character of the administrative massacres of European colonial rule and the militarism of small massacres of more recent wars. But the administration and justification of these latter deaths—and the effect of the refusal to admit responsibility—is reminiscent of the mentality of the imperial bureaucrat that Arendt so powerfully described.

The soulless, technical specialists that ruled Empire by violence had nothing with which to identify, Arendt wrote, except some 'superstition of a possible and magic identification … with the forces of history. The ideal of such a political body will always be the man behind the scenes who pulls the strings of history' (OT 216). Prior to his removal from the Department of Defense, Donald Rumsfeld said, 'I'm not a lawyer and I'm not in to that end of the business'.[37] But life and death for many was nonetheless decided by his decree. In the bureaucratic chain of command it *appears* 'impossible to localize responsibility and to identify an enemy' (CR 138). 'In governments by bureaucracy,' Arendt wrote, 'decrees appear in their naked purity as though they were no longer issued by powerful men, but were the incarnation of power itself and the administrator only its accidental agent' (OT 244). Bureaucratic rule makes possible the thoughtless use of public power and diffuses responsibility. Although nobody is held responsible for such deaths, this 'nobody' still rules. All that remains, the 'one thing that counts [is] the brutal naked event itself ' (OT 245), the event of thousands of civilian deaths.

[37] Donald Rumsfeld, Pentagon Briefing, 22 January 2002. Available at <http://transcripts.cnn.com/TRANSCRIPTS/0201/22/se.01.html>.

14

Hannah Arendt's Judgement of Bureaucracy

LEORA BILSKY

THE HOLOCAUST POSED a difficult dilemma for the law: how to judge bureaucratically organised crimes. In her postscript to *Eichmann in Jerusalem*,[1] Hannah Arendt argued that the problem stemmed from the attempt to apply a legal system and juridical concepts that were not meant to deal with 'the facts of administrative massacres organized by state apparatus'. Later, in her critique of the Frankfurt-Auschwitz trial, she pointed to the absurdity created when a trial addressing the symbol of evil in the twentieth century—the death machine of Auschwitz—ends up dealing with individual infringements of the law by sadistic perpetrators. While Arendt was quick to identify the disjunction between the idiom of law and the facts of bureaucratic crimes, she continued to insist on the need to establish individual criminal responsibility.

Law's continued encounter with State-organised crimes since the end of the Second World War has brought about radical legal transformations. New crimes were developed, such as crimes against humanity and genocide, the temporal and spatial boundaries of jurisdiction were redefined, and the focus of adjudication has shifted from the defendant to the victim. These changes have matured into a new corpus of international criminal law amounting to a 'jurisprudence of atrocity'.[2]

Notwithstanding these transformations in the form and content of the law, the demand to establish individual liability according to the dictates of traditional criminal law has not been abandoned, and in some aspects has strengthened since the Nuremberg trials. This continuity is perplexing, as it was often this very focus on individual guilt that was shown to undermine law's attempt to make bureaucratic organisations accountable.

* I would like to thank Natalie Davidson for her superb research assistance. This paper is part of a book length research project on the Holocaust restitution litigation, which was made possible by funding from the Minerva Center for Human Rights, the Cegla Center for Interdisciplinary Research of Law, and the Israel Science Foundation.

[1] H Arendt, *Eichmann in Jerusalem* (New York, Penguin, 1977) (hereafter 'EJ').

[2] L Douglas, 'Shattering Nuremberg, Toward a Jurisprudence of Atrocity' (2007) *Harvard International Review*, available at <http://hir.harvard.edu/shattering-nuremberg>.

Contrary to Arendt, I suggest that it is not the law as such, but rather the dominance of criminal law that has obstructed the law from addressing the involvement of bureaucracy (both State and private) in the Holocaust. Arendt's argument that criminal law cannot retain its basic moral integrity if it abandons the requirement of individual guilt is persuasive, but it is not true of all areas of law. I conclude by identifying a shift away from the limitations of criminal law in the wave of Holocaust restitution lawsuits filed against German and European companies in American courts during the 1990s. I suggest that this litigation may offer a solution to a problem that has haunted Holocaust jurisprudence for more than six decades. Most importantly, the class-action suit dispenses with the need to establish the liability of individual perpetrators within private bureaucratic organisations, and in this way allows the courts to confront bureaucracy on its own terms. Thus, while Arendt was right to point out the need to develop new legal tools to adjudicate the involvement of bureaucratic organisation in the Holocaust, she wrongly assumed that the only legal road open to handle the problem is through criminal law.

I. FIRST ENCOUNTER: ARENDT AND THE EICHMANN TRIAL

The phrase 'the banality of evil' was coined by Hannah Arendt in relation to the defendant Adolf Eichmann, in the subtitle to her book *Eichmann in Jerusalem*. With this term Arendt points to a new kind of evil appearing under the Nazi regime. Using the term 'banal' to describe Eichmann's acts caused immediate controversy in Israel and in the international community.[3] Many saw this as an unfortunate term, a provocative and misleading description that trivialises the Holocaust and undermines Eichmann's culpability.[4] Furthermore, the choice of the term 'banal' to depict Nazi evil-doing surprised those familiar with Arendt's previous book, *The Origins of Totalitarianism*,[5] where she used the term 'radical evil' to describe the crimes of the Nazi regime. Richard Bernstein, one of the most sophisticated readers of Arendt's work, argues that in fact there is no contradiction. We should understand the two terms as relating to different aspects of the same phenomenon. Radical evil refers to the socio-structural dimensions of the Holocaust, while banal evil refers to the psychological-ethical constitution of the perpetrators.[6] In other words, with the provocative term 'banal', Arendt exposes the new mindset of the functionary that makes him the ideal actor in a bureaucratic organisation of mass murder and extermination. However, this explanation does not help us

[3] L Bilsky, *Transformative Justice: Israeli Identity of Trial* (Ann Arbor, Michigan University Press, 2004).

[4] The most famous critic is Gershom Scholem. H Arendt, *The Jew as Pariah* (RH Feldman ed) (New York, Grove, 1978) 245. For elaboration on the controversy about the term, see E Young-Bruehl, *Hannah Arendt: For Love of the World* (New Haven, Conn, Yale University Press, 1982) 337–40.

[5] H Arendt, *The Origins of Totalitarianism* (New York, Harcourt Brace, 1973) (hereafter 'OT').

[6] RJ Bernstein, *Hannah Arendt and the Jewish Question* (Cambridge, Mass, MIT Press, 1996) 137–53. For further elaboration, see D Pendas, 'Eichmann in Jerusalem, Arendt in Frankfort: The Eichmann Trial, the Auschwitz Trial, and the *Banality of Justice*' (2007) 34 *New German Critique* 77.

understand whether the law has the capacity to bridge the rift that opens between the enormity of the crimes and the banality of the motives.

In this essay I do not intend to engage the problem of evil as a philosophical question that the banality of evil invokes.[7] The question that interests me here is more specific to the law and points, I believe, to a crisis of judgement that the law has been facing in its various attempts to judge the crimes of the Nazi regime. Specifically, I ask how and in what way bureaucratically organised slave-work and mass-murder challenge the foundations of criminal responsibility. I argue that Arendt accurately identified the dilemma created for the law by the new type of murderer who sends millions to their death while understanding his own role in bureaucratic terms, as a 'specialist' in immigration and an 'expert' on the Jewish problem. The challenge that this new type of perpetrator created for traditional conception of *mens rea* was connected to the bureaucratic setting of the crime. However, most of the scholarly attempts to address the problem have focused on the *mens rea* requirement and ignored, for the most part, the need to develop tools to judge the bureaucratic organisation as such.

In identifying the novelty of the crimes, Arendt points time and again to the bureaucratic setting in which they are carried out. In the epilogue to *Eichmann in Jerusalem* Arendt writes: 'The fundamental problems posed by crimes of this kind … [is] that they were, and could only be, committed under a criminal law and by a criminal state.'[8] Furthermore, Arendt underscores the fundamental implications of this shift: the State that is ordinarily taken to be the source of legality under positive criminal law is transformed under the Nazi regime into the source of organised crime. Indeed, this is one of the unique aspects of Nazi crimes: their systematic and organised nature due to the fact that a State bureaucracy stands behind them. Arendt is well aware that bureaucracy can help render individual motivation irrelevant to institutional outcomes, and that this carries important implications for our understanding of the *mens rea* requirement of criminal law. And yet, this recognition does not lead Arendt to question the very attempt to use criminal law, and in particular to establish the individual culpability of the Nazi perpetrators. There is an unexplained gap in Arendt's argument, a leap between the descriptive (a social-science understanding of bureaucratic action) and the normative (a demand to establish individual guilt according to the strictures of criminal law).[9]

[7] See S Neiman, *Evil in Modern Thought: An Alternative History of Philosophy* (Princeton, NJ, Princeton University Press, 2002) 299–304.

[8] EJ 262.

[9] Here I follow Pendas, who identifies this tension in Arendt's writings. See Pendas above n 6. Pendas argues that while in *Eichmann in Jerusalem* Arendt calls for a recognition of the new type of desk-murderer, in her analysis of the Frankfurt-Auschwitz trial she 'balked at the implications of her own earlier insights' by characterising the killers as 'simple sadists'. I agree with Pendas that a tension exists in Arendt's analysis between understanding the working of bureaucratic organisations and the demand from the law to prove individual guilt. However, as I shall argue, Arendt is critical of German law's emphasis on the individual sadist, and in her analysis of the Auschwitz trial she pushes her readers further to understand the limitations, and even paradoxes, to which traditional criminal law, with

Arendt, who was not a jurist, objected to the legalistic way of thinking, to the precedent-orientated reasoning that attempts to fit the new into pre-existing legal categories. As a critical thinker she undertook to expose the unprecedented nature of the new crime. In her book the *The Origins of Totalitarianism*, she investigated the different ways in which the totalitarian State works to destroy the spaces of civic and political action. She was among the first to identify the ways in which this regime undermines freedom of action and even the conscience of the individual. Furthermore, she writes that totalitarian governments operated

> according to a system of values so radically different from all others, that none of our traditional legal, moral, or common sense utilitarian categories could any longer help us to come to terms with, or judge, or predict their course of action.[10]

However, in a letter to Karl Jaspers, from December 1960, shortly before she went to Jerusalem to report on the Eichmann trial, she writes that

> We have no tools to hand except legal ones with which to judge and pass sentence on something that cannot even be adequately represented either in legal terms or in political terms.[11]

Arendt admits that her change of mind can be attributed to an American influence of relying on juridical thinking to solve political problems. Indeed, American jurists insisted on conducting the Nuremberg trials against the oppositions of their allies.[12] Given Arendt's sophisticated understanding of the administration of the Holocaust, can the law fulfil her expectations?

Arendt was among the first to point to the limits of criminal law in relation to the new crimes. Yet, unlike later critics who questioned the very turn to the law as the dominant way to deal with the Holocaust,[13] Arendt affirms the recourse to the law, and upholds its demand to establish individual culpability. One explanation is her attempt to wear simultaneously the hats of both the spectator and the actor. As a historian, a social scientist and a philosopher, she undertook to identify the novelty of the crimes (of genocide and crimes against humanity) committed by the administration of a criminal State, and made possible by a network of public and private bureaucratic organisations. Yet putting herself in the place of an actor in the legal drama, that is, wearing the juridical hat, Arendt upholds the normative and moral commitments of criminal law that require proof of

its central focus on the individual, can lead, in respect to understanding Auschwitz as a bureaucratic mass-murder machine.

[10] OT 360.

[11] H Arendt and K Jaspers, *Correspondence 1926–1969* (L Kohler and H Saner (eds)) (New York, Harcourt Brace & Company, 1992), letter 274 (23 December 1960) 417.

[12] GJ Bass, *Stay the Hand of Vengeance* (Princeton, NJ, Princeton University Press, 2000) 147–81.

[13] See G Agamben, *Remnants of Auschwitz: The Witness and the Archive* (DH Roazen trans) (New York, Zone Books, 2002) 19–20, criticising law's limited understanding of testimonies of the Holocaust.

individual guilt. Arendt is well aware of the difference between these two points of view, writing:

> Of course it is important to the political and social sciences that the essence of totalitarian government, and perhaps the nature of every bureaucracy, is to make functionaries and mere cogs in the administrative machinery out of men, and thus to dehumanize them … [Yet] one must realize clearly that the administration of justice can consider these factors only to the extent that they are circumstances of the crime.[14]

Such a stance, of deliberate legal blindness to social circumstances, is a well-known technique of legal reasoning, generally known as legal formalism. What is surprising here is that this position is upheld by one of the strongest critiques of legalism.[15] Indeed, aware of the limits of old precedents, Arendt calls to construct new crimes that can respond to the novel social and political conditions of the totalitarian State. Moreover, she does not limit their application to future cases notwithstanding their apparent retroactivity, but rather articulates interpretations that can allow the judges to apply the new crimes to Eichmann's actions. Indeed, Arendt chooses to end her book with a warning about the danger of not developing new legal tools that respond to the unprecedented nature of these crimes.[16] Arendt is willing to go a long way in changing the requirements of criminal law, including a move from subjective to objective standard liability.[17] And yet she is not willing to abandon the principle of individual responsibility. This seeming contradiction leads one commentator to argue that Arendt is trying to reconcile the two points of view: 'Part of what Arendt tries to do in *Eichmann in Jerusalem* is to find a way to resolve this paradox by encompassing banal evil and individual criminal guilt within the same conceptual apparatus.'[18]

The difficulty in reconciling the two points of view of the historian and the judge is evident in the epilogue to *Eichmann in Jerusalem*, where Arendt tries both to point out the dilemma that judging the crimes of the Holocaust poses to the law and offer her solution. She writes:

> Foremost among the larger issues at stake in the Eichmann trial was the assumption current in all modern legal systems that intent to do wrong is necessary for the commission of a crime. On nothing, perhaps, has civilized jurisprudence prided itself more than on this taking into account of the subjective factor. Where this intent is absent, where, for whatever reasons … the ability to distinguish between right and wrong is impaired, we feel no crime has been committed.[19]

[14] EJ 289. Arendt repeats and elaborates this position in her essay, 'Personal Responsibility Under Dictatorship' in J Kohn (ed), *Responsibility and Judgment* (New York, Schocken Books, 2003).

[15] For elaboration on 'legalism' as a distinct form of legal reasoning connected to liberal theory, see JN Shklar, *Legalism: Law, Morals, and Political Trials* (Cambridge, Mass, Harvard University Press, 1964).

[16] EJ 273.

[17] For elaboration, see S Neiman, 'Banality Reconsidered' in S Benhabib (ed), *Politics in Dark Times: Encounters with Hannah Arendt* (Cambridge, Cambridge University Press, 2010) 305, 311.

[18] Pendas, above n 6, 78.

[19] EJ 277.

But immediately after she points out the fundamental premise of modern criminal law that seems to be undermined by the bureaucratic organisation of the crime, and right before she provides her own solution to this problem, a strange thing occurs. Arendt abandons the point of view of the 'spectator' that she occupies throughout her book and takes on the insider's position to address the defendant as the judge:

> You admitted that the crime committed against the Jewish people during the war was the greatest crime in recorded history, and you admitted your role in it. But you said you had never acted from base motives, that you had never had any inclination to kill anybody … What you meant to say was that where all, or almost all, are guilty, nobody is.[20]

Arendt is quick to dismiss these claims:

> Let us assume, for the sake of argument, that it was nothing more than misfortune that made you a willing instrument in the organization of mass murder; there still remains the fact that you have carried out, and therefore actively supported, a policy of mass murder. For politics is not like the nursery; in politics obedience and support are the same.[21]

With this answer we witness Arendt's vacillation between the objective standard (obedience to orders) and the subjective standard (inferring 'support' or subjective intention from objective facts). However, this brief answer does not deal with the considerable difficulties of judging actors in a bureaucratic organisation, let alone a criminal State. Specifically, it does not address the systematic undermining of cognitive and moral capacities of individuals acting under such conditions. Indeed, in her later essay, *On Violence*, Arendt describes the bureaucratic phenomenon as a novel form of governance of 'rule by Nobody'.[22] It might be that Arendt can dismiss the strength of such arguments in relation to Eichmann due to the unique position that he held in the Nazi bureaucracy, a position that allowed him considerable control and knowledge in relation to the fate of the Jews that he persecuted. Still, one can raise doubts as to how satisfying are the answers that Arendt formulates as a judge, to the questions she has raised as a historian.[23] It is

[20] EJ 277–78.

[21] EJ 279.

[22] '[T]he latest and perhaps most formidable form of … dominion: bureaucracy or the rule of an intricate system of bureaus in which no men neither one nor the best, neither the few nor the many, can be held responsible, and which could be properly called rule by Nobody. (If, in accord with traditional political thought, we identify tyranny as government that is not held to give account of itself, rule by Nobody is clearly the most tyrannical of all, since there is no one left who could even be asked to answer for what is being done. It is … impossible to localize responsibility and to identify the enemy.' H Arendt, *On Violence* (San Diego, Cal, New York, Harcourt Brace Jovanovich, Publishers, 1970) 38–39.

[23] Neiman, above n 17, suggests that Arendt upholds an objective standard of liability that is independent of the actor's subjective intention and instead focuses on the objective harm his actions have brought about. In her view, this move from subjective guilt to objective fact is similar to the conception of guilt articulated in Greek tragedies. However, the replacement of subjective intention with

not reconciliation that we witness in the epilogue to *Eichmann in Jerusalem*, but rather an unexplained shift of perspectives from spectator to judge that covers an unresolved tension.

What can explain this shift from the detached historian to the involved judge? Would the answer to the dilemma that Arendt formulated as a historian be any different from the one she articulated under her assumed position as judge? Instead of trying to solve these questions, I suggest that this abrupt shift points to something fundamental about the act of legal judgment. The act of judging the perpetrator seems to undermine the understanding of the historian about the power of the bureaucratic organisation over the individual will.[24] Is it possible that the very leap to the position of judge necessarily results in a certain blindness to the historical facts? Does this leap in Arendt's writing represent a deeper antinomy between legal judgment and historical understanding of the Holocaust, one that cannot be reconciled simply by defining new crimes? I would like to argue that Arendt's unexplained shift from historian to judge, at the very critical moment in which she recognises the abyss of judgment, is meaningful. It seems to hide, not just from her readers, but also from herself, the crisis of judgment faced by liberal criminal law. The leap from historian to judge helps cover the fundamental way in which bureaucracy undermines the liberal foundations of criminal law. I argue that facing this crisis demands nothing less than a shift in our conception of legal judgment. In other words, the encounter of law with bureaucratically organised crime might demand the abandonment of a conception of justice based on individual guilt.

II. SECOND ENCOUNTER—ARENDT AND THE AUSCHWITZ-FRANKFURT TRIAL

Arendt had another opportunity to clarify the relation between individual liability and the organised nature of Nazi crimes in her review of the Frankfurt-Auschwitz trial (1963–65), in which 22 defendants were charged under German criminal law for their roles as mid- and lower-level officials in the Auschwitz-Birkenau concentration camp.[25] Whereas Eichmann's trial dealt with the 'desk-murderer' who planned the extermination, here the law turned its attention to the direct perpetrators of 'administrative-massacre' who operated the Auschwitz concentration

objective harm undermines the basis of liberal criminal law and raises doubts as to the very possibility of conducting a liberal criminal trial for Eichmann, an endeavour that Arendt upholds.

[24] For elaboration on the tension between judging and understanding, see L Bilsky, 'Judging and Understanding: Response to Prof Douglas and Prof Luban' (2001) 19 *Law and History Review* 184. See also Neiman, above n 17, at 307.

[25] Reappeared in Kohn (ed), above n 14, at 227–56. Originally appeared as H Arendt, *Introduction to Bernd Naumann, Auschwitz: A Report on the Proceedings against Robert Karl Ludwig Mulka and Others before the Court at Frankfurt* (J Steinberg trans) (London, Pall Mall, 1966).

camp, those who implemented the Nazi genocide, those who actually shot, gassed or tortured their victims to death.[26]

In her critique of the Frankfurt trial, Arendt is quick to point to the immense gap between the old categories of the German criminal code and the new crimes committed by the Nazi regime. She writes that 'what the old penal code had utterly failed to take into account was nothing less than the everyday reality of Nazi Germany in general and of Auschwitz in particular'.[27] As a result of this,

> a man who had caused the death of thousands because he was one of the few whose job it was to throw the gas pellets into the chambers could be criminally less guilty than another man who had killed 'only' hundreds, but upon his own initiative according to his perverted fantasies.[28]

Here again, Arendt points to the gap between subjective intentions and objective results. While criminal law creates grades of liability that increase according to the subjective intention of the actor, it fails to account for the way in which the organisation of mass-murder in the concentration camp was dependent upon the subordination of individual will to the needs of the organisation. Arendt explains that ignoring this background, ignoring Auschwitz as an institution, resulted in a failure of understanding, a blurring of the distinction between murder and mass-murder.[29] The tension between individual liability and the bureaucratic organisation of the crime increased in the Frankfurt trial as a result of the application of the nineteenth-century German criminal code with its subjectivist emphasis. Missing were the categories of 'crimes against humanity' and 'genocide' that were created after the Holocaust and which were meant to address mass-murder. Moreover, in 1965 all crimes but murder were barred under a statute of limitation, and murder, according to the German code, required a special subjective motive.[30] A third obstacle stemmed from the distinction that the German code makes between perpetrator and accomplice.[31] These legal obstacles led the Frankfurt court to focus, as Arendt points out, on the 'extraordinary' sadistic perpetrators, failing to come to terms with 'ordinary' perpetrators of Auschwitz. In other words, the structure of German penal law prevented it from judging the ordinary perpetrators of the 'mass production of murder'. This frustration with

[26] Pendas, above n 6.

[27] H Arendt, *Auschwitz on Trial*, reprinted in Kohn (ed), above n 14, 243.

[28] *Ibid* 243.

[29] *Ibid* 242.

[30] Art 211 of the *Strafgesetzbuch* (StGB) (Penal Code) defines murder (*Mord*) as follows: 'A murderer is anyone who kills a human being out of blood lust, in order to satisfy their sexual desire, out of greed or other base motives, maliciously or treacherously or by means dangerous to the public at large or in order to enable or conceal another crime.' For elaboration on the limitations of the German criminal code in this respect, see D Pendas, *The Frankfurt Auschwitz Trial, 1963-1965: Genocide, History and the Limits of Law* (Cambridge, Cambridge University Press, 2006) 53–79.

[31] Pendas, *ibid*.

the law leads Arendt to observe the limits of criminal law when dealing with the organisation of mass murder:

> The background here was administrative massacres on a gigantic scale committed with the means of mass production—the mass production of corpses. Mass murder and complicity in mass murder was a charge that could and should be leveled against every single SS man who had ever done duty in any of the extermination camps and against many who had never set foot into one.[32]

This insight, however, was not applied during the Frankfurt-Auschwitz trial. Indeed, not until 2010, when German prosecutors indicted John Demjanjuk for mass murder for allegedly serving as a guard in an extermination camp, did the law try to make good on this observation.[33]

In 1965, when Arendt wrote her review of the Frankfurt trial, and out of frustration with the criminal law, she entertained the idea that the foundation of individual liability, the assumption of innocence, should be reversed in this trial. She writes:

> Within the setting of Auschwitz, there was indeed 'no one who was not guilty,' as the witness said, which for the purposes of the trial clearly meant that 'intolerable' guilt was to be measured by rather unusual yardsticks not to be found in any penal code.[34]

In trying to explain the unique nature of the mass-murder at Auschwitz, Arendt emphasises its bureaucratic structure that stands in tension with the individualist orientation of criminal law, and in particular the legal definition of 'murder' in the 1897 German penal code.[35] Again, Arendt's insights about the limitations of criminal law to deal with administrative massacre do not lead her to rethink the reliance on criminal law. She limits her criticism to the German criminal code. At most, she is willing to entertain the possibility of changing the legal presumption of innocence. But she is not seriously considering a change of direction for the law.

From the perspective of the law's capacity to cope with the bureaucratic aspects of the Holocaust, the Frankfurt-Auschwitz trial was clearly a regression from the

[32] *Auschwitz on Trial*, above n 27, 243–44.

[33] For elaboration see ch 15 of this volume by Lawrence Douglas. John Demjanjuk's trial began in Munich on 30 November 2009, on charges of being an accessory to over 27,000 counts of murder. This was the second attempt to bring Demjanjuk to trial, after his conviction in Israel for offences under the Nazi and Nazi Collaborators (Punishment) Law (1950) was overturned by the Israeli Supreme Court in 1993 due to a finding of reasonable doubt based on evidence suggesting that Demjanjuk was not 'Ivan the Terrible' from Treblinka. For further elaboration, see L Douglas, *The Memory of Judgment* (New Haven, Conn, and London, Yale University Press, 2001) 185–211.

[34] *Auschwitz on Trial*, n 27 above, 244.

[35] 'Reading the trial proceedings, one must always keep in mind that Auschwitz had been established for *administrative* massacres that were to be executed according to the strictest rules and regulations. These rules and regulations had been laid down by the desk murderers, and they seemed to exclude—probably they were meant to exclude—all individual initiative … The extermination of millions was planned to function like a machine …' (*ibid* 252).

advances made in the Nuremberg trials, where a systematic attempt was made to handle the organised nature of the crime. First, with respect to piercing the shield of State sovereignty, the Nuremberg charter abolished the defences of 'act of State' immunity and superior orders, thus allowing judgment of those who kill upon orders.[36] Secondly, in relation to the collective aspects of the crime, the charter created the new crime of participation in a criminal organisation.[37] Lastly, and most importantly, the American prosecution relied on the doctrine of 'conspiracy' taken from American anti-trust litigation in order to overcome the immense gap between the planners and the actual perpetrators.[38] The Frankfurt-Auschwitz trial retreated from the understanding that there is a need for a profound reform of criminal law in order to handle Nazi crimes. However, these difficulties were not unique to German law; rather, they stemmed from traditional conceptions of criminal law about individual liability.[39] The most important innovation of the Nuremberg trials was the notion that international law cannot remain focused on the behaviour of States but should pierce the veil of sovereignty to reach the individual perpetrator of the crimes.[40] However, in doing so, international law had to rely on traditional concepts of criminal law which emphasise the subjective state of mind of the individual and thus frustrate the understanding of the administration of mass-murder. The move from international tribunals to domestic courts (in Jerusalem, Frankfurt and elsewhere) only strengthened this tendency, but was not the source of the problem. The problem, as I pointed out, was the result of the lack of legal tools to address the liability of organisations. This problem, which was somehow mitigated in the Nuremberg trials, resurfaced in later years when the central innovations of Nuremberg in relation to the organised nature of the crime (of criminalising whole organisations and relying on criminal conspiracy)

[36] Charter of the International Military Tribunal, Arts 7 and 8.

[37] Charter of the International Military Tribunal, Arts 9 and 10.

[38] JA Bush, 'The Prehistory of Corporations and Conspiracy in International Criminal Law: What Nuremberg Really Said' (2009) 109 *Columbia Law Review* 1094.

[39] Unique to German law is the problem that arises out of the 'continuity of the State' hypothesis. In order to avoid charges of retroactivity of the penal law, the court had to answer the defence's argument that 'a State cannot possibly punish that which it ordered in another phase'. In response, the court emphasised that 'National Socialism was also subject to the rule of law', and hence the 1897 code applied. Arendt is critical of this fiction, given the radical change taken in the meaning of 'law' under National Socialism, where the will of the Fuhrer was the source of law and the Fuhrer's order was valid law (*Auschwitz on Trial*, n 27, at 244).

[40] S Ratner, JS Abrams and JL Bischoff, *Accountability for Human Rights Atrocities in International Law: Beyond the Nuremberg Legacy*, 3rd edn (Oxford, Oxford University Press, 2009) 6: '[T]he watershed for the development of the principle of individual accountability for human rights abuses was the exercise undertaken by the WWII victors … The creation of the International Military Tribunal at Nuremberg … evinced a decision by the Allies that individual officials bear personal responsibility for outrageous conduct towards their own citizens and foreigners during wartime and ought to be accountable. As a result, the IMT Charter provided for individual criminal responsibility …' The authors explain that the notion that international law would prescribe accountability for individuals for their misconduct was anathema to the whole conception that international law governed principally relations between States (*ibid* 4).

fell into disfavour, thereby undermining the ability of the criminal law to cope with the organised aspects of the Holocaust.[41]

Legal theorists struggling with the bureaucratic aspects of modern genocide and mass-murder have tried to develop doctrines that overcome the gap between the individualist assumptions of criminal law and the reality of administrative massacre.[42] For example, with respect to the problem of the interchangeability of the perpetrator, the question arose whether responsibility can simultaneously be attributed to the direct perpetrator who physically committed the crime and to the indirect perpetrator who instigated or planned it. The positive answer articulated by Arendt was not part of domestic Israeli criminal law at the time of the Eichmann trial. Faced with this dilemma, German jurist Klaus Roxin later developed a doctrinal solution known as the doctrine of the 'perpetrator behind a perpetrator'.[43] This solution, later to be incorporated in part into Israeli criminal law, was meant to overcome one of the problems of bureaucratic crimes—the functional division within every administration.[44] Other legal theorists have attempted to explain the way in which administrative massacres undermine the conditions for establishing individual criminal culpability, emphasising the shaky assumptions about the individual's conscience and the moral judgement upon which criminal law relies,[45] the weakening of individual will, the lack of full control by the individual, or the way in which bureaucracy undermines the ability of individual perpetrators to know and understand the full implications of their actions.[46] These authors have tried to develop doctrines that overcome the gap between the individualist assumptions of criminal law and the reality of administrative massacre.[47] However, these proposals have not become part of international criminal law, where, as we shall see below, the commitment to the principle of individual guilt has only strengthened over the years.

[41] A Cassese, *International Criminal Law*, 2nd edn (Oxford, Oxford University Press, 2008) 33–34, 227.

[42] See D Luban, A Strudler and D Wasserman, 'Moral Responsibility in the Age of Bureaucracy' (1992) 90 *Michigan Law Review* 2348, suggesting the use of principles of culpable ignorance to hold individuals in organisations culpable for wrongdoing; and M Osiel, *Mass Atrocity, Ordinary Evil and Hannah Arendt* (New Haven, Conn, Yale University Press, 2001) 149–64, proposing to turn the legal presumption about manifest illegality into a factual presumption that can be rebutted because of the bureaucratic organisation of administrative massacre.

[43] The first formulation of the theory of 'indirect perpetration' through control over an organised system of power dates back to 1963. Claus Roxin offered a novel way of conceptualising the relationship between different actors who had clearly contributed to the crime: instead of qualifying those who are far removed from the commission of the crimes as instigators or mere accomplices, Roxin proposed to see them as perpetrators behind the perpetrators. See C Wilke, 'Traveling Responsibilities', paper presented at the ASLCH Meeting in Boston in April 2009. Wilke examines the application of the theory in Argentina during the 1980s, Germany during the 1990s and by the International Criminal Court after 2000. Wilke explains that the attempt to apply this doctrine in trials of genocide or mass-murder, such as the Argentine 'dirty war', faced considerable difficulties.

[44] Section 29 of the Penal Law, 5737-1977 (39th amendment, 1994).

[45] Osiel, above n 42,149–64.

[46] Luban, Strudler, and Wasserman, above n 42, 38.

[47] *Ibid*.

III. THE INTERNATIONAL CRIMINAL LAW OF ATROCITY SINCE NUREMBERG

An overview of the evolving international criminal law of atrocity, as developed by international tribunals and in the Rome Statute of the ICC, reveals that following Nuremberg, the primacy of the principle of individual guilt has only strengthened, through the development of a regime of individual responsibility clearly distinct from that of State responsibility,[48] as well as the failure of the doctrines of conspiracy[49] and participation in a criminal organisation[50] to become firmly accepted in international criminal law. These doctrines were short-lived and subsequently rejected in 1998 by the Rome Statute.[51] In addition, though the doctrine of joint criminal enterprise has emerged in the jurisprudence of the International Criminal Tribunal for the former Yugoslavia (ICTY),[52] it is not clear whether it has gained widespread recognition.[53] What we see in the area of international criminal law is that alongside the ability to overcome limitations of space and time (the development of universal jurisdiction and the inapplicability of statutes of limitation to heinous crimes under customary international law),[54] the law has not abandoned its commitment to individual liability.

During the many criminal trials that followed the Second World War, the unquestioned assumption of the law was that it is possible, indeed necessary, to establish the individual culpability of the perpetrator of international crimes. However, this normative position was not supported by the social facts revealed in these trials. For the most part the courts failed to address the bureaucratic structure within which the perpetrators worked, and, as a result, many of these trials, with their emphasis on individual responsibility, failed to reflect the historical realities. It therefore seems that the normative commitment of the law to judge the individual according to the traditional strictures of criminal law stands in tension with the need to clarify the historical truth about the bureaucratic nature of the Holocaust.

[48] A Bianchi, 'State Responsibility and Criminal Liability of Individuals' in A Cassese (ed), *The Oxford Companion to International Criminal Justice* (Oxford, Oxford University Press, 2009).

[49] Cassese, above n 41, 227.

[50] Eg, the Rome statute does not provide for liability stemming from mere participation in a criminal organisation.

[51] Cassese, above n 41, 33–34; MC Bassiouni, *Introduction to International Criminal Law* (New York, Hotei Publishing, 2003) 82–84; R Cryer, *Prosecuting International Crimes—Selectivity and the International Criminal Law Regime* (Cambridge, Cambridge University Press, 2005) 316; A Eser, 'Individual Criminal Responsibility' in A Cassese, P Gaeta and JPWD Jones (eds), *The Rome Statute of the International Criminal Court: A Commentary* (Oxford, Oxford University Press, 2002) 767, 784–85; Bush, above n 38, 1094-1100; Osiel, above n 42, 6.

[52] K Gustafson, 'Joint Criminal Enterprise' in Cassese (ed), above n 48, 391–96.

[53] For the view that this form of criminal liability is implicitly permitted under Art 25(1) of the Rome Statute of the ICC, see Cassese, above n 41, 212. But see M Osiel, *Making Sense of Mass Atrocity* (Cambridge, New York, Cambridge University Press, 2009) 114, claiming that the ICC is showing reluctance to use the doctrine of joint criminal liability.

[54] Cassese (ed), above n 48.

Lawrence Douglas rejects this criticism, arguing that it misses the profound transformations that the law has undertaken through its contact with atrocity.[55] The last two decades, he argues, have seen the development of a large body of writing that analyses the major changes that occurred in international criminal law as a result of its ongoing involvement with the Holocaust and subsequent atrocities. Douglas suggests that we should not view these changes sporadically, as isolated reforms meant to overcome certain legal obstacles, but rather as amounting to a paradigm shift in our understanding of the substance and processes of criminal law. In fact, he argues that the contact of the law with atrocity has led to remarkable innovations which form a 'jurisprudence of atrocity', a coherent body of doctrines and theories that aim to submit the most heinous crimes to adjudication. As indicated above, at the centre of the law's transformation stands the puncturing of the shield of national sovereignty and the recognition of new crimes such as crimes against humanity and genocide. The post-Nuremberg jurisprudence concerning these supranational crimes has in turn severed the Nuremberg paradigm of connecting international crimes to the protection of the system of sovereign Nation States, further reducing the relevance of the Nation State as the unit of analysis.[56] In fact Douglas argues that these crimes explode the spatio-temporal limitations on prosecution, as they are not governed by prescriptive periods and can be tried under universal jurisdiction. And this in turn has resulted in a radical transformation of criminal procedure, which has shifted from being mainly concerned with the rights of the accused to a preoccupation with facilitating prosecution and developing the rights of victims.

Having outlined the profound transformations of the legal landscape, Douglas calls for a radical revision of the goals of the criminal trial. Contra Arendt, he supports replacing traditional objectives such as correction, retribution and deterrence with expressive, didactic purposes of ostracism of the defendant, clarifying the historical truth and building a collective memory, with the ultimate hope of remedying the violations experienced by specific groups and communities. With this he joins a line of modern writers who uphold the expressive function of international criminal trials as their main justification.[57] It is important to note that criminal law traditionally has tried to minimise its didactic role, as this has put it in dangerous proximity with 'show trials' and the risk of betraying justice for politics. Indeed, this was precisely Arendt's criticism of the Israeli prosecution of Eichmann. Moreover, it is worth noting that there is an internal logic connecting individual liability with the aim of retribution, and once we recognise the legitimacy of the expressive goals of the criminal trial, it is not clear why we should

[55] Douglas, above n 2.

[56] Eg, Art 7 of the Rome Statute of the ICC abandons the requirement elaborated at Nuremberg of a nexus to war in the definition of 'crimes against humanity'.

[57] See Osiel, above n 42; J Shklar, *Legalism: Law, Morals, and Political Trials* (Cambridge, Mass, Harvard University Press, 1964); M Koskenniemi, 'Between Impunity and Show Trials' (2002) 6 *Max Planck Yearbook of United Nations Law* 1.

insist on individual liability.[58] The irony is that current support for the recognition of the didactic role of the criminal trial of supranational crimes is not accompanied with a willingness to abandon the need to establish individual guilt. Thus, we witness again a divide, this time between the expressive goals of the trial and the commitment to individual responsibility.

The continued insistence on individual liability, notwithstanding the major changes in the jurisprudence of atrocity, can only be explained, in my view, as stemming from the choice of criminal law as legal tool. The heart of criminal liability is the autonomy of the individual, and without it we cannot justify the taking of liberty. However, it is this very demand that undermines the ability of criminal law to address the bureaucratic organisation of the crimes, as is further shown by the criminal law's poor record in dealing with business involvement in the Holocaust.

IV. PRIVATE BUSINESS AND THE PROBLEM OF CORPORATE LIABILITY

Private corporations and their managers were rarely the subject of criminal trials for their involvement in the Holocaust.[59] Even when they were, courts have been reluctant to convict defendants in the absence of unquestionable criminal intent.[60] In this area we can identify a pattern similar to the one we identified in relation to State bureaucracy: the brave beginnings that were undertaken in Nuremberg, in what came to be known as the industrialists' trials, were short-lived and were discontinued throughout the cold war.

During the subsequent trials at Nuremberg,[61] the American prosecution attempted to bring under legal judgment the involvement of various sectors of civil society in enabling the commissions of heinous crimes, including that of private businesses. However, lacking jurisdiction over the business corporation

[58] This question has become all the more urgent in the trial of Milosevic (Case IT-02-54-T *Prosecutor v Slobodan Milosevic*, Order Terminating the Proceedings, 14 March 2006). After having conducted a long trial aimed at clarifying the historical truth, the unexpected death of the defendant has terminated the legal proceedings without a definitive judgment. Given the expressive purpose of the trial, it remains unclear why the trial should be terminated without a judgment if it is mainly directed towards clarifying history?

[59] As Bush, above n 38, 1098, emphasises, no corporation has ever been charged with or convicted for an international war crime or similar offence; only individuals were charged in the first trials at Nuremberg and Tokyo, as well as in the four subsequent trials at Nuremberg that focused on managers, directors and owners of the giant German enterprises such as Krupp, Flick, IG Farben.

[60] For further discussion see AL Zuppi, 'Slave Labor in Nuremberg's IG Farben Case: The Lonely Voice of Paul M. Hebert' (2005–2006) 66 *Louisiana Law Review* 495.

[61] At Nuremberg, the International Military Tribunal (IMT) did not try any industrialists for their use of forced labour. Subsequently, however, the United States Military Tribunal (USMT) did try executives from three German firms: IG Farben, Flick and Krupp.

as an entity,[62] the prosecution attempted to deal with the criminal complicity of private corporations by indicting their directors and managers as individuals. The court, however, routinely spoke in terms of corporate responsibility and obligations in its judgment of the individual managers.[63]

These trials of the industrialists were conducted by the US military tribunals under the Allied forces' Control Council Law No 10. In three cases, *United States v Flick*,[64] *United States v Krauch*[65] (the *IG Farben Case*) and *United States v Krupp*,[66] the leaders of large German industries were prosecuted for crimes against peace (ie, initiating the Second World War), war crimes and crimes against humanity. The charges stemmed from the active involvement of the defendants in Nazi practices such as slave labour and deportations.[67] Notwithstanding the important precedents created by these trials for the use of criminal law to deal with the conduct of private corporations, their success was partial, due to criminal law's narrow definition of the intent required to establish liability, which involves independent initiative and choice, and not mere contribution to the commission of the crime.[68] The problem of bringing the conduct of the private corporations under the judgment of criminal law has proven especially perplexing with relation to the use of slave and forced labourers. For example, most members of the board of IG Farben were acquitted of charges relating to the use of slave labour due to lack of clear evidence of their knowledge and direct engagement.[69] The trial targeted, among other things, IG Farben's participation in the 'slave labor program' of the Third Reich.[70] Even though the fact that IG Farben exploited a large number of forced labourers was not even disputed by the defence, they argued that they acted out of 'necessity', specifically that IG Farben had yielded to the pressure of the Reich labour office to employ foreign labourers. The tribunal, working under the strictures of criminal law based on subjective intention and free will, accepted this argument and acquitted (Judge Herbert dissenting).[71]

[62] International law at the time of the Nuremberg trials did not recognise the criminal liability of corporations. See SR Ratner, 'Corporations and Human Rights: A Theory of Legal Responsibility' (2001) 111 *Yale Law Journal* 443.

[63] Ratner, *ibid* 477–78, cites the IG Farben decision as an example. See also A Ramasastry, 'Corporate Complicity: From Nuremberg to Rangoon: An Examination of Forced Labor Cases and Their Impact on the Liability of Multinational Corporations' (2002) 20 *Berkeley Journal of International Law* 91.

[64] 6 Trials of War Criminals Before the Nuernberg (*sic*) Military Tribunals Under Control Council Law no 10 (1949).

[65] 8 Trials of War Criminals Before the Nuernberg (*sic*) Military Tribunals Under Control Council Law no 10 (1949).

[66] 9 Trials of War Criminals Before the Nuernberg (*sic*) Military Tribunals Under Control Council Law no 10 (1949).

[67] Ratner, above n 62, 477.

[68] See below n 69 and accompanying text.

[69] Nine of the 23 Farben directors were found guilty of corporate plunder in occupied territories. Only five were held liable for the abuse of slave labour.

[70] Bush, above n 38, 1172–74.

[71] For further discussion see Zuppi, above n 60. The tribunal held that '[t]he defendants here on trial have invoked what has been termed the defense of necessity. They say that the utilization of slave labor in Farben plants was the necessary result of compulsory production quotas imposed upon them

As we see, no corporation has ever been charged with or convicted for an international war crime or similar offence, and only individuals were charged in the first trials at Nuremberg and Tokyo, as well as in the four subsequent trials at Nuremberg that focused on managers, directors and owners of giant German enterprises such as Krupp, Flick, and IG Farben. This preference for individual liability has not changed with the establishment of a permanent international criminal court (ICC), as the Rome Statute did not include corporations as permissible subjects of jurisdiction and rejected the doctrine of criminal conspiracy.[72] As a consequence of these developments, one commentator observes that 'the law concerning both corporations and conspiracies is in knots'.[73]

by the government agencies, on the one hand, and the equally obligatory measures requiring them to use slave labor to achieve such production, on the other. Numerous decrees … have been brought to our attention, from which it appears that said agency assumed dictatorial control over the commitment, allotment, and supervision of all available labor within the Reich … Heavy penalties, including commitment to concentration camps and even death, were set forth for violation of these regulations. The defendants who were involved in the utilization of slave labor have testified that they were under such oppressive coercion and compulsion that they cannot be said to have acted with intent which is a necessary ingredient of every criminal offense … In view of these indisputable facts … this Tribunal is not prepared to say that these defendants did not speak the truth …' *United States v Krauch*, above n 65, 1174 cited in F Jessberger, 'On the Origins of Individual Criminal Responsibility under International Law for Business Activity' (2010) 8 *Journal Of International Criminal Justice* 783, 792–93. Judge Herbert criticised the broad application of necessity. Herbert wrote that 'Such doctrine constitutes … unbridled license for the commission of war crimes and crimes against humanity … through the simple expedience of the issuance of compulsory governmental regulations.' (*United States v Krauch*, above n 65, at 1310, cited in Zuppi at 517). He thought that the officers of Farben should be held guilty: 'I cannot agree that there was an absence of a moral choice. In utilizing slave labor within Farben the will of the actors coincided with the will of those controlling the Government and who had directed or ordered the doing of criminal acts.' (*ibid* 1309). The disagreement among the judges involved issues of both historical facts and standards of interpretation. As to the former, the restitution litigation of the 1990s ignited the debate among historians about the scope of choice enjoyed by the corporations under the Third Reich. See P Hayes, 'Corporate Freedom of Action in Nazi Germany' (2009) 45 *Bulletin of the German Historical Institute* 29–42, 51.

[72] See P Saland, 'International Criminal Law Principles' in R Lee (ed), *The International Criminal Court: The Making of the Rome Statute* (The Hague, Kluwer Law International, 1999) 189, 198–99. After considerable discussion, the drafters did not include criminal liability of corporations. The reasons cited for the rejection of corporate liability were that it would shift the ICC's focus away from individual liability, and that there was no common international standard for corporate liability. See M Kremnitzer, 'A Possible Case for Imposing Criminal Liability on Corporations in International Criminal Law' (2010) 8 *Journal of International Criminal Justice* 909, 917. Thus, notwithstanding the growing recognition of criminal liability of corporations by various European States, the Rome Statute establishing the ICC limited its jurisdiction to natural persons and rejected the introduction of criminal liability for corporations. In addition, the American doctrine of criminal conspiracy was rejected, largely at the insistence of lawyers from civil law countries whose domestic traditions generally do not include criminal or civil liability for conspiracy (see Bush, above n 38, 1100). Instead, the ICC's jurisdiction includes crimes similar to conspiracy, like joint enterprise and aiding and abetting, as well as liability for 'contributing to a common purpose', as a surrogate for conspiracy. See Rome Statute of the International Criminal Court, Art 25(3), July 17, 1998, 2187 UNTS 90, 105 (extending ICC jurisdiction to a person who 'contributes to the commission or attempted commission of such a crime by a group of persons acting with a common purpose').

[73] Bush, above n 38, 1101. See also WA Schabas, *An Introduction to the International Criminal Court*, 2nd edn (Cambridge, Cambridge University Press, 2004) 101–05, interpreting from Art 25 of the Rome Statute that it does not recognise corporate criminal responsibility and relies instead on the

V. JUDGING BUREAUCRACY: BETWEEN SPECTATOR AND JUDGE

We began our journey of reflection on the crisis of judging bureaucracy posed by the Holocaust, by pointing out the apparent contradiction in Arendt's argument. It seems that Arendt urges us to understand the novelty of the Holocaust as a bureaucratic crime, while exposing the failure of traditional juridical concepts in dealing with the Holocaust's bureaucratic aspect. However, this recognition does not lead Arendt to question the resort to criminal law. On the contrary, she upholds its emphasis on attributing individual responsibility. Arendt is of the opinion that all that is required in the legal arena is to recognise changes in substantive law (recognition of the new crimes of crime against humanity and genocide) without the need to alter the reliance of criminal process on the principle of individual culpability. To the contrary, in the face of the bureaucratisation of the crimes, Arendt appears to stress the importance of proving the individual guilt of the perpetrators. A review of the jurisprudence of atrocity since the Second World War reveals that notwithstanding the changes in substantive criminal law, the emphasis on individual culpability has remained strong. In light of the development of historical knowledge on the complex bureaucratic aspects of the Holocaust, it seems that the gap between the historical understanding and the legal tools has only increased with the years. Is there a way out of this impasse?

One route would be to try to alter criminal law further, by extending criminal liability to corporations under international law.[74] In light of Hannah Arendt's insights discussed throughout this essay, in order for corporate criminal liability to provide an adequate legal response to bureaucratic involvement in atrocity, criminal law's focus on a subjective intent traceable to an individual would have to be relaxed. However, as I have argued above, this subjective focus is at the heart of criminal liability. Indeed, it appears to be retained by contemporary proponents of corporate criminal liability in international law.[75] I should like to

concept of common purpose complicity, which the judges of the ICTY developed into the theory of 'joint criminal enterprise'.

[74] For arguments to this effect, see A Clapham, 'Extending International Criminal Law beyond the Individual to Corporations and Armed Opposition Groups' (2008) 6 *Journal of International Criminal Justice* 899, and Kremnitzer, above n 72, 909–08. Criminal liability of corporations is well-established in common law jurisdictions, but has recently spread to some civil law jurisdictions as well (see T Weigend, 'Societas delinquere non potest? A German Perspective' (2008) 6(5) *Journal of International Criminal Justice* 927).

[75] Eg, Kremnitzer, above n 72, 911, writes that 'criminal liability should not be imposed on conduct that is not significantly anti-social or that can not be defined with reasonable prediction and clarity ... The area appropriate for criminal law should, as a rule, be restricted to acts accompanied by a subjective mental element, not including negligence. The subjective mental element may be stretched as far as the case of an organ of a company who suspects that criminal activity is taking place by a subordinate employee in the framework of the corporation (even when the suspicion relates only to a specific crime in general and does not include details concerning the concrete circumstances of the crime), and encourages, by omission or commission, this criminal activity.' It is doubtful whether such

conclude by suggesting that only by turning to private law have jurists found a way to address the bureaucratic organisation of the crimes of the Holocaust.

The industrialists' trials at Nuremberg did not signal the beginning of the systematic criminal adjudication of private businesses for their involvement in the Holocaust. Neither did the civil domestic road prove any better. German compensation legislation failed to relate to inmates' labour for private firms, and the few private lawsuits brought against the largest industrial firms in Germany resulted in paltry settlements.[76]

Claims for reparations made their debut in American courts in the mid-1990s.[77] Swiss banks were the first target of mass class actions suits filed in US federal courts on behalf of Holocaust survivors. Soon to follow were claims for life insurance plans, and demands for compensation for slave and forced labour. Litigation also expanded to include banks in other countries and other private corporations.[78] In 1998, Swiss banks were the first to settle a claim, for an unprecedented US$1.25 billion.[79] Shortly thereafter, a series of claims against German corporations led to the establishment of a US$5 billion fund to which the German Government and corporations contributed in equal shares, and to a signing of

a 'stretched' subjective element would answer Arendt's concerns, as it requires a definite knowledge and intent on the part of an individual or perhaps group of individuals who compose the corporate organ.

[76] Ferencz explains that the German compensation legislation did not include payment for unpaid wages or for companies' unjust enrichment when inmates were assigned to work for private firms, as they were considered relatively minor obligations that could be dealt with by companies themselves. The failure to pay 'slave labourers' gave rise to lawsuits against a few of the big industrial firms whose abuses had been revealed in the Nuremberg trials. Despite intensive litigation in many test cases, Germany's highest court held that all such claims, being in the nature of reparations, could be considered only as part of a peace treaty with a united Germany. (The exception to this rule was in a case brought against IG Farben which ended in negotiated compensation. A civil division of the district court in Frankfurt AM allowed the claim for compensation of DM 10,000 of the former prisoner and forced labourer Norbert Wollheim against IG Farben (in liquidation); subsequently IG Farben (in liquidation) came to an agreement with those prisoners having worked in Auschwitz and Monowitz about total compensation of DM 30 million.) See BB Ferencz, *Less Than Slaves, Jewish Forced Labor and the Quest for Compensation* (Indiana, Indiana University Press, 2002) 34–67. Interestingly, one of the early attempts to overcome the hurdles imposed by German legislation by turning to American courts was by a survivor of IG Farben's plant in Monowitz, whose claim for indemnification had been rejected because he was neither a German national nor a 'refugee' at the time of his enslavement (see *Princz v Federal Republic of Germany* [1994] 26 F 3d 1166 (DC Cir 1994) *cert denied*, 513 US 1121, 115 SCt 923. See Zuppi, above n 60, 524. We can thus trace the origins of forced labour and restitution litigation in American courts to the unsatisfactory treatment by the German legal system of IG Farben's involvement with Auschwitz.

[77] Note, however, that some sporadic claims have been recorded prior to this date. See MJ Bazyler and RP Alford (eds), *Holocaust Restitution: Perspectives on the Litigation and its Legacy* (New York, London, New York University Press, 2006) xiii.

[78] M Marrus, *Some Measure of Justice: The Holocaust Era Restitution Campaign of the 1990s* (Madison, The University of Wisconsin Press, 2009) 4.

[79] See *ibid* 10–25. For a detailed exposition of the settlement mechanism, see M Domes, 'Compensation for Survivors of Slave and Forced Labor: The Swiss Bank Settlement and the German Foundation Provide Options for Recovery for Holocaust Victims' (2001) 14 *The Transnational Lawyer* 171, 175–92.

an Executive Agreement between the Governments of Germany and the United States.[80]

None of the restitution suits was ultimately resolved on the merits of the case. The legal pressure, however, did yield historical findings in a turnabout way. Swiss banks agreed to a comprehensive audit, and German corporations established historical committees and opened their archives to historians whom they appointed to investigate their involvement in the Holocaust.[81] Though the courts did not make any pronouncement of liability, they were actively involved in the negotiation process as well as in the implementation of the settlements, issuing numerous rulings as to the proper categorisation of claims and allocation of funds.[82] Commenting on the legal design of lawsuits launched in court with the aim of reaching out-of-court settlements, Holocaust historian Michael Marrus writes that the problem that Arendt identified about the inadequacy of 'juristic concepts' to deal with matters such as genocide was only exacerbated in this litigation, since the class actions were not really about law but about political, diplomatic and media pressures.[83]

Is this a pre-ordained failure? Is the law doomed to fail when trying to address the bureaucratic aspects of the Holocaust? I would like to suggest that the restitution class actions of the 1990s provide us with the first instance in which the idiom of the law corresponded to the bureaucratic aspects of the crimes.[84] Indeed, because the claims were grounded in tort and property law, the restitution litigation removed one of the most formidable obstacles to bringing Auschwitz under

[80] Under Secretary Eizenstat played a pivotal role in the shaping of this agreement. See Domes, above n 79. Concurrently, an Agreement Concerning Holocaust Era Insurance Claims was concluded between the 'Remembrance, Responsibility, and Future' Foundation, the newly-introduced International Commission on Holocaust Era Insurance Claims (ICHEIC) and the German Insurance Association. This detailed agreement set out the mechanism for settling 'individual claims on unpaid or confiscated and not otherwise compensated policies of German insurance companies', Agreement preamble, available at <http://www.icheic.org/pdf/agreement-GFA.pdf>. These settlements did not bring the sprawling litigation campaigns to a halt, however. For an overview of litigation campaigns by 2006, see Bazyler and Alford, above n 77.

[81] In 1996, in the wake of the restitution campaigns, the Swiss Bankers Association formed a committee of accountants to audit their records and determine the extent of dormant accounts belonging to Holocaust victims. Later that year, the Swiss Government appointed a committee of historians to assess the role of Switzerland in the Second World War. That committee was headed by Swiss historian Jean-Francois Bergier. Both committees published extensive reports. See E Barkan, *The Guilt of Nations: Restitution and Negotiating Historical Injustices* (Baltimore, Md, The Johns Hopkins University Press, 2001) ch 5. For the final report published in 2002 by the Bergier Committee, see *Final Report of the Independent Commission of Experts, Switzerland—Second World War*, 276–77, available at <http:www.uek.ch>. Holocaust historian Saul Friedlander was appointed as a head of an independent historical commission with the aim of investigating the corporate history of Bertelsmann AG, a German media corporation, during the years 1921–51. The commission issued an extensive report that was accepted as the official institutional history. See S Friedlander *et al*, *Bertelsmann im Dritten Reich* (München, Bertelsmann, 2002) (In German).

[82] For a detailed outline of the courts' involvement in the Swiss Banks Settlement, for example, see the official website of the settlement at <http://www.swissbankclaims.com/Chronology.aspx>.

[83] Marrus, above n 78, 27.

[84] See L Bilsky, 'Transnational Holocaust Litigation' *European Journal of International Law* (forthcoming 2012).

legal judgment: the need to establish subjective individual intent, which does not stem from the law itself (as Arendt seemed to assume) but is connected to the logic of criminal law.[85] Thus, I suggest considering the development of restitution lawsuits in the 1990s as opening the possibility of combining the historical understandings of the bureaucratic aspects of the Holocaust with the legal tools of the class action. In a certain way, it can be said that the law has undergone the same process as Arendt underwent in the Epilogue to *Eichmann in Jerusalem.* By trying to address the involvement of bureaucratic organisations in the Holocaust, the judge abandoned his traditional judicial stance as an umpire and became an involved actor, a judge-manager-bureaucrat of mass claims whose main task is to facilitate monetary settlement. We saw that Arendt did not manage to preserve the separation between the two stances of 'spectator' and 'actor'. Maybe, in order to judge the Holocaust, there is no choice for the law but to adopt the tools and language of bureaucracy itself. This necessarily involves abandoning the principle of individual liability which has been central until now in judging the Holocaust.

[85] Although the restitution claims of the 1990s operated in the field of private law, they reflected certain elements of the international criminal law of atrocity outlined above, in particular the lack of spatio-temporal limitations on litigation and the centrality of the victims. Nevertheless, the Holocaust restitution suits should be read primarily in light of the American structural class action against human rights violations, which abandons the focus on individual liability to tackle social conditions and the ways that large bureaucratic organisations determine those conditions.

15

Arendt in Jerusalem, Demjanjuk in Munich

LAWRENCE DOUGLAS

I. FROM MUNICH TO JERUSALEM AND BACK AGAIN

THE MUNICH TRIAL of John (Ivan) Demjanjuk was in certain respects unremarkable. The Ukrainian-born Demjanjuk stood accused of complicity in the deaths of 28,060 Jews during his service as a guard at the Sobibor extermination camp. The figure was surely horrific, and yet the crime itself—accessory to murder—was relatively inconsequential against the larger sweep of Nazi genocide. Demjanjuk himself remains a limited man. No longer the bulky, histrionic defendant tried in Jerusalem over twenty years ago, the ostensibly ailing Demjanjuk was more an absence than a presence in his Munich trial, both because his numerous medical complaints required frequent cancellations of court dates and because at trial he chose to remain silent, gurney-bound and hidden behind dark glasses. The German case against Demjanjuk was almost exclusively built on documentary evidence—no more than a handful of Sobibor survivors remain alive and none could recollect the defendant, much less identify him. And so the trial at times was dull, as trials often are; Rebecca West memorably called the Nuremberg trial, also a case built around documents, a 'citadel of boredom'.[1] Originally expected to last four months, the trial limped on for eighteen as court days were short—only three hours per day of trial, a gesture of accommodation to the nonagenarian accused—and frustratingly intermittent, in part because of medical cancellations, in part because the single courtroom in Munich large enough to accommodate the press and spectators was also booked for other high-profile trials, and thus had to be run something like a repertory theatre.

The verdict announced on May 12, 2011, in which the court sentenced Demjanjuk to five year's prison and then promptly released him pending appeal, seemed only to cast doubt on the importance of the proceeding. And while Demjanjuk's conviction promises to bring to a close the era of high-profile Nazi atrocity trials that reaches back to Nuremberg and brought us other memorable proceedings, such as the Eichmann trial in Jerusalem in 1961, the Frankfurt-Auschwitz trial (1963–65), and the French trials of Klaus Barbie (1987) and Maurice Papon (1997–98), the

[1] R West, *A Train of Powder* (New York, Viking Press, 1955) 3.

fact that this era should end with Demjanjuk in the dock represents a stunning denouement. For it is undeniably the case that Demjanjuk would never have been tried in Munich if he had not once been mistaken for someone else.

Ivan Demjanjuk emigrated to the United States in 1952 and became a citizen in 1958, changing his first name to John. He worked for decades as a machinist at a Ford plant while raising a family in suburban Cleveland.[2] His legal problems began over thirty years ago, when prosecutors in what became the Office of Special Investigations (OSI) in the Justice Department received material, passed on from Soviet sources, indicating that the native Ukrainian had been trained at the Trawniki camp, an SS training facility, and subsequently had served as a guard at Sobibor, one of the three 'pure' extermination facilities, along with Treblinka and Belzec, constructed by the SS in the spring of 1942 in Poland as part of Operation Reinhard, the planned elimination of the Jews of Poland. Of the 250,000 Jews who passed through Sobibor less than sixty survived, and the greatest number of these settled in Israel. But when the OSI asked the Israeli Police to assist its investigation, an odd thing happened at the identification parades conducted by the Israelis. Sobibor survivors failed to recognise a contemporaneous photo of Demjanjuk, while a number of Treblinka survivors, enlisted to assist the investigation of a completely unrelated case, blanched at a photo of Demjanjuk. This, they insisted, was the operator of the Treblinka gas chamber, a guard whose unusual cruelty had earned him the sobriquet *Ivan Grozny*, 'Ivan the Terrible'. As far back as the Eichmann trial, witnesses had testified about the legendary sadism of Treblinka's 'Ivan the Terrible'; now, after a lengthy extradition process, Demjanjuk was flown to Israel to stand trial as the notorious Treblinka guard.

Demjanjuk's arrival in Israel in 1986 created a stir that reminded many of the capture of Adolf Eichmann a quarter-century earlier. The trial of 'Ivan the Terrible' would be the first Nazi perpetrator trial in Israel since that of Eichmann. Capturing the spectacle-like quality of the proceeding, the Demjanjuk trial, like the Eichmann proceeding before it, was to be staged not in a conventional courtroom, but in a theatre-like public space retrofitted to accommodate over 300 spectators. In 1961, Israelis had followed the Eichmann trial live on radio, the first trial so broadcast; now they could watch the Demjanjuk trial live on television, the first trial to be televised in Israel's history. And both trials were staged to serve explicitly didactic purposes: to instruct successive generations of Israelis of the horrors out of which the Zionist state was created.

Only Demjanjuk's Jerusalem trial turned into less a re-enactment than a pathetic caricature of its famous predecessor. Part of this had to do with the contrasts between the two men. I think it is fair to say that Eichmann helped make his trial a tremendous success. In contrast to the hectoring, belligerent courtroom behaviour of, say, Slobodan Milosevic or Saddam Hussein, Eichmann was an ideal

[2] For a discussion of the American investigation and the Israeli trial, see L Douglas, *The Memory of Judgment: Making Law and History in the Trials of the Holocaust* (New Haven, Conn, Yale University Press, 2001) 196–207.

defendant, snapping to his feet when the judges entered the chamber, answering their questions with precision and deference. Arguably the very craven obedience to authority that helped turn Eichmann into a perpetrator of genocide made him into a model defendant. And with his dour bank teller appearance, humourless demeanour and formal manners, Eichmann delivered an unforgettable image of Arendt's 'banality of evil'.

Demjanjuk, by contrast, looked like he had just been plucked from a beer hall. Big, beefy and boisterous, Demjanjuk enjoyed, during lulls in the trial, entertaining his guards with the bits of mangled Hebrew he had picked up in his jail cell. On the stand he proved to be a terrible witness on his own behalf—not because he betrayed traces of his alleged former cruelty, but because he seemed incapable of telling a coherent story. He claimed never to have set foot in the Trawniki SS facility and never to have worked as a camp guard anywhere at any time. He insisted that he spent the last years of the war as a prisoner of war, surviving in a brutal German POW camp. But when asked to name the camp, he could not; and when pressed to describe his activities as a POW, he openly contradicted himself. His story was so implausible, the gaps in his memory so large and unbelievable, his alibi so riddled with contradictions, that the presiding judge felt obliged to interrupt his testimony to explain the importance of a coherent alibi in a criminal trial. But if anything, Demjanjuk appeared baffled by the very need to account for his actions.

In part thanks to his incoherent alibi, Demjanjuk found himself condemned to death, only the second person in Israeli history, after Eichmann, to be convicted of a capital crime (Israel had abolished the death penalty except for the most extreme crimes such as genocide). The lengthy process of appeals, automatic in Israeli law in capital cases, coincided with the unravelling of the Soviet Union, and so both Demjanjuk's prosecutors and the defence attorneys were able to gain access to long-mouldering KGB files that suggested precisely what the Israeli trial court had considered and dismissed as far-fetched: that there had been two Ukrainian 'Ivans', one at Sobibor and one at Treblinka, who bore a small but not entirely negligible resemblance to one another—both, for example, had round heads, thinning hair and protruding ears. This information suggested that 'Ivan the Terrible' had been one Ivan Marchenko, a Ukrainian who, after serving at Treblinka, was apparently killed in fighting in the Balkans toward the war's end. This material did not entirely exculpate Demjanjuk—to the contrary, it only strengthened the certainty that Demjanjuk had been a guard at Sobibor, what the OSI evidence had originally suggested. But the Israelis had tried, convicted and sentenced Demjanjuk to death as 'Ivan the Terrible of Treblinka', and the new material did cast doubt on whether Israel was about to execute the right 'Ivan'. And so the Israeli Supreme Court voided the conviction—at the same time that it excused the trial court of any mishandling of the proceeding.[3] The latter gesture was disingenuous. The three-judge trial court had treated the proceeding

[3] See *Criminal Appeal 377/88 Ivan (John) Demjanjuk v The State of Israel: Judgment of the Supreme Court* (Jerusalem, Supreme Court, 1993).

as a national oral history and Holocaust commemoration project. For the court, the living memory of survivors was to serve not only as the instrument of indictment and as a tool for preparing the gallows; it was also to provide a means for vouchsafing history against Holocaust deniers. Swept up in its historic mission, the trial court fatally insisted that the intensity of survivors' memories of the camp provided the surest measure of the accuracy of their identifications of Demjanjuk. This assumption, born more of a respect for the lived trauma of survivors than of a sober legal assessment of testimony, was quietly but emphatically rejected by the Supreme Court.

After his release from Israeli prison, Demjanjuk returned to suburban Cleveland and succeeded in having his US citizenship reinstated. This triggered a fresh struggle between Demjanjuk and the OSI, which, embarrassed by the collapse of the Israeli case and by a finding by a Federal court that it had suppressed evidence of its own doubts about Ivan the Terrible, redoubled its efforts to see the Sobibor guard deported. Since the early 1950s, the United States had adopted a distinctive policy, strengthened through federal law, of dealing with suspected Nazi perpetrators who had settled in the country after the war. Rather than try them under domestic criminal law, a course that would have raised thorny jurisdictional problems, the United States brought civil charges against persons suspected of lying on immigration forms; in cases of successful denaturalisation, the United States would deport the suspect to his or her country of origin, or to another country that could claim proper jurisdiction for a criminal trial. The Justice Department achieved its goal of having Demjanjuk's citizenship revoked for a second time in 2002; only now the United States could find no country willing to accept him. That struggle ended when German prosecutors expressed a willingness to bring charges, and in May 2009, Demjanjuk found himself bundled onto a small government jet and flown to Germany. Half a year later, in the end of November 2009, his trial started in Munich.

II. ARENDT AND THE IDIOM OF ATROCITY

Hannah Arendt famously argued that the Eichmann trial 'never rose to the challenge of the unprecedented',[4] an argument that she repeated several years later at the time of the Frankfurt-Auschwitz trial. For Arendt, it was crucial that the law use or forge the proper idiom of criminality, the adequate legal incrimination, capable of naming and condemning the unprecedented nature of Nazi atrocities. This idiom, she argued, was available at the time of the Eichmann trial—it was the most significant conceptual innovation of the Nuremberg trial of the major war criminals—only the Jerusalem court largely ignored it. The Eichmann court's

[4] H Arendt, *Eichmann in Jerusalem: A Report on the Banality of Evil* (New York, Penguin Books, 1992) 263.

failure to build on Nuremberg's understanding of crimes against humanity was, for Arendt, one of the trial's many shortcomings. The gravamen of the prosecution's case against Eichmann was so-called 'Crimes against the Jewish People', which, Arendt lamented, made the Holocaust sound like simply a more elaborate form of a nineteenth-century pogrom.[5] Worse, the incrimination introduced an untenable and vaguely incoherent specificity into criminal law, as if the legal definition of 'murder' could turn on the ethnicity of the victim: *The defendant is charged with murder of a Jew, a crime different than murdering a Catholic.*

The notion of crimes against humanity, Arendt insisted, captured the unprecedented quality of Nazi atrocity as a 'crime against the human status' and as an 'attack upon human diversity as such'.[6] That Arendt understood the incrimination in a manner different from the jurists at Nuremberg is beside the point. Arendt, after all, was not interested in a timid recapitulation of legal precedent; instead, she sought to push legal discourse toward a more robust conceptual grasp of the meaning and distinctiveness of the crime of mass atrocity.

Still unanswered, however, is *why* exactly Arendt believed so strongly in the necessity and power of the proper legal idiom. Her argument most emphatically does not insist that framing the proper idiom is a key to rendering legal justice in the conventional sense of handling the accused in a procedurally fair fashion. Arendt never seriously doubts the fairness of Eichmann's conviction; nor does she call into the doubt, as did many thinkers at the time, the wisdom of sentencing Eichmann to death. Likewise, she never calls into question the fairness of the convictions in the Frankfurt-Auschwitz trial—if anything, she laments the acquittals. Put another way, if judgment framed in wrong or inadequate legal concepts occasions an injustice, it is not an injustice to the accused.

Arendt wants, rather, to insist that the law's failure to frame and use proper idioms constitutes a failure to do conceptual justice to the distinctive nature of mass, state-sponsored atrocity. What this distinctive nature or essence is, need not in the moment concern us. At times, she identifies it with the bureaucratic nature of a crime which invites the shifting of responsibility to superiors; at others, she speaks of the functional subdivision of tasks that fragments and dilutes a sense of individual blameworthiness; and at others still, she talks about the distinctive dehumanisation visited upon actors in bureaucratic structures embedded in totalitarian regimes.

At first blush, this concern with framing legal concepts adequate to the task of grasping the essence of crimes of atrocity appears to sit uncomfortably with Arendt's louder, more persistent argument that the criminal trial must not be burdened with doing the work of the historian.[7] But the contradiction dissolves on further analysis. For Arendt's interest is not historical and retrospective.[8] Less

[5] *Ibid* 267–70.
[6] *Ibid* 268–69.
[7] *Ibid* 253.
[8] I am grateful to Awol Kassim Allo for this insight.

concerned with framing an accurate representation of the crime as an artifact or as a moment of history, Arendt's interest is prospective, directed toward grasping the crime of atrocity as a phenomenon that remains present, real and capable of repetition. Arendt makes this argument most explicitly toward the end of *Eichmann in Jerusalem*:

> It is essentially for this reason: that the unprecedented, once it has appeared, may become a precedent for the future, that all trials touching upon 'crimes against humanity' must be judged according to a standard that is today still and 'ideal.' If genocide is an actual possibility of the future, then no people on earth—least of all, of course, the Jewish people, in Israel or elsewhere—can feel reasonably sure of its continued existence without the help and protection of international law. Success or failure in dealing with the hitherto unprecedented can lie only in the extent to which this dealing may serve as a valid precedent on the road to international penal law.[9]

Remarkable in this quotation is both the existential exigency, the sceptre of genocidal extinction, that Arendt gives word to, and also the conventional logic of deterrence that appears to lies at the heart of her advocacy for a conceptually revamped legal discourse. International law, if it is to offer an adequate prophylactic against genocide, must adequately digest the nature of the crime as a juridical matter.

This interest in deterrence appears also to inform the connection that Arendt draws between idioms and institutions. Arendt laments, for example, the fact that the Eichmann trial took place before an Israeli court. Having already identified Eichmann's crime as in essence a crime against humanity, Arendt insists that 'it [the crime] needed an international tribunal to do justice to it'.[10] Here again Arendt obviously is not speaking of justice in the conventional sense but in the sense of comprehending a conceptually unprecedented event. It is in this latter sense that crimes against humanity require an international court, as '[t]he very monstrousness of the events is "minimized" before a tribunal that represents one nation only'.[11] An international trial, Arendt argues, even before an ad hoc tribunal, such as those constituted in Nuremberg and Tokyo to deal with Axis crimes in the European and Pacific theatres in World War II, would have been far preferable to a trial before a domestic national court in Israel. An international court, even of an ad hoc nature, would have better conjured the spectre of 'constant repetition'—that genocide is 'an actual possibility of the future'—and so would have made 'imperative' the need for a permanent international criminal court, an institution that had been twice rejected by the United Nations at the time of Arendt's writing, but which, as we all know, is now a fledgling reality.

Admittedly there is something odd about Arendt's appeal to the logic of deterrence. In 'Personal Responsibility under Dictatorship', Arendt notes that legal

[9] *Ibid* 273.
[10] *Ibid* 269.
[11] *Ibid* 270.

punishment is typically justified in terms of the 'need of society to be protected against the crime, the deterring force of the warning example for the potential criminal, and, finally retributive justice'—only then insightfully to observe, 'none of these grounds is valid for the punishment of the so-called war criminals'.[12] In this essay, written after *Eichmann in Jerusalem* and before her introduction to Bernd Naumann's report on the Frankfurt-Auschwitz trial, Arendt reaches a conclusion no less insightful for being paradoxical: '[H]ere we are, demanding justice and meting out punishment in accordance with our sense of justice, while, on the other hand, this same sense of justice informs us that all our previous notions about punishment and its justification have failed us.'[13] And yet in *Eichmann in Jerusalem*, Arendt offers a robust defence of the need for adequate idioms and institutions to do justice to crimes of atrocity, a defence that does less to rethink these 'previous notions' than to recapitulate them.

Arendt's interest in deterrence appears, then, to contradict her position in 'Personal Responsibility under Dictatorship' at the same time that it sounds disturbingly naive, coming as it does from a thinker interested in framing novel concepts to grasp extraordinary crimes. International prosecutors invariably speak of the importance of trying perpetrators as a means of deterrence, and the enabling charters of recent international courts—the ad hoc tribunals for Yugoslavia (ICTY) and Rwanda (ICTR), and the International Criminal Court—all wave at the goal of deterrence. But however obligatory this rhetorical appeal, it seems dreadfully obvious that the Nuremberg and Eichmann trials did little to deter Pol Pot, and that the work of the ICTY and ICTR has done little to put a brake on genocide in Darfur. This might simply be a consequence of the fact that prosecutions of perpetrators of crimes of atrocity have until now been extremely rare, and as institutions of supranational justice gain greater traction, their deterrent effects will become more visible. But even this seems highly questionable. Even in the case of conventional domestic crimes, deterrence—which, after all, is a negative effect—is notoriously difficult to measure; in the case of supranational crimes, involving complex organisations and often direct state sponsorship, it may be altogether impossible. Deterrence, as a justification for punishing crimes of atrocity, remains almost entirely speculative if not fanciful.

I believe, then, that Arendt's concern with idioms and institutions can better be understood as a reflection of her belief in the humanising act of rendering *judgment*—not as a narrowly instrumental means to some additional goal (deterrence), but as a meaning-sustaining activity in times of crisis. Drawing on both Kant and Aristotle, Arendt understands the act of judging (*urteilen*) as 'one, if not the most important activity in which … sharing-the-world-with-others comes to pass'.[14]

[12] H Arendt, 'Personal Responsibility under Dictatorship' in J Kohn (ed), *Responsibility and Judgment* (New York, Schocken, 2003) 25.

[13] *Ibid* 26.

[14] H Arendt, *Between Past and Future: Six Exercises in Political Thought* (New York, Viking Press, 1968) 221.

It is the task of judgment to grasp and comprehend unprecedented realities without recourse to 'reductive commonplaces'.[15] Judging makes good on the human project to 'begin anew', to fashion fresh standards in the face of 'something that has ruined our categories of thought'.[16] This belief in the centrality of judgment to the project of being human is perhaps nowhere more poignantly captured than in Arendt's own effort in *Eichmann in Jerusalem* to wed two forms of judgment, the deliberative and the juridical, *urteilen* and *verurteilen*.

In the last pages of *Eichmann in Jerusalem*, Arendt assumes the voice of the judge, addressing Eichmann directly. Her discourse of condemnation (*verurteilen*) liberates itself from the law's 'preconceived categories' and 'customary rules'[17] to supply the terms of deliberative judgment (*urteilen*) missing in the court's verdict. Indeed, Arendt appears to condemn Eichmann precisely because his crimes represent such a complete evacuation of thought as to create a crisis of judgment: '[W]e find that no one, that is, no member of the human race, can be expected to want to share the earth with you.'[18] What is remarkable about these words is how they echo her understanding of judgment as a 'sharing-the-world-with-others'. Only now, judgment must redeem itself through an aggressive gesture of purging and exclusion. Only through a coercive act of ejection can judgment demonstrate and renew itself as an inclusive non-coercive human activity. As the ultimate refusal to share the world with others, the crime of atrocity demands an act of restorative judgment that both speaks to the perpetrator and ejects him. Thus despite Arendt's own disappointingly instrumental appeal to the logic of deterrence, her insistence on the importance of novel legal idioms can be better understood in terms of the centrality of judgment to her vision of the activity of being human. Reimagined idioms and institutions critically supply the necessary tools by which *verurteilen* can answer the challenge that extreme atrocities pose to *urteilen*. Ultimately, then, Arendt is concerned with preserving the integrity of understanding and judgment in the face of unprecedented acts. And it is the continuing importance of this concern that ultimately, despite its anomalous character, made the Demjanjuk trial a coherent and important project.

III. DEMJANJUK AND THE IDIOM OF JUDGMENT

Let us linger for a moment over Arendt's observation that 'nothing is more pernicious to an understanding of these new crimes … than the common illusion that the crime of murder and the crime of genocide are essentially the same'.[19]

[15] M Dietz, 'Arendt and the Holocaust' in D Villa (ed), *The Cambridge Companion to Hannah Arendt* (Cambridge, Cambridge University Press, 2000) 87.

[16] H Arendt, 'Understanding and Politics' (1953) 20 *Partisan Review* 379. See also, MP d'Entrèves, 'Arendt's Theory of Judgment' in Villa (ed), above n 14, 245.

[17] *Ibid*.

[18] Arendt, above n 4, 279.

[19] *Ibid* 272.

For decades, this illusion had been no more disastrously inscribed than in the numerous atrocity trials conducted by the courts of the Federal Republic of Germany. To appreciate this, we need go no further than the charges levelled against Demjanjuk. To the foreign observer, these charges pose something of a riddle. Why try Demjanjuk as an accessory to murder, and not, say, genocide or crimes against humanity?

Germany is one of the few countries in the world successfully to have tried and convicted persons for the crime of genocide. And yet these trials are all of recent vintage, involving crimes committed in the Balkans in the 1990s.[20] No perpetrator of Nazi-era atrocities, by contrast, has ever been charged with genocide by a German court, this despite the fact that the incrimination was incorporated into the German legal code as far back as 1954. German courts are also among the few domestic national courts to have experience with trying persons for crimes against humanity. And yet here we encounter a fresh oddity: these latter trials are all *old* cases, conducted by German courts in occupation zones in the late 1940s. The assumption of sovereignty by the Federal Republic marked the abrupt end of trials involving crimes against humanity in West German courts (although they continued in East Germany).[21] And so we encounter the anomalous fact that no Nazi perpetrator or accomplice has been tried before a domestic court in the Federal Republic for genocide or crimes against humanity in over six decades. Adding to the anomaly is the fact that crimes against humanity and genocide were fashioned, as Arendt reminds us, as incriminations designed to facilitate the prosecution of Nazi-like atrocities. All the more curious, then, that German[22] courts have consistently refused or failed to use the very incriminations designed to facilitate the prosecution of Nazi atrocities.

The answer to our riddle lies in the principle of retroactivity. German jurists long ago concluded that because crimes against humanity and genocide were recognised as crimes only after 1945, their use by German courts against former Nazis would violate the *Rückwirkungsverbot* (the bar against retroactivity), anchored both in the German Basic Law (GG Artikel 103, Abs 2) and in the Criminal Law, where it appears as the first and most fundamental norm (§ 1 StGB).[23] And yet the answer does less to settle the matter than it begs the question. Bars against retroactivity are familiar to virtually all theories of jurisprudence and legal systems. Montesquieu and Beccaria describe the bar as a basic requirement of

[20] See, eg, the case of *Public Prosecutor v Djajic*, Bayerisches Oberstes Landesgericht, 23 May 1997, and the discussion in L Reydams, *Universal Jurisdiction: International and Municipal Legal Perspectives* (Oxford, Oxford University Press, 2003) 150–57.

[21] See A Weinke, *Die Verfolgung von NS-Tätern im geteilten Deutschland. Vergangenheitsbewältigungen 1949–1969 oder: Eine deutsch-deutsche Beziehungsgeschichte im Kalten Krieg* (Paderborn, Schöningh, 2002).

[22] Unless otherwise indicated, the term 'German' refers to the courts and laws of the Federal Republic.

[23] *Grundgesetz für die Bundesrepublik Deutschland, vom 23.5.1949, veröffentlichte und bereinigte Fassung. Zuletzt geändert durch Gesetz vom 21.7.2010*, BGBl I, 944.

justice, and the German legal theorist Feuerbach is credited with formulating the principle into the Latin maxims dutifully committed to memory by all students of international law: *nullum crimen sine lege, nulla poena sine lege.*[24] Yet French jurists, operating in a civil law system that takes the bar against retroactivity every bit as seriously as the German, found the bar as raising no obstacle to trying Klaus Barbie, the so-called 'Butcher of Lyon', and Maurice Papon, the former senior police official in the Vichy Government and later French Budget Minister, for crimes against humanity.[25]

Certainly many German jurists in the post-war era understandably associated the complete collapse of liberal legality under Nazism with Nazi jurists' attack on the bar against retroactivity. This began as early as March 1933 with the passage of the *Gesetz über Verhängung und Vollzug der Todesstrafe*, the notorious law that retroactively introduced the death penalty for the crime of arson, thus enabling the execution of the alleged *Reichstag* arsonist, Marinus van der Lubbe.[26] Carl Schmitt offered a jurisprudential gloss on the attack on the *Rückwirkungsverbot*, arguing in 1935 (a decade before he would rediscover its attractions) that *nulla poena* had transformed the German criminal code into a 'Magna Charta des Verbrechens', as it limited the ability of German law to be flexible and adaptive.[27] Schmitt's broadside against *nulla poena* found echoes in the writings of other legal theorists, who similarly sought to liberate Nazi jurisprudence from what they termed the straitjacket of liberal positivism. The Federal Republic's overly rigorous application of the ban on retroactivity can, at least in part, be understood as an attempt to exorcise the ghost of Nazism from the body of German law.

But only in part. Also playing a role were highly contentious political struggles over the Nazi past that played themselves out in the early years of the Federal Republic. Symptomatic was the backlash against Nuremberg and the Allied trial program in Germany. Although supported by the German public at the time of its original staging, the Nuremberg trial experienced a dramatic erosion of support and perceived legitimacy in Germany in the late 1940s and early 1950s. A sharpening of the *nulla poena* debate was both cause and consequence of the turn against the Allies' trial program.[28] This was all of a piece with a messy and often conscious instrumentalisation of the term 'war crimes trial', as revanchist jurists

[24] See KS Gallant, *The Principle of Legality in International and Comparative Criminal Law* (Cambridge, Cambridge University Press, 2008). Technically speaking, *nulla poena* includes, in addition to the bar against retroactivity, a bar against 'analogical' jurisprudence, and a stipulation of statutory precision in the specification of a crime. Although the last of these played a role in some arguments detailed in this essay, the largest debates involved the question of retroactivity.

[25] R Golsan (ed), *The Papon Affair: Memory and Justice on Trial* (London, Routledge, 2000).

[26] See I Müller, *Hitler's Justice: The Courts of the Third Reich* (Cambridge, Mass, Harvard University Press, 1992) 27–35.

[27] C Schmitt, 'Der Führer schütz das Recht. Zur Reichstagsrede Adolf Hitlers vom 13. Juli 1934', *Deutsche Juristen-Zeitung* 39 (1934), 1947. See also B Rüthers, *Entartetes Recht: Rechtslehren und Kronjuristen im Dritten Reich* (München, DTV, 1994).

[28] See M Broszat, 'Siegerjustiz oder strafrechtliche "Selbstreinigung"' (1981) 29 *Vierteljahrshefte für Zeitgeschichte* 477.

and politicians in the Federal Republic came to conflate acts of extermination and atrocity with acts of armed conflict.[29] The fact that the *Rückwirkungsverbot* came to bar the use of crimes against humanity and genocide against former Nazis did not, then, follow ineluctably from a sober application of legal logic. Rather, it served clear political interests that sought to liberate the Federal Republic—and its statesman—from a vexatious and often inconvenient preoccupation with past crimes. Here we need only recall that thousands of former Nazi jurists—from the lowest judicial officer to judges on the nation's highest courts—enjoyed successful legal careers in the Federal Republic.[30]

And yet as a result of the *nulla poena* controversy, the most serious crime that a perpetrator of Nazi atrocity could be tried with in the Federal Republic was murder. This remains the case. Whatever else we might say about this restriction, it had disastrous consequences for the trial of Holocaust crimes in German courts. Acts of genocide had to be juridically digested through the category of simple murder, with this incrimination's specific statutory peculiarities. Two deserve special attention. As a statutory matter, *Mord* (murder) is distinguished from *Totschlag* (manslaughter) in that murder is the killing of a 'human being out of … base motives [*niedrige Beweggründe*], maliciously [*Grausam*] or treacherously [*heimtückisch*]'.[31] As the statute of limitations on manslaughter had expired within a decade of the war's end, German prosecutors could indict only in cases of killings motivated by base motives or demonstrating malice or treachery, thus dramatically restricting the universe of perpetrators who could be tried for Nazi atrocities.[32]

As a second matter, German law long drew a strong, indeed bizarre, distinction between the perpetrator (*Täter*) and the accessory (*Gehilfe*), limiting the former to acts in which a criminal evinced 'individual initiative' in his criminal activity.[33] As a consequence, the physical act of killing—the act, say, of pulling the trigger—did not necessarily make a killer a perpetrator in German law. Only if it was found that one killed, or authorised killing, out of base motives (or maliciously or treacherously) *and* demonstrated personal initiative, could one be convicted as a perpetrator of murder under German law. These statutory restrictions limited the universe of perpetrators to the point that it often appeared that, for the purposes of German law, Nazi

[29] See N Frei, *Vergangenheitspolitik: Die Anfänge der Bundesrepublik und die NS-Vergangenheit* (München, DTV, 1999).

[30] J Reinhold, *Der Wiederaufbau der Justiz in Nordwestdeutschland 1945 bis 1949* (Königstein, Athenaum, 1979) 103ff, 130ff.

[31] § 211 StGB, available at <http://www.gesetze-im-internet.de/stgb/__211.html> (accessed 11 February 2011).

[32] See D Pendas, *The Frankfurt Auschwitz Trial, 1963–1965: Genocide, History and the Limits of Law* (Cambridge, Cambridge University Press, 2006) 56–61. Also K Freudiger, *Die Juristische Aufarbeitung der NS-Verbrechen* (Tübingen, Mohr Siebeck, 2002) 138–42.

[33] For a discussion that this limitation placed on German trials of Nazi criminals, see H Friedlander, 'Nazi Crimes and German Law' in N Stoltzfuss and H Friedlander (eds), *Nazi Crimes and the Law* (Cambridge, Cambridge University Press, 2008) 15–34.

genocide was perpetrated by only three men: Hitler, Himmler and Heydrich.[34] Precious few participants in the genocidal machine could be considered guilty of murder, and the vast majority of those who did satisfy this first condition could be found guilty only as accessories.

Not only did this drastically restrict the reach of the criminal law, it also badly distorted the picture of the perpetrator. For the purposes of German law, those who had served in concentration and death camps could be convicted of murder only if they had behaved as *Exzeßtäter*. Prosecutors had to demonstrate that camp functionaries had engaged in excessive or supererogatory acts of killing, that is, had killed without orders to do so, or, to put it another way, had killed in violation of even the law in effect under the Nazis.[35] Ironically, then, post-war German law essentially employed SS standards of legality in evaluating the conduct of those who served in concentration and death camps, limiting the crime of murder to individuals who could have been condemned by the SS's own courts.

Arendt was keenly aware of the gaps and distortions this produced at the Frankfurt-Auschwitz trial. 'What the old penal code [*viz*, the statutory definition of murder] failed to take into account,' Arendt notes, 'was nothing less than the everyday reality of Nazi Germany in general and of Auschwitz in particular.'[36] As a result of this insufficiency, 'a man who had caused the death of thousands because he was one of the few whose job it was to throw the gas pellets into the chambers could be criminally less guilty than another man who had killed "only" hundreds, but upon his own initiative and according to his perverted fantasies.'[37] To correct this mangling of legal categories, Arendt insists, '"mass murder and complicity in mass murder" was a charge that could and should be leveled against every single SS man who had ever done duty in any of the extermination camps'.[38] Arendt wrote these words in the mid-1960s, and no German court paid heed—that is, until the Demjanjuk court in Munich.

IV. IVAN THE ACCESSORY

It goes without saying that Demjanjuk was not an architect or a leading implementer of SS policy. As he himself memorably put it at the time of his Jerusalem trial, '[w]hy are you making such a fuss of my matter, like with Eichmann? Eichmann was big, while Ivan is little'.[39] In Munich, his defence tried to paint him as a victim of Nazism—as much a victim, in his attorney's tendentious formulation,

[34] See A Rückerl, *NS-Verbrechen vor Gericht: Versuch einer Vergangenheitsbewältigung* (Heidelberg, CF Müller, 1984) 274–81.

[35] See G Werle and T Wandres, *Auschwitz vor Gericht: Völkermord und bundesdeutsche Strafjustiz* (München, CH Beck, 1995) 31–33.

[36] H Arendt, 'Auschwitz on Trial' in Kohn (ed), above n 11, 243.

[37] *Ibid*.

[38] *Ibid* 243–44.

[39] *Demjanjuk v Israel: Judgment of the Supreme Court*, 381.

as Jewish survivors of Sobibor such as Thomas Blatt, who testified as a witness for the prosecution. However absurd this claim, it is true that Demjanjuk was first drafted into the Soviet Red Army, was taken as a prisoner of war by the Wehrmacht; and only after landing in a POW camp was he recruited, along with other Ukrainian and Baltic POWs to be trained at Trawniki, the SS *Ausbildungslager*, for service as a death camp guard. As a *Trawniki* trained *Wachmann* (guard), Demjanjuk occupied the bottom rung in the official death camp hierarchy. He does not appear to have distinguished himself through his cruelty; if he did, no material evidence indicated this. In fact, the Munich trial was able to adduce scant evidence showing exactly what Demjanjuk did at Sobibor, beside the evidence that demonstrated, incontestably, that he served there as a guard.[40]

These facts return us to the question that haunted the proceeding: why *was* Demjanjuk tried? What purpose did the trial serve? If Arendt believed that the classical goals of retribution, correction and deterrence imperfectly apply to atrocity trials, these reservations would seem to apply with all the greater force in the case of a low-level perpetrator, now in his ninety-second year, whose crimes were committed two generations ago. But if Arendt implicitly problematises the proceeding, she also helps us locate its importance—on the level of legal idiom. As a juridical matter, the framing of a proper legal idiom conventionally is conceived as a means of enabling prosecution. At Nuremberg, for example, the concept of crimes against humanity was designed to plug juridical gaps—legal interstices—not formally covered by war crimes. In the Demjanjuk trial, the obverse phenomenon came into play. Instead of a novel idiom serving as a means of enabling a trial, here a trial served to frame a fresh idiom. In making this claim, I do not mean to purview the motivations of prosecutors and judges; rather, my aim is conceptual: it is to reconstruct a logic that makes an otherwise problematic trial intelligible.

While nominally working within the confines of the statutory construction of murder, the Demjanjuk court in fact achieved something quite radical. In convicting Demjanjuk, it effectively adopted the jurisprudential theory that Arendt defended nearly 50 years ago. Against the defence's argument that no evidence indicated what precise acts *Wachmann* Demjanjuk committed at Sobibor, the prosecution and court answered, *it does not matter.* According to the court's theory, the mere fact that Demjanjuk served as a guard *necessarily* meant that he was an accessory to murder. It should be made clear that this theory was specifically tailored to

[40] This evidence includes Demjanjujk's Trawniki ID that indicates his assignment to Sobibor; a Sobibor Transfer roster, indicating Demjanjuk's transfer from Sobibor back to Trawniki; and the record of interrogations that the Soviets did with another guard, Ignat Danilchenko, who has since died. After being trained at Trawniki and before being assigned to Sobibor, Demjanjuk first served at Majdanek, where there is a record of his being disciplined. After Sobibor, Demjanjuk was assigned as a guard at Flossenbürg; German prosecutors presented the testimony of a fellow Ukrainian guard, Alexander Nagorny, who testified in Munich, and also presented several documents, including the Flossenbürg transfer roster, the assignment of weapons to the guards, and a list of guard duties, all of which name Demjanjuk. This later evidence does not prove Demjanjuk's assignment to Sobibor, but it does challenge his insistence that he never served as a guard anywhere at any time.

the reality of Sobibor, a pure death camp; it would not and could not apply even in the case of Auschwitz, which maintained a substantial slave labour population. Sobibor was a factory of death pure and simple; its sole purpose was to exterminate. It is worth recalling that of the 1.2 million persons deported to Auschwitz, approximately 100,000 survived. Of the 1.3 million Jews sent to Treblinka, Belzec, and Sobibor, around 120 survived.[41] A guard at such a facility, whether he spent all his time manning a guard tower or escorting Jews to gas chambers, was by necessity an accessory to murder.

The theory was quite simple and its logic is, I believe, irresistible. Still, its embrace by a German court marks a dramatic transformation in the theory and conduct of German atrocity prosecutions. Some may find it regrettable that this change was so long in coming; others might criticise the fact that the new theory was adopted in the prosecution of a Ukrainian *Wachmann* and not in the trial of a German SS camp official. But it cannot be denied that the Demjanjuk trial marks a fundamental conceptual reorientation. Here we need only note that no guard or death camp officer had ever before been convicted in the Federal Republic under the theory adopted in Munich. Whether the theory will prove successful in future prosecutions is beside the point. The importance of this belated jurisprudential understanding is not to be measured in terms of the prosecutions it sponsors or the convictions it secures; its importance, *pace* Arendt, lies in the renewal of judgment as a meaning-positing act.

So let us agree: Demjanjuk himself is an irrelevancy. At stake is the law's belated conceptual reorientation. For decades a fatally misplaced concern with retroactivity forced German trials to torture history by pigeonholing Nazi atrocities into the conventional murder statute; now, while still working within the strictures of murder, the Munich court found a way to accommodate the logic of genocide. The Demjanjuk trial delivered a belated correction to the 'pernicious … understanding' and the 'common illusion' that the 'crime of murder and the crime of genocide are essentially the same'.[42] That the banishing of this illusion should coincide with the passing of the perpetrators is as ironic as it is unsurprising.

[41] T Snyder, *Bloodlands: Europe Between Hitler and Stalin* (New York, Basic Books, 2010) 275–76.
[42] Arendt, above n 4, 272.

Part IV

The Right to Have Rights

16

Between Politics and Law: Hannah Arendt and the Subject of Rights

CHARLES BARBOUR

I. INTRODUCTION

ARGUABLY THE BEST-KNOWN and most frequently cited text in all of Arendt's work—certainly in recent years—is the famous section of *The Origins of Totalitarianism* on 'The Perplexities of the Rights of Man', in which she argues that stateless people and refugees expose the limits of so-called human rights, inasmuch as these rights appear suddenly to vanish at precisely that moment when they might be required or invoked—that is, when one is no longer a citizen of a particular State, but a mere human, or nothing more than a human being. And arguably the most frequently-cited phrase in that text is 'the right to have rights', or the right, as Arendt puts it, to 'belong to some kind of organized community'.[1] But if the phrase 'the right to have rights' is well-known, it has not been especially well-received. More than a few commentators have pointed out its manifest circularity, or the sense in which it seems to place an effect before its cause. How can one have a right, they wonder, before one has any rights? And if one could have such a thing, than would not the same stateless people and refugees who, in Arendt's estimation, reveal the paucity of all universal rights also reveal, and more explicitly reveal, that of 'the right to have rights'? In what sense might it make sense to speak of a right to have rights?

In this essay, I want to offer an account of 'the right to have rights' that locates it within the context of Arendt's treatment of the relationship between politics and the law, especially as it concerns her theory of action. I propose that, for Arendt, a right is not a property or a possession, but a capacity to act, and that we cannot divorce her discussion of rights from her theory of action. Moreover, I contend that, for Arendt, action—and by extension rights—cannot be neatly located either inside or outside of a formally constituted legal order, but emerges, as it were, on the border in-between lawlessness and the law, or the realm of the human and that of the citizen—what, more recently,

[1] H Arendt, *The Origins of Totalitarianism* (Orlando, Harcourt, 1978) 296 (hereafter 'OT').

Giorgio Agamben has dubbed '*zoe*' and '*bios*', or 'bare life' and a 'form of life'.[2] Or, to put the same point differently, according to Arendt, the capacity to act is *both* an ontological given (in that it is related to what she calls 'natality', or the 'new beginning' represented by the birth of each singular human) *and* an existential achievement (in that it requires, or is concomitant with, the creation of what Arendt calls a 'space of appearance', or a space of human plurality). Arendt's extensive consideration of this paradoxical or circular aspect of action provides, I maintain, a framework or basis for interpreting the paradoxical, circular aspects of the phrase 'the right to have rights'.

While Arendt's work has always sparked controversy, and has never been without its detractors, the recent past has also witnessed the emergence of a new set of criticisms—criticisms levelled by a group of contemporary political philosophers who want to challenge what they see as the soft pluralism and nascent institutionalism inherent in her approach. For some, such as Alain Badiou, this involves returning in a surprising and iconoclastic manner to 'the politics of truth'—of axioms and statements rather than opinions and debates.[3] For others, like Jacques Rancière, it means rethinking the subject of rights, and characterising politics as that which concerns not the citizens of a constituted order, but what he calls 'the part that has no part', or those whose undeniable presence disrupts every order.[4] Here I want to suggest that the vehemence of these critiques of Arendt overshadows what Rancière in particular might take away from her project. While I agree with Andrew Schaap's assessment that Rancière is not, as Schaap puts it, 'a closet Arendtian',[5] or committed to Arendtian principles in spite of himself, I nevertheless believe there is something to be gained by thinking of Arendt as 'a closet Rancierian', or that elements of her work inform elements of his.

II. ACTION AND THE LAW

It is unfortunate that even among extremely sophisticated political thinkers, 'The Perplexities of the Rights of Man' is often read in isolation—excised not only from the rest of *The Origins of Totalitarianism*, but from the rest of Arendt's career as well. For unless it is provided with some context, this relatively short piece could easily be misconstrued as an uncomplicated, straightforward defence of institutions, or any formally constituted legal order. In other words, if we focus exclusively on 'The Perplexities of the Rights of Man', and allow it to stand in for Arendt's

[2] G Agamben, *Homo Sacer: Sovereign Power and Bare Life* (D Heller-Roazen trans) (Stanford, Cal, Stanford University Press, 1998).

[3] A Badiou, 'Against Political Philosophy' in A Badiou, *Metapolitics* (J Barker trans) (London, Verso, 2005).

[4] J Rancière, 'Who is the Subject of the Rights of Man?' (2004) 103(2) *South Atlantic Quarterly* 197.

[5] A Schaap, 'Enacting the Right to Have Rights: Jacques Rancière's Critique of Hannah Arendt' (2011) 10(1) *European Journal of Political Theory* 22, 37.

work in general, or allow it to become what Susannah Young-ah Gottlieb calls a 'synecdoche ... for her entire political thought',[6] we could be misled into believing that Arendt wants to locate politics entirely within the law, and that she sees no possibility for action, or for the benefits of public life, without the prior establishment of the law. As I hope to show here, however, Arendt's position is hardly this simple. And there is more to be gained from considering a greater portion of her work than from using 'The Perplexities of the Rights of Man' as a foil, or as a tool for constructing an alternative to 'Arendtianism'.

The effort to contextualise 'The Perplexities of the Rights of Man' could head in an inexhaustible number of directions, from its location at the very end of Arendt's long consideration of 'Imperialism', to its relationship with Arendt's biography and her own experience of statelessness. But in this essay I want to remain, initially at least, within the realm of political and legal theory, and with what we might call Arendt's 'major' texts—those which she published in her lifetime, and which have since received a significant amount of critical attention, with particular emphasis on *The Human Condition* and *On Revolution*. I do so because, while I want to suggest that Arendt's position is complex, I do not want to suggest that it is arcane, or that, up until now, it has somehow been hidden from view. On the contrary, Arendt set out her opposition to institutionalism, and to any exclusively juridical or constitutional conception of the public sphere, in documents that are themselves entirely public and available to almost anyone who chooses to read them.

The general framework for my interpretation of Arendt's career is indebted to a recent article by Peg Birmingham, entitled 'On Action: The Appearance of the Law'. Here Birmingham proposes that, between *The Human Condition* and *On Revolution*, there is a kind of break in Arendt's work, and especially in her treatment of the law. If, in the former, Arendt relies on a recognisably Greek model of the law as a wall or a border, and thus something that can be established only by a sovereign decision, in the latter, she adopts a more Roman conception of law as alliance, or as something that emerges not out of a decision, but out of political *praxis*. Inasmuch as it emerges out of politics, Arendt concludes, law can also be altered by politics, or by human action.[7] In other words, not just violence and sacrifice, but words and deeds constitute the law.

While I am not entirely certain that this break is as sharp as Birmingham implies, I nevertheless agree that Arendt's work represents an alternative to the Schmittian theory of the exception, and that it reveals the copious space that exists between the law and its suspension. Drawing on Birmingham's insights, I propose that, in her earlier work, and especially *The Human Condition*, Arendt develops a complex *topography* of the law, or of the relationship between politics or action and the law. In the

[6] S Young-ah Gottlieb, *Regions of Sorrow: Anxiety and Messianism in Hannah Arendt and WH Auden* (Stanford, Cal, Stanford University Press, 2003) 34.

[7] P Birmingham, 'On Action: The Appearance of the Law' in A Yeatman, P Hansen, M Zolkos and C Barbour (eds), *Action and Appearance: Ethics and the Politics of Writing in Hannah Arendt* (London, Continuum, 2011) 103, 115.

later work, on the other hand, she supplements this topography with a *temporality*, or an account of the relationship between the event of the revolutionary act and the duration of the laws that it constitutes. The result is a kind of political ontology, or a model of the space and the time of the political, that might serve as a ground for our understanding of 'the right to have rights'.

The simplest gloss of 'The Perplexities of the Rights of Man' would treat it as a reinvention of Edmund Burke's argument that we cannot have rights as humans but only as members of some particular, limited national or political community—an argument to which Arendt explicitly refers, although not without some measure of irony.[8] Outside of such a community, Arendt seems to suggest, in what she calls the 'mere givenness' of our natural existence, humans are essentially different and discrete. Inside of one, on the other hand, they are able to construct an artificial 'second nature', or a world in which they can meet one another as equals, capable of articulating their own opinions and making meaningful judgements about the opinions of others. In this interpretation, 'the right to have rights' would be nothing more than a right to belong to an order or a State—a right, in other words, to something more than a natural existence, or a right to a form of life that has been conventionally arranged.

That Arendt would reject such a reading is already signalled—however minimally—in 'The Perplexities of the Rights of Man' itself, where she notes that no matter how organised a political community might be, it is always, as it were, threatened by that which lies outside of it and by the 'mere givenness' that it endeavours to exclude. 'Since the Greeks,' Arendt writes, 'we have known that highly developed political life breeds … a deep resentment against the disturbing miracle contained in the fact that each of us is made as he is—single, unique, unchangeable. The whole sphere of the merely given,' she continues, 'is a permanent threat to the public sphere, because the public sphere is as consistently based on the law of equality as the private sphere is based on the law of universal difference and differentiation'.[9] Thus, already in 'The Perplexities of the Rights of Man', there is a sense in which, even while it gets excluded from the public sphere, the 'disturbing miracle' of 'mere givenness', or the singularity of each human birth, is also included in the form of a threat—indeed, a 'permanent threat'.

The topology, then, of inclusion and exclusion, citizen and human, or the one who is a member of an 'organized community' and the one who is a member of nothing more than humanity as such, is considerably more tangled than it appears at first glance. And this complexity is developed much further in *The Human Condition*, which was first published seven years after *The Origins of Totalitarianism*, in 1958. Here Arendt associates politics, not with institutions, but with action, or the uniquely human ability to begin something new. She distinguishes, as is well known, between work and action. Whereas work involves creating an object, and

8 OT 296.
9 *Ibid* 301.

is typically conducted in isolation, action involves performing before an audience, and has no objective remains, save the memory and the judgement of others. Thus Arendt associates action with what she calls a 'space of appearance'. And she insists that this space 'comes into being wherever men are together in the manner of speech and action', and thus 'predates all formal constitution of the public realm and the various forms of government' or 'the various forms in which the public realm can be organized'.[10] In this sense, then, politics precedes the law. It is already 'there', or potentially there, as soon as humans appear before one another.

But, for Arendt, this does not mean that politics can be entirely divorced from the law, or that it can remain independent of every regulating limit. Rather, according to the position Arendt proffers in *The Human Condition*, politics or action and the law exist in a kind of interminable and unstable tension with one another. On the one hand, Arendt says, action is essentially 'boundless' and 'unpredictable.' It operates by creating new relations between people, and thereby creating new public spaces, as well as new forms of power. On the other hand, she continues, this process is inherently insecure; for action has a tendency to exceed the public space that it creates. The law functions as a boundary or a wall that encloses the space of action in order to protect it—from external enemies, to be certain, but also from action itself. As Arendt puts it, 'action not only has the most intimate relationship to the public part of the world common to us all, but is the one activity which constitutes it'. But this public world 'could not endure' or 'survive the moment of action and speech itself' without what Arendt calls the 'stabilizing protection' of 'the wall of the *polis* and the boundaries of the law'.[11]

Quite clearly, then, Arendt does not believe that action can emerge only within the bounds of a formally-constituted legal order. And, quite clearly, her conception of action is designed to repudiate this kind of institutionalism, or any suggestion that only citizens can engage meaningfully in politics. Rather, on Arendt's account, action constitutes a public world, or is coextensive with a public world, while the law encircles it, or establishes the boundaries that, almost by definition, the 'boundlessness' and 'unpredictability' of action is destined to challenge again. Action, in other words, both conditions and threatens the law—making it possible on the one hand and impossible on the other. Or, to put the matter differently, action opens up a space in-between law and life, or the *bios* of the recognised citizen and the *zoe* of the mere human, or 'bare life'. Rather than a decision separating law and its exception, action creates ever-new relations and connections, and thus power—which, as Arendt explains in her essay *On Violence*, 'corresponds to the human ability not just to act but to act in concert' and 'is never the property of an individual' but 'belongs to a group and remains in existence only so long as the group keeps together'.[12]

[10] H Arendt, *The Human Condition* (Chicago, Ill, University of Chicago Press, 1998) 199 (hereafter 'HC').

[11] *Ibid* 198.

[12] H Arendt, *On Violence* (San Diego, Cal, Harcourt, 1970) 44.

This line of thought is extended, as well as altered, in *On Revolution*, which first appeared in 1963, five years after *The Human Condition*. Like many of Arendt's books, *On Revolution* has been mired in controversy since its publication, particularly for its treatment of Marxism, and for its very rigid distinction between the social and the political, or the realm of necessity and that of freedom. As is well known, Arendt organises *On Revolution* as a comparison of two revolutionary traditions, one extending back to the American experience, and the other to the French. The first, Arendt suggests, was initially more promising, it not exactly more successful, because it endeavoured to constitute a new space of freedom, or political action. The second, on the other hand, despite the fact that it would become the model for more than a century of subsequent revolutionary events, was inherently flawed. For it sought not to constitute a space of freedom, but to liberate humanity from necessity—and especially from the destitution of the poor. It consequently took on the character not of a sequence of free acts, but of a desperate effort to keep pace, as it were, with the forces of necessity, whether that meant the irresistible movement of the masses, or the irresistible march of history.

It seems to me that, despite the vehemence of the debates that were sparked by Arendt's distinction between the social and the political, the more interesting aspect of *On Revolution* is its consideration of the relationship between politics and law, or the event of revolutionary action, and the new order it is designed to create. The American Revolution is more compelling for Arendt, not because its instigators realised that political freedom can be achieved only inasmuch as it gets separated from the problem of social liberation—or what, following the political economists of the nineteenth century, Arendt calls 'the social question'—but because, in the crucible of the event, they came to realise that their aim was not to liberate themselves from arbitrary taxation but to generalise the experience of the revolution itself—the experience, that is to say, of freedom, or of constituting new beginnings. How, then, can the event that creates the new order be sustained in that order? How can newness itself endure?

In 'On Action', Birmingham proposes that the shift in Arendt's conception of the law, from the Greek model of the wall to the Roman notion of alliance, was the result, in part, of her reading of Walter Benjamin, and particularly Benjamin's 'Critique of Violence'—the essay in which Benjamin posits his enigmatic, almost gnomic concept of 'divine violence', setting it off against 'mythic violence', which entails an endless dialectic or oscillation between 'law-making' and 'law-preserving' violence, or the kind of violence that constitutes order, and the kind that defends it.[13] She argues that, somewhat furtively, Arendt borrows this distinction between mythic and divine violence, but recasts it as the difference between violence and power, or what Birmingham calls 'the deadly force of instrumental violence' and 'the living spirit of power'.[14] In this interpretation, which Birmingham attributes to

[13] W Benjamin, 'Theses on the Philosophy of History' in W Benjamin, *Illuminations* (H Zohn trans) (New York, Schocken, 1968).

[14] Birmingham, above n 7, 105.

Arendt, if 'mythic violence' is a means to an end (whether that end is the creation or the protection of the law), 'divine violence' is the enigma of pure means without end—or, in more concrete terms, an order that is infused at each moment with the miracle of its beginnings.

While Birmingham does not put it this way, her reading suggests that what we find in Arendt's later work is not a topology, or a spatial formulation of the relationship between politics and law, but a temporality, or a way of thinking the time of politics and the time of law. The question is less one of the inside and the outside, or what gets included and what gets excluded by law's boundary, than of means and ends, or the event and its duration. In this sense, and in order to expand on Birmingham's characterisation of Arendt's debt to Benjamin, we might propose that it is not only the 'Critique of Violence' that informs her later work, but his 'Theses on the Philosophy of History' as well, and especially the famous notion of 'the time of the now' that he advances there—in which 'every second of time' is 'the strait gate through which the messiah might enter'.[15] The time of revolution that Arendt wants to depict is not what Benjamin calls 'homogeneous, empty time', or a totality that holds together past, present and future, thus making history rational or complete, but, as Arendt puts it in the title of a collection of essays that span what Birmingham characterises as the break in her career, 'between past and future'.

The same temporality is no doubt operative in Arendt's frequent discussions of the performative character of political action, or the sense in which, as in performing arts, the political act creates no objective remains but exhausts itself in its expression—or, as Arendt puts it in her essay 'What is Freedom?', the sense in which, in both the performing arts and politics, 'the accomplishment lies in the performance itself and not in the end product'.[16] Action, then, is extracted from the logic of means and ends, or the logic that, for Benjamin, characterises both mythic violence and homogeneous, empty time. It is 'miraculous', as Arendt occasionally puts it, because it is not the expression of an essence, or even the fulfilment of a potential, but something on the order of an event. And inasmuch as any legal order keeps open the possibility or the space of action, it is infused with the spirit of its founding moment—the revolutionary spirit, or the ever-present possibility of the new.

III. THE PERFORMANCE OF RIGHTS

In an important recent paper on Hannah Arendt and Jacques Rancière, Andrew Schaap argues vigorously that Arendt's 'right to have rights' can only really apply to those who, as speaking animals, are in some sense destined for politics from the

[15] *Ibid* 264.

[16] H Arendt, 'What is Freedom?' in H Arendt, *Between Past and Future: Eight Exercises in Political Thought* (New York, Penguin, 1993) 153 (hereafter 'BPF').

outset, or destined to have an audible political voice. Rancière, on the other hand, provides an analysis of rights that presupposes, indeed axiomatically presupposes, what Arendt takes to be the achievement of human interaction—namely equality. If, for Arendt, politics involves 'world-disclosing public action through which individuals reveal their humanness … in the presence of equals', for Rancière it entails 'the staging of a dissensus in which those who are deemed to lack speech make themselves heard'. And if Arendt constructs rights 'as a precondition for politics' inasmuch as they 'institutionalize an artificial equality that is constitutive of the public sphere', Rancière understands them in terms of 'contesting political exclusion by *enacting* equality' or 'the enactment of equality within the conditions of inequality'.[17] Taking the struggles of the *sans papiers* in France as his principal example, Schaap maintains that it is what he calls 'the performative dimension' of radical political action that 'eludes a consistent Arendtian analysis', or a consistent application of her principles. 'By acting *as if* they have the rights that they lack,' Schaap concludes, 'the *sans papiers* actualize their political equality'.[18]

It would be difficult to deny that Arendt and Rancière are at odds when it comes to the question of equality. Whereas Arendt treats it as something that must be constructed, and as a particularly fragile construction at that, Rancière takes it to be axiomatic—something that needs to be neither created nor proven, only asserted and, in being asserted, enacted. At the same time, the claim that Arendt somehow misses 'the performative dimension' of politics, or the element of what we might call political make-believe (the 'as if', as Schaap says), seems a little hasty. For surely one of the central features of Arendt's understanding of action is its performative dimension, or what many Arendt scholars call the 'dramaturgy' of public life. And surely anyone who, like Arendt, derives a politics not from Kant's Second Critique, but from his Third, is aware of the role of the imagination, and of the 'as if', in political discourse and events. In this section, I should like to begin by proposing that, while a great deal of his analysis is sound, and cannot easily be circumvented, Schaap makes the error of thinking that, for Arendt, a right is something like a property or possession, rather than a capacity to act. In positioning Arendt as an essentialist, or someone committed to an Aristotelian conception of potential and actual, or what he calls 'flourishing', Schaap overlooks the sense in which 'the right to have rights' is also an enactment of equality—something that exists only inasmuch as it is practised, or asserted and performed.

A very common interpretation of 'the right to have rights'—an interpretation that, following Frank Michelman, Schaap quickly, and I think correctly, rules out—suggests that it is ethical or normative, or the moment when, whether or not she is fully aware of it, Arendt places an ethical framework around the political. Thus, for example, Selya Benhabib insists that there is an 'asymmetry', as she puts it, between the first and the second use of the term 'right' in Arendt's phrase.

[17] Schaap, above n 5, 23.
[18] *Ibid* 30.

While the second connotes the rights of the citizen, or political rights in general, the first must refer to what Benhabib calls 'a moral claim to membership', or a claim to 'recognition' of '[o]ne's status as a rights-bearing person'.[19] But resolving the circularity of 'the right to have rights' in this fashion has at least one crucial drawback—it serves to dislocate it from political action, or from the capacity to act that, in Arendt's work, characterises every other meaningful right. It has the potential to transform 'the right to have rights' into a passive experience of being recognised, rendering it politically neutral.

That Arendt associates rights with action is already apparent in 'The Perplexities of the Rights of Man', where she emphatically privileges the kinds of rights that allow one to engage in politics over all others. Thus, Arendt insists that, whatever other supposed rights one might lose, '[t]he fundamental deprivation of human rights is manifested first and above all in the deprivation of a place in the world which makes opinions significant and actions effective.' Thus stateless people and refugees 'are deprived, not of the right to freedom [here understood in the conventional liberal sense of the word, and not in the sense given to it by Arendt in her essay 'What is Freedom?', which is to say public rather than private freedom], but of the right to action; not of the right to think whatever they please, but of the right to opinion'.[20]

One approach to these comments—the one, I think, that Schaap and Rancière assume—is to suggest that, in them, Arendt is proposing that, inasmuch as they have been expelled from one political community, the stateless are politically impotent, or incapable of any action whatsoever. But it seem to me that when Arendt talks about 'the right to have rights', she is referring precisely to the possibility of action and politics that remains *after* one has been expelled from a particular legal order—the capacity to act that remains, as it were, outside of the legal order, or on the border in-between law and lawlessness. For, as seen above, in other texts Arendt is very clear that action requires nothing more than, and indeed is concomitant with, a 'space of appearances', and that this space takes shape not only within the bounds of the law, but anywhere humans come together in word and deed.

Beyond the passages from *The Human Condition* analysed in the previous section of this essay, one striking example from Arendt's work stands out—namely her discussion of Rene Char and the French Resistance in the preface to her collection *Between Past and Future.* Because, in it, Arendt calls into question many of the easy distinctions and oppositions upon which she is generally believed to have insisted, and generally criticised (by both her supporters and her detractors), it is worth quoting the text at length. Here Arendt refers to the peculiar sense of melancholy—the '*epasseur triste*' or 'sad opaqueness'—that Char claims to have experienced at the end

[19] S Benhabib, '"The Right to Have Rights": Hannah Arendt on the Contradictions of the Nation-State', in S Benhabib, *The Rights of Others: Aliens, Residents and Citizens* (Cambridge, Cambridge University Press, 2008) 57.

[20] OT 297.

of the war, and thus of the Resistance as well. It was, Char says, as though they had lost a 'treasure'. 'What was this treasure?' Arendt then wonders, and proceeds to respond to her own question while quoting bits of Char:

> As they themselves understood it, it seems to have consisted, as if were, of two interconnected parts: they had discovered that he who 'joined the Resistance found himself', that he ceased to be 'in quest of [himself] without mastery, in naked unsatisfaction', that he no longer suspected himself of 'insincerity', of being 'a carping, suspicious actor of life', that he could afford 'to go naked'. In this nakedness, stripped of all masks—of those which society assigns to its members as well as those which the individual fabricates for himself in his psychological reactions against society—they had been visited for the first time in their lives by an apparition of freedom … because they … had taken the initiative upon themselves and therefore, without knowing or even noticing it, had begun to create that public space between themselves where freedom could appear, [or] a public realm where—without the paraphernalia of officialdom and hidden from the eyes of friend and foe—all relevant business in the affairs of the country was transacted in word and deed.[21]

This story opens up Arendt's work in a number of fascinating ways, revealing, I think, the limits of the standard interpretations. For, in other places, Arendt seems to be adamant that one cannot, indeed should not, 'go naked' in the political realm—that politics requires costumes and masks, or the '*personae*' that, at one and the same time, conceal our private self and amplify our public voice.[22] She also seems adamant that we cannot hope to 'find ourselves' in public life, and that intimate passions—such as pity and love—are both perverted by and perverting of politics.[23] Nevertheless, here Char is not only seen to cross these boundaries, but he is also celebrated for doing so.

I should like to propose that, in this example, Char and the Resistance figures to whom Arendt refers are enacting what she means by 'the right to have rights', or the right, beyond every established order and law, to belong to a meaningful political community or a meaningful community of freedom. Thus, despite living under occupation, and despite living in a country where politics has been utterly transformed into violence, the men and women of the Resistance manage to compose a real public sphere—one that, even while it is a clandestine public sphere, composed and operated in secret, and even though it has exactly no access to the mechanisms of the State and no protection of the law, is able, somehow and enigmatically, to transact 'all relevant business in the affairs of the country'.

That, for Arendt, the right to have rights, or the capacity to act, is universal, and not the possession or the vocation of a limited number of 'speaking animals', as Schaap puts it, seems undeniable, at least at the theoretical level. For, on Arendt's account, it is not merely the case that each individual possesses the ability to act or to begin something new. Rather, and far more fundamentally, inasmuch as they

[21] BPF 2–3.
[22] H Arendt, *On Revolution* (New York, Penguin, 1990) 106–07 (hereafter 'OR').
[23] HC 52–53, 242.

are born, or as a result of what Arendt calls the miracle of 'natality', each singular human *is* a new beginning. The practical expression of this principle of universality is most explicit, perhaps, in Arendt's defence of revolutionary councils, and direct as opposed to representative democracy. For Arendt, the American Revolution failed precisely inasmuch as it abandoned the former in the name of the latter. For while representative democracy can achieve what Arendt calls a 'certain control of rulers by those who are ruled', only the latter allows for 'the power that arises out of joint action and deliberation'.[24] Or, alternatively, while representative democracy makes it possible, and even likely, to 'mistake civil liberties for political freedom', council democracy is based on the assumption that 'political freedom, generally speaking, means the right to be a participator in government or it means nothing'.[25] As Arendt frequently points out, not everyone will take up the task of political action, certainly not at all times. But every individual can.

In this sense, despite their very different approaches to the word equality, the kinds of democracy that Arendt and Rancière advocate have at least something in common. It would not be too much of a stretch to say that Rancière's most significant contribution to contemporary political theory, democratic theory in particular, is not so much his suggestion that democracy involves dissensus and disagreement rather than the unified will of a homogeneous people (many other thinkers make this same point, including Arendt), but that it involves not the rule of everyone, or even that of the majority, but the rule of anyone at all—that it has more in common with the picking of lots than it does with the casting of votes.[26] Here equality refers not to a formal legal equality, or equality before the law, but an equal capacity to act. And there is little doubt that, while she might not be inclined to call it 'equality', Arendt would agree that this is a universal capacity—that literally anyone may take up the task of appearing before others in word and deed, and that not some natural essence or predetermined predilection for glory but the completely unpredictable nature of action itself—or the unpredictable interplay of virtue and fortune—will determine who does so.

IV. CONCLUSION

In what is perhaps the most unusual, and strangely revealing, moment in his criticism of Arendt, Rancière identifies her with the perspective he calls 'archi-political'.[27] From this perspective, exemplified by Plato's division of his republic into producers, warriors and rulers, politics involves the complete organisation of the social field, or the relegation of every one to a pre-ordained social part, and thus the exclusion or the erasure of what Rancière calls 'the part that has no

[24] OR 296.
[25] *Ibid* 218.
[26] J Rancière, *Hatred of Democracy* (S Corcoran trans) (London, Verso, 2006).
[27] Rancière, above n 4, 299.

part'—which is also the part that constitutes the proper subject of politics.[28] While he does not really elaborate on this claim, Rancière seems to be suggesting that, despite her explicit distaste for Plato, and for any effort to understand the world of human affairs in terms of philosophical truth rather than political opinion, Arendt also sought to divide up society, or to impose what Rancière would call a single 'distribution of the sensible'.[29] Inasmuch as she distinguished between the 'mere givenness' of the human and the qualified life of the citizen, Arendt wanted to place a definite frame around the political. And in doing so, Rancière implies, she heralded the end of politics itself.

As I hope to have shown here, however, this reading of Arendt, while compelling at moments, is also limited and incomplete. It begins by focusing our attention greatly if not exclusively on certain passages from 'The Perplexities of the Rights of Man', at the expense of other, often very well-known statements and works. And it operates by ignoring the complexity of what Arendt means by action, and of her treatment of the relationship between politics and the law. For, on Arendt's account, action is never localised in a single sphere or realm but enigmatically conditions and threatens every such realm—being the effect not of a secured legal order, but of what Arendt calls 'natality', or the new beginning that, before everything else, each human already 'is'. Attending to this larger understanding of action does not, of course, allow us to suggest a homology between Arendt and Rancière. It does not suggest that, as Schaap put it, Rancière is a 'closet Arendtian'. But it does suggest that, on some issues if not others, the two thinkers can be placed in proximity to one another, often in ways that cast new light, or new patterns of light and shadow, across each.

The argument that Arendt relies too heavily on extremely rigid distinctions and oppositions is hardly new. It has been made countless times in the past, by friends and foes alike. Thus, and to pick just one example, Benhabib accuses Arendt of what she calls 'phenomenological essentialism', or the assumption that 'each type of human activity has a proper "place" in which it can be carried out'.[30] But, depending on how we read Arendt, it seems to me that this point is routinely overstated. For in the details of her work, and especially in the examples she uses and the stories she recounts, Arendt clearly explores everything that comes in-between the categories and concepts for which she is best known—everything that skirts back and forth across their borders, and that cannot be contained by them. The example of the story about Char recounted above is just one among many, some of which I discuss elsewhere. In any case, it seems to me that, as much as she is a thinker of distinct categories, Arendt is a thinker of that which relates and

[28] J Rancière, *Disagreement: Politics and Philosophy* (J Rose trans) (Minneapolis, University of Minnesota Press, 1999) 69.

[29] J Rancière, *Aesthetics and its Discontents* (S Corcoran trans) (London, Polity, 2009) 25.

[30] S Benhabib, *The Reluctant Modernism of Hannah Arendt* (Thousand Oaks, Cal, Sage, 1996) 123–24.

separates such things, or the in-between that holds them together while holding them apart.

One of those enigmatic in-betweens, I think, is what Arendt calls 'the right to have rights'. For, as the circular construction of the phrase suggests, this right is neither inside nor outside of the law. It is neither a purely positive right or the right of a citizen of a constituted order, nor a fully natural right or a right one possesses by virtue of one's birth. Rather, it is that which makes this distinction both possible and impossible. It allows for the distinction between the qualified life of the citizen and the 'mere givenness' of the human, but it cannot be contained by that distinction. Rather, and like action, the right to have rights exists inasmuch as someone, and perhaps ultimately everyone, is in-between these states, creating public spaces out of the very words and deeds that have the capacity to dismantle them, or that condition and threaten them at one and the same time.

17

Citizens and Persons: Legal Status and Human Rights in Hannah Arendt

JAMES BOHMAN

I. INTRODUCTION

JUDGING FROM THE wealth of the discussion of 'the right to rights', Hannah Arendt's analysis of the perplexities of human rights and the decline of the Nation State still resonates deeply in thinking about a just global order. Writing in the period after two world wars, Arendt called refugees 'the most symptomatic group in contemporary politics'.[1] Displaced from every State and welcome nowhere, such people were a symptom of a fundamental conflict between national sovereignty and the rights of persons who belonged to no political community, much less one that could protect their rights. Arendt argues these persons lack both citizenship rights and human rights, and thus 'the right to have rights', understood in terms of what refugees lacked: membership in a political community.[2] It might seem that the answer to this perplexity might be to establish some form of citizenship beyond the State, but for Arendt that merely repeats the same problem at a higher level, since that world organisation (or even world government) could not guarantee human rights anymore than can the Nation State. As Arendt formulates the problem, the perplexities of human rights are not solved by promoting new laws, new instruments to assure compliance, or even new enforcement mechanisms. Yet Arendt holds that the right to have rights is 'the only human right, the one right without which no other can materialize'.

Refugees are still the most symptomatic group in contemporary politics, but in a sense different from Arendt's analysis of the right to have rights. While many conflicts emerge when the enforcement of human rights is considered, there is now at the very least a variety of functioning human rights institutions, including international and regional courts, and the International Criminal Court. With respect to displaced persons and refugees due to armed conflicts, there are now effective international treaties and formal organisations concerned with issues

[1] H Arendt, *The Origins of Totalitarianism* (New York, Harcourt Brace, 1971) 277 (hereafter 'OT').
[2] *Ibid* 302.

related to refugees and stateless persons, including the Geneva Convention Related to the Status of Refugees and the UN High Commissioner on Refugees. Given the expansion of international law in the post-war period, States are not the only institutions that can, however imperfectly, address the claims of denationalised, stateless and persecuted persons. However, refugees are symptomatic of the present era, to the extent that they are not only 'stateless', but often denied access to political membership. They have membership, but it is insufficient for a worthwhile human life. As such they are forced to migrate, and in so doing they are even more dominated than before. They do not, strictly speaking, lack the 'right to have rights' or membership in a political community; these descriptions seems ill-suited to current forms of vulnerability and 'rightlessness'. They are not so much persecuted as denied entrance; and once they have entered, they have neither documents, nor legal status or citizenship. To assume that their predicament would be made better by citizenship as membership is to deny a now pervasive fact of modern polities: citizens live out their lives with many non-citizens in their midst, many of whom have no legal status. Only properly nested cosmopolitan institutions that preserve human dignity regardless of borders would help them beyond their double bind of domination at home and abroad. Perhaps their situation would be better addressed by Arendt's republicanism; but the point of contrast is more republican, the distinction between citizen and slave, between those with recognised status and those who have none within their State of residence. These changes in the circumstances of politics make it likely that many democracies have become dominators, practising what Walzer calls 'the oldest form of domination', the domination of non-citizens by citizens.

Despite an astronomical increase in numbers of people who live their lives apart from their place of birth, this phenomenon is hardly new. The Greeks had their metics, who were integral to their economic life, and the status of denizenship was widely recognised in Europe and often entailed many enforceable rights, claims and protections. Today, domination, in the sense of falling under the control of another, is, more often than not, due to the difficult circumstances in which many people who lack legal and civil status live in the world today. To have a status, as Hegel remarks, is to be someone; to lack it is to be a nobody, the existence of whom is not even to be counted. As persons with no legal or civil status, these people are often subjected to coercive labour practices, which some consider forms of modern slavery. As John Bowe points out, American agribusiness takes it for granted that existing labour laws and standards do not extend to illegal aliens. This private domination is then reinforced by police violence and threats against illegal agricultural workers, who are constantly under the threat of deportation and State violence due to their lack of legal status.[3] Migration patterns within developing States have produced a similar rise in the numbers who have left their entitlement

[3] See J Bowe, *Nobodies: American Slave Labor and the Dark Side of the Global Economy* (New York, Random House, 2007).

and legal status in their community of origin. In India, for example, millions have migrated internally from rural areas to cities, in which they illegally occupy public lands, such as railway rights of way or public parks. Partha Chatterjee estimates that currently perhaps millions of Indians 'may live in illegal squatter settlements, make illegal use of water and electricity, and other criminal acts'.[4] Both internal and external migrants live without security and are treated as having the status of illegality by territorial States. For many populations within States but without status, the very conditions of life are subject to ongoing negotiation in a complex *modus vivendi*, often punctuated by violence and the threat of imprisonment, deportation and resettlement by political authorities. Illegality is thus a pervasive fact of liberal democracies.

The clear implication of this form of exclusion is that illegal immigrants or destitute persons are silently dominated by those who live in civil society and by the ongoing willingness of governments to ignore many of their own laws, such as those concerning safe labour conditions, minimum wage, and other forms of security from exploitation and violence. When State and local institutions are unwilling or unable to cope with pervasive illegality, the result is the failure of the rule of law in the republican sense, to the extent that the condition of illegality creates a form of law that fails to provide a space for freedom for millions of people. As the treatment of undocumented immigrants in developed countries such as the United States shows, such long-term and open violations of the rule of law do not consist merely in permitting illegal persons to continue residence and then deporting them with or without administrative hearings; they also involve granting an associated implicit permission for employers to engage in open and illegal practices of forced labour and confinement. It is for this reason that those without the appropriate status also lack the power to change their legal situation, while those having this status can unilaterally extinguish whatever statuses the dominated person may currently have.

The appeal to citizenship does not seem to designate a status that provides the basis for the 'right to have rights' as the 'single human right'. But it does deepen the problematic character of citizenship, since citizens now dominate non-citizens, a fact that seems to colour such advancements as the right to asylum, the acceptance rate of which is remarkably low in most Northern countries. As internal migrants in countries like India show so compellingly, having citizenship somewhere can hardly be the basis for claims of inclusion and fair treatment. As compelling as the right to have rights is when thinking about the fate of the sort of stateless person that Arendt has in mind, I shall argue that such a derivation of rights status from some other status is plagued with irresolvable regress problems, since there would also be the right to have the right to have rights. This is because citizenship is after all not the right sort of universal status. As Arendt herself points out, we may generalise the discussion of status by deriving their membership from the

[4] P Chatterjee, *The Politics of the Governed* (New York, Columbia University Press, 2004) 40.

human community as such, a claim which would be intelligibile only if there were something like that World State. I argue instead that Kant is correct: the statuses that bearers of rights have cannot be derived from anything else or prescribed by something else. Republicanism instead suggests that to be statelessness or to lack citizenship is to be a slave; to be treated as having 'no rights but only duties'. Even Kant's formulation is different: 'the right to right' rather than 'the right to have rights'. The right sort of status is thus not something to be granted *qua* citizen but rather the universal status of being a person, that is, a legal status that is the basis for inclusion.

I shall argue for a non-derivable conception of legal person as a universal status, as a response to current dilemmas of membership, in three steps. First, I want to elaborate the philosophical differences between Kant and Arendt, but put them in the context of the republican arguments that they share. While Arendt thinks a world republic would be subject to the same difficulties as the State (and more, because of the lack of freedom is generalised), Kant held that freedom requires fundamental commitments to the rights of persons. Secondly, I develop the republican dimensions of this argument further, once it can be shown that there is a cosmopolitan form of republicanism that sees the rights of persons as central toward achieving non-domination. Lastly, I turn to the issue of legal status, and argue that the various forms of legal protections of the rights of persons, particularly their rights to freedom, are central to any non-statist understanding of a cosmopolitan legal order. In this context, we can sensibly describe the motivations for a cosmopolitan political order that might transform our understanding of personhood without reducing these demands to citizenship in a particular State. In a certain sense this will vindicate Arendt's claim that there is no way to think of human rights 'independent of all specific political statuses and deriving solely from the fact of being human'.[5] Although it is clear that Arendt understands the significance of statelessness in terms of a republican conception of freedom, she does not seem to make the legal status of persons central to her analysis of freedom. The first step in this argument is to locate Arendt in the republican tradition, so that we can make the rather non-republican argument that refugees and stateless persons are dominated by citizens in such a way that it is now only contingently true that *civitas* is *libertas*.

II. KANT, ARENDT AND NON-DOMINATION

Whether considered in republican or liberal terms, a central aim of the rule of law is to avoid arbitrary rule. Law imposes fundamental constraints on the exercise of power, including generality, publicity and non-retroactivity, and in this way

[5] See C Menke, 'The Aporias of Human Rights and the One Human Right' (2007) 74 *Social Research* 744.

helps to create, as Harrington puts it, 'the empire of law, not of men'.[6] In sharp contrast to Filmer's view that 'it is no law except it restrains liberty'[7], law is seen as a necessary condition of freedom, at least in the sense of freedom from domination, here understood as arbitrary rule. Or, to quote Harrington again, any just political community aims at 'freedom by the laws, and not freedom from the law'.[8] But what is it to be ruled by laws and yet free? The familiar formal constraints of the empire of law and not men may lessen some forms of domination, but they hardly make it impossible, neither do they constitute all conditions for non-domination directly.

It might be thought that besides these constraints that limit the loss of freedom for subjects of the law, the rule of law also requires further conditions related to authorship of the laws. The ideal that the subjects of the laws must also be their author presupposes the citizenship of all those who live in the political community. Being the author of the law that binds one is not all that there is to the richer and more complex statuses that are themselves the creation of the law. Accordingly, the rule of law is not merely instrumental in bringing about some antecedently present form of freedom but is in part constitutive of it as political freedom—a status that can be had in no other way than through the laws shared by a community. Indeed, for Pettit, non-domination is achieved not through threats or coercion, but 'by introducing constitutional authority' that is so organised that it cannot itself become a dominator. These institutional conditions 'will not just inhibit domination, but bring it to an end'.[9] This authority of a 'non-dominating interferer' is thus constitutive of freedom. But this refers inescapably to the non-domination of each other *qua* citizens, and not to the non-domination of others as such.

But there is another, more individualistic and instrumental way in which Pettit talks about the constitutive role of citizenship as a status. Non-domination is also a form of power possessed by individuals who have control over their own destiny, and such control negatively requires 'the power of any agent' that is sufficient to 'prevent various ills from happening to them'.[10] This power makes the agent's freedom from interference 'particularly secure and resilient', rather than being irreducibly contingent on the circumstances in which the agent acts. But what is it that gives these agents the necessary control to avoid such insecurity? It cannot be simply that constitutional authority comes with a list of rights and immunities that constrain its regime. Such authority does not even begin to address the possibility that it may even dominate those who do not have such rights because they lack citizenship status. The difficulty with Pettit's republicanism can be traced to the use of 'legal status' as an unanalysed term, especially with regard to constitutional

[6] Harrington, as quoted by P Pettit, *Republicanism: A Theory of Freedom and Government* (Oxford, Oxford University Press, 1998) 39.

[7] Filmer quoted by Pettit, *ibid*, 38.

[8] Harrington, quoted by Pettit, *ibid*, 38–39.

[9] Pettit, *ibid*, 82.

[10] *Ibid* 69, 132.

forms of authority that deal with laws and principles that require the courts and other institutional actors not to discriminate between citizens and non-citizens. What is lacking here is not some pre-given set of rights removed from the political process, but rather something that is closer to Arendt's idea of 'the right to have rights'.[11] Arendt proposed this conception in order to express the perplexity concerning the status of human rights for stateless persons and refugees, thus to discuss the status of increasing numbers of people without status. But what sort of status should we accord such 'a right to have rights'? Arendt's aim is clearly to show that simply attributing human rights to anyone does not supply them with 'a place in the world' or the standing that that stateless person had and lost with their 'right to belong to an organized political community'. Besides domination of migrants, this perplexity has become regularised into a persistent social fact unrelated to war, now that many residents live with no right of residence in the midst of secure, democratic political communities. For our purposes, among her many descriptions of the 'right to rights', Arendt correctly alludes to their lack of legal status for stateless persons, even if she does not offer any possible solution for their fate: '[T]heir plight is not that they are not equal before the law, but that no law exists for them.'[12] While the diagnosis may be correct, the orientation in her account to citizenship in an organised political community eliminates any universal solution to the lack of legal standing. In this regard, Arendt simply did not recognise the long-held achievement of democratic States to embrace both the rights of citizens and the rights of persons of political status in a particular community and of legal status that applies to all persons. Neither did she consider the full implication of republican ideas of freedom, in which the freedom of each depends on the freedom of all. Here Kant's insight is to separate the acquired status of citizens from the universal and underived status of persons before the law. As such, most modern conceptions of law include universal statuses that are often found in enumerated rights of all persons.

For all their disagreements, Pettit and Arendt share a common presumption present in the republican tradition: that free status generally and legal status in particular derive from citizenship, from membership in a political community. But in the case of stateless persons and migrants without legal status, this presumption that legal status is derivative of civil status simply restates the problem and not the solution. We can get closer to a solution only if such legal status is unlinked from membership in a particular community for good republican reasons. Whatever the basis for non-domination, it cannot leave some in a well-ordered political community without status at all; indeed, the status that is the basis of freedom from domination cannot be acquired through nor derived from some other status, however important this status might be. In a key republican passage in the *Metaphysics of Morals*, Kant argues instead that any just political

[11] OT 297–98.
[12] *Ibid* 296–97.

order is based on a universal and for that reason 'innate right to freedom'.[13] As 'the only original right' that applies to 'all persons in virtue of their humanity', the right to freedom is neither an 'acquired right' nor one that depends on some antecedent status such as citizenship or any other membership.[14] It is, for Kant, 'the right of humanity in one's person'.[15] As Rawls points out, the claim to freedom does not await some further derivation of this sort. Kant, he argues, sees that all such claims as claims of reason are 'self-originating and self-authenticating'.[16] Accordingly, moral freedom simply consists in regarding oneself and others as 'self-originating and self-authenticating sources of valid claims'.[17] Using the familiar republican trope, Rawls sees slavery as the violation of the right to freedom, since 'slaves are not counted as self-originating sources of claims at all'.[18] If the right to freedom consists in a self-originating and self-authenticating status, or if the demand for freedom is its own justification, Rawls helps clarify why the right to freedom is imprescriptable and unacquired and original in ways that the civil status cannot be.

On the basis of this contrast between original and acquired right, Kant goes further and specifies the form of equality in claim-making that this original right demands. If all possess this original right, non-domination is required as a fundamental equality not among citizens, but among *persons* whose independence 'from being bound by others to more than they can bind them'[19] allows them to be free from domination. This account of equal freedom avoids the conceptual difficulties of Pettit's idea of arbitrary interference by giving the republican contrast between master and slave a normative twist, arguing that without this original right, human beings would be 'persons without personality', 'beings who have only duties and no rights', and thus 'slaves or serfs',[20] dominated by others who deny that they are self-originating sources of claims and impose duties upon them through private and public forms of coercion, including expulsion and servitude. Those who live as non-citizens among citizens are dominated in just this normative sense: the moral harm of domination is not just the psychological and other costs of the capacity arbitrarily to interfere in the life of another, but rather that when one is so dependent and subordinated, 'one ceases to be a person'.[21] The injustice of domination is to have no status at all.

[13] I Kant, *Metaphysics of Morals* (M Gregor trans) (Cambridge, Cambridge University Press, 1996) 29–30.

[14] *Ibid*, 30.

[15] *Ibid.*

[16] J Rawls, *Political Liberalism* (New York, Columbia University Press, 2003) 100.

[17] *Ibid* 32.

[18] J Rawls, 'Kantian Constructivism and Moral Theory' in J Rawls (S Freeman ed), *Collected Papers* (Cambridge, Mass, Harvard University Press, 2001) 331.

[19] Kant, above n 11, 630–31.

[20] *Ibid* 241.

[21] For this reason, the voluntary surrender of one's freedom entirely to another is impossible for Kant, since it is only as a person that one may enter into a contract. Thus, the right to freedom is imprescriptible and unalienable. See *ibid* 104. Hegel similarly argues that 'my right to my distinct

The turn to such a universal status is an answer to the question of *whose* freedom is important in assessing a just legal order. The only possible answer consistent with non-domination is '*all* persons'. Without this scope, the right to freedom would be distributed according to the contingencies of membership, or upon the entirely counterfactual assumption that all residents of any polity also have the status of citizens. But this empirical assumption clearly no longer holds, if it ever has. Thus, with regard to Pettit's properly historical claim that '*libertas* is *civitas*', the state in which such freedom is exercised would be based on a distinction between those who have freedom from domination and those who do not. Such domination causes its ills through the denial of full legal status. Such treatment is inconsistent with the further republican precept that each can share in freedom from domination if and only if all are so free. Pettit argues, for example, that individuals enjoy non-domination only if it is ensured for all members of the vulnerability class to which they belong. The requirement is stronger, even for citizens who never directly face the power of sovereign States as others do. 'To the extent that those others are exposed to arbitrary interference, you too are exposed; to the extent that they are dominated you too are dominated.'[22] The limit of the extension of the freedom of all from domination is the whole political community. But even if that inference were made, there would still be a range of persons who lack the status, which leaves them vulnerable to domination.

Such a strategy of securing non-domination through domination cannot succeed, since it creates at the same time new vulnerabilities for subclasses and minorities among citizens, vulnerabilities that they share with resident non-citizens. The vulnerability class created by such policies cannot be so limited, precisely because the freedoms at stake apply to persons whether they are citizens or not. To the extent that resident non-citizens are dominated as persons, their vulnerability is twofold: neither the *imperium* of the State nor the *dominium* of private persons is limited by the rule of law in the requisitely substantive sense. The difficulty with Pettit's 'empire of law' condition as sufficient for non-domination is that it does not answer the question: 'Freedom for whom?' Historically, residence has not automatically entailed citizenship status. As the history of many democracies show, many groups, from women to African Americans, continued to be dominated as persons as members of minority groups. Due to pervasive sexism and racism, women and African Americans stood in functionally equivalent relationship to the legal system as do current groups living without freedom. Lacking the effective capacity to address institutions and officials directly in their legal capacity, these dominated citizens could nonetheless address each other and other citizens as members of a public, whose response entails their recognition of a shared communicative freedom. This communicative status provides a location in which to

personality in general and to my universal freedom of the will' are all imprescriptible and inalienable. See GWF Hegel, *Philosophy of Right* (Cambridge, Cambridge University Press, 1991) 92.

[22] Pettit, above n 6, 124.

become a 'self-originating source of claims', and may also be recognised by social movements that aim to achieve the protections of legal status for migrants and others who lack citizenship. Like the status of person, such recognition of shared communicative status in the public sphere is cosmopolitan in the sense that in this it is not derived from some other membership, but rather from mutually granted and thus shared communicative freedom. In general, such forms of communicative freedom that generate communicative power point to possibilities of transformation that correspond to the constituent powers of the people.

III. PERSONHOOD AS LEGAL STATUS

In the last section, the republican argument for a shared right to freedom applies to citizens and non-citizens alike in those cases where the vulnerability class is persons. If this is true then *civitas* is no longer a sufficient condition for *libertas*. A common republican claim is that war and other mechanisms that increase the *imperium* of the State undermine civic freedom. The very attempt to limit migration may have such effects on the freedom of citizens. But those persons without the protections of status, especially the travellers, migrants, nomadic and aboriginal peoples, and the immigrants about whom Kant was concerned, are vulnerable to both the *dominium* of private persons, from whom they are not protected, and the *imperium* of the State, to which they cannot make claims or appeals. For example, when sodomy laws made being gay an illegal status, gays were subject to arbitrary arrest and police harassment that became the object of contention in the Stonewall riots. It is clear that such persons, *qua* illegal, are subjects and not equal before the law, and in this way laws may not protect their most basic interests.[23] Call those provisions that recognise the universal legal status of persons the 'cosmopolitan constitution'.

Such cosmopolitanism is reflected in the United States Constitution in the scope of *habeas corpus* and other legal and procedural rights that are included, particularly in Amendments Four through Eight of the Bill of Rights, as well as in the Fourteenth Amendment to the United States Constitution. Or we might appeal to Article Six of the Universal Declaration of Human Rights: 'Everyone has the right to recognition everywhere as a person before the law.' To the extent that they have such a recognised legal status, they have more specific rights. Or, as Höffe put it in his discussion of Kant's right to freedom, what they lack is the 'right to right', or, more accurately, the right to law—'the right to be reckoned with in this legal capacity and to integration in the community of persons living in a legal form'.[24] It is thus a universal right to legal standing itself that is a necessary

[23] I Young, 'Equality of Whom? Social Groups and Judgments of Injustice' (2001) 9 *Journal of Political Philosophy* 1.

[24] O Höffe, *Kant's Cosmopolitan Theory of Law and Peace* (Cambridge, Cambridge University Press, 2005) 121. The pun '*Recht auf Recht*' that Höffe employs exploits the well-known ambiguity of *Recht* as both right and law; it is thus both the 'right to right' and the 'right to law', where the latter specifies the meaning of the former.

condition for external freedom. Among the people who have no status and thus cannot avoid being dominated are included illegal immigrants and squatters, prisoners and 'illegal enemy combatants', and all others who can make no claims to justice or right because there is no one to whom they may make their appeal. Even if they do not have the authorial status of democratic citizenship, their legal status as persons gives them an important editorial capacity to revise decisions and policies that deny their right to freedom. Arendt is correct that persons without legal status gain rights to freedom when they are arrested, since they then must be treated as persons. Hundreds of people are detained and deported without due process and other minimum guarantees, and it is they who lack the basic legal status of persons. As mere subjects, it is clear that the instrumental benefits of the rule of law do not necessarily extend to all those who live in a polity but primarily to citizens, and to that extent law can be a means for the domination of those without legal status. Even in a fairly robust space for politics, there remains a strong distinction between those who govern and those who are governed, and thus between those who are secure in their rights and those who live only on the uncertain dispensation of authorities.

Once it is clear that domination is always tied to the lack of various statuses, it becomes possible to begin to develop appropriate republican remedies for the central form of domination by states: the denial of the most basic legal status, the status of being a *person* Here we should emphasise those aspects of the law that apply to citizens and non-citizens alike as persons, such as the Fifth Amendment to the United States Constitution, or those federal and Supreme Court decisions based on the Fourteenth Amendment which recognise the entitlements of all residents to minimal procedural justice and to such goods as schooling and emergency medical care, regardless of their legal or illegal status. At the same time, these cosmopolitan legal guarantees are quite limited, when they exist at all. Because the United States Constitution does not protect those without legal status systematically, its extension of some rights does not map clearly on what are now considered distinctly human rights as such. Even in a constitutional democracy (such as the United States) that grants *habeas corpus* to all persons—citizens and non-citizens alike—immigration authorities still do not require a warrant for detentions, and have broad authority to question people about their legal status and to search their homes without reasonable suspicion. The absence of legal status makes it possible for institutions to track the interests of citizens in such a way as to dominate non-citizens. If citizens must be protected as persons, all persons as such must also be protected from domination.

Besides constitutional distinctions, there are also particular kinds of law that regulate relations among persons as such; for example, the 1789 Alien Tort Claims Act that was part of the authorisation of the judicial branch to provide individuals, whether nationals or non-nationals, such rights of appeal to the United States courts (even when the alleged actions did not take place within United States' territory). This is an example of a cosmopolitan normative power practised at home. Further legalisation of such claims may be found in the 1991 Torture Victim

Protection Act, which also extends the power of district courts to hear such cases and offer remedies to non-citizens. On this same basis, the capacity to protect persons within its borders requires the United States to participate in a regional human rights court (such as the Inter-American (and hence regional) Court of Human Rights, which should also be strengthened so as to include individual appeals), itself modelled on the success of the independent European Court of Human Rights. The Supreme Court, as a constitutional court, is not necessarily the best forum to consider human rights claims in a period in which the unprecedented numbers of non-citizens make it difficult to imagine any other way to organise a status which would give them the right of individual appeal as a normative power of persons against domination by States and their citizens. Indeed, the European Convention on Human Rights already entitles foreigners without nationality of any EU Member State to appeal to the European Court of Human Rights and to the Court of Justice of the EU for the ongoing juridical recognition of their rights.[25] In addition to the powers contained in the legal status of EU citizenship, the multiplication of institutions whose task it is to preserve the conditions of non-domination makes such powers and statuses more robust. Institutions at EU level can thus 'serve to make these States more democratic'.[26] The extension of the protection of human rights in the EU even to non-citizens shows the advantages of multiply realising human rights in differentiated institutions, even as these powers are a source of further political contestation by anti-immigrant parties.

How do multiple levels and sites promote the powers of citizens and persons, and especially the central normative power of initiating deliberation about claims to justice? We can answer this question in two ways. One way is to see how the institutional design and practices of the EU could be used to promote this fundamental normative power, the power that is basic to the right to have rights. The European Court of Human Rights could do so by providing a forum and a variety of locations and sites for deliberation, around which transnational publics can emerge in order to challenge the exercise of institutional powers and authorities whatever they are. Just as in the role of the US Supreme Court as a forum, significant cases mobilise civil society actors to participate in forming public opinion. A second way to promote deliberation follows from these features. To achieve more robust interaction across various levels and diverse locales, and to promote citizens' capacity to initiate deliberation at multiple levels, large federal institutions require a written constitution. In order to become legitimate enough to reform itself democratically, the EU not only has to promote European citizenship as a status, it must also create those institutional contexts and forums in which such a

[25] Joseph Weiler points to the case of *Gaygusuz v Austria* that went to the European Court of Human Rights and led to the extension of social security benefits to third country nationals. See JH Weiler, 'An "Ever Closer Union" in Need of a Human Rights Policy' (1998) 9 *European Journal of International Law* 658, 719.

[26] On the rights of immigrants, regardless of status, to political participation in the EU, see I Honohan, *Civic Republicanism* (London, Routledge, 2002) 238–39.

status is linked to powers that can be exercised effectively in deliberation on issues that affect their status. This same understanding of non-domination suggests that those powers necessary for non-domination be extended to all human beings, who as persons have the right to freedom.[27] A United States Court of Human Rights (or a regional version of such a court) would not only make freedom from domination for aliens more robust, it would also promote non-domination of citizens as well, who have the very same rights of appeal.

IV. BEYOND THE RIGHT TO HAVE RIGHTS

This discussion of persons allows us to think beyond the right to have rights. It may well be that Arendt's understanding of republicanism led her to argue that only States provided the basis for speaking and acting. In order to be able to contest those conditions that undermine non-domination, the protective reach of democracy has to extend beyond citizens. Robust non-domination, even for citizens, is often a matter of improving democratic practice. If it aims at achieving non-domination, the republican rule of law must secure these two preconditions of the right to freedom, and thereby constitute a robust form of non-domination that is not simply due to the fact that republican governments act according to the common interest or common good, but attempts to extend the protective reach of democracy to non-citizens and those without legal status. These instrumental benefits require protecting important active and minimally authorial aspects of the legal status of persons, such as the right of individuals to appeal to the appropriate legal body that acts as a forum for deliberation about the statuses of persons. While citizenship and membership within a State are often the basis for exclusion from exercising what Kant saw as the 'right of humanity in one's person', any just State has its own cosmopolitan constitution in which the rights of persons is a status that provides a basis for claims against exclusion. The fundamental requirement of the republican rule of law is just this 'right to freedom', that is, the legal status which allows the independence of persons to resist having duties imposed upon them by private and public actors.

These Kantian demands for universal statuses require a twofold revision of republican theories of freedom. First, when understood in terms of such an original right to freedom, freedom as non-domination is neither freedom from arbitrary interference nor realised through civil status and constitutional rule alone. Doing justice to those without status required a cosmopolitan dimension to the rule of

[27] Besides grounding the universal legal status of all persons in the cosmopolitan constitutions, the extension of political status to all human beings could be fulfilled in the political community of humanity. While such a conception can be shown to be desirable on republican grounds, I do not offer such a defence here. See J Bohman, *Democracy across Borders: From Demos to Dêmoi* (Cambridge, Mass, The MIT Press, 2010) ch 3. See also J Bohman, 'Democratizing the Global Order: From Communicative Freedom to Communicative Power' (2010) 36 *Review of International Studies* 431.

law. Without it, freedom from domination remains irreducibly contingent, and thus cannot accommodate the constitutive nature of the rule of law. Secondly, it cannot account fully for the active aspects of the legal status of persons, particularly the capacity to make universal claims on citizens. The original right to freedom exists only when the persons are self-originating and self-authenticating sources of claims that must find some address at some location within the legal order. Whatever the instrumental benefits of legal status, they cannot be independent of these freedoms.

In introducing 'the right to have rights', Arendt parsed the idea in two distinct ways: first, as 'a right to belong to some kind of political community'; and, secondly, as 'the right of every individual to belong to humanity'.[28] As Michelman points out, the first formulation makes sense given the prevalence of States; but the second is a 'moral claim' to citizenship, or at least 'juridical personhood', within a State. It may be that the right to belong to some kind of political community is no longer as significant, for the kind of migrants and refugees encountered now are not strictly speaking without some sort of political entity in which they belong so much as unable to lead a full human life within their State of origin. The second aspect of the right to have rights is in fact still a reality, regardless of whether one has a political status or not. But, as I have argued, Michelman is correct when he says that the right to have rights is at least about 'juridical personhood' within a State (or politically organised community), so as to treat illegal or undocumented persons in such a way as to recognise their humanity. The difference here is that this is demanded of them by their own commitments to a cosmopolitan constitution, and its understanding of the requirements of any just legal order. It remains true nonetheless that the political recognition of this legal status may require the extension of *political status* to all human beings that could be fulfilled only in the political community of humanity. This status set the bar for the burden of justification, the terms of which must be consistent with the cosmopolitan constitution in each just political community.

It might be objected that such a constitutive conception of legal status is too strong to be realised beyond the context of bounded political communities and their shared moral commitments and sovereign self-rule. However, most constitutional democracies already have these republican and cosmopolitan features with respect to the rights of persons. If we consider the possibility of the domination of non-citizens by citizens that is now a pervasive fact of modern societies, then it is clear that many of these powers and liberties must be shared by all within a republican polity. Citizens and non-citizens, then, as persons do in fact have a say over the scope of political authority in a free community. Without shared liberties, both citizens and non-citizens are insecure in their own non-domination *qua* persons. Republics need to heed Seneca's cosmopolitan injunction never to dominate others, if they are themselves to honour their constitutive commitments to non-domination

[28] OT 296–97.

and are not themselves to become dominated through the institutional means by which they dominate others.

Given the many international forms of private and public authority today that are potential and actual sources of domination, the republican project must be to extend the rule of law to the global level so that it too can be organised in terms of the right to freedom, which now includes a universal legal status that comes with external freedom in Kant's sense. Indeed, in a world of extensive social, economic and political interaction across borders, citizens may come to be dominated by distant others with whom they are not in an extant political community. Because domination and non-domination are not all-or-nothing properties in such a situation, the best way to attain a global legal and political order is neither in a unitary set of institutions, nor through the functional division of institutional labour. Rather, there must be a set of overlapping and intersecting institutions, each with its own distinctive powers and capabilities. Such a form of cosmopolitanism continues that cosmopolitan strand of republican theory that has always seen all political communities as transnational, pluralistic and complex, and yet for that very reason better able to attain the instrumental benefits of non-domination and to fulfil the constitutive demands of the rule of law. Such an institutional order would provide not merely a minimal legal status, but also a variety of means to secure, if not political status, at least the right to freedom for persons transnationally. Since no constitution would be able to fulfil the demands of the rule of law without some cosmopolitan components concerned with the universal status and protections, the prospect of a world in which all persons have basic freedoms and underived legal status is a realistic extension of current constitutional practices.

18

The Right to Have Rights: From Human Rights to Citizens' Rights and Back

SAMANTHA BESSON

We become aware of the existence of a right to have rights (and that means to live in a framework where one is judged by one's actions and opinions) and a right to belong to some kind of organized community, only when millions of people emerge who had lost and could not regain these rights because of the new global political situation … The right that corresponds to this loss and that was never even mentioned among the human rights cannot be expressed in the categories of the eighteenth-century because they presume that rights spring immediately from the 'nature' of man … Man of the twentieth century has become just as emancipated from nature as eighteenth century man was from history … This new situation in which 'humanity' has in effect assumed the role formerly ascribed to nature or history, would mean in this context that *the right to have rights, or the right of every individual to belong to humanity, should be guaranteed by humanity itself. It is by no means certain whether this is possible.* For, contrary to the best-intentioned humanitarian attempts to obtain new declarations of human rights from international organizations, it should be understood that this idea transcends the present sphere of international law which still operates in terms of reciprocal agreements and treaties between sovereign states; and for the time being a sphere that is above the nations does not exist. Furthermore, this dilemma would by no means be eliminated by the establishment of a 'world government'. Such a world government is indeed within the realm of possibility, but one may suspect that in reality it might differ considerably from the version promoted by idealistic-minded organizations.[1]

[1] H Arendt, 'The Decline of the Nation-State and the End of the Rights of Man', in *The Origins of Totalitarianism* (London, Penguin, 1951) 177–78 (emphasis added).

I. INTRODUCTION

(INTERNATIONAL)[2] HUMAN RIGHTS[3] theory is *en vogue*. It has been the case for quite some years in Germany,[4] and is now also the case in Anglo-American circles.[5] The main accounts put forward in the last 15 years are

[2] In the course of this essay it will become clear why, in view of the interlocking human rights practice, and in particular in view of the fact that subjects of international and national human rights are the same and that the locus of application of human rights is domestic in priority (see, eg, S Gardbaum, 'Human Rights as International Constitutional Rights' (2008) 19 *European Journal of International Law* 749; G Neumann, 'Human Rights and Constitutional Rights' (2003) 55 *Stanford Law Review* 1863), a theory of human rights has to be a theory of both domestic and international human rights. And this is even more the case of a legal theory of human rights, assuming of course that international law can be regarded as law (see, for that argument and refutation of different forms of scepticism relative to the legality of international law and to ethical thinking about international law, S Besson and J Tasioulas, 'Introduction' in S Besson and J Tasioulas (eds), *The Philosophy of International Law* (Oxford, Oxford University Press, 2010) 1). There should therefore be one concept of human rights that can capture not only their moral and legal dimensions, but also their legal guarantees at the domestic, regional and international levels. For a similar view about the human rights continuum, see R Forst, 'The Justification of Human Rights and the Basic Right to Justification. A Reflexive Approach' (2010) 120(4) *Ethics* 711 (depending on the existence of a political system, whether domestic or international). For human rights theories that focus exclusively on international (legal or political) human rights, see J Rawls, *The Law of Peoples* (Cambridge, Mass, Harvard University Press, 1999); CR Beitz, *The Idea of Human Rights* (Oxford, Oxford University Press, 2009); J Raz, 'Human Rights without Foundations' in S Besson and J Tasioulas (eds), *The Philosophy of International Law* (Oxford, Oxford University Press, 2010) 321; J Raz, 'Human Rights in the Emerging World Order' (2010) 1 *Transnational Legal Theory* 31. And for human rights theories that focus on human rights independently from any political or legal system whether national or international, see J Tasioulas, 'Are Human Rights Essentially Triggers for Intervention?' (2009) 4 *Philosophical Compass* 938; J Tasioulas, 'Taking Rights out of Human Rights' (2010) 120(4) *Ethics* 647; J Griffin, *On Human Rights* (Oxford, Oxford University Press, 2008).

[3] The concept of human rights I am trying to elucidate in this essay is the modern and post-1945 concept of human rights. See also A Buchanan, *Justice, Legitimacy, and Self-Determination: Moral Foundations for International Law* (Oxford, Oxford University Press, 2004); JW Nickel, *Making Sense of Human Rights,* 2nd edn (Oxford, Blackwell Publishing, 2007).

[4] See, eg, R Alexy, *Theorie der Grundrechte*, 3rd edn (Frankfurt am Main, Suhrkamp, 1996); S Gosepath and G Lohmann (eds), *Die Philosophie der Menschenrechte*, 2nd edn (Frankfurt am Main, Suhrkamp, 1999); H Bielefeldt, *Philosophie der Menschenrechte. Grundlagen eines weltweiten Freiheitsethos* (Darmstadt, Primus, 1998); H Brunkhorst, WR Köhler and M Lutz-Bachmann (eds), *Recht auf Menschenrechte* (Frankfurt am Main, Suhrkamp, 1999); KP Fritzsche and G Lohmann (eds), *Menschenrechte zwischen Anspruch und Wirklichkeit* (Würzburg, Ergon, 2000); G Lohmann *et al*, *Die Menschrechte: Unteilbar und Gleichgewichtig?* (Potsdam, University Press, 2005); R Forst, *Das Recht auf Rechtfertigung. Elemente einer konstruktivistischen Theorie der Gerechtigkeit* (Frankfurt am Main, Suhrkamp, 2007); C Menke and A Pollmann, *Philosophie der Menschenrechte. Zur Einführung* (Hamburg, Junius Verlag, 2007); KP Fritzsche, *Menschenrechte*, 2nd edn (Paderborn, F Schöningh, 2009).

[5] See, eg, H Shue, *Basic Rights: Subsistence, Affluence and US Foreign Policy*, 2nd edn (Princeton, NJ, Princeton University Press, 1996); Rawls, *The Law of Peoples*, above n 2; Buchanan, above n 3; JW Nickel, above n 3; MJ Perry, *Toward a Theory of Human Rights: Religion, Law, Courts* (New York, Cambridge University Press, 2007); G Letsas, *A Theory of Interpretation of the European Convention on Human Rights* (Oxford, Oxford University Press, 2008); Griffin, above n 2; J Griffin, 'Human Rights and the Autonomy of International Law' in S Besson and J Tasioulas (eds), *The Philosophy of International Law* (Oxford, Oxford University Press, 2010) 339; J Tasioulas, 'Human Rights, Universality and the Values of Personhood: Retracting Griffin's Steps' (2002) 10 *European Journal of Philosophy* 79; J Tasioulas, 'The Moral Reality of Human Rights' in T Pogge (ed), *Freedom from Poverty as a Human Right: Who Owes What to the Very Poor* (Oxford, Oxford University Press, 2007) 75;

organised across a (self-imposed) divide between so-called ethical or traditional accounts of human rights[6] and political or functional accounts of human rights.[7] Recent attempts have been made to bridge this divide through moral-political accounts of human rights,[8] or, more recently in the field of legal theory, through a moral-legal approach to human rights.[9] Despite their differences, which will become clear in the course of this essay, the latter proposals share a republican conception of politics and hence of international human rights. In that context, they draw their original inspiration from Hannah Arendt's 1949 idea of 'the right to have rights',[10] and usually flag a reference to her argument about the relationship between (universal) human rights and (particular) democratic membership.[11]

In this essay, I should like to take a closer look at this argument. It is important indeed at the outset of, and as groundwork to, a republican account of international human rights,[12] to assess more precisely how human rights and democratic membership—or, as I understand it here, democratic citizenship—relate.[13] This is essential to the understanding of the nature and legitimacy of international human rights, both aspects being connected.[14] If democracy and human rights are

Tasioulas, 'Are Human Rights Essentially Triggers?', above n 2; Tasioulas, 'Taking Rights out of Human Rights', above n 2; Beitz, above n 2; Raz, 'Human Rights without Foundations', above n 2; Raz, 'Human Rights in the Emerging World Order', above n 2. See also the special issue of *Ethics* (2010) 120(4) edited by Allen Buchanan on Griffin's book (Griffin, *On Human Rights*); and CR Beitz and R Goodin (eds), *Global Basic Rights* (Oxford, Oxford University Press, 2009), an edited collection assessing the impact of Shue's book (Shue, *Basic Rights*) 30 years after the publication of its first edition.

[6] Eg Griffin, above n 2; Tasioulas, 'Taking Rights out of Human Rights', above n 2. For an excellent critique, see Forst, above n 2.

[7] Eg Rawls, *The Law of Peoples*, above n 2; Beitz, above n 2; Raz, 'Human Rights without Foundations', above n 2; Raz, 'Human Rights in the Emerging World Order', above n 2. For an excellent critique, see Forst, above n 2; JL Cohen, 'Rethinking Human Rights, Democracy and Sovereignty in the Age of Globalization' (2008) 36 *Political Theory* 578.

[8] Eg S Benhabib, 'Another Universalism: On the Unity and Diversity of Human Rights' (2007) 81 *Proceedings and Addresses of The American Philosophical Association* 7; Cohen, above n 7; Forst, above n 2. See also D Baynes, 'Discourse Ethics and the Political Conception of Human Rights' (2009) 2 *Ethics and Global Politics* 1, 2 and 18.

[9] Eg S Besson, 'Human Rights *qua* Normative Practises—*Sui generis* or Legal?' (2010) 1 *Transnational Legal Theory* 127; S Besson, 'Human Rights—Ethical, Political … or Legal? First Steps in a Legal Theory of Human Rights' in D Childress (ed), *The Role of Ethics in International Law* (Cambridge, Cambridge University Press, 2011) 211–45.

[10] See H Arendt, '"The Rights of Man": What Are They?' (1949) 3 *Modern Review* 24.

[11] See, eg, Forst, above n 2; Cohen, above n 7; Benhabib, above n 8; S Benhabib, 'The Legitimacy of Human Rights' (2008) 137(3) *Deadalus* 94; S Benhabib, 'Claiming Rights across Borders: International Human Rights and Democratic Sovereignty' (2009) 103(4) *American Political Science Review* 691; D Ivison, 'Republican Human Rights?' (2010) 9 *European Journal of Political Theory* 31.

[12] My starting point in this essay, and my angle of approach to the 'right to have rights', is not citizenship theory (unlike S Benhabib, '"The right to have rights": Hannah Arendt on the contradictions of the nation-state' in *The Rights of Others: Aliens, Residents, and Citizens* (Cambridge, Cambridge University Press, 2004) 49) but human rights theory.

[13] In the rest of the essay, I shall be using 'citizenship' to mean democratic membership. Of course, one may be a citizen of a non-democratic State or a non-democratic post-national political community more generally, but this will not be my concern here.

[14] See, eg, S Besson, 'The *Authority* of International Law—Lifting the State Veil' (2009) 31(3) *Sydney Law Review* 343.

mutually dependent sources of legitimacy in the domestic context, it is important to wonder how they relate once decoupled by the internationalisation of human rights and potentially re-coupled, both across governance levels and at the same supranational governance level,[15] and whence international human rights draw their legitimacy. And this in turn implies assessing how Arendt's famous argument as regards their connection can still be of relevance more than 50 years after she first articulated her challenge to international human rights, and especially after half a century of steady development of international and regional law and institutions, on the one hand, and of entrenchment of international and regional human rights guarantees and adjudication, on the other.

Of course, there may be good reasons for not digging deeper than the usual passing reference to Arendt's argument one finds in most recent discussions in human rights theory. Some may indeed object to the obsolete nature of Arendt's arguments pertaining to international human rights, and reduce her contribution to an historical curiosity or a relic of modernity. Fears of anachronism expressed before using a 1949 argument in 2011 may, however, be placated by the legendary indeterminacy of Arendt's political theory. Furthermore, from a theoretical perspective, the limitations of Arendt's moral philosophy are well known; she was not a foundationalist thinker, and was clearly not interested in the philosophical justification of human rights. As a result, her argument leaves it to the moral philosopher to reconstruct a complete account of the nature of human rights. Neither are her views about the law and its relationship to morality sufficiently clear to draw conclusive arguments about the relationship between moral and legal rights. In any case, the present essay is not a contribution to a detailed exegesis of Arendt's ideas about international law[16] and human rights in particular,[17] and hence to the

[15] See, eg, S Besson, 'Human Rights and Democracy in a Global Context—Decoupling and Recoupling' (2011) 4(1) *Ethics and Global Politics* 19; I Maus, 'Menschenrechte als Ermächtigungsnormen internationaler Politik oder: der zerstörte Zusammenhang von Menschenrechten und Demokratie' in H Brunkhorst, G Köhler and M Lutz-Bachmann (eds), *Recht auf Menschenrechte* (Frankfurt am Main, Suhrkamp, 1999) 276; C Gould, *Globalizing Democracy and Human Rights* (Cambridge, Cambridge University Press, 2004); E Erman, *Human Rights and Democracy: Discourse Theory and Global Rights Institutions* (Aldershot, Ashgate, 2005).

[16] See, eg, J Klabbers, 'Possible Islands of Predictability: The Legal Thought of Hannah Arendt' (2007) 20 *Leiden Journal of International Law* 1; P Owens, *Between War and Politics: International Relations in the Thought of Hannah Arendt* (Oxford, Oxford University Press, 2007).

[17] See, eg, JL Cohen, 'Rights, Citizenship, and the Modern Form of the Social: Dilemmas of Arendtian Republicanism' (1996) 3 *Constellations* 164; FI Michelman, 'Parsing "A Right to Have Rights"' (1996) 3 *Constellations* 200; H Brunkhorst, 'Are Human Rights Self-Contradictory? Critical Remarks on a Hypothesis by Hannah Arendt' (1996) 3 *Constellations* 190; S Benhabib, *The Reluctant Modernism of Hannah Arendt* (New York, Rowman & Littlefield, 2000); Benhabib, above n 12; P Birmingham, *Hannah Arendt and Human Rights: The Predicament of Common Responsibility* (Bloomington, Indiana University Press, 2006); S Gosepath, 'Hannah Arendts Kritik der Menschenrechte und ihr "Recht, Rechte zu haben"' in Heinrich Böll-Stiftung (ed), *Hannah Arendt: Verborgene Tradition—Unzeitgemäße Aktualität?* (Berlin, Akademie Verlag, 2007) 279; JL Cohen, 'Sovereignty and Rights: Thinking with and beyond Hannah Arendt' in Heinrich Böll-Stiftung (ed), *Hannah Arendt: Verborgene Tradition—Unzeitgemäße Aktualität?* (Berlin, Akademie Verlag, 2007) 291; C Menke, 'The "aporias of human rights" and the "one human right": regarding the coherence of Hannah Arendt's argument' (2007) 74 *Social Research Paper* 739, available at <http://findarticles.com/p/articles/mi_m2267/is_3_74/ai_n24943363/print>; S Parekh,

growing field of 'Arendtology' in those contexts. It develops a self-standing and contemporary argument for the moral-political nature of human rights, using Arendt's original intuition as a starting point.

Arendt's argument about the right to have rights can best be read from her essay 'The Decline of the Nation-State and the End of the Rights of Man', published in 1951 in *The Origins of Totalitarianism*.[18] Her argument was primarily based on a theoretical critique of the eighteenth-century idea of the 'Rights of Man', according to which human beings have rights based on their human nature or reason alone. She draws a further argument against the classical idea of human rights from her sociological and political observations: the development of nationalism and statelessness in the first half of the twentieth century, and the atrocities of the Second World War have demonstrated that no rights can be guaranteed when one is deprived of membership in a political community. As a result, there can only be one human right *stricto sensu* that human beings have by virtue of their humanity, and that is the 'right to have rights' in a given political community and hence to become a member of that community. All other rights can be guaranteed only within a given political community, and more specifically in Arendt's account, the domestic political community.[19] From that first conclusion, Arendt quickly moved to her famous aporia, however.[20] That aporia resides in the inherent limitations of the Nation State and nationalism, on the one hand, and the necessary exclusions triggered by political membership, on the other, hence her legendary distrust of national sovereignty. The domestic political community becomes the solution to its own problems, in other words, but also as a result the reason for its failure to succeed where it has just failed. Faithful to her republicanism of fear,[21] Arendt did not consider any alternatives plausible. She disregards the idea of a World State as potentially dangerous and hence as undesirable. Later on, in a more optimistic move, however, she placed her (dimmed) hopes in an embryonic international community; this is best exemplified in her critical report on the Eichmann trial, and her discussion of the need and possibility to develop international criminal law and to establish the jurisdiction of international criminal tribunals to try those who have become *hostes humani generis*.[22]

Hannah Arendt and the Challenge of Modernity (Oxford, Routledge 2008); J Ingram, 'What is a "Right to have Rights"? Three Images of the Politics of Human Rights' (2008) 102 *American Political Science Review* 401.

18 Arendt, above n 1, 177.

19 *Ibid*, 299.

20 For a detailed discussion of this aporia or dilemma, see Gosepath, above n 17; and Menke, above n 17.

21 See, eg, R Forst, 'Republikanismus der Furcht und der Rettung. Zur Aktualität der politischen Theorie Hannah Arendts', in Heinrich Böll-Stiftung (ed), *Hannah Arendt: Verborgene Tradition—Unzeitgemäße Aktualität?* (Berlin, Akademie Verlag, 2007) 229.

22 H Arendt, *Eichmann in Jerusalem* (London, Penguin, 1965) ch 1, Epilogue and Postscript. See, eg, S Benhabib, 'International Law and Human Plurality in the Shadow of Totalitarianism: Hannah Arendt and Raphael Lemkin' (2009) 16(2) *Constellations* 331; T Mertens, 'Memory, Politics and Law—The Eichmann Trial: Hannah Arendt's View on the Jerusalem Court's Competence' (2005) 6 *German Law Journal* 407.

From a contemporary perspective, one may quibble with Arendt's aporia and disagree in particular with her grim views about the inherent limitations of domestic politics and the absolute nature of sovereignty, on the one hand, and the underdeveloped political nature of international law and the international community, on the other.[23] However, her groundbreaking analysis of the problem raised by the idea of universal human rights retains its original force more than 50 years after its first statement. Expressed at the dawn of the modern international human rights system, her argument even has the potential to lead us well beyond the intrinsic limitations of that system and provide an interesting reference in view of the development of democratic structures beyond the State.

More specifically, Arendt's idea of a 'right to have rights' remains still extraordinarily actual in three related respects: first, its ability to straddle the universal and the particular by putting universal human rights and particular political membership in a mutual equilibrium and tension; secondly, its sense of the hybrid nature of human rights that Arendt situates between politics and morality, thus laying the ground for a republican notion of legality distinct from positivity[24]; and, lastly, her intuition about membership in a modern international community, where all of us are both insiders and outsiders at the same time depending on the political level in consideration. At the same time and despite the strength of those realisations encapsulated in one single idea, three fundamental questions remain open in Arendt's resolutely non-foundationalist account of the right to have rights: the idea of human rights, and whether they are 'rights' or not and what makes them 'human' rights by contrast to other rights such as contractual rights for instance; the nature of those rights, and whether they are moral or legal rights; and, lastly, the level of legalisation of those rights, and who are their right-holders and duty-bearers.

Interestingly, those three questions are still at the core of most contemporary discussions of human rights.[25] I shall take all three questions in turn in the following sections of this essay. I shall first argue for a moral-political account of human rights and emphasise the inherently legal nature of human rights (section II.), and then explain the relationship between international and domestic guarantees of human rights (III.).

[23] See the critiques by Cohen, 'Rights, Citizenship, and the Modern Form of the Social', above n 17; Cohen, 'Sovereignty and Rights', above n 17; A Arato and J Cohen, 'Banishing the Sovereign? Internal and External Sovereignty in Arendt' (2009) 16 *Constellations* 307; Benhabib, above n 12; and Gosepath, above n 17.

[24] See, eg, S Besson and JL Marti Marmol (eds), *Legal Republicanism: National and International Perspectives* (Oxford, Oxford University Press, 2009).

[25] They have not yet been broached head-on by proponents of the moral-political account of human rights (eg Forst, above n 4, and Forst, above n 2; Benhabib, above n 12; Benhabib, above n 8; and Benhabib, Benhabib, 'Claiming Rights across Borders', above n 11). The closest one gets to obtaining answers to those questions is Cohen's 2008 remarkable essay, 'Rethinking Human Rights', above n 7.

II. HUMAN RIGHTS: MORAL AND LEGAL

One of the first questions one should ask about human rights pertains to their nature.[26] It is also the *prima facie* paradox raised by the idea of a 'right to have rights'. One way to dissolve the paradox is indeed to look more closely at the nature of human rights and to understand, as some authors do, the former as a moral right and the latter as legal rights.[27] As I shall argue, this understanding does not do full justice to Arendt's fundamental intuition, nor, more specifically, to the intrinsic legality of human rights or to the interaction between international and domestic human rights law.

In this section, I start by arguing that human rights may be understood as moral propositions, and more specifically as universal moral rights that ground moral duties. When the fundamental interests that found human rights are legally recognised, I go on to explain how human rights ought also to be described as legal rights, and how those legal rights relate to the universal moral rights they recognise, modulate or create. Even though those two dimensions of human rights are addressed separately and one after the other for the sake of the exposition, they cannot be dissociated, as will transpire in the course of the argument.

A. The Morality of Human Rights

Human rights are a sub-set of universal moral rights (i) that protect fundamental and general human interests (ii) against the intervention, or in some cases non-intervention of (national, regional or international) public institutions (iii). Those three elements will be discussed in turn.

To start with, a human right exists *qua* moral right when an interest is a sufficient ground or reason to hold someone else (the duty-bearer) under a (categorical and exclusionary) duty to respect that interest vis-à-vis the right-holder.[28] For a right to be recognised, a sufficient interest must be established and weighed against other interests and other considerations with which it might conflict in a particular social context.[29] Rights are, on this account, intermediaries between interests and duties.[30] Turning to the second element in the definition, human rights are moral rights of a special intensity, in that the interests protected are regarded as fundamental and general human interests that all human beings have by virtue of their humanity and not of a given status or circumstance. They include individual interests when these constitute part of a person's well-being in an objective

[26] See Besson, 'Human Rights—Ethical, Political ... or Legal?', above n 9.

[27] See Benhabib, *The Reluctant Modernism of Hannah Arendt*, above n 17; Benhabib, above n 12, 56–61; Gosepath, above n 17.

[28] J Raz, 'On the Nature of Rights' (1984) 93 *Mind* 194, 195.

[29] *Ibid* 200, 209.

[30] *Ibid* 208.

sense. The fundamental nature of the protected interests has to be determined by reference to the context and time rather than established once and for all.[31]

What makes it the case that a given individual interest is regarded as sufficiently fundamental or important to generate a duty, and that, in other words, the threshold of importance and point of passage from a general and fundamental interest to a human right is reached, may be found in the normative status of each individual *qua* equal member of the moral-political community.[32] A person's interests merit equal respect in virtue of her status as member of the community; those interests are recognised as socio-comparatively important by members of the community, and only then can they be recognised as human rights. This relationship to political equality bridges the sterile opposition between the individual and the group.[33] The recognition of human rights is done mutually and not simply vertically, and as a result human rights are not externally promulgated as such but mutually granted by members of a given political community.[34] However, human rights are not merely a consequence of individuals' equal status, but also a way of actually earning that equal status and consolidating it. Without human rights, political equality would remain an abstract guarantee; through human rights, individuals become actors of their own equality and members of their political community.[35] Human rights are power-mediators[36]: they both enable political equality and stem from it. Borrowing Arendt's words, 'we are not born equal; we become equal as members of a group on the strength of our decision to guarantee ourselves mutually equal rights'.[37]

[31] See, on the ahistorical and synchronic universality of human rights: Tasioulas, 'Human Rights, Universality and the Values of Personhood', above n 5; Tasioulas, 'The Moral Reality of Human Rights', above n 5, 76–77. *Contra* J Griffin, 'First Steps in an Account of Human Rights' (2001) 9 *European Journal of Philosophy* 306. See also Raz, 'Human Rights in the Emerging World Order', above n 2.

[32] See Forst, above n 2; R Forst, 'The Basic Right to Justification: Toward a Constructivist Conception of Human Rights' (1999) 6 *Constellations* 35, 48. On the relationship between political equality and human rights more generally, see T Christiano, *The Constitution of Equality* (Oxford, Oxford University Press, 2008) 138, 156, on public equality as ground for liberal rights; and A Buchanan, 'The Egalitarianism of Human Rights' (2010) 120(4) *Ethics* 679.

[33] The proposed account comes very close to Forst, above n 2; Forst, 'The Basic Right to Justification', above n 32, 48–50; and Forst, above n 4. My account differs ultimately as Forst's is based on a reflexive *right* to political justification, whereas the present account is based on political equality and its mediation through human rights (see also Christiano, above n 32, 156). Both accounts, of course, rely on Habermas's idea of co-originality between democratic sovereignty and human rights (J Habermas, *Faktizität und Geltung* (Frankfurt am Main, Suhrkamp, 1998) ch III), although they provide different variations of that idea, notably by referring to an external right or value as a foundation for their co-originality. See C Brettschneider, *Democratic Rights—The Substance of Self-government* (Princeton, NJ, Princeton University Press, 2007) 29–38 for a similar interpretation of Habermas's co-originality.

[34] See JL Cohen, 'Minimalism about Human Rights: The Most We Can Hope For?' (2004) 12 *The Journal of Political Philosophy* 190, 197–98; Forst, above n 2.

[35] See Cohen, above n 34, 197–98; Cohen, above n 7, 585–86.

[36] For the original idea of mediating duties, see H Shue, 'Mediating Duties' (1988) 98 *Ethics* 687, 703. See also C Reus-Smit, 'On Rights and Institutions' in CR Beitz and RE Goodin (eds), *Global Basic Rights* (New York, Oxford University Press, 2009) 25, on human rights and power mediation. On liberal rights and the exercise of power in general, see Christiano, above n 32, 134.

[37] Arendt, above n 1, 301.

In short, the proposed account of the nature of human rights follows a modified interest-based theory: it is modified by reference to considerations of equal moral-political status in a given community. Under a purely status-based or interest-based model, the manichean opposition between the individual and the group, and between his private and public autonomy would lead to unjustifiable conclusions.[38] It is important to pause at this stage and clarify what is meant by political membership or inclusion into an organised political society. This will then enable me to clarify how it is neither a parochial nor an exclusive criterion, and can account for both the universality and the generality of human rights.

Political membership is a normative idea according to which a person's interests are to be treated equally and taken into consideration in a given political group's decision.[39] Human rights protect those interests tied to membership and disrespect of which would be tantamount to treating them as outsiders. Of course, some human rights, such as civic and political rights, are more closely tied to actual membership, while others, such as the right to life, are closer to basic demands of humanity and hence to access to political membership. Even the latter rights, however, constrain what equal membership can mean if it is to be legitimate and the kind of interests it must protect. This is in line with the republican idea of the political community *qua* locus of rights.[40] By submitting individuals to genocide, torture and other extreme forms of cruel treatment, a community excludes them and no longer treats them as equal members, thus violating the threshold of recognition of human rights: political equality.[41]

Of course, there can be many overlapping political communities (eg international organisations), and this argument is not limited to a national polity and to the State. Neither is the argument limited to citizens only, or at least to those citizens who are also nationals; membership ought to include to varying degrees all those normatively affected by the activities of political authorities and who are subject to the laws or decisions of the community. This includes asylum seekers, economic migrants, stateless persons and so on. As we shall see, human rights work as a political irritant and as mechanisms of gradual inclusion that lead to the extension of the political franchise, and in some cases of citizenship itself to new stakeholders in the community. Lastly, the argument does not imply that human rights apply only within national borders; if national political authorities affect the fundamental interests of other individuals outside national borders, those individuals deserve equal protection. This includes individuals and groups normatively affected by and subjected to law-making and decision-making abroad by military—and also by economic—interventions.

[38] See Tasioulas's critique of Griffin, *On Human Rights*: Tasioulas, 'Taking Rights out of Human Rights', above n 2.

[39] The following argument is a development of Cohen's argument, above n 34, 197–98.

[40] See Cohen, above n 7, 604, fn 47.

[41] As a result, it is not possible to distinguish, among human rights, between those that are connected to political equality and to democracy, and those that are not.

This brings me to the third element in the definition: human rights are entitlements against public institutions (national, regional or international). They generate duties on the part of public authorities to protect not only equal individual interests, but also individuals' political status *qua* equal political actors. Public institutions are necessary for collective endeavour and political self-determination, but may also endanger them. Human rights enable the functioning of those institutions in exchange for political equality and protection from abuse of political power. This is why one can say that human rights both are protected by public institutions and provide protection against them; they exist because of collective endeavour in order both to favour and constrain it.[42] Of course, other individuals may individually violate the interests protected by human rights, and ought to be prevented from doing so by public institutions and in particular through legal means.[43] This ought to be the case whether those individuals' actions and omissions may be attributed to public authorities or not *qua de jure* or *de facto* organs. However, public institutions remain the primary addressees of human rights claims and the primary duty-bearers.[44]

In short, the proposed account is moral in the justification it provides for human rights, and political in the function with which it sees them vested: they are indeed regarded both as shields against the State and as guarantees of political inclusion. In terms of justification, its moral-political dimension differs not only from accounts based on a purely ethical justification of human rights, but also from accounts that seek a political form of minimalist justification of human rights.[45] In other words, the proposed moral-political account of human rights can salvage the political role of human rights without diluting their moral justification.[46]

B. The Legality of Human Rights

It follows from the moral-political nature of human rights that the law is an important dimension of their recognition and existence. It is time to understand exactly how this is the case, and to unpack the inherently legal dimension of human rights.

[42] See A Buchanan, 'Equality and Human Rights' (2005) 4 *Politics, Philosophy & Economics* 69, 74; Buchanan, above n 32.

[43] See Shue, above n 5, on the different types of negative and positive duties corresponding to a human right, including duties to prevent other agents from violating them.

[44] This normative argument actually corresponds to the state of international human rights law that only directly binds States and/or international organisations to date and no other subjects (eg individuals and groups of individuals). The universality of human rights obligations does not imply the generality of the duty-bearers of the corresponding duties, ie a personal scope that reaches beyond institutional agents whether domestic or international (*contra* O O'Neill, 'The Dark Side of Human Rights' (2005) 81 *International Affairs* 427; C Lafont, 'Accountability and global governance: challenging the state-centric conception of human rights' (2010) 3 *Ethics & Global Politics* 193, 203).

[45] See Cohen, above n 34.

[46] See also Forst, above n 2; Forst, above n 32, 48–50.

Just as moral rights are moral propositions and sources of moral duties, legal rights are legal propositions and sources of legal duties. They are moral interests recognised by the law as sufficiently important to generate moral duties.[47] The same may be said of legal human rights: legal human rights are fundamental and general moral interests recognised by the law as sufficiently important to generate moral duties.

Generally speaking, moral rights can exist independently from legal rights, but legal rights recognise, modify or create moral rights by recognising moral interests as sufficiently important to generate moral duties.[48] Of course, there may be ways of protecting moral interests or even independent moral rights legally without recognising them as legal 'rights'. Conversely, some legal rights may not actually protect pre-existing moral rights or create moral rights, thus only bearing the name of 'rights' and generating legal duties at the most.[49] The same cannot be said of human rights more specifically, however. True, universal moral interests and rights may be legally protected without being recognised as legal 'rights'. But, as we shall see, human rights *stricto sensu* can only exist as moral rights *qua* legal rights. Conversely, one may imagine legal norms referred to as human rights that do not correspond to moral human rights. In such a case, the legal norms named 'human rights' would give rise only to legal duties and not to moral (rights-based) duties. Legal human rights, however, can be regarded as rights *stricto sensu* only when their corresponding duties are not only legal, but also moral.

Two additional remarks are in order on the relationship between moral and legal rights, and on the relationship between moral and legal human rights. The differences between rights and human rights, on the one hand, and between their respective moral and legal dimensions, on the other, can be quite important given the moral-political nature of human rights and what this implies in turn for their inherently moral and legal nature.

Not all moral rights are legally recognised as legal rights, on the one hand. There are many examples of moral rights which have not been recognised as legal rights. Neither should all moral rights be recognised and protected legally. Respect for them should be a matter of individual conscience in priority.

The same cannot be said about human rights, however. True, not all universal moral rights have been or are legally recognised as legal human rights. Some are even expressly recognised as universal moral rights by the law even though they

[47] J Raz, 'Legal Rights' (1984) 4 *OJLS* 1, 12. For a recent restatement of his theory of moral and legal rights and their relationship, see Raz, 'Human Rights in the Emerging World Order', above n 2.

[48] Legal recognition of human rights can therefore be taken to mean, depending on the context, both the legal recognition of an interest *qua* human right and the legal recognition of a pre-existing human right.

[49] Note that this duty is the primary moral duty to protect the interest that founds the legal human right, and not the secondary moral duty to obey the legal norm 'human right': see S Besson, 'The Democratic Authority of International Human Rights' in A Follesdal (ed), *The Legitimacy of Human Rights* (Cambridge, Cambridge University Press, 2012) forthcoming.

are not made into legal rights or modulated by the law.[50] A distinct question is whether they ought to be legalised and hence protected by law. Again, respect for universal moral rights ought to be voluntary in priority, and this independently from any institutional involvement. However, the universal moral rights that will become human rights create moral duties for institutions, and hence for the law as well, to recognise and protect human rights.[51] Based on the moral-political account of human rights presented previously, the law provides the best and perhaps the only way of mutually recognising the comparative importance of those interests in a political community of equals.[52] It enables the weighing of those interests against each other and the drawing of the political equality threshold or comparative line. In short, the law makes them human rights *stricto sensu*. As a result, in the moral-political account of human rights propounded here, the legal recognition of a fundamental human interest, in conditions of political equality, is part of the creation of a moral-political human right. In other words, while being independently justified morally and having a universal and general scope, human rights *qua* subset of universal moral rights are also of an inherently legal nature. To quote Jürgen Habermas, 'they are conceptually oriented towards positive enactment by legislative bodies'.[53] Thus, while legal rights *stricto sensu* are necessarily moral in nature (*qua* rights), human rights (*qua* rights) are not only necessarily moral but also legal, and they are as a result both moral and legal rights.

Neither, on the other hand, do legal rights necessarily always pre-exist as independent moral rights. Most do, and are legally recognised moral rights,[54] but others are legally-created or legally specified moral rights.[55] In some cases, law and politics may affect a person's interests, thus in a sense enhancing the moral interest and/or its moral-political significance which are necessary for that interest to be recognised as a source of duties and hence as a right. One may think of zoning rights in the context of land planning, for instance, or of government bond-holders' rights.[56]

[50] One may think here of the moral rights mentioned by the 9th Amendment to the US Constitution.

[51] See Raz, 'Human Rights in the Emerging World Order', above n 2.

[52] See, eg, Cohen, above n 7, 599–600; Forst, above n 2; Forst, above n 32, 48–50. See even T Pogge, 'Human Rights and Human Responsibilities' in A Kuper (ed), *Global Responsibilities: Who Must Deliver on Human Rights* (New York, Routledge, 2005) 3, fn 26, who concedes this point in the case of civil and political rights. It seems, however, that the egalitarian dimension of human rights, and hence their inherently legal nature, would apply even more to the case of social and economic rights.

[53] J Habermas, 'Die Legitimation durch Menschenrechte' in *Die postnationale Konstellation. Politische Essays* (Frankfurt am Main, Suhrkamp, 1998) 183. See also Habermas, above n 33, 310–12.

[54] The legalisation of pre-existing moral rights is rarely a mere translation; it usually specifies and somehow changes the moral right. See S Meckled-Garcia and B Cali, 'Lost in Translation: The Human Rights Ideal and International Human Rights Law' in B Cali and S Meckled-Garcia (eds), *The Legalization of Human Rights, Multidisciplinarity Perspectives on Human Rights and Human Rights Law* (London, Routledge, 2006) 11; and B Cali and S Meckled-Garcia, 'Introduction: Human Rights' in Cali and Meckled-Garcia (eds), *ibid* 1.

[55] See Raz, 'Legal Rights', above n 47, 16–17. See also: Raz, 'Human Rights in the Emerging World Order', above n 2.

[56] Both examples are given by Raz, *ibid*.

The same cannot be said about legal human rights, however: all of them necessarily also pre-exist as independent universal moral rights. However, the law can specify and weigh moral human interests when recognising them as legal human rights. One may imagine certain political interests the moral-political significance of which may stem from the very moral-political circumstances of life in a polity. As a result, the law does not create universal moral rights, but it can modulate them when recognising them. Furthermore, the inherently legal nature of human rights and the role the law plays in recognising given interests as sufficiently important in a group as to generate duties and hence human rights, make it the case that the law turns pre-existing universal moral rights into human rights and hence actually turns them into human rights. As a result, human rights cannot pre-exist their legalisation as independent moral human rights *stricto sensu*, but only as independent universal moral rights.

III. HUMAN RIGHTS: INTERNATIONAL AND DOMESTIC

Once the moral-political nature and hence inherent legality of human rights has been clarified, the next question pertains to the level of legalisation of those rights.[57] To address this question adequately, it is useful to start by explaining the idea of the international right to have domestic rights, before turning to how this idea can illuminate the current international human rights practice and how international and domestic human rights are articulated. The third subsection below pertains to the relationship of mutual reinforcement between human and citizens' rights.

A. The Right to Have Rights

Theoretically, the legalisation of human rights, ie the legal recognition and modulation of universal moral rights *qua* human rights, could take place at the domestic or at the international level: through national or international legalisation.

Given what was said about the interdependence between human rights and democracy, however, the political process through which their legalisation takes place ought to be democratic and include all those whose rights are affected and whose equality is at stake. As a result, using international law to recognise fundamental and general human interests as sufficiently important to generate State duties at the domestic level is delicate. Not only does international law-making include many other States and subjects than those affected, but the democratic

[57] The argument presented in this section is a summary of a lengthier argument developed in Besson, 'Human Rights—Ethical, Political … or Legal?', above n 9.

quality of its processes is not yet secured.[58] To be democratic, the primary locus of legitimation and accordingly of legalisation of human rights ought therefore to be domestic.

It is important at this stage to distinguish between two categories of human rights: human rights that pertain to the access to membership in a political community; and those that pertain to actual membership in the political community. Interestingly, this distinction helps in delineating two competing readings of Arendt's 1949 idea of the 'right to have rights'.

Starting with the former category of human rights, ie rights to membership, the distinction between domestic or international legalisation does not apply. That category pertains to human rights that contribute to constituting our political equality, and not to those that condition it in the first place as the rights that pertain to equal membership in a political community. Those rights prohibit, for instance, submitting individuals to genocide, torture and other extreme forms of cruel treatment through which a community excludes individuals and does not treat them as equal members.[59] They include also rights to asylum[60] and the customary right to *non-refoulement*. Those rights cannot be guaranteed first within a given political community since they work as constraints on democratic sovereignty and self-determination. They are to be legalised internationally as a result. However, to be legitimate, they have to be recognised legally through inclusive and deliberative processes of the kind that are incrementally developed in international law-making, and I shall get back to those.[61] Rights to membership correspond to a first reading of Arendt's right to have rights: those universal moral rights, and potentially also legal rights, to membership are the only human rights that may be and have to be guaranteed legally from the outside a political community and that aim at guaranteeing the ulterior benefit of domestic rights within each political community, ie human rights *per se*.[62]

By contrast, it is pertaining to the second group of human rights that guarantee membership in the political community, ie most human rights, that the locus of legalisation becomes most sensitive. As we saw before, they can be recognised only by those whose political equality they contribute to create and guarantee. Following the categories of rights presented before, this second group of international human rights as they stand under current international law can at least be regarded as legally protected universal moral rights, and most of the time as legal

[58] See, eg, T Christiano, 'Democratic Legitimacy and International Institutions' in S Besson and J Tasioulas (eds), *The Philosophy of International Law* (Oxford, Oxford University Press, 2010) 119–37, on the lack of representativeness and the asymmetry of international law-making processes from a democratic theory's perspective. See also Cohen, above n 7, 599–600; Besson, above n 49.

[59] See Cohen, above n 7, 587.

[60] Universal Declaration of Human Rights, Art 14.

[61] On the bootstrapping between international human rights law-making and their democratic reception and interpretation at domestic level, see Buchanan, above n 3; A Buchanan, 'Human Rights and the Legitimacy of the International Order' (2008) 14 *Legal Theory* 39. See also section II.B. below.

[62] See, eg, Cohen, above n 7; Benhabib, above n 12, 56–61.

rights as well. However, unless they refer to and correspond to existing domestic (moral-political and legal) human rights, they cannot (yet) be regarded as human rights *stricto sensu* for lack of a moral-political community.[63]

Qua legal rights, those international human rights norms guarantee rights to individuals under a given State's jurisdiction, on the one hand, and to other States (or arguably international organisations) (international human rights are usually guaranteed *erga omnes*), on the other, to have those rights guaranteed as 'human rights' within a given domestic community. They correspond to States' (and/or arguably international organisations') duties to secure and ensure respect for those rights as 'human rights' within their own jurisdiction.[64] In that sense, international human rights duties are second-order duties for States (and/or arguably international organisations) to generate first-order human rights duties for themselves under domestic law, ie international duties to have domestic duties. What those international human rights norms do, in other words, is protect legally the universal moral right to have rights, ie the right to equal membership in a moral-political community, with all the other human rights this status implies. Unlike most readings of Arendt's right to have rights,[65] however, this reading understands those rights as universal moral rights which may also be protected as international legal rights. They are not human rights themselves but are rights to have human rights, the latter being at once moral and legal rights and not only positive legal rights.

In short, there are two groups of universal moral rights: the first group (that may be termed 'rights to membership'[66]), which may and ought to be legalised internationally without yet being guaranteed domestically; by contrast, rights belonging to the second group ('members' rights') have to be legalised in domestic law in a given political community before they can be recognised as human rights *stricto sensu* under international law. In the meantime, international law's human rights norms that protect rights in the latter category guarantee rights to have human rights protected under domestic law. Those two groups of moral rights can be matched under Arendt's notion of rights to have (human) rights.

Of course, the situation would be altogether different if the moral-political community bound by legal human rights was an international one: the right-holders and duty-bearers would be the equal members, political actors and law-makers of that international community. In that case, all international human rights could be

[63] There is, in other words, a form of political parochialism or legal contingency of human rights that conditions their recognition as international legal human rights, well before parochialism arises as a problem for the scope of legitimacy of an existing legal human right. See also Raz, 'Human Rights in the Emerging World Order', above n 2.

[64] See O'Neill, above n 44, 433, on the distinction between the first-order human rights duties at domestic level and second-order human rights duties generated by international human rights law.

[65] See, eg, Benhabib, above n 12; Gosepath, above n 17.

[66] For a detailed discussion of the human right to democratic membership and participation, see S Besson, 'The Human Right to Democracy—A Moral Defence, with a Legal Nuance' in *Souveraineté populaire et droits de l'homme*, Collection Science et Technique de la Société, Strasbourg: Editions du Conseil de l'Europe 2010, available at <http://www.venice.coe.int/docs/2010/CDL-UD%282010%29003-e.pdf>.

regarded as human rights *stricto sensu*. True, this would require a minimal level of democratic organisation of that community, which to date is not yet given.[67]

The European Union (EU) constitutes an interesting example of a supranational political community where human rights and democracy have developed hand-in-hand beyond the State in reaction to the increasingly direct impact of EU law over individuals.[68] There, EU institutions, and EU Member States when they apply EU law and act as indirect EU institutions as a result, are bound by human rights duties under EU law. And EU decision-making processes may be considered by and large democratic in terms of representative inclusion of all those normatively affected in their fundamental interests by and subject to EU laws and decisions. However, those supranational communities, whether European or international, are not what is usually aimed at in the context of international human rights law: most international human rights instruments existing to date bind national authorities exclusively, and only vis-à-vis individuals under their (territorial and extra-territorial) jurisdiction.

One may not exclude, of course, further institutional developments, whether at a regional or functional level. The idea of a worldwide political community, and hence of a global democracy *stricto sensu*, however, is not only implausible, but normatively undesirable.[69] One may as a result share Arendt's fears about an unchecked global sovereign. And given what has just been said about the externally-guaranteed international legal rights to have human rights on the inside, and the beneficial tensions between those international rights and duties and the corresponding internal ones, conceiving of the international community as a political one with its own human rights-holders and human rights duties-bearers would undermine the productive tension between human rights and political membership, and the equilibrium that may be reached between the universalising process of the particular and the particularisation of the universal.[70]

B. International and Domestic Human Rights Law

Interestingly, the normative considerations presented before about the locus of legitimation and legalisation of human rights are reflected in actual processes of legalisation of human rights under domestic and international law.

[67] See S Besson, '*Ubi Ius, Ibi Civitas.* A Republican Account of the International Community' in S Besson and JL Martí (eds), *Legal Republicanism—National and Post-National Perspectives* (Oxford, Oxford University Press, 2009) 204.

[68] On EU institutions as human rights duty-bearers, however, see S Besson, 'The European Union and Human Rights: Towards a New Kind of Post-national Human Rights Institution'(2006) 6 *Human Rights Law Review* 323.

[69] See, eg, Besson, above n 67; S Besson, 'Institutionalizing global demoi-cracy' in L Meyer (ed), *Justice, Legitimacy and Public International Law* (Cambridge, Cambridge University Press, 2009) 58.

[70] For a similar position, see Benhabib, above n 12; Benhabib, above n 8; and Benhabib, 'Claiming Rights across Borders', above n 11.

To start with, one observes that human rights guarantees in international law are usually minimal. They rely on national guarantees to formulate a minimal threshold which they reflect and entrench internationally.[71] More importantly, they are usually abstract and meant to be fleshed out at domestic level, not only in terms of the specific duties attached to a given right but also in terms of the right itself.[72] Both levels of protection are usually regarded as complementary and as serving different functions, therefore, rather than as providing competing guarantees. This complementarity between international and domestic guarantees explains why the national reception of international human rights within domestic law is favoured or even required by international human rights instruments.[73] Domestic human rights law does more than merely implement international human rights: it contextualises and specifies them. One actually often talks of 'reception' within the domestic legal order in that respect.[74] Through domestic legal reception, national authorities determine democratically what the actual threshold of importance of various human interests is to be and what duties that human right will give rise to in practice. In turn, this explains why, in the case where domestic guarantees of the same human rights exist, international guarantees are usually subsumed into domestic ones in practice.

The role played by the minimal threshold constituted by international human rights is not to be underestimated. States are bound, through international human rights and duties, to keep the level of human rights protection they have achieved domestically and not to fall back below that minimal threshold. International human rights are guarantees against levelling-down. There is nothing vacuous as a result in international human rights minimalism.[75] Quite the contrary: it corresponds not only to the current state of legality of international human rights, but also to their moral-political reality and democratic legitimacy.

Besides its explanatory value once faced with the reality of international human rights law and the latter's coordination with domestic human rights, the proposed

[71] This is confirmed by the way in which democratic States usually ratify human rights instruments and hence generate international human rights duties for themselves only once they have recognised minimal international human rights standards in domestic law (eg Switzerland and the European Convention on Human Rights in the 1970s, and currently in the context of the ratification of the additional Protocol to the International Covenant on Economic, Social and Cultural Rights or the European Social Charter).

[72] It is important to note that the contextualisation of human rights ought to take place through the form of domestic legal rights according to this essay's moral-political argument. Of course, this does not yet mean that it will be the only way to make them effective (see, eg, SE Merry, *Human Rights and Gender Violence: Translating International Law into Local Justice* (Chicago, Ill, University of Chicago Press, 2006); SE Merry and M Goodale (eds), *The Practice of Human Rights: Tracking Law Between the Global and the Local* (Cambridge, Cambridge University Press, 2007)).

[73] Some international human rights instruments expressly establish positive duties to implement international human rights through domestic law (whether through domestic rights or not): eg Art 4 of the UN Convention on the Rights of the Child.

[74] On this term, see A Stone Sweet and H Keller, 'Introduction' in *A Europe of Rights. The Impact of the ECHR on National Legal Systems* (Oxford, Oxford University Press, 2008) 3.

[75] *Contra* Raz, 'Human Rights without Foundations', above n 2, section IV.

normative approach has the further benefit of fitting the structure of the international legal order more generally. It puts international human rights law back into its political context. State sovereignty and political self-determination indeed form one of the pillars of the international order, a pillar which is complemented and not replaced —or even restricted as one often reads—by the second pillar of international human rights law.[76] The international legal order protects indeed the very interdependence between democracy and human rights alluded to before, by guaranteeing the basic conditions for political equality through State sovereignty and political self-determination, on the one hand, and the possibility to use them through human rights and the right to have rights, on the other. It is actually through the relationship of mutual reinforcement between citizens' rights and human rights to which we shall turn now, that this dualistic structure of the international legal order appears most clearly.

C. From Human Rights to Citizens' Rights and Back

If human rights are to be democratically legitimate, they ought to be the outcome of a legalisation process in which human rights-holders can also be the authors of their own rights. Human rights ought to be citizens' rights, in other words. Having human rights *qua* citizens' rights means both having them by virtue of one's own laws and authoring them as author of one's own laws.

International human rights guarantees usually also benefit non-citizens domestically, however, and have a broader personal scope therefore than the rights that belong to citizens or members of a domestic or regional polity. This cleavage between citizens and non-citizens is problematic. Obviously, the nexus between human rights and citizens' rights is not respected as long as political rights pertain to the holding of nationality; all resident non-nationals are excluded from political participation, despite these people being potentially equally affected by the laws and regulations of their host State. Needless to say, in circumstances of globalisation, increased mobility and constant migration, the exclusion of non-nationals from the polity they actually live in is ever harder to justify.[77] At the same time, however, whether the criterion for citizenship remains nationality or shifts towards residence, and whether certain political rights are granted to members of the political community without naturalisation and full citizenship, it should be clear that boundaries still have to be drawn between members of

[76] See, for a similar argument, P Macklem, 'What is International Human Rights Law? Three Applications of a Distributive Account' (2007) 52 *McGill Law Journal* 575, 577; Cohen, above n 7, 595–97.

[77] Inevitably, problems of under-inclusiveness, but also over-inclusiveness, will be growing; see in more detail: J Carens, 'Membership and Morality: Admission to Citizenship in Liberal Democratic States' in WR Brubaker (ed), *Immigration and the Politics of Citizenship in Europe and North America* (Lanham, Md, University Press of America, 1989); L Beckman, 'Citizenship and Voting Rights: Should Resident Aliens Vote?' (2006) 10 *Citizenship Studies* 153.

any given political community and non-members. As a matter of fact, the effect of human rights is not so much to exclude those boundaries but to make sure those boundaries are constantly being questioned and potentially pushed further to include more stakeholders among decision-makers. This is the result of the fruitful albeit irresolvable tension that exists between human rights and citizens' rights.

This constant interaction between human rights and citizens' rights is reminiscent of Arendt's universal right to have particular rights, and the to-ing and fro-ing between the universal and the particular. Human rights are specified as citizens' rights, but citizens' rights progressively consolidate into human rights in return. Thus, the legalisation of human rights is a two-way street that is not limited to a top-down reception or a bottom-up crystallisation. Only those polities that respect international human rights (of both kinds discussed before) are legitimate in specifying the content of those rights *qua* citizens' rights, and hence in contributing to the recognition and existence of those rights *qua* international human rights that constrain polities in return.[78]

This virtuous circle can actually be exemplified by recent human rights practice, whether it is of a customary, conventional or even judicial nature. On the one hand, citizens' rights contribute to the development of the corresponding international human rights' judicial or quasi-judicial interpretations. This is clearly so in the case law of the European Court of Human Rights, where common ground is a constant concern and is sought after when interpreting Convention rights. Consolidations of national best practices and benchmarking also occur, for instance, through general comments issued by the United Nations human rights committees. Within the EU, this actually occurs through the recognition of common constitutional traditions *qua* non-written general principles of EU law.[79] More broadly, one observes in international law the gradual development of general principles of law derived from domestic and regional human rights.[80] One should also mention, on the other hand, mechanisms of transnational consolidation of human rights. This takes place, for instance, through comparative constitutional borrowings in national courts and legislatures.

IV. CONCLUSION

If there is one idea in Arendt's political theory that cannot be regarded as obsolete whatever changes have occurred in international law since 1949, it is her idea of a 'right to have rights'.

[78] This virtuous circularity is reminiscent of Buchanan, above n 3, 187–89.

[79] Treaty on the EU, Art 6(3); EU Fundamental Rights Charter, Art 52(4).

[80] See eg JF Flauss, 'La protection des droits de l'homme et les sources du droit international' in Société Française pour le Droit International (ed), *La protection des droits de l'homme et l'évolution du droit international* (Paris, Pédone, 1998) 11.

Based on a contemporary and self-standing argument about the nature of human rights, this essay has demonstrated how Arendt had already, at the dawn of the post-1945 human rights regime, put her finger on the three questions that are still at the core of contemporary discussions in human rights theory: the rights-nature of human rights; the relationship between moral and legal human rights; and the relationship between international and domestic human rights guarantees. Although Arendt was not interested for philosophical reasons in giving full answers to those three interrogations, she was a precursor in proposing a resolutely modern conception of human rights that situates them in the constant tension between the universal and the particular, between politics and morality, and at the intersection of various levels of political integration. Sixty years later, the developments of European and international human rights law and practice have proved her right. An international community is nowhere to be seen *qua* full-blown political community, and remains undesirable from a normative perspective. However, international human rights law and multi-level citizenship have developed, and have generated a productive and mutual relationship with domestic politics, thus proving a greater resilience and power of transformation of both democratic sovereignty and international law than Arendt could have hoped for.

More specifically, and following Arendt's original republican intuition about human rights, and based on the relationship between democracy and individual rights, I have argued that human rights are inherently moral and legal: the law cannot create universal moral rights but it can recognise or even modulate them, and turn them into human rights *stricto sensu*. Of course, there can be universal moral rights that are not matched by legal rights, and legal norms that go by the name of human rights which are not human rights. However, there cannot be human rights which are not *à la fois* universal moral rights and legal rights.

By virtue of human rights' close relationship to democracy, I have argued further that the legalisation of human rights ought to take place in each given political community, and hence, for the time being, at domestic level in priority. International human rights norms can be regarded as human rights only if they match, in a minimal way, an existing set of domestic human rights. This occurs through the mutual relationship of reception and consolidation I have described between international legal human rights norms and citizens' rights. In the absence of such a set of domestic human rights, international human rights are legal rights that correspond at the most to the universal moral rights to have human rights in every given jurisdiction. To those rights to have human rights correspond second-order State duties to have human rights duties under domestic law and procedures. The only human rights that may and ought to be recognised legally at the international level only and in the absence of corresponding domestic rights are a second group of human rights: human rights to membership and to all the human rights those rights require for their realisation in a given political community. Those human rights may be guaranteed only from outside a political community, and through inclusive and representative mechanisms of international law-making. Those two kinds of human rights are two complementary interpretations of Arendt's right to have rights that go beyond a sterile opposition between moral and legal rights.

These rather modest and sobering conclusions about the nature and the existence of international human rights need not be a source of concern, however. International democratisation is developing fast, following the development of common fundamental interests and the need to address them together in an inclusive fashion. In those conditions, the recognition of human rights in international law will be required by the expansion of political equality and new ways of political inclusion in international law-making, and hence legitimised at the same time. The European Union is a good example of these *demoi*-cratic developments at regional level, with EU human rights and EU citizenship reinforcing each other mutually. Those political developments within regional or functional international organisations trigger difficult questions though. It yet remains unclear, for instance, how the combination of multi-level citizenship and human rights standards beyond the State will and ought to impact on States' democratic and human rights regimes. But that will have to be the topic for another essay.[81]

[81] See, eg, Besson, above n 15.

Index